Mircea A. Tamas

THE WRATH OF GODS

Esoteric and Occult in the Modern World

A REVISED EDITION

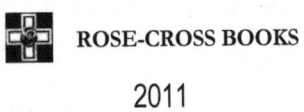

ROSE-CROSS BOOKS

2011

Copyright © 2004 by Mircea A. Tamas

This revised edition is published by **Rose-Cross Books**
TORONTO
www.rose-crossbooks.com

Printed in Canada   Toronto 2011

Text editing by *Deanna Winger*
Cover design by *Imre Szekely*
Text revision by *Ariana Ananda Tamas*

National Library of Canada Cataloguing in Publication

Tamas, Mircea A. (Mircea Alexandru), 1949-
    The wrath of gods : esoteric and occult in the modern world / Mircea A. Tamas.

Includes bibliographical references.
ISBN 0-9731191-4-4

    1. Occultism--Religious aspects--Christianity. 2. Church history--Primitive and early church, ca. 30-600. I. Title.

BF1411.T35 2004   261.5'13   C2004-902217-2

CONTENTS

5	INTRODUCTION: *THE WRATH OF GODS*
8	CHAPTER I: *THE GREAT DISARRAY*
25	CHAPTER II: *ESOTERICISM AND EXOTERICISM*
37	CHAPTER III: *ESOTERICISM AND OUTSIDE DARNESS*
52	CHAPTER IV: *INITIATION AND SALVATION*
76	CHAPTER V: *INITIATION AND HESYCHASM*
95	CHAPTER VI: *RENÉ GUÉNON AND INITIATION*
106	CHAPTER VII: *RENÉ GUÉNON AND TRADITION*
118	CHAPTER VIII: *THE WRATH OF TRADITIONALISTS*
132	CHAPTER IX: *RENÉ GUÉNON AND HIS SOURCES*
153	CHAPTER X: *RENÉ GUÉNON AND AGARTTHA*
168	CHAPTER XI: *GNOSIS AND GNOSTICISM*
185	CHAPTER XII: *GNOSTICISM AND OCCULTISM*
200	CHAPTER XIII: *THE NEAR-WEST*
216	CHAPTER XIV: *NOAH AND THE NEAR-EAST*
233	CHAPTER XV: *SAINT PAUL AND HISTORICISM*
251	CHAPTER XVI: *GREAT TRIAD AND HOLY TRINITY*
267	CHAPTER XVII: *THE THREE MARYS*
284	CHAPTER XVIII: *PILGRIMAGE AND TOURISM*
293	CHAPTER XIX: *MASONRY AND THE CONSPIRACY THEORY*
310	CHAPTER XX: *ROSICRUCIANISM AND TYPOGRAPHY*
323	CHAPTER XXI: *LANGUAGE DISARRAY*
343	CHAPTER XXII: *THE MODERN WORLD AND THE ANTI-GRAIL*
352	CHAPTER XXIII: *ORIENS AND OCCIDENS*
370	CHAPTER XXIV: *UNITY AT THE END OF TIMES*
387	CONCLUSION: *THE WRATH OF GODS?*

INTRODUCTION

THE WRATH OF GODS

THE HIGHEST NAME OF GOD IS "the Merciful," not "the Wrathful." Comparing the "Golden Age" to the "Iron Age," the former is supposed to last four times longer than the latter, illustrating God's Mercy; moreover, the darkest period of the "Iron Age" will be the shortest one of the entire human cycle, and will depend on the righteousness of people rather than on Wrath of the Gods.[1]

Nevertheless, this Wrath has its purpose.

The lord saw how great man's wickedness on the earth had become, and that every inclination of the thoughts of his heart was only evil all the time. The Lord was grieved that he had made man on the earth, and his heart was filled with pain. So the Lord said, «I will wipe mankind, whom I have created, from the face of the earth – men and animals, and creatures that move along the ground, and birds of the air [the Three Worlds][2] – for I am grieved that I have made them.» But Noah found favour [mercy][3] in the eyes of the Lord. (**Genesis** 6:5-8)

---

[1] We use the plural "gods" in accord with the significance of the Hebrew name for God, *Elohim*, a name which allows the multiple within the Godhead and represents God in connection to creation and judgment (wrath). "The Holy One, Blessed be He, said to those, You want to know my name? I am called according to my actions. When I judge the creatures I am Elohim, and when I have mercy with My world, I am named YHVH" (**Exodus Rabbah** 3:6).

[2] The notes between the square brackets are ours.

[3] Here "favour" has to be understood as grace and blessing, as divine mercy.

The Judaic and Christian traditions consider that, at one time, God became angry with humankind. In these traditions, Melchizedek, who represents the Lord of the World,[1] is both, King (*Melki-Zedeq* means "the king of justice") and Priest (as the emperor of *Salem*, that is, of the Peace).[2] Justice or Rigor is the fundamental attribute of the temporal power, sometimes designated by the left hand; Peace or Mercy is the attribute of the spiritual authority, being the right hand (Guénon, **Roi**, p. 25). In the Islamic tradition, the "right way" is "the way of those upon whom You release Your mercy, and not of those upon whom is Your wrath, neither of those who are in error" (*çirâta elladhîna anamta alayihim, ghayri el-maghdûbi alayhim wa lâ ed-dâllîn*).[3] Considering what the **Bible** says, "Noah found favour [the mercy of God]," it seems that the others stirred the wrath of God.[4]

In the Sumerian tradition, the gods are angry as well. **The Epic of Gilgamesh** describes how the gods, angry with humankind, destroyed it, starting storms, flood and fire, the only survivor being, like Noah, Utnapishtim. Yet, "when Enlil had come, when he saw the boat, he was wrath and swelled with anger..."[5]

In Greek mythology, Zeus (but also the other Olympian gods) is often angry, punishing mortals. Hesiod stressed a special episode, about the "race of silver" that "could not keep from sinning and from wronging one another, nor would they serve the immortals, nor sacrifice on the holy altars of the blessed ones. Then Zeus the son of Cronos was angry and put them away, because they would not give honour to the blessed gods who live on Olympus" (**Works and Days**, 130-140).[6] Ovid retold the episode: "And Jove was witness from his lofty throne of all the evil, and groaned as he

---

[1] René Guénon, **Le Roi du Monde**, Gallimard, 1981, p. 48.
[2] Christ is also Lord of the World, "in the order of Melchizedek."
[3] René Guénon, **Le Symbolisme de la Croix**, Guy Trédaniel, 1984, p. 134.
[4] It is stated in the **Bible** that not only the human race, but also the whole world declined.
[5] **The Epic of Gilgamesh**, Penguin Books, 1968, p. 109.
[6] Hesiod, **The Homeric hymns and Homerica**, William Heinemann Ltd., 1936, p. 13.

The Wrath of Gods

remembered the wicked revels of Lycaon's table, the latest guilt, a story still unknown to the high gods. In awful indignation [and anger] he summoned them to council." And Jupiter (Zeus) sent the flood from the sky, storms and thunders, to destroy the humankind. "And Jove's anger, unbounded by his own domain [the superior, freshwaters], was given help by his dark blue brother [Neptune, the inferior, saltwaters]."[1]

There is no doubt: the gods, Sumerian, Judeo-Christian or Greek, were always disappointed with the human race. Humankind succeeded, it seems, to make a fool of itself to such an extent that it awoke the Wrath of the Gods. And we have to understand that it is not easy to rouse the Wrath of the Gods, who, by definition, have mercy as their essence: that is why the human race instead of perishing completely, was saved each time when the gods favoured an "elected" one, who was variously called Noah, Utnapishtim or Deucalion.

One could object that these sinful races have long been dust, and we have nothing in common with them. Yet today, humankind stirs again the Wrath of the Gods.

---

[1] Ovid, **Metamorphoses**, Indiana Univ. Press, 1955, pp. 8, 11.

CHAPTER I

THE GREAT DISARRAY

NOW, AT THE BEGINNING OF the 21st century, we live a completely illegal life; and we don't refer to human legality, but to cosmic law. In respect to the law of the cosmic cycles, our humankind should not exist anymore, because the Wrath of the Gods is wide-awake. As death is considered an unfit subject for discussions, and it is tacitly avoided, likewise the end of times is considered a ridiculous and obsolete subject. Of course, it is something different to talk about somebody else's death, the same, as it is different to mention the end of other planetary systems or the disappearance of other species. In fact, we note a curious phenomenon: the closer the end of times seems to be, the more often issues such as death and calamities are in the public eye. There is no daily news without highlighting a fatal accident, a fire, a storm or a murder; we can say that there is no news if it doesn't contain something deadly. It would be unfair to blame the media for "morbidizing" the information the public "has the right" to know, when, in fact, the public itself is thirsty of such kind of news.

The more interested the public seems to become in "catastrophic" news, the more reluctant people appear to be talking about their own deaths. This shyness extends beyond the individual and we remark the same reluctance in admitting and discussing the end of times or of all humankind. People today prefer to hide behind some bizarre theories that promise continuous progress and eternal existence. The moderns prefer to ridicule any allusion to the end of times, covering themselves with a very comfortable, but illusory "scientific" perspective. And yet, it is not difficult to grasp the truth. As human beings are born and die, as the seasons and the phases of the moon flow in cycles, the same will occur with humankind, which was born and will have to die. The only concession that was made to us, if we can call it a concession, is that we ignore the time when the end will come.

Four main stations could mark the journey of a humankind as ours. The partition in four derives from geometric symbolism; as the planetary orbits are closed curves, as the hands of the clock cover a circumference, the same could be said of the cyclical evolution of the world with four stations corresponding to the four quarters of a circle. It is nothing unusual, because we also have four cardinal points that divide a circle into quarters, and there are four solar stations, two solstices and two equinoxes, often represented in correspondence to the cardinal points, quartering the circle. The ancient people called the four milestones of humanity's evolvement "ages" and considered them in a qualitative descending hierarchy.

As we said, one concession was made to us: we don't know how much time we still have and when it will be exhausted.[1] Nevertheless, it doesn't mean that we cannot guess and read the "signs of the times." Various sacred writings suggest humankind is now living its last moments; more than that, using some indications related to the duration of the equinoctial precession, humankind should already have been dead.

And if we honestly and without bias read the "signs of the times" we understand that what the Hindu tradition predicted will now occur: "When reign the deceit, falseness, inertia, sleep, wickedness, consternation, dismay, confusion, fright, sadness, that is called Kali-

---

[1] "As it was in the days of Noah, so it will be at the coming of the Son of Man. For in the days before the flood, people were eating and drinking, marrying and giving in marriage, up to the day Noah entered the ark; and they knew nothing about what would happen until the flood came and took them all away. That is how it will be at the coming of the Son of Man" (**Matthew** 24:37-39).

yuga, which is the dark age" (**Bhagavata Purana**)[1]; a witness of such a dark era describes it almost with the same words: "They have become filled with every kind of wickedness, evil, greed and depravity. They are full of envy, murder, strife, deceit and malice. They are gossips, slanderers, God-haters, insolent, arrogant and boastful; they invent ways of doing evil; they disobey their parents; they are senseless, faithless, heartless, ruthless." Looking around us, we would discover all these negative characteristics without too much effort. However, the last quotation is from a letter written by Saint Paul to the Romans two thousand years ago (**Romans** 1:29-31).

Saint Paul was an absolutely outstanding character of the Christian tradition and his role deserves special attention. Though we will come back to this, let us say here that one of the "signs of the times" is also the fact that today there is a collaborative attempt to trivialize, even to contest the Paulician mission. Saint Paul's letter describes a gloomy picture, very suitable for the end of times, and yet humankind survived for another two thousand years after that. This is one of the modern arguments: those who complain about naughty children, increasing prices, calamities, government, lack of education and culture do not describe anything new; our ancestors, in Plato's or Saint Paul's time, have complained the same way. *Nil novi sub sole.* "Nothing is new under the sun"; in other words, those who complain are doing this since this is the human nature and not because humankind is more and more deteriorated and the world is in greater agony.

This argument is at least curious. On the one hand, modern science states that mankind has a significant age, and our world has an age measured in millions of years. With every new analysis, due to a linear perspective, this age swells. On the other hand, archeological vestiges regarding lost civilizations are limited to some thousands of years, and known history to even less. Without too much care, these

---

[1] We find the same description in the *enigma* or the *prophetic riddle* uncovered in the foundations of the Thélème Abbey (Rabelais, **Gargantua & Pantagruel**, Penguin Books, 1969, pp. 160 ff).

two aspects are mixed and we have a false picture of present humanity. In fact, what we know for sure about human history is confined to the last "age," to *Kali-yuga*, that is, the "Iron Age" of Hesiod and Ovid. We see the same illusion as the one regarding the earth's surface: for a local zone, we have the feeling that the earth is flat, and with a good approximation we can replace the curve with a straight line tangent to it; in the same way, the historical period we are talking about is a "local" one, a very short period.

For this reason, what Saint Paul and other ancient authors affirmed should not surprise us. They lived, like us, in the same "Iron Age" to which **Bhagavata Purana** referred. The period of two thousand years is much too short – approximately the thirtieth part of the whole cycle – to permit us to observe a notable difference. More than that, the Greco-Roman civilization is much too close to our modern mentality, and therefore, by comparison, we can expect the differences to be even more difficult to notice.

It is important to stress that our perspective is a purely traditional one, or, in the historian of religions' language, a "mythical" one. In other words, everything we state here is from this "mythical" point of view and we want to interfere as little as possible with aspects belonging to the modern sciences or with elements connected to the present political and social situation. What we are interested in, and that is the reason for this work, is to find out how it is possible today to reconcile traditional perspective and spiritual realization with modern life. We have no taste for polemics, fights about concepts or sterile criticism. We are not interested in specific individuals or historical facts. We are not looking for scapegoats. If we will consider the modern world, highlighting its flaws, these flaws will appear from a traditional and sacred point of view; from a modern perspective, they could appear, on the contrary, as positive developments. As we saw in the *Introduction*, Hesiod uttered that Zeus destroyed humankind "because they would not give honour to the blessed gods." From a traditional vision, the present lack of sincere religiosity is enough reason to stir the Wrath of the Gods; from the point of view of an atheist or of a "Sunday believer," the liberation from "the fear of God" means progress and emancipation.

The Great Disarray

In this context, we consider it suitable to use Saint Paul's letters as examples, because, translating them, we can depict the present situation, without being forced to refer to elements that could be misinterpreted.[1]

Great disarray reigned in the times of Saint Paul. In that epoch, the Roman Empire, considered the only super-power and "civilization," reached its climax. Openly, the Republic was changed to an Empire and it is interesting to note that Jesus Christ came into the world at exactly the time of the first Roman emperor, Augustus. That period is usually called the "golden age" of Augustus, and of course, Vergil, Horace and Ovid contributed to this fame; we shouldn't forget that Vergil was Dante's guide, the Florentine poet recognizing his initiatory quality[2]; and Ovid gave us a thorough description of the four ages. Obviously, we witness the operation of the law of analogy: each cycle, longer or shorter, primary or secondary, is analogous to the whole cycle; we could expect then that after this so-called "golden age" a decline would follow and an intensification of disarray, and, indeed, that is what happened. We cannot talk though about a linear fall, even though many people would like to simplify everything at all costs. Augustus' successors, Tiberius, Caligula, Claudius and Nero, were remembered in the history books as wicked emperors, and in their time Saint Paul accomplished his mission. However, even though the Roman Empire will have some more success, soon, close to the year 400

---

[1] Similarly, what the Islamic tradition stressed in its Holy Book is applicable to the whole humankind. "And of mankind are some who say: We believe in Allâh and the Last Day [how many really believe in the end of times, today?], when they believe not. They think to beguile Allâh and those who believe, and they beguile none save themselves; but they perceive not. In their hearts is a disease, and Allâh increases their disease. A painful doom is theirs because they lie. And when it is said unto them: Make not mischief in the earth, they say: We are peacemakers only. Are not they indeed the mischief-makers? But they perceive not" **(Qur'ân 2: 8-12).**

[2] "For if we review the ages and the dispositions of men from the fall of our first parents, we shall not find that there ever was peace throughout the world except under the immortal Augustus, when a perfect monarchy existed. That mankind was then happy in the calm of universal peace is attested by all historians and by famous poets" (Dante, **Monarhia**, I, 16).

A.D., it will be forced to split in two, and the Western Roman Empire will cease to exist shortly after. The barbarian invasions had an obvious dissolving effect, specific to the end of a cycle; there are other apocalyptical signs, such as the arson of Rome, and above all, the destruction of the Temple of Jerusalem in the year 70 A.D., followed by the obliteration of the cities of Pompeii and Herculaneum by the eruption of Mount Vesuvius.

Under these circumstances, the birth of the Christian tradition appears providential, allowing the beginning of a new cycle. René Guénon wrote:

> If we consider what was, at that time, the situation of the Western world, that is, the assembly of countries contained in the Roman Empire, we can easily understand that, if Christianity wouldn't have «descended» in the exoteric domain, this world as a whole would have been soon without any tradition, what existed at that time, and especially the Greco-Roman tradition that normally became predominant, reaching an extreme decadence – a sign that its cycle of existence was close to an end (of course, speaking of the Western world as a whole, we make exception for an elite that not only understood its own tradition from an outer point of view, but also continued to receive an initiation in the Mysteries). This «descent» was not an accident or a deviation, but has to be seen, on the contrary, as a «providential» event, because it saved the Occident of that time from a fall to a state comparable to the one in which it is now. Anyway, the moment when a general loss of the tradition should have taken place, as the one that characterizes the modern times, hadn't come yet; it means that a «straightening» had to occur, and only Christianity could operate it, with the condition of giving up the esoteric and exclusive characteristic that it had initially.[1]

---

[1] René Guénon, **Aperçus sur L'Ésotérisme Chrétien**, Éd. Traditionnelles, 1983, p. 27. Guénon also wrote: "This age [of crisis] is that of the beginning and expansion of Christianity, coinciding, on the one hand, with the dispersion of the Jewish people, and on the other hand, with the last phase of the Greco-Latin civilization. ... Many common characteristics were noticed between the antique decline and that of the present age; without pushing the parallel too far, we have to admit the existence of some striking similarities. The pure «profane» philosophy gained terrain... At the same time, the old sacred doctrines, which almost nobody understood, have degenerated, due to this incomprehension, in «paganism,» in the true sense of the word, that is, they became just «superstitions,» things that have lost their profound significance, surviving in a superficial way... The Greco-Latin civilization had to

The Great Disarray

We remark how the symbolic rules regarding the end of a world, found in diverse sacred texts, are obeyed, including the intervention of an *avatâra* to regenerate the world and start the Wheel of Law, as described in the Hindu tradition: "Whenever there is a decay of the Law [*dharma*, rectitude, sacred regulation, tradition, virtue], O, Bharata, and an ascendancy of unlawfulness [*adharma*, vice, profane, crooked], then I manifest Myself [through *Mâyâ*]. For the protection of the good, for the destruction of the evil-doers, for the firm establishment of the Law [*dharma*], I am born in every age [*yuga*]" (**Bhagavad-Gîtâ**, IV, 7-8).

The great disarray of those years, when Christianity was born, had spread to all the levels of existence; from immorality and decadence, notorious not only in Rome, but also in the other parts of the Empire, to the "religious" sectarianism, everything suggested a corruption of life. In those days, the "religious" sects had tremendously multiplied and the Greek and Oriental *Mysteries* were celebrated everywhere; the Mythraic Mysteries, the Mysteries of Isis and the Orphism functioned side by side. In Rome, all the gods of the Empire were brought together; the proliferation of the sects was a sure sign of the end, being not a unifying synthesis, but a dangerous syncretism. The division more and more intense that illustrates the multiplicity disconnected from the Principle[1] is one of the strongest signs of the end of the cycle. To this we should add the innumerable vices, which Saint Paul, we saw, had condemned merciless, after he warned "The wrath of God is being revealed from heaven against all the godlessness and wickedness of men who suppress the truth by their wickedness" (**Romans** 1:18).

---

come to an end, and the straightening had to come from outside and in another mode. Christianity was the one that operated this transformation… After a confused period of barbarian invasions, needed to finalize the destruction of the old world, a normal order was restored for some centuries" (René Guénon, **La Crise du monde moderne**, Gallimard, 1975, pp. 27-28).

[1] We use the words "principle" and "principial" in the original sense, as derived from Latin *principium, principialis*, "primitive, origin, first, beginning, fundament"; we didn't choose "principal" due to its modern usage.

It is the time of the snakes, which, from a microcosmic point of view, represent our visceral desires, the numerous "sins" that swallow the human being. They are Medusa's serpents. Even though her true meaning was lost in the time of "classical" Greece, Medusa is a symbol of the Pole; that is why she is painted as a *swastika*.[1] The snakes that compose her hair are equivalent to Shiva and Samson's locks. Shiva's hair, in which Gangâ, the celestial river, stopped, symbolizes the texture of the Universe (Guénon, **Croix**, p. 88) and has the same meaning as Samson's hair. The cutting of Samson's locks describes the severance between the World and the Principle, followed, as a consequence, by its decay and death.[2] It means that Medusa's snakes got loose, without any control, and instead of a multiplicity rooted in Unity, there is only a divided and sectarian multiplicity, floating in disarray.

This sectarianism reigned in the Roman Empire, but also in Jerusalem, that is, in the old Palestine: Essenes, Nazoraeans, Ebionites, Pharisees, Sadducees, Zealots, Sabaeans, Sicarii, Heodians, Elchasaites, were names uttered more or less publicly. It is true that some names designated almost the same sect; regarding their objective, we are not interested, we care only about the fact that they supported a sectarianism that illustrated the disaccord and disarray typical of the entire Roman Empire.[3]

Even primeval Christianity didn't escape division. We shouldn't be surprised, considering that it was born in a region and in a time when sectarianism and the wrath between gods were flourishing. As controversial as Saint Paul appears, his letters state without possibility of denial that his mission was "to unify" and to reattach the multiplicity to Unity, in the name of Christ. The Christian Church was built on this basis; and to end the continuous division, it

---

[1] Many centuries before being desecrated, *swastika*, a symbol found in all genuine traditional forms, was a sign of the Pole.
[2] See our work, **The Everlasting Sacred Kernel**, Rose-Cross Books, 2002.
[3] Guénon wrote: "And the Gospel says: «If a house is divided against itself, that house cannot stand» [**Mark** 3:25]; these words apply precisely to the modern world, with its materialistic civilization, that cannot, by its own nature, but generate division and struggle" (Guénon, **Crise**, p. 148).

was forced to become dogmatic and intolerant, to banish the so-called "heresies," and to fuse (not "to confuse") the nations in one form, that of the Christian traditional society. Only in this way could the old cycle (the Roman Empire) be replaced with a new one (the Christian Empire), which, unfortunately, taking into account the moment of the present cycle and the advanced state of the "Iron Age," soon started to decline: close to the first Millennium the Great Schism took place (between "Catholic" and "Orthodox"), and the destruction of the Templars, at the beginning of the 14th century, marked the major fall of the traditional Christian society.[1]

Saint Paul wrote: "For we were all baptized by one Spirit into one body – whether Jews or Greeks, slave or free – and we were all given the one Spirit to drink" (**1 Corinthians** 12:13). That is why he tried to spread the Word of Jesus Christ only in those regions where nobody had been before him ("It has always been my ambition to preach the gospel where Christ was not known, so that I would not be building on someone else's foundation," **Romans** 15:20); that is why, even though disapproved of, he continued to obey the Jerusalem Church (the Jerusalem Assembly, *Ecclesia*), accepting James, "the brother of the Lord," as leader of the Christians. On the contrary, some exponents of the Jerusalem Church would hunt him, and there, where Paul founded Christian communities, they would bring disarray and division, stirring the Corinthians, Galatians and Ephesians against his teachings. Christianity, just born, had to face almost immediately the menace of sectarianism; here we have to insert the dispute between Paul and Peter, and the divergences between Paul and James, "the brother of Jesus." The fact that Paul went to Jerusalem (where he stayed only fifteen days), seeing just Peter and James, and after that he was approved by the Jerusalem Church to spread the Gospel among nations, and the fact that he considered Peter, John and James as the three pillars of the Church

---

[1] One of the reasons of such a relatively fast disintegration was the lack of a sacred language (Latin and Greek were only liturgical languages and they challenged each other).

(**Galatians** 2:9),[1] shows not his hostility with regard to the Jerusalem Church, but his attachment. "As they traveled from town to town [Paul and Timothy], they delivered the decisions reached by the apostles and elders in Jerusalem for the people to obey" (**Acts** 16:4).

"The people of the city [Iconium] were divided; some sided with the Jews, others with the Apostles." (**Acts** 14:4). The troubles and division that appeared were mainly of an individual order. It was impossible for Saint Paul to understand why he, who was invested directly by Jesus Christ to spread the Word among the nations (the Gentiles), should be attacked and denied by the exponents of the Jerusalem Church; his distress and shock are easily understandable. In the same way we can understand, from a human and individual point of view, the intransigence of the Judaic Christians, who, actually, didn't do anything but repeat the intransigence of a part of the Jews regarding Christ himself. Saint Paul's message to the Corinthians reveals implicitly the disarray created by the different points of view, similar to the Tower of Babel episode.

I appeal to you, brothers, in the name of our Lord Jesus Christ, that all of you have a common speech and agree with one another so that there may be no divisions among you and that you may be perfectly united in mind and thought. My brothers, some from Chloe's household have informed me that there are quarrels among you. What I mean is this: One of you says, «I follow Paul»; another, «I follow Apollos»; another, «I follow Cephas»; still another, «I follow Christ.» Is Christ divided? (**1 Corinthians** 1:10-13)

The *Gospel* of Paul has in its essence two fundamental elements: peace and union, which are a reflection of the spiritual center. In his letters, Saint Paul spoke often about peace and union, his words being somehow an exteriorization and a revelation of a secret doctrine, of a sacred kernel. René Guénon, explaining the Evangelic phrase *Gloria in excelsis Deo, et in terra Pax hominibus bonae voluntatis,*

---

[1] These three pillars could be compared to the three pillars of Masonry. Dante suggested the correspondence between the three theological virtues (hope, faith and charity) and Peter, John and James (see also René Guénon, **L'ésotérisme de Dante**, Gallimard, 1981, p. 27).

wrote that "Peace," in an esoteric sense, is one of the fundamental attributes of the spiritual centers established in our world (*in terra*); "*Gloria* and *Pax* refer to the inner aspect, with respect to the Principle, and the outer aspect, with respect to the manifested world." Guénon added: "we could explain in a precise mode the numerous Evangelic texts in which «Peace» is mentioned (however, the Gospel states explicitly that it is not about the peace as the common people understand it)."[1] The peace Saint Paul talks about is exactly an explanation of *in terra Pax hominibus bonae voluntatis*. We will not know what Saint Paul thought about this, yet it is not difficult to observe that he appears as a Christian messenger that translates to an outer domain an inner doctrine, many of his words hiding a meaning beyond the "religious" sense.

To make us understood let us give another example. The creation of the world imposed the birth, or better yet, an "explication" of the multiplicity from One.[2] Some traditions say that God created the world as an indefinite plane expanse, and Satan produced the uneven, the mountains, the valleys, etc., that is, the multiplicity. In consequence, the return to One, the spiritual realization through which the union with the Principle takes place, means to restore the plane expanse and the primordial indistinctness. It is the state announced by the prophet Isaiah: "A voice of one calling in the desert: «Prepare the way for the Lord; make straight in the wilderness a highway for our God, make straight the paths of our God. Every valley shall be raised up, every mountain and hill made low; the rough ground shall become level, the rugged places a plain. And the glory of the Lord will be revealed, and all mankind together will see it. For the mouth of the Lord has spoken»" (40:3-5); and Saint Luke described it also: "Every valley shall be filled in, every mountain and hill made low. The crooked roads shall become

---

[1] Guénon, **Roi**, pp. 23-24. "Peace I leave with you; my peace I give you. I do not give to you as the world gives. Do not let your hearts be troubled and do not be afraid" (**John** 14:27).
[2] The words "complication" and "explication" have the same Latin root and Nicholas of Cusa used them to define God (as complication) and the World (as explication).

straight, the rough ways smooth" (**Luke** 3:5). The glory of the Lord mentioned by Isaiah is, of course, *Gloria in excelsis Deo*.

Genesis gives the same illustration of the production of multiplicity:

> Now the whole world had one language and a common speech. ... But the Lord came down to see the city and the tower that the men were building. The Lord said, «If as one people speaking the same language they have begun to do this, then nothing they plan to do will be impossible for them. Come, let us go down and confuse their language so they will not understand each other» ... That is why it was called Babel – because there the Lord confused the language of the whole world. From there the Lord scattered them over the face of the whole earth. (**Genesis** 11:1-9)

Here multiplicity appears as a divine punishment. To explain this episode, the law of inverted analogy, specific to traditional symbolism, has to be applied. The divine Will imposes the multiplicity just because it is possible. Without developing doctrinal questions, we may say that the supreme Principle as universal Possibility comprises both, non-manifestation and manifestation,[1] hence the Lord's incentive: "Then God blessed Noah and his sons, saying to them, «Be fruitful and increase in number and fill the earth»" (**Genesis** 9:1); this multiplication is one blessed by God, that is, a multiplication from Unity, not a deviated one, detached from the Principle. In the Tower of Babel episode, we find also a "unity," but an inverted one, a "human" (if we may say so), not a "divine" one; this "human unity" is, in fact, extreme sectarianism, the total severance from Divinity. Human beings started to be more and more conceited and to believe that they were similar to gods and the

---

[1] Universal manifestation as a whole comprises the Three Worlds, which from human perspective can be named: corporeal, subtle or psychical (understood at its full extension, not only as the part connected to the human body), and angelic or spiritual; the first two compose the individual domain; the last is the super-individual domain. The non-manifestation "is" beyond manifestation and alludes to the super-luminous Darkness. The manifestation (word that we are constantly using in our work) is equivalent to the universal Existence and has as direct principle the Supreme Being.

Tower of Babel was the token of this vanity.[1] God's punishment was not so much the multiplicity, but the "dispersal," and of course, considering the inverted analogy, human beings, dreaming about a "union" outside God, generated this scattering.[2] The construction of the Tower of Babel symbolizes, in an extended perspective, the moment when the present humanity started to fall, but represents more precisely the moment when the world stepped into *Kali-yuga*. The Tower of Babel indicates a false unity, an outer union, completely different from the one preached by Saint Paul; that is why the sixteenth card of the Tarot shows a tower destroyed by the divine thunderbolt, illustrating the Wrath of the Gods. In this context, Saint Paul's words appear in their full brightness. His encouragement regarding the union in the name of God and the use of a common tongue is just the opposite of division and the confusion of languages from the Tower of Babel episode; it means the straightening of the mountains and valleys.

In Masonry, there is an initiatory formula regarding the "reuniting of what was scattered"; Saint Paul speaks about this "reuniting" too, his fight against division being, in fact, the remedy against the great disarray that gained ground at the same time as sectarianism and extreme multiplicity. "I urge you, brothers, to watch out for those who cause divisions and put obstacles in your way that are contrary to the teaching you have learned. Keep away from them. For such people are not serving our Lord Christ, but their own appetites. By smooth talk and flattery they deceive the minds of naive people" (**Romans** 16:17-18). The "appetites" mentioned by Saint Paul refer to the devils within us; in various traditions the intestines were compared to the snakes of the inferior desires, they are Medusa's

---

[1] In the Judaic Kabbalah, the invitation, "Come, let us build us a city, and a tower, with its top in heaven," underlines a revolt against the Holy One, blessed be He, connected to Nimrod, about whom it is said, "and the beginning of his kingdom was Babel" (**Zohar**, I, 74 b, see **The Zohar**, Rebecca Bennet Publ., 1956, vol. I, pp. 253-4). In Masonry, in the Scottish Rite, the 21st degree, called *Patriarch Noachite*, contains Nimrod and the construction of the Tower of Babel as central elements; also, the sacred words of this degree are the names of Noah's sons.

[2] "It is the dispersion in multiplicity, and in such a multiplicity that is not anymore united by the admittance of a superior principle" (Guénon, **Crise**, p. 62).

snakes that broke with the Principle and at the end of times multiplied by themselves.

Saint Paul asked: "Is Christ divided?" And here is suggested the essence of the Eucharist. The Holy Communion is a formidable and sublime mystery of the Church, through which is repeated Christ's sacrifice made at the Last Supper. Jesus announced to the nations: "I tell you the truth, unless you eat the flesh of the Son of Man and drink his blood, you have no life in you. Whoever eats my flesh and drinks my blood has eternal life, and I will raise him up at the last day" (**John** 6:53-54).

The word "communion" derives from Latin. In Latin, there is the word *comminuo*, composed of *com*, "with" (or even "together with") and *minuo*, "to tear apart," "to cut into pieces," "to mince" (hence, other words as "minus," "minute," "minuscule").[1] Therefore, "communion" means, "to mince with somebody," "to impart," "to share the pieces with others." A second Latin word deserves attention: *communico*, meaning "to impart," "to mingle," "to put together," "to unite"; it is composed of *com*, "together with," and *munico*, this one being derived from *munus*, "duty," "task," "remuneration"; *munus* refers to solving a task together, but also of being paid together (from this word resulted "municipality" and "community", and of course, "communication"). Even from this succinct linguistic study, we understand an important aspect of Holy Communion: it is not about a sectarian sacrifice through which Jesus is "cut into pieces," divided, and his parts scattered all over the corporeal world, but a sacrifice that unites, imparts, and brings together a community. In the Christian tradition, it is said that Christ wore one-piece clothing, without any sewing, symbolizing unity. The same concept is considered about his body: a unity that is only apparently divided at the Last Supper, because the profound meaning of Holy Communion is the common participation of the believers, their gathering to communicate and impart the divine grace; and not to enjoy as individual, in a selfish mode, his or her

---

[1] To this *minuo* the name of Friar John of the Hashes alludes (Rabelais 98).

"own piece," his or her "own sect": "«I follow Paul»; another, «I follow Apollos»; another, «I follow Cephas»."[1]

Many writings were created regarding these first years of Christianity and, as usually, the fundamental error was to reduce to an historical and human plane events of spiritual and transcendental order. It is not our task to research in detail the various views related to primitive Christianity, but, since modern Western society is directly connected to the Christian tradition (even though today it doesn't effectively possess it anymore), it is natural to use examples from this tradition. Guénon wrote: "everything that can be valid in the modern world came from Christianity, or at least through Christianity, which brought the whole heritage of the anterior traditions" (Guénon, **Crise**, p. 151).[2]

Some tried to create an artificial competition between Peter, Paul and James ("the brother of Jesus"), as if these three would have been members of a political party running for leadership.[3] In fact, what we should stress is that, in the early years after Christ's resurrection, some disarray and sectarianism emerged, because the process of

---

[1] Without any doubt, in the early years of Christianity many teachers functioned in Asia Minor, Jerusalem, Rome, etc., pretending that only they know "the true doctrine of Christ," the others being false prophets.

[2] It is true that René Guénon remarked as well: "It is said that the modern Occident is Christian, yet that is a mistake: the modern mentality is anti-Christian, because is essentially anti-religious; and it is anti-religious because it is anti-traditional. ... Of course, some Christian elements survived in this anti-Christian civilization of our age. ... The Occident was Christian in the Middle Ages, but not anymore" (Guénon, **Crise**, pp. 150-152, see also René Guénon, **Saint Bernard**, Éd. Trad., 1984, p. 17). And Coomaraswamy underlined in a letter: "My objection to most Christians is not bigotry but that they compromise with modernism. I think consistently highly of Guénon. Speaking of the desirability of a return (for Europe) to Christianity, he remarks, «if this could be, the modern *world would automatically disappear*»" (Ananda K. Coomaraswamy, **Selected letters**, Oxford Univ. Press, 1988, p. 308).

[3] It was also said that the doctrine of the body's resurrection served a political objective, regarding the legitimacy of the Church's leadership and the supremacy of Rome, because the risen Jesus appeared to Peter first. Yet it is known that some versions consider that Mary Magdalene was the first witness of the resurrection, or that James, "the brother of the Lord," was first to see the risen Christ. In fact, **The New Testament** states that Jesus, after resurrection, appeared to many people. Without developing theological questions, we mention that before the resurrection, even the disciples didn't believe that this would happen, though Christ told them so.

cyclical change is a painful and sacrificial one, and the confusion that reigned among the first Christians suggests that invisible forces played a subtle role. These forces that guided Christianity to become a traditional society dressed in a Catholic religion,[1] are not historical characters, which could be identified by the modern scientists. Regarding those who criticize Saint Paul's role, considering that he somehow "hijacked" Christianity from its original idea, they touch a forbidden domain. The only thing that, we, the common people, can observe is that, in spite of disarray and divisions of the early years, the mission of Christianity was not to remain a small sect, which would have been pulverized when the Temple of Jerusalem was destroyed, in year 70 A.D., but to become an orthodox tradition, which made it possible for the Occident to continue to exist. That is the lesson for modern people.[2]

---

[1] In Greek, *katholicos* means "general, universal."
[2] Charles-André Gilis advanced the opinion that Jesus' mission was "a failure," which means, if we accept his hypothesis, that the crusaders' immense desire to conquer Jerusalem was an inept endeavour, since who would want to fight for "the place of defeat," a place where existed a "Palestinian Christianity," different from the triumphant Western Christianity. Jesus' "failure" (**La papauté contre l'islam**, Le Turban Noir, 2007, p. 93) is a question of perspective. From the point of view of the Judaic tradition, we could imagine a "failure," but likewise we could talk about Judas' failure as an Apostle. In fact, Christ revealed well in advance that Judas will betray Him and that He will be crucified, in other words, He revealed (and not only once) the divine plan; even though, at that specific moment of the cycle, the Jewish society was in a process of hardening itself and shutting out the spiritual influences from above, the Jews were the keepers of a genuine tradition, from which Christ used the seeds needed to generate an orthodox and true tradition for the West, which was on the threshold of dissolution (Gilis himself says a little bit further: "the divine plan targeted the straightening of the Western world," **La papauté**, p. 111). Charles-André Gilis believes that the Jews brought the divine wrath upon themselves because they could not recognize Christ as *avatâra* and for this reason they were scattered. Actually, the Jews' role, positive (the Apostles and Christ's disciples) and negative (the "jurists" and the people who wanted Him dead), was part of the divine plan. Guénon said the same thing about the "counter-initiatory" forces: these forces believed that they could oppose *Spiritus*, when, in fact, they obeyed it, without knowing it, because everything must obey the divine will; the "counter-initiatory" forces are used, after all, even if against their will and even if they think otherwise, for the realization of "the divine plan into the human domain," in accord with their nature (the same way Judas was used, for example), as "providential" tools for the world's development (**Le règne**, pp. 259-260). Gilis' "eso-exoterical" position, and also his desire to support his

We may suppose, therefore, that Christianity was, originally, an initiatory doctrine, restricted to an elite. Due to the agony of the Roman world, regeneration was necessary and the replacement of the old cycle with a new one; all these would require a sacred, divine kernel, and thus, "Christianity" accepted the task of sacrificing and unveiling itself to the crowd, passing from esotericism to exotericism. This "sacrifice," illustrated by Christ himself, has produced a strange thing though: the new tradition, perfectly orthodox and valid, remained without an esoteric side, even if a hidden and initiatory kernel continued to exist more or less dormant. It is true that later, Hermetism, Masonry, and Chivalry, rebuilding an initiatory marrow, grafted onto the Christian tree, but maybe because of this "grafting" the marrow dried out after the 14th century, and in our days is almost dead.

---

point of view at any price, leads him to the strange situation of being in accord precisely with those he battles most. Robert Eisenman wrote 1035 pages (!) about Christ's "failure" (**James the Brother of Jesus**, Penguin Books, 1997), where he strives ineffectively and with lamentable arguments to rewrite the sacred history, declaring St. Paul an anti-Semite, the Gospels some Greek anti-Semitic writings, and Christianity a "Paulician" or Greek Christianity (see also Gilis, **Introduction à l'enseignement et mystère de René Guénon**, Éditions Traditionnelles, 2001, p. 114), a counterfeit in comparison with the real Judaic Christianity, of James, the brother of Jesus; the author thinks little of St. Paul because he did not know Jesus physically, the idea of a direct illumination being, obviously, unscientific and, therefore, impossible to be accepted; St. Paul only "felt" that he was in touch with Jesus (p. 51), which illustrates the profane, antitraditional and materialistic mentality of this author.

CHAPTER II

ESOTERICISM AND EXOTERICISM

RENÉ GUÉNON WAS CRITICIZED in many ways. Some of his most fierce contestants were the Catholics, and one of his great "weaknesses" was considered to be his lack of understanding of Christianity. It is impossible though to talk about Tradition and the modern world without taking into account the essential role played by Guénon, and because he was labeled as "refractory" regarding the Christian religion, we think it is helpful to see what René Guénon really thought about this theme; nobody would dare to accuse him of being biased and in favour of the Christian tradition. And we stress right now that the few pages written by Guénon about the Christian tradition are worth much more than thousands of tomes issued by profanes who could not surpass the narrow horizon of the body.

Guénon wrote around Christmas, in 1949:

Only with regrets we decided [to write about Christianity], given that, we must confess, we never felt an attraction to tackle this subject in particular, due to different reasons, among which the first one is the almost impenetrable obscurity that enveloped everything regarding the origins and the first years of Christianity, obscurity which, if we think about it, seems not to be accidentally, but deliberately. (Guénon, **Ésot. Chrét.**, pp. 21-22)

However, around Easter, in 1947, Guénon had already stated: "Almost everything referring to the origins and the first years of

Christianity is covered, unfortunately, with a lot of obscurity," and then added: "Remembering that some Christian rites appear somehow as an «exteriorization» of the initiatory rites, we could ask ourselves if the original Christianity was not, in fact, something totally different from what we would think today it is" (Guénon, **Ésot. Chrét.**, p. 18). Yet the decisive paragraph is to be found in the same article, **Christianisme et Initiation**, of 1949, already quoted, in which Guénon tried to answer those who stubbornly maintained an illusory view about the great disarray; these people, though they affirmed to be partisans of the traditional perspective and so they admitted without reticence the theory of the cosmic cycles (that describes the decadence of the world from "age" to "age"), couldn't leave the individualism, and consequently, they needed an illusory optimism: they convinced themselves that the Christian religion maintained an initiatory characteristic until the present days.

Far from being the religion or the exoteric tradition that is known today under this name, Christianity, at its origins, had, both due to its rites and doctrine, an essentially esoteric characteristic, and therefore, an initiatory one. We can find a confirmation in the fact that the Islamic tradition considers primitive Christianity as a real *tarîqah*, that is, an initiatory way, and not a *sharîyah*, or a legislation of the social order, and open to everybody; the more so as, after that, we see the lack of legislation needed to be supplied by constituting a «canonic» law, which is in fact not other than the old Roman law, that is, something brought from outside. ... Such a lacuna would be not only inexplicable, but really inconceivable for an orthodox and regular tradition, if this tradition should have encompassed both an exotericism and an esotericism. ... However, if Christianity had an initiatory character, then everything is easily explained, being a question not of a lacuna, but of an intentional restraint to intervene in a domain that, by definition, couldn't present interest in these conditions. (Guénon, **Ésot. Chrét.**, pp. 22-23)

We may note that it would be then a mistake to put on the same level primitive Christianity and the political and quasi-messianic sects, which troubled Palestine in those times; anyway, even some words used by Saint Paul suggest its esoteric and initiatory origins. Guénon continued:

To be possible, the Christian Church had to be, in the first years, a close and exclusive organization, in which were admitted, not anybody without distinction, but only those who proved to have the necessary qualifications to obtain a valid initiation under a form that we could call «Christian»; and we could find enough indications that this was the case, even though, due to our modern tendency to deny esotericism, their true signification is too often detoured.

For modern people, Guénon's words don't mean much. Even for the common Christian believer, who diligently attends the Sunday mass, prays and listens to the Gospels, Guénon's sayings don't rouse any reaction. On the contrary, the word "esotericism" suggests something dubious or related to *New Age* and Occultism, something secret and mysterious, and consequently, dangerous and maybe illegal. To illustrate what we are trying to say, let us give an example, pretty well-known as a matter of fact. Yoga is a *darshana*, that is, an orthodox "point of view" of the Hindu tradition, having as its final objective the "union" with the Principle and being, therefore, a spiritual discipline. In the modern world, Yoga is usually considered a psychophysical method for health improvement, to attain, as Latin axiom says, *mens sana in corpore sano*. This pseudo-yoga is freely practiced everywhere, using some *Hatha-Yoga* and *Raja-Yoga* elements; we see individuals in gym classes executing postures (*asanas*) in a totally inadequate ambience, surrounded by noise or by modern music. These individuals don't know much. Yet there are others who have some knowledge from studying more or less serious books, and who have the illusion that, participating without any real guidance in this pseudo-yoga, will achieve a high degree of perfection.

Of course, we have to keep things in proportion, but the modern "religious" man proceeds somehow similarly. Even if the Christian tradition is purely orthodox, in comparison to the pseudo-yoga, some common believers participate to the exoteric rites in a very superficial manner, unaware of their real import; moreover, the ambience in the churches is not always adequate and traditional. In addition, the common believer has no clue that, beside this exoteric aspect, there could exist also an esoteric side. For this believer, the

Christian tradition represents the exoteric rites and sometimes just the Sunday mass. There are others though, who have from different sources learned information about initiation and esotericism, and they have the illusion that applying the information to the Christian rites, they become "initiates."[1] This illusion is extremely dangerous and can be found in any tradition, not only in Christianity, because, by definition, human beings function in the world at the "I" level, and so, it is very difficult to get rid of "egoism," when the "ego" makes them exist in this world.

As a result, we have to ask the question: does it make sense in the modern world to use notions such as "esotericism" and "exotericism," now, when the majority of people don't care to think about them or even more, don't know these two domains exist? First of all, the two notions have to be defined because they exist independently of individuals and their degree of ignorance in this respect[2]; secondly, the great danger is that, in our days, the term "esotericism" is employed far from its origins and meanings, unwittingly or on purpose, hence being a source of disarray. Thirdly, the traditional perspective is not a fatalistic one. The texts of the Far-Eastern tradition stress that the initiates or the seers, due to their nature, cannot remain impassive and fatalist seeing the fall of the world; even if they know this fall obeys the inexorable law of cyclic "evolution," they will try hard to influence the decadence, opposing it and trying to stop it. Of course, an eloquent example is precisely the birth of Christianity. Yet we could also give as illustration the

---

[1] Some of them, purely and simply, confound esotericism with symbolism. René Guénon, describing "new confusions" with regard to esotericism, noted that some individuals belonging to religious circles, forced to admit the concept of esotericism, camouflaged it under the cover of symbolism (See Guénon's article **Nouvelles confusions**, Études Traditionnelles, no. 271, Oct.-Nov., 1948, reprinted in **Initiation et Réalisation spirituelle**, Éd. Traditionnelles, 1980, pp. 116 ff.). Today, this tactic is still in use.

[2] Regarding this autonomy, it is so much harder to understand expressions like "Guénonian esotericism" and "Christian Guénonian" used by some modern authors. The names of these authors are not important; these and others are for us, in this work, merely examples illustrating how ignorant (or /and malevolent) some of the traditionalists and, all the more, the anti-traditionalists are.

case of René Guénon, who, even though he knew exactly the status of the modern world, wrote his whole life for the Westerners to modify their mentality and open their eyes.[1] Those who, considering themselves disciples of the traditional perspective, turn with wrath (and nothing else) against the modern world replace the Wrath of the Gods, and so, they are in error. In spite of the moment of the cycle and the inevitable end, the sacred operation cannot stop. That is why Saint Paul, even though he announced to those he Christianized that the end of times is nearby, and the second coming of Christ is close, accomplished his mission without pause.

The differentiation between "esoteric" and "exoteric" is not unknown to Christianity, since Clement of Alexandria wrote about this. At the end of the second century, A.D., he wrote: "And the disciples of Aristotle say that some of their treatises are esoteric, and others common and exoteric. Further, those who instituted the mysteries, being philosophers, buried their doctrines in myths, so as not to be obvious to all."[2] Clement of Alexandria stated without equivocation the necessity of the esoteric domain; more than that, he alluded to the initiatory characteristic, which the Christian tradition, in these early years, still possessed.[3]

---

[1] Guénon wrote in 1927: "There is a quite favorable symptom, the indication of a possible straightening of the contemporary mentality" (Guénon, **Crise**, p. 8); and even after twenty years, René Guénon, who knew better than anybody else the real situation of the modern world, continued to write in order to start a regeneration. Also, it is important to clarify here a point, which too often was misinterpreted: many were surprised and disappointed that Guénon, instead of using his free time to write more books, "wasted" it answering tens of letters received from all over the world, among which some were just nonsense. But what René Guénon did (very similar to Ramana Maharshi, who answered any question, doesn't matter how naive that was), regards his function and his continuous endeavour to change the modern mentality; if his works were written for the public (even though especially for an elite), the letters were meant for some specific individuals, but to Guénon they were of equal importance (that is why his letters cannot always be considered a public good).

[2] **The Writings of Clement of Alexandria**, T. and T. Clark, Edinburgh, 1869, vol. II, pp. 255-256, **Stromata** V, 9.

[3] In all cases, the esoteric domain is identical to the initiatory one, Guénon affirms; the exoteric domain is identical to the religious one only in some traditional forms (René Guénon, **Y a-t-il encore des possibilités initiatiques dans les formes traditionnelles occidentales?**, Études Traditionnelles, no. 435, 1973, p. 2; this

For he who is still blind and dumb, not having understanding, or the undazzled and keen vision of the contemplative soul [that is, *Spiritus*], which the Saviour confers, like the uninitiated at the mysteries, or the unmusical at dances, not being yet pure and worthy of the pure truth, but still discordant and disordered and material, must stand outside of the divine choir. (Clement V, 4)

Clement of Alexandria added:

In accordance with the method of concealment, the truly sacred Word, truly divine and most necessary for us, deposited in the shrine of truth, was indicated by the Egyptians by what were called among them *adyta*, and by the Hebrews by the veil. Only the consecrated – that is, those devoted to God, circumcised in the desires of the passions for the sake of love to that which is alone divine – were allowed access to them [to the spiritual things].[1]

The idea that only some "elected" people had access to the esoteric domain appears as a real insult to modern man, and the fact that there is a limitation to knowledge looks like a brutal discrimination and an injustice. But, of course, it is nothing of this kind! First of all, the esoteric domain is esoteric not because somebody wanted to institute a secret "association" or because some individuals founded a select "sect" with a hidden status in which only some special carefully selected members had the right to participate. Clement of Alexandria's example is very good: it is useless for the unmusical to sing, let us say in **La Bohème**; they would not be chosen for the simple reason that they don't have the required voice; it is not a question of discrimination or human rights violation, nor of the fact that the music is kept hidden from public ears. The same thing happens with esotericism. Here it is not so much about hiding some particular mysteries regarding the divine order from the common people, but about the fact that, in conformity with the natural law,

---

article, written in 1935, was composed for the Romanian traditional journal *Memra*, of Father Avramescu, yet, unfortunately, the journal ceased its ephemeral existence and Guénon's article remained unpublished).

[1] We may note Clement's expression, "devoted to God"; it is what the Judaic tradition calls *nazirite*.

not everybody has the capacity or the qualification to understand what it is all about. In other words, the celestial mysteries are esoteric, mainly, because human beings have no power and capability to comprehend them. Secondly, and as a result, people could replace true knowledge and comprehension with imaginary ones, that is, with dangerous ones; therefore, and just therefore, these mysteries were guarded from common people, who could misinterpret or wrongly understand them, generating serious consequences. "Thence the prophecies and oracles are spoken in enigmas, and the mysteries are not exhibited incontinently to all and sundry, but only after certain purifications and previous instructions" (Clement V, 4).[1] And: "All then, in a word, who have spoken of divine things, both Barbarians and Greeks, have veiled the first principles of things, and delivered the truth in enigmas, and symbols, and allegories, and metaphors, and such like tropes" (Clement V, 4).

Even Christianity, though shifting from the initiatory and esoteric domain to the exoteric one, continued to keep a veiled lore, because, by its own nature, let us say it again, the divine wisdom contains an ineffable kernel. "O my people, hear my teaching; listen to the words of my mouth. I will open my mouth in parables, I will utter hidden things, mysteries from our past" (**Psalms** 78:1-2). And Saint Paul stated: "We do, however, speak a message of wisdom among the mature [perfects], but not the wisdom of this age or of the rulers of this age, who are coming to nothing. No, we speak of God's secret wisdom, a wisdom that has been hidden and that God destined for our glory before time began" (**1 Corinthians** 2:6-7).

"The secret wisdom," even though Christianity became a religion, that is, an exoteric tradition, remained present, and, of course, still inaccessible to the "unmusical" or "uninitiated," or to the "unspiritual" man. "For [the Spirit] recognizes the spiritual man and the

---

[1] The reference to "purification" is important because, in the early years, when baptism was an initiatory rite that allowed the entrance to the *Lesser Mysteries* (Guénon, **Ésot. Chrét.**, p. 33), before to be baptized the neophyte followed a rigorous preparation composed of purifications and instructions; the baptism itself was a purification through elements.

gnostic as the disciple of the Holy Spirit, dispensed by God, which is the mind of Christ" (Clement V, 4). Saint Paul stressed:

The man without the Spirit does not accept the things that come from the Spirit of God, for they are foolishness to him, and he cannot understand them, because they are spiritually discerned. The spiritual man makes judgments about all things, but he himself is not subject to any man's judgment: «For who has known the mind of the Lord that he may instruct him?» But we have the mind of Christ (**1 Corinthians** 2:14-16).

And more:

Brothers, I could not address you as spiritual but as worldly [corporeally] – mere infants in Christ. I gave you milk, not solid food, for you were not yet ready for it. Indeed, you are still not ready. You are still worldly [corporeally]. For since there is jealousy and quarreling among you, are you not worldly? Are you not acting like mere men? For when one says, «I follow Paul,» and another, «I follow Apollos,» are you not mere men? (**1 Corinthians** 3:1-4)

At the highest level, Saint Paul's "spiritual man" is exactly the initiate of the esoteric domain, but for the Christian tradition, "descended" into the world, he is the man embarked on the path of salvation.[1]

René Guénon wrote: "We could say the passing [of Christianity] from esoteric to exoteric constitutes a real «sacrifice,» which is true for any descent of the Spirit" (Guénon, **Ésot. Chrét.**, p. 28). Therefore, the exoteric domain doesn't have to be understood as a profane one. It is, in a traditional society, a sacred and legitimate domain, since the Spirit descended into it; that is why even in this domain we can talk, in a relative way, about mysteries and secrets.

Therefore also the Egyptians place Sphinxes before their temples, to signify that the doctrine respecting God is enigmatical and obscure; perhaps also that we ought both to love and fear the Divine Being: to love Him as gentle and benign to the pious; to fear Him as inexorably just [and angry] to the

---

[1] The neophyte, the Man, can be male or female; here Man should be understood as Sanskrit *mânava* "a mental being," image of Hindu *Manu*, the Lord of the World.

impious; for the sphinx shows the image of a wild beast and of a man together (Clement V, 5).[1]

Even in the exoteric domain we see a partition between the worldly men, who don't have the capacity to understand the secret wisdom and can only fear God, and the spiritual men, who love God with a Love identical with the knowledge of the Divine. It is the difference between the right hand way and the left hand way, or the difference of what the Pythagoreans symbolized with the letter Y, the two branches representing the virtue and the vice; yet we note that between these two there is the central branch, invisible, which corresponds to the esoteric domain. Of course, if we raise the symbolism to its highest level, then the two branches of the letter Y correspond to esotericism (*déva-yâna*, the way of gods, *Ianua Coeli*) and exotericism (*pitri-yâna*, the way of men, *Ianua Inferni*), and the vertical invisible line is a way leading to an immediate Liberation.[2]

It is impossible to know how the Christian passage from esoteric to exoteric took place and when the initiatory side became completely obscured. We saw in Saint Paul's letters, and after 150 years, in Clement of Alexandria's writings, a language persisting with an initiatory perfume.

It is probably impossible to establish a precise date for this change that made Christianity a religion in the proper sense of the word and a traditional form addressed to everybody without discrimination; what it is sure is that in the time of Constantine and of the Council of Nicaea it was already a consummated fact, so that this one had only to «sanction» it, inaugurating the age of «dogmatic» formulations designated to constitute a pure exoteric presentation of the doctrine. At the same time, Constantine's «conversion»

---

[1] Vol. II, p. 239.
[2] See René Guénon, **Symboles fondamentaux de la Science sacrée**, Gallimard, 1980, p. 251. Michel Vâlsan considered the difference between esotericism and exotericism as being illustrated by the "spirit of servitude" and the "filial spirit" (see Saint Paul's sayings, **Galatians** 4:7), since it is not a question of different mentality but of different spiritual influences conferred; Origen wrote that those who are God's servants are so because they received the spirit of servitude due to fear, and they don't advance to receive the filial spirit (Michel Vâlsan, **L'Initiation Chrétienne**, Études Traditionnelles, no. 389-390, 1965, p. 167).

implied the recognition, through a somehow official act of the imperial authority, of the fact that the Greco-Roman tradition had from now on to be considered extinct, even though it still survived for many years. (Guénon, **Ésot. Chrét.**, p. 28)

The changing from esotericism to exotericism, Guénon also added, could not take place without some inconvenience, but this did not oppose the foundation of Christianity as an exoteric traditional form and did not contest its legitimacy, "due to its huge advantage to the Western world; however, if Christianity as such ceased to be initiatory, there still remained the possibility to subsist, in its core, an initiation specific to Christianity, for an elite" (Guénon, **Ésot. Chrét.**, p. 29). And he concluded:

We should note that this change of the essential characteristic and, we may say, even of the nature of Christianity, perfectly explains why, as we already said, everything that preceded it, was willingly covered with obscurity. It is obvious that the nature of the original Christianity, that is, essentially initiatory and esoteric, had to remain completely ignored by those who now were admitted into the exoteric Christianity. (Guénon, **Ésot. Chrét.**, p. 29)

Nevertheless, a tradition is complete only if it contains both sides, exoteric and esoteric. In other words, the Christian tradition, established as an exoteric domain, and being therefore the fundament of an orthodox traditional society in the Occident,[1] would have been lame without an initiatory kernel. Wherefore, it was normal and necessary, the same way the mistletoe grows on the oak – its host, for various initiatory currents to grow supported by Christianity, they constituting Christian esotericism. And it is not about some kind of syncretism or an artificial cohabitation. Hermetism with its branches, Masonry, Chivalry, Rose-Cross and

---

[1] We understand the Occident to be composed of three main parts: the Near-West (containing the Greek-Orthodox Christianity), the Middle-West containing the European Catholicism and Protestantism, and the Far-West (mostly America). See our article **The Near West**, in **Sophia**, The Journal of Traditional Studies, volume 9, no. 1, summer 2003, Oakton, USA.

others, all were pure Christian initiatory organizations, that is, intimately linked to the Christian tradition, forming its sacred kernel.

Theoretically, as Dante stated, temporal (imperial) power allowed salvation and the realization of the *Lesser Mysteries*, namely the entrance into the Earthly Paradise; on the other hand, spiritual authority (Papacy) guided the path of the *Greater Mysteries* and the entrance into the Heavenly Paradise. In reality, Christian exotericism could only lead, in the best of the cases, to salvation (in its religious sense), often a virtual one, spiritual men being few. Christian rites, changed from initiatory to exoteric, lost their spiritual efficacy, so to say, because they became public and open to everybody; they did not operate anymore in the deepest region of the being, as an initiatory rite would have operated. "Now, then, it is not wished that all things should be exposed indiscriminately to all and sundry, or the benefits of wisdom communicated to those who have not even in a dream been purified in soul; nor are the mysteries of the word to be expounded to the profane" (Clement V, 9).[1]

Clement of Alexandria also said: "Whence also the Egyptians did not entrust the mysteries they possessed to all and sundry, and did not divulge the knowledge of divine things to the profane; but only to those destined to ascend the throne, and those of the priests that were judged the worthiest" (Clement V, 7). Likewise, in the Christian tradition, sacred monks, fasting, praying, purifying their heart of ignorance and consuming a lot of personal effort, have reached the perfection and the spiritual station, like Saint Gregory Palamas; they followed a way that we could call initiatory,[2] and which could, for example, survive under the cover of the religious orders, but which was not accessible to the crowd.

Christian esotericism, in contrast, had the capacity to offer an initiation not only to "priests" or "kings," but to each one who was qualified, helping the neophyte to achieve a real spiritual realization; yet, even in this case, the station obtained was that of the primordial

---

[1] Vol. II, p. 255.
[2] The Hesychastic way of the Greek-Orthodox tradition has an initiatory characteristic, which is difficult to contest.

man, that is, the Earthly Paradise (the integral of the individual being), since Hermetism and Masonry did not possess a metaphysical characteristic, but only a cosmologic one, and Rose-Cross was an initiatory station corresponding only to the Earthly Paradise.[1]

Today, unfortunately, this Christian esotericism doesn't exist anymore. Or, what exists is very poorly represented, being either hidden or almost inaccessible, or having just a virtual efficacy. And it is not difficult to understand why and to accept this truth. Guénon wrote:

To obey and follow the exoteric rites is totally sufficient for «salvation»; it is already a lot, of course, and it is all that the majority of the human beings can ask in a legitimate way, today more than before; but what will do, in these circumstances, those for whom, in conformity with the expression of some *mutaçawwufin*, «Paradise is still a prison»? (Guénon, **Ésot. Chrét.**, p. 26).

---

[1] It doesn't mean that there was no possibility of attaining a complete initiation, with the two steps, the *Lesser* and the *Greater Mysteries*, as proved by Dante or even by Alchemy, where *albedo* (the white phase) corresponds to the *Lesser Mysteries*, and *rubedo* (the red phase) to the *Greater Mysteries*. We may note, as Guénon remarked, that the "adept" (a word so much abused today) represents the perfect one, i.e., the neophyte who has reached spiritual perfection, and who, with regard to the *Lesser Mysteries* is called *adeptus minor*, and with regard to the *Greater Mysteries*, *adeptus major* equivalent to *jîvan-mukta* of the Hindu tradition.

CHAPTER III

ESOTERICISM AND OUTSIDE DARKNESS

THERE IS A GREAT DIFFERENCE between exotericism and the "outside darkness." The exotericism is a perfectly legitimate domain (in the sense of *dharma* of the Hindu tradition), while the "outside darkness" is completely illegitimate (*adharma*). Exotericism represents the side of the tradition open to all the members of that tradition, without distinction, allowing them to participate, as much as each one's capacity permits, in the sacredness. The "outside darkness," in contrast, designates chaos, the counter-initiatory and even the profane perspective, any traditional element being excluded. Exotericism does not oppose esotericism, representing, on the contrary, a precondition to reaching esotericism, and even after initiation it cannot be neglected.[1] Those who do not participate to exotericism allow the profane to invade their lives; in other words, they throw themselves gradually into the "outside darkness."

"But the subjects of the kingdom will be thrown outside, into the darkness, where there will be weeping and gnashing of teeth" (**Matthew** 8:12); "Then the king told the attendants, «Tie him hand and foot, and throw him outside, into the darkness, where there will be weeping and gnashing of teeth»" (**Matthew** 22:13); "And throw that worthless servant outside, into the darkness, where there will be weeping and gnashing of teeth" (**Matthew** 25:30). The "outside

---

[1] René Guénon, **Initiation et Réalisation spirituelle**, Éd. Traditionnelles, 1980, p. 74.

darkness" must not be confused with the exoteric domain, not even with the infernal states. When Dante descended into Hell, at the beginning of his initiatory voyage, he did not enter the "outside darkness"; rather, his state before the initiation corresponded to this darkness.[1]

Even though exotericism is needed to shelter the esoteric, the same way skin is needed to cover and keep the kernel inside,[2] the two domains are profoundly distinct; one who participates more or less in the exoteric aspect has to accept its limits and reject the illusion that, by some miracle, it is possible to obtain an initiation. For this reason, when Christianity was open to all, that is, to exotericism, all its initiatory tracks were carefully obscured, to prevent any disarray, even though, some of the "heresies" born in the early years are proof that the initiatory origins could not be completely wiped away.

We cannot in any way accredit this «obscuring» of the origins to ignorance, such ignorance being evidently impossible for those who should be the more so conscious of this as they participated in it; also, we cannot consider this a «political» and selfish maneuver... the truth is exactly the opposite, that is, [the concealment] was a natural one, required to maintain, in concert with the traditional orthodoxy, the profound distinction between the exoteric and esoteric domains.[3] As we said before, the confusion between the two domains is one of the most probable causes that generated the heterodox «sects,» and, no doubt, among the ancient Christian heresies, there were some which had no other origin but this confusion.[4] (Guénon, **Ésot. Chrét.**, p. 30)

---

[1] However, Guénon uttered explicitly that the descent to Hell also takes place in the initiatory cavern, and so "we must avoid to consider crossing of the labyrinth [the labyrinth drawn at the entrance of the cavern] as designating this descent, and we can ask ourselves to what the labyrinth corresponds: it is the «outside darkness» to which the state of wandering can be perfectly applied" (Guénon, **Symboles**, p. 217).
[2] It seems a "sign of the times" that today we are tempted with artificial fruits without seeds.
[3] "Due to an error inherent to the analytical spirit, it is forgotten that distinction does not mean at all separation" (Guénon, **Crise**, p. 75); such an error is made by many "traditionalists" even today.
[4] A good example is Gnosticism, about which we will talk in a separate chapter.

The Pythagoreans also suggested this profound difference between the esoteric and exoteric domains. Iamblichus tells that the Pythagoreans unveiled their doctrine only to the qualified ones:

And with respect to these probationers, those who appeared to be worthy to participate of his dogmas, from the judgment he had formed of them from their life and the modesty of their behaviour, after the quinquennial silence, then became *Esoterics*, and both heard and saw Pythagoras himself within the veil.[1]

Clement of Alexandria said, we remember, that the Hebrew method to hide was the veil. Iamblichus wrote as well:

Their writings also, and all the books which they published, most of which have been preserved even to our time, were not composed by them in a popular and vulgar diction, and in a manner usual with all other writers, so as to be immediately understood, but in such a way as not to be easily apprehended by those that read them. For they adopted that taciturnity which was instituted by Pythagoras as a law, in concealing after an arcane mode, divine mysteries from the uninitiated, and obscuring their writings and conferences with each other. (Iamblichus 56)

As we already said, the esoteric domain is essentially secretive, not because somebody desired, driven by jealousy or selfishness, to keep hidden some special teachings, but because these teachings were of a super-human nature, and thus, they were inexpressible. In other words, they are mysterious since the common man cannot truly comprehend them, which, of course, generates a reaction, often aggressive and full of fantasy, from those who think they are being held outside.[2] Only secondarily, the initiatory teachings were guarded and it was forbidden to unveil them to the uninitiated, that is, to the worldly people; even though secondary, the "law of secretiveness [or

---

[1] Iamblichus, **Life of Pythagoras**, transl. by Thomas Taylor, Inner Traditions International, 1986, p. 38.
[2] As Clement of Alexandria said, it is not about an imposed secret, but about the incapacity of some people to understand the supernal truth.

of silence]" has a very serious motivation, related to the danger implied by this unveiling.

Let us remark that the mystery which covered the esoteric domain for many years inflamed the fantasy of numerous individuals; today still, there are many attempts to solve the enigma for the public, since for modern man it is impossible to understand that the mystery refers to the spiritual domain, namely, to something completely opposite to the worldly realm[1]; for this reason, various modern works assumed that the secret was about a hidden material treasure, or a political secret, or some made up phantasmagorias.

The "law of secretiveness" is important from both points of view, outer and inner. From an outer point of view, it is important the uninitiated not to have access to some elements which, in their hands, would become dangerous for themselves first, and then for the others. From an inner point of view, any revealing would have produced a weakening of the esoteric aspect, and there are sufficient proofs regarding some Western initiatory organizations, which, admitting as members, without any discrimination, all kind of unqualified individuals, decayed without any chance of recovery; it is as if the spiritual influences ceased to activate in the spiritual plane, restricting themselves to the individual order. For this reason, those admitted inside an initiatory organization had to utter a very strong oath regarding the "law of secretiveness," and this oath was not only formal, because the initiates who betrayed it were as guilty as the profanes that "stole" the mystery. "Conceal it, then, from those who are unfit to receive the depth of knowledge, and so cover the pit. The owner of the pit, then, the Gnostic, shall himself be punished, incurring the blame of the others stumbling" (Clement V, 8). And also: "They say, then, that Hipparchus the Pythagorean, being guilty of writing the tenets of Pythagoras in plain language, was expelled from the school, and a pillar raised for him as if he had been dead" (Clement V, 9). The death penalty was the punishment for anyone

---

[1] Of course, we consider "spiritual" in a traditional sense, that is, something divine.

who revealed the Eleusinian Mysteries.[1] Hermetism stated the same thing: "For it would be impiety to make public through the presence of many witnesses a discussion which is replete with God in all his majesty" (**Corpus Hermeticum, Asclepius I**).[2]

[The Pythagoreans] perpetually preserved among their arcana, the most principal dogmas in which their discipline was chiefly contained, keeping them with the greatest silence from being divulged to strangers, committing them unwritten to the memory, and transmitting them orally to their successors, as if they were the mysteries of the Gods. Hence it happened, that nothing of their philosophy worth mentioning was made public, and that though for a long time it had been taught and learnt, it was alone known within their walls [esoteric]. But to those out of their walls [the exoteric ones], and as I may say, to the profane, if they happened to be present, these men spoke obscurely to each other through symbols. (Iamblichus 116)

This last quotation is most interesting, since it envisions not only the distinction between the esoteric and exoteric domains, even though the "exoteric" ones are mentioned, but that between the esoteric and "outside darkness," with the image of the wall separating the two domains being very strong. Saint Paul also used this image when he wrote: "For he himself is our peace, who has made the two [worlds, Judaic and pagan] one and has destroyed the barrier, the dividing wall of hostility" (**Ephesians** 2:14); we note again the importance of peace and unity, yet here the wall is purely and simply a mark of division. In Iamblichus' text though, the wall replaces the veil, and distinctly and irremediably separates what is within from what is without. If the veil, diaphanous or transparent, is an excellent symbol to show the distinction between esotericism and exotericism, the wall on the other hand, solid and opaque, appears as a barrier, as a battlement defending the inside against the outside. Yet, as we said, even though the exoteric is distinct from the esoteric, the two domains are like the skin and the kernel, and therefore the

---

[1] George E. Mylonas, **Eleusis and the Eleusinian Mysteries**, Princeton Univ. Press, 1974, pp. 224-225.
[2] **Hermetica**, ed. and transl. by Walter Scott, Shambhala, 1993, p. 289.

irreconcilable separation produced by the wall leads us rather to the opposition between esotericism and the outside darkness.[1]

As we explained on another occasion,[2] the word "temple" comes from the Greek *temno*, "to cut"; hence, Greek *temenos* "a piece of land cut off" and "a piece of land sacred to a god"; hence, Latin *templum*, "a sacred place." Cutting off a piece of land means actually to separate somehow this portion from adjoining land. The adjoining land becomes in this case the "outside darkness," the wild woods, a profane and tenebrous place. The land inside the cut becomes the sacred kernel, the self-illuminated place, the "temple," and the city of Troy. In Latin, we find an Indo-European word *seco*, "to cut"; its root provided the words *sacer*, "saint, sacred," *sica*, "dagger" and the English *scythe*. The Latin *sacer* has the same spiritual meaning as the Greek *temenos*. The related Latin word *sacrificium*, "sacrifice, immolation," means "to render sacred" and from there, "to perform a sacred rite." It implies that a *sacrificium* requires a "cutting": cut a piece of land, and it becomes sacred; cut bread or an animal, and that means performing a sacrifice. The sacrifice with its "cutting" automatically establishes a distinction between the *templum*, or the "sacred place," and the rest of the world, which becomes the labyrinth as "outside darkness," the maze of profanity and

---

[1] The Evangelic statement, "At that moment the curtain [veil] of the temple was torn in two from top to bottom" (**Matthew** 27:51), some interpreted it as a proof that in Christianity the barrier between esotericism and exotericism has disappeared, the religious rites having initiatory powers. If we really want to interpret the tearing of the veil, we could say that it is equivalent to what Saint Paul affirmed regarding the wall of partition, meaning rather the access of nations, beside the Jews, to Christ's word. On the other hand, we should observe that, if in the Catholic churches this veil or wall doesn't exist, in the Orthodox churches there is the *iconostasis* or *catapetasma* wall; the word *catapetasma* comes from Greek, where *cata* means "downwards" and *petasma* derives from a verb, "to unfold," hence the significance of veil, curtain, the *catapetasma* being that very veil. It is almost useless to insist that, contrary to what some people think, the area outside the *catapetasma*, which should represent, in a relative way, exotericism, is also sacred (some individuals stubbornly persist in considering Christian exotericism some kind of eso-exotericism, just because they don't really understand what exotericism means). About the rejection of this idea of eso-exotericism see Vâlsan, **Initiation**, pp. 148 ff.

[2] See our work, **The Everlasting Sacred Kernel**.

ignorance,¹ and also, in the worst case, the abode of the counter-initiatory forces.²

In the Islamic tradition, the wall as a "cutting" is the "rampart" that protects against Gog and Magog (**Qur'ân** 18:92-99) and many *hadîth* tell about the crack in the wall, which will bring the end of the world.³ The Great Wall is the "cutting" which protects and separates the whole Cosmos from the "outside darkness," and so any wall is, from a traditional point of view, a specification of the Great Wall, having the same functions. As the Cosmos degenerates, the protective Wall cracks and fissures start to appear. Through these fissures the satanic, tenebrous forces (Gog and Magog) begin to break in; Guénon also wrote about these fissures.⁴

The "cutting" represents not only a protection against the evil forces or an obstacle against ignorance, but also a frame to sustain and order the elements of the enclosure. Any alteration of the sacred frame would shatter harmony, balance, and peace, leading to chaos and devils' invasion. Remus, Romulus' twin brother, was punished and killed because he jumped over the sacred "cutting" of Rome.⁵ After that, a Roman rule stipulated the death penalty for the soldier who crossed the wall of the camp instead of using the gate.⁶

As Plutarch said, the trespasser was called a "profane." Macrobius (**Saturnalia** III, 3, 3) wrote: "about *profanum* almost everybody agrees

---

[1] "The initiatory cave is illuminated within, and, on the contrary, the darkness is outside the cave, the profane world being, of course, assimilated to the «outside darkness»" (Guénon, **Symboles**, pp. 212, 232).

[2] Reviewing the cave's symbolism, as explained by Guénon, we note that the cave represents the Cosmos, but only as formal manifestation, and exiting it symbolizes the super-individual journey of the *Greater Mysteries* (Guénon, **Symboles**, p. 232); in accordance with this specific symbolism, and with respect to the Microcosm, we may say that the cave represents the individuality, and in particular *Anima*, while the "outside darkness" is a sort of infra- or anti-*Anima*.

[3] Émile Dermenghem, **Muhammad**, Harper & Bros. 1958, pp. 20-1.

[4] René Guénon, **Le règne de la quantité et les signes des temps**, Gallimard, 1970, pp. 230 ff.

[5] Plutarch, **The Lives of the Noble Grecians and Romans**, Encyclopaedia Britannica, 1952, p. 19.

[6] Jackson Knight, **Vergil, Epic and Anthropology**, Barnes & Noble Inc., 1967, p. 219.

that it means «what is outside the temple,» «far away from a sacred place»" and gave Vergil as an example, who "talking about a sacred oak grove and the entrance to Hell, also sacred, says: «Keep far away, you, *profanes* – shouts the Sybille – do not come close to the sacred oak grove.»" Indeed, *profanum* (Latin *fanum* means not as much "temple" as any "sacred place"[1]) refers to the "outside darkness" located outside the walls of the temple or of the "cutting." Trespassing the "cutting" represents then the fall from order (Gr. *cosmos*) to chaos. The wall mentioned by Iamblichus is this "cutting" and, in the case of the Pythagoreans, if the inside is the esoteric domain and the "sacred place," the outside designates the "outside darkness." Nicholas of Cusa, for whom "the vision of God" takes place in the dark,[2] beyond the rational limits, where *coincidentia oppositorum* and the Truth reign, said: "The place wherein Thou art found unveiled is girt round with coincidence of contradictories, and this is the wall of Paradise wherein Thou dost abide."[3]

If we can associate esotericism and exotericism, without mixing them, we cannot correlate esotericism with the "outside darkness," except maybe if we consider them as initiation and counter-initiation. This seems evidently; and yet, today, because of the great disarray, we witness exactly such a phenomenon. Often, even members of the exoteric order have anathematized the esoteric, throwing it into the "outside darkness." There are many examples, the attacks against Masonry being one of the best known. It seems weird that apparently serious supporters of the exoteric order could be so aggressive and scared regarding esotericism, when the Fathers of the Church stated it without reservation.

---

[1] "Profane" in Greek is Βεβηλος, a word that might be derived either from Hebrew "in confusion," since a profane person confounds the differences of things (lacks the power of discrimination), or from the particle βε, denoting privation or separation, and βηλος, "the threshold of a temple" (see John Parkhurst, **A Greek and English Lexicon to the New Testament,** William Baynes and Son, London, 1822, p. 94).
[2] This type of darkness corresponds to the Super-luminous Darkness and has nothing to do with the "outside darkness" or with the infernal darkness.
[3] Nicholas of Cusa, **The Vision of God,** The Book Tree, 1999, pp. 43-44.

For the prophet says, «Who shall understand the Lord's parable but the wise and understanding, and he that loves his Lord?» It is but for few to comprehend these things... [Saint Paul] thus inculcates the caution against the divulging of his words to the multitude in the following terms: «And I, brethren, could not speak to you as to spiritual, but as to carnal, even to babes in Christ. I have fed you with milk, not with meat: for ye were not yet able; neither are ye now able. For ye are yet carnal.» (Clement V, 10)

And let us quote again Saint Paul:

That is, the mystery was made known to me by revelation, as I have already written briefly. In reading this, then, you will be able to understand my insight into the mystery of Christ, which was not made known to men in other generations as it has now been revealed by the Spirit to God's holy apostles and prophets. (**Ephesians** 3:3-5)

In a way, though, we can understand the exoteric representatives' apprehension. As Guénon said, "it is admissible for an exoteric one to ignore the esoteric, even though this ignorance does not justify its denial; yet, on the contrary, it is inadmissible that someone who claims to be esoteric, would ignore the exoteric" (**Initiation**, p. 71). However, what happens when, in this great disarray that reigns today, the esoteric domain is mischievously replaced with the "outside darkness"? It is very easy for some exoteric people, in good faith, to ignore what genuine esotericism means and to deny it without discussion. On the other hand, the fall of the world seizes all the levels, and exotericism itself has many fissures in its rampart. Here it is a very complicated situation.

Today, in our modern world, we witness, with dismay, a brutal counterfeit of the esoteric. We are not mistaken when suggesting that, what commonly is labeled as esotericism belongs, in fact, to the "outside darkness." There are some keywords used to confuse the common human minds: *New Age*, occult, magic, Tarot, Runes, yet, the term "esotericism" is also used (actually "abused"), being considered an equivalent of the others. The fundamental difference between genuine esotericism and the counterfeit one is that the former has a kernel of super-human origins, being not a human invention; while the latter (and here we include all kind of elements with various names) is the product of human fantasy, will and ingeniousness, being a construction similar to the Tower of Babel. Modern pseudo-esotericism betrays itself immediately because it is widely open to the public, not requiring any spiritual qualification; in other words it is, in fact, anti-esoteric. Modern pseudo-esotericism, regardless of the name, often appears as one of the mankind's garbage bags, since it gathers without discrimination or comprehension all kind of vestiges collected from lost civilizations, or syncretizes various elements from living traditions, generating bizarre and illusory theories. The lack of any link with the Principle, that is, the lack of super-human or divine element, makes modern pseudo-esotericism a favorite support of the antitraditional and counter-initiatory forces.[1]

There is a difference between antitradition and counter-tradition, comparable to the difference between deviation and subversion (Guénon, **Le règne**, p. 348). To facilitate somehow a better understanding we will present a diagram, which – we have to stress – is just a pale illustration, and limited by its own schematic. The Hindu tradition describes four conditions of *Âtmâ*: the supreme state (which is the abode of *Âtmâ* itself, corresponding to non-manifestation), the informal state, the subtle state and the corporeal state (the last two composing the formal domain). Translated in a Western language, we notice a "hierarchy" having at the top *Âtmâ*, followed by *Spiritus*, *Anima* and *Corpus*. In general, as it appears in

---

[1] Yet even those who claim to be "traditionalists" have a confused image about esotericism. Recently, at a conference about esotericism, held in a university in Paris, its author, even though it seems that he has read and praised Guénon's work, promoted a Christian eso-exotericism, thinking that the esoteric domain refers only to "human knowledge" (which makes the Christian religion something exclusive human), and saw the initiation, not as something reserved for an elite, but as an individual initiation, for each of us. Eventually, the author mistook the esoteric for the exoteric, even though Guénon showed, for example, that the rites, either esoteric or exoteric, have an essentially symbolic character, which means that the symbols have efficacy in different regions with different effects, not belonging exclusively to esotericism (René Guénon, **Introduction génerale à l'étude des doctrines hindoues**, Guy Trédaniel, 1987, pp. 107 ff.).

various initiatory stories, *Spiritus* is masculine and *Anima* feminine, as Purusha is masculine and Prakriti feminine. For this pair, the Plenitude, Pleroma, the Mountain, and *vajra* represent the masculine principle, and the emptiness, the void, the cave, and the shell are tokens of the feminine principle.

In the Far-Eastern tradition, the Void corresponds to *Âtmâ* (without conditions), but there is a median void as well (an immanent projection of the Void), and also the feminine emptiness. Such a projection could be observed in **Yi Jing**, considering the seventh and the eighth hexagrams, *Shi* and *Bi*. *Shi* is composed of *Kun* (earth) up and *Kan* (water) down, that is, of five broken lines and a continuous one (the second line, considered as usually, from inside toward outside); *Bi* is composed of *Kan* up and *Kun* down, that is, of five broken lines and a continuous one (the fifth). The continuous line of *Bi* has as a reflection the continuous line of *Shi*, corresponding to each other with respect to the inverse analogy; the former represents the Emperor's position, the latter indicates the army general's (temporal power, feminine).

In the Hindu tradition, the Void, projected into the plane of the being, constitutes the cave of the heart, the residence of *jivâtmâ*, "the living soul (*anima*)," reflection of *Âtmâ*, the immortal Self. From a worldly point of view, the cave means emptiness, and therefore the feminine principle (with its emblems: womb, receptacle, vessel, bell, calyx) corresponds to this emptiness. We should add another example of such a projection, also from the Hindu tradition: *Brahma saguna*, the Supreme Being, is represented in manifestation by a triad, *Trimurti*, in which the median term is also Brahmâ, but masculine not neutral.

Returning to the initial diagram, we may say that the projection of *Âtmâ* in the microcosm is not *Spiritus* but the median term (between *Spiritus* and *Corpus*), *Anima*; hence the translation "living soul" for *jivâtmâ*. This is, of course, a worldly perspective, with respect to which the initiation means Psyche's quest (the feminine *anima*) of Eros (the masculine *Spiritus*). From the same perspective, as long as *Anima* is wedding *Spiritus*, the world enjoys a traditional life. When the divorce between these two occurs and the viewpoint from *sattwic* shifts to *tamasic*, reaching *Corpus*, the world is invaded by antitradition. The antitraditional point of view is a "materialistic" and "corporeal" one.[1]

Yet, there is more. Through a monkey-like projection, imitating the projection of *Âtmâ* as *jivâtmâ*, it is possible to envisage a sort of anti-*Anima*, beyond the *Corpus*, that is, "infra-human," which represents the counter-tradition. For this reason it is said that the devils have our souls as abode; and therefore, *Corpus* is not the counter-initiatory obstacle, but our soul, our sentiments and desires, our mind and our thoughts.[2] As initiation is the spirit of tradition, so counter-initiation is the "kernel" of counter-tradition (Guénon, **Le règne**, p. 350).

From the diagram it would seem that counter-initiation is an illusion, since the anti-*Anima* appears as a sort of phantasm. In fact, counter-initiation is very real. Guénon wrote: "«Counter-initiation,» we must say, cannot be assimilated to a purely human invention, which would be no different from «pseudo-initiation.» In fact, it must, with regard to its origin, derive from the unique source to which every initiation is attached, and, generally speaking, everything that manifests in our world a «non-human» element" (Guénon, **Le règne**, p. 351). At the end of the cycle, when *Anima* breaks up with *Spiritus*, the counter-initiation becomes fully active and imposes its own projection, *Anima* receiving the reflection of the anti-*Anima*.

---

[1] Schuon considered that "One of the effects of what monotheist symbolism calls the «fall of Adam,» was the separation between the soul and the body, conjointly with the separation between heaven and earth and between the spirit and the soul" (Frithjof Schuon, **From the Divine to the Human**, World Wisdom Books, 1982, p. 99). Yet there is an essential difference between the two kinds of separation and we should be careful when comparing them. Only the modern philosophy, starting with Descartes, assumed that we have two separated principles, the soul (erroneously considered "spirit") and the body; in spite of this differentiation, the modern mentality regarded them from the same "materialistic" perspective, illustrating somehow the fact that, after the divorce between the spirit and the soul, the soul drifted closer and closer to the body; in the end, when anti-*Anima* became active, the profane people "lost their souls."

[2] However, it can be noticed that the counter-initiation has no access to *Spiritus*.

Contrary to pseudo-initiation, which is just an illusory counterfeit of the modern disarray, and a product of the counter-initiation without its own reality, the counter-initiation is very real. It is a counterfeit as well, but only because it imitates initiation like an inverted shadow, yet its intention is not to imitate but to oppose (even if it is impossible, since counter-initiation cannot go beyond the subtle or psychic domain) (Guénon, **Le règne**, pp. 323-4). As the spiritual influence, even though "supra-human," operates through authorized human beings, counter-initiation tries so much more to use human beings by directing them toward the anti-*Anima*, that is, the "infra-human" domain. Counter-initiation is the most suitable term to define the "anti-*Anima*" to which are attached, to different degrees, the human agents through whom the antitraditional action is accomplished, and this – Guénon stressed – is not something conventional but it refers to very precise realities (Guénon, **Le règne**, p. 256).

The antitraditional action had as a goal both to change the general mentality and to destroy all the Western traditional institutions; its first and direct manifestation occurred in the Occident, and from here it started to extend into the entire world, using the Occidental mentality as an instrument (Guénon, **Le règne**, p. 257).[1] There were two phases. During the first one, the mentality became a "materialistic" one, and it considered real only the corporeal domain (Guénon, **Le règne**, p. 258); this phase corresponded to antitradition and blocked the communication with the superior domains. The second phase, much more dangerous in comparison to the solidification produced by materialism, corresponds to counter-initiation, and it launched the subtle dissolvent forces of an inferior nature (Guénon, **Le règne**, pp. 260-1).[2]

---

[1] "[Counter-initiation] is against any tradition, either Oriental or Occidental, including Judaism. With respect to Masonry, ... it is not an agent of the «conspiracy,» but on the contrary one of its first victims" (René Guénon, **Études sur la Franc-Maçonnerie et le Compagnonnage**, Éd. Traditionnelles, 1980, I, p. 110).

[2] These forces belong to the inferior subtle (or "psychic") manifestation, connected to what we called "anti-*Anima*."

Antitradition was just deviation – a step by step deviation away from the traditional doctrines and mentality; it was a voyage from quality to quantity, the humanism of the Renaissance, with rationalism and eventually materialism being the stages encountered by the modern world during this voyage (Guénon, **Le règne**, p. 262). Yet at the end a "reversal" took place, a last degree of deviation, which was the subversion, the great parody, and the monkey-like imitation of tradition.

Guénon considered that the origins of such subversion should be connected to some ancient lost civilization, where a revolt and a perversion occurred, and traditional data point to the revolt of the giants (and of the warrior caste).[1] René Guénon compared this subversion to "the fall of the angels," since the exponents of the counter-initiation, like the profane persons, were ignorant ones who lost *Spiritus*; for them, "the doors of Heaven became closed" (Guénon, **Le règne**, p. 352). Therefore, counter-initiation, having lost the capability to guide human beings toward the super-individual (angelic) states, could only lead them toward the "infra-human" domain, toward anti-*Anima*. Guénon said that in the Islamic tradition those who tried to enter illegitimately a gate saw the gate closing in front of them, and they were forced to return, not as simple profanes, but as *sâher* (magician or sorcerer).[2]

---

[1] The Tower of Babel episode alludes to a similar subversion.
[2] The closing of the heavenly doors represents a symbol used at different levels. An Orphic text affirms: "I'll speak to whom 'tis lawful, but these doors O! shut 'gainst the profane." D'Alveydre considered it was around 3200 B.C. when the Center started to be known as Agarttha, and then it occurred what he called "Irshou's schism." The date of the schism should correspond to the date when the "Iron Age" began. Saint-Yves d'Alveydre regarded Buddhism as another schism; in consequence, Buddha's access to Agarttha became forbidden (Saint-Yves d'Alveydre, **Mission de l'Inde en Europe**, Dorbon, 1949, pp. 84, 96). In **Le Roi du Monde**, first edition, Guénon embraced Saint-Yves and Ossendowski's opinion when he wrote: "Shâkya-Muni, alors qu'il projetait sa révolte contre le Brâhmanisme, aurait vu les portes de l'*Agarttha* se fermer devant lui" (**Roi**, 1939, p. 17); this part was suppressed in other editions.

Yet, despite the real menace represented by the counter-initiation — which could be linked to the Wrath of the Gods —, René Guénon gave us as well a "merciful" statement:

> But, here is the «devil's stupidity»: the exponents of the «counter-initiation,» acting like this, have the illusion that they oppose the spirit itself; but nothing can oppose the spirit. At the same time, unwittingly, they are in fact subordinated to the spirit and they cannot stop being, in the same way as everything that exists, even if unconsciously and involuntarily, subordinated to the divine will, from which nothing can escape. Therefore, the agents of counter-initiation are used as well, even if against their will, to the realization of «the divine plan in the human domain»; they play, like the others, a role in accordance with their nature, but, instead of being conscious of this role, as the real initiates are, they are conscious only of the negative and inverse aspect; thus, they are also deceived [even if they strive to deceive everybody], in a mode which is much worse for them than the pure and simple ignorance of the profanes, since, as a result they will be rejected farther and farther away from the *principial* center until they will fall into the «outside darkness.» (Guénon, **Le règne**, p. 355)

It is no doubt that in the modern world the authentic initiatory domain has disappeared; we will not find anything actively and effectively esoteric. And this leads us to the question: what sense would it make then to talk about esotericism, or does this term have to be eliminated? Yet, regardless of how intense the disarray is in the modern world, there is a chance that some people have access to theoretical esoteric training. An authentic theoretical instruction, especially today, is an indispensable condition for anyone who has a vocation toward the divine things. That is why, concepts as "esotericism" and "initiation" must not be excluded. What has to be opposed is the "outside darkness."

CHAPTER IV

INITIATION AND SALVATION

RENÉ GUÉNON LEVELS THE ESOTERIC domain with the initiatory one. If we clarified to some extent what esotericism means and why it is needed, we would still have to see if the term "initiation" makes any sense in the modern world. The word "initiation" derives from Latin *initium*, meaning "beginning" but also "entrance"; it alludes to the "second birth," to a new commencement, new dawn, a new sunrise (a spiritual one, of course).[1] Consider the Latin tri-part meaning of *initium*: *in-i-tium*, composed of the preposition *in*, *i* from *ire* (derived from *eo*, "to go," related to Sanskrit *êmi*, "go"[2]), and the suffix *tium*; hence the meaning "to enter a gate or a way" for *initiatio*, derived from *in-ire*, and its relation with the god Janus, the protector of initiation. Macrobius (**Saturnalia** I, 9, 11) noted an etymology that connects the name Janus to *ire*, "to go," yet we shouldn't forget that Janus is as well the master of the gates. The significance of *initium* is quite general, but the ancient Latin authors, like Varro and Cicero, used this term to translate the meaning of the Greek word "mysteries," of course, not just any type of mysteries, but precisely the *Mysteries*. Varro wrote: "Initia vocantur potissimum ea, quae Cereri fiunt sacra," that is, "Especially those sacred rites celebrating the goddess Ceres are called

---

[1] From this symbolic solar perspective, we note Jesus Christ's two titles, *Oriens* and *Sol Justitiae*.
[2] X. Delamarre, **Le Vocabulaire Indo-Européen**, Maisonneuve, 1984, p. 254.

initiations" (M. Terentius Varro, **De re rustica**, III, 1, 5). Cicero also said: "nihil melius illis mysteriis, quibus ex agresti immanique vita exculti ad humanitatem et mitigati sumus; initiaque ut appellantur, ita re vera principia vitae cognovimus", that is, "there is nothing better than those mysteries, through which, after a barbarian and wild life, we were cultivated for civilization and we were tamed; they are named initiations, because through them we found out the true principles of life" (M. Tullius Cicero, **De legibus**, II, 14). Eventually, Rufus called the Mysteries of Samothrace *Samothracum initia*, (Q. Curtius Rufus, **Historiae Alexandri Magni Macedonis**, VIII, 1), and Titus Livius wrote about *per initiorum dies*, "during the initiatory days" (Titus Livius, **Ab Urbe condita**, XXXI, 14, 7).[1] It is sure that in the Greco-Roman world the word *mysteria*, "mysteries," referred to the esoteric domain, to something reserved for an elite, for the initiates, and this is the meaning of the Latin word *initium*.

In Greek, μυείσθαι τά μεγάλα means "to be initiated into the Greater Mysteries," the verb *mueo* being translated as "to be initiated into mysteries" or "to instruct." In the Eleusinian Mysteries, *muesis* was the initiation preceding that of the *Greater Mysteries* (called *telete*, Gr. *teleo* meaning "to initiate"). Both the words "mysteries" and *mueo* (and also *mystai*, "initiate") derive from a common radical *mu*, signifying a closed mouth, that is, silence,[2] but also with the eyes closed. Guénon stressed that *mueo*, "to initiate," indicates also "to consecrate," namely, to transmit a spiritual influence, which actually is the essence of initiation.[3] It is very important that the Greeks correlated "the initiation into mysteries" with silence and with darkness (closing of the eyes). Regarding the silence, as Guénon explained, the initiatory teachings contain an inexpressible part, which clarifies the function of the symbols and myths (a word derived from the same radical, *mu*). At the same time, obviously the initiation takes place in a "speaking silence," that is to say, the initiate

---

[1] We owe these quotations to Claudio Mutti.
[2] Eustathius affirmed that the initiates had "to shut their mouths, and not discover what they were taught in the mysteries" (μυειν το στομα, και μη εκφαινειν ά μεμυηνται).
[3] René Guénon, **Aperçus sur l'Initiation**, Éd. Traditionnelles, 1992, p. 123.

becomes mute, closing the mouth as far as the world is concerned, annihilating the multiplicity of words, and regaining the lost Word. In the same way, the initiate becomes blind with regard to the world, opening the "eye of the heart" in exchange; but we could say that through initiation the neophyte enters the darkness of non-manifestation, and also the darkness inside the veil. Various reliefs show the initiate of the Dionysian Mysteries covered with a veil; similarly, Heracles, when he was initiated into the *Mysteries*, had his head covered with a veil, this veil being the same as the one we mentioned before, parting the esoteric and exoteric domains.[1] Finally, we could add Plato's sayings, who, in **Symposium** (218 b), asks the uninitiated to close their ears.

However, the profound meaning of the *Mysteries* and the equivalence between Greek *mueo* and Latin *initio*, lead to the conclusion that the term "initiation" refers to entering the esoteric field, the domain of mysteries, of the invisible and the inexpressible.

Since Western society was built on Greco-Roman heritage, it is no surprise that the Christian esoteric domain took over the two terms "initiation" and "mysteries" in a spiritual sense, yet from the beginning of Christianity we saw the Fathers of the Church using the word "mysteries" with the same significance, following Jesus' example. "He said, «The knowledge of the secrets [*mysteria*] of the kingdom of God has been given to you, but to others I speak in parables, so that, though seeing, they may not see; though hearing, they may not understand»" (**Luke** 8:10). Or: "He told them, «The secret [*mysterion*] of the kingdom of God has been given to you. But to those on the outside [the outsiders, the exoteric people] everything is said in parables so that, they may be ever seeing but never perceiving, and ever hearing but never understanding; otherwise they might turn and be forgiven!»" (**Mark** 4:11-12). And also:

---

[1] It is interesting that the brides also wear veils and it seems that at the beginning of Christianity, both the bride and the groom were covered by a veil, which alludes to *hieros gamos*.

The disciples came to him and asked, «Why do you speak to the people in parables?» He replied, «The knowledge of the secrets [*mysteria*] of the kingdom of heaven has been given to you, but not to them. ... This is why I speak to them in parables: Though seeing, they do not see; though hearing, they do not hear or understand. In them is fulfilled the prophecy of Isaiah: You will be ever hearing but never understanding; you will be ever seeing but never perceiving. For the heart of this nation has become calloused; they hardly hear with their ears, and they have closed their eyes. Otherwise they might see with their eyes, hear with their ears, understand with their hearts and turn, and I would heal them. But blessed are your eyes because they see, and your ears because they hear.» (**Matthew** 13:10-16)

We should note first the unanimity of the Gospels regarding this episode, which suggests its special importance. There is in these quotations a transparent hint of the "Wrath of God," Jesus using in this sense the authority of the prophet Isaiah (6:9-13), who described the end of times, an end of a secondary cycle, when "the cities lie ruined and without inhabitant, until the houses are left deserted and the fields ruined and ravaged, until the Lord has sent everyone far away and the land is utterly forsaken. And though a tenth remains in the land, it will again be laid waste"; the image of the desert, in various traditions, symbolizes precisely the end of times. Like in the Tower of Babel episode, where the "scattering" of the population that, apparently, wanted "unity," is God's Will, the same Will orders now to Isaiah: "Make the heart of this people calloused; make their ears dull and close their eyes. Otherwise they might see with their eyes, hear with their ears, understand with their hearts, and turn and be healed." What Isaiah described is, of course, the Wrath of God, which throws humankind (regardless of the amplitude of the cycle) into the "outside darkness." The fact that God Himself generates the "callousness" ("solidification") of the heart,[1] suggests, somehow, that any Age, from the "Golden" to the "Iron Age," is in conformity to the divine Will, and all partial disorders contribute to total order, that nothing which happens should not have happened. On the

---

[1] In Hesychasm, the *Prayer of the Heart* has "de-solidification" as result, the "dissolving" of the heart.

other hand, in conformity with the inverted analogy, the "solidification" of the heart triggers in fact the Wrath of God and not vice-versa.

Equally interesting is the interdiction to hear, see and understand. We note that the understanding is done with the heart, which is profoundly traditional, the intellect being "situated" in the heart, and the initiatory seeing being accomplished with the "eye of the heart," as Sufism and Hesychasm utter. Regarding the hearing and seeing, we should refer to what Plato said related to mysteries and the uninitiated. The profanes, those thrown into the "outside darkness," outside the wall, do not hear and do not see, and we perceive again the inverted analogy, because the initiates also have their mouths and the eyes closed; yet, their closure is with regard to the world, a withdrawal into the heart, inside the veil.

Concerning the Christian reference to the mysteries, we observe that it appears in all the Gospels, as an answer to the disciples' question, "Why do you speak to the people in parables?" Already the psalmist declared: "I will open my mouth in parables, I will utter hidden things, mysteries from our past" (**Psalms** 78:1-2). Sallust wrote that the parables or fables imitate the gods, according to the effable and ineffable, unapparent and apparent, wise and ignorant. Since, he added, "to inform all men of the truth concerning the gods, produces contempt in the unwise, from their incapacity of learning, and negligence in the studious; but concealing truth in fables, prevents the contempt of the former, and compels the latter to philosophize."[1] *Sûrah* **Ibrâhîm** underlined that God Himself spoke in parables, and presented the parable of the blessed tree[2]; "So

---

[1] Sallust, **On the Gods and the World**, transl. by Thomas Taylor, The Philosophical Research Society, Ca., 1976, pp. 9-11. We may note the words fable, effable and ineffable, which derive from Latin *fari, for*, "to talk." As with the myth, which, even if it comes from the Greek *mu* (referring to silence), breaks the silence expressing the ineffable in a symbolic mode, the same occurs with the sacred fable (and not the one invented by individuals), which tries to translate the ineffable. We also observe that the Latin *for* meant initially "to prophesize, to talk inspired by the gods," and from here derived the Latin *fatum*, "prophecy" and only later "fate."
[2] Noah's family was considered a blessed tree.

Allâh sets forth parables for men, in order that they may receive admonition" (**Qur'ân**, 14:24-26).

Finally, the information that Jesus used the term *mysterion* (pl. *mysteria*) suggests not only the initiatory characteristic of primitive Christianity, but also the concordance, so contested, between Saint Paul and Christ.[1] Yet what interests us most is the evidence that there was from the beginning a clear understanding of the terms "initiation" and "mysteries."[2]

All the more strange appears the fact that the moderns took over the word *initium*, abusing it copiously. And we are not talking about the typical language abuse of the profane world, where we encounter expressions such as "initiation into cooking," "initiation into geology," "initiation into economics," etc., but about the abuse of the spiritual sense by scientists, scholars and academic researchers, who should show responsibility in such matters. At the very moment when we comprehend that initiation refers to divine things and transmits a spiritual influence and a divine blessing, we become shocked by the absurdity of some expressions such as "initiation into geology," which nothing can justify, since here it is not about the "evolution" of the language, or about the "progress" of the human mentality, but purely and simply –why should we lie to ourselves? – about a decline from the sacred to the profane. The most shocking abuse though appears to be the use of this notion, "initiation," to describe various social and even religious rites, especially after modern man discovered the so-called "primitive societies" as source of information. Without any distinction, the term "initiation" was taken over by anthropologists, ethnologists, historians of religions,

---

[1] Sure, some have disputed the fact that Jesus used the word *mysterion*, accrediting it to His disciples, who employed the language of their time; it is a weak argument, bearing in mind that the *Mysteries* were celebrated in the Roman Empire long before Christ's crucifixion; on the other hand, Jesus belonged to the initiatory Christianity more than anybody else. The individuals, who try to promote discordance between the teachings of Christ and those of Saint Paul, are exponents of that division combated so fiercely by Saint Paul.

[2] When Saint Paul wrote: "I have learned the *secret* of being content in any and every situation, whether well fed or hungry, whether living in plenty or in want" (**Philippians** 4:12), he alluded to the initiation into sacred mysteries.

etc., and used to describe rites of passage from adolescence to maturity, from celibate to marriage, the entrance into some associations or groups, and so on. The modern idea, in flagrant contradiction with its own Western traditional heritage, that initiation means "rites of passage" (regardless of what passage we are talking about) is very dangerous because, eventually, it could lead to the passage to the "outside darkness."

Even in the sacred domain of orthodox exotericism the notion of "initiation" has no place. Some tried to argue that the Christian tradition, even though as a religion it is exoteric, has preserved its initiatory trait and the Holy Sacraments still offer an initiation in the normal sense of the word, and access to the *Mysteries*. René Guénon is categorical in this respect: "At this hour we cannot anymore consider the Christian rites as having an initiatory feature" (Guénon, **Ésot. Chrét.**, p. 26). But it doesn't mean that he succeeded in convincing those who supported the illusion of an "esoteric exotericism." Among them were close associates, who should have understood better the difference between religion and initiation, and only because of them Guénon decided to insist upon the early years of Christianity. We shouldn't be surprised. Saint Paul sent three letters to the Corinthians (one of which was lost), striving again and again to bring them back to his teachings, and yet the Corinthians remained hostile to their own Apostle. But Saint Peter himself, though devoted completely to Christ, rejected Him three times, and this episode was kept in the Gospel as an admonition for us to see how weak, ephemeral and inconstant the human ego is.[1]

As we have already seen, René Guénon declared: "Only with regrets we decided [to write about Christianity]," stressing "the almost impenetrable obscurity that enveloped everything regarding the origins and the first years of Christianity"; yet who had ears to hear? "Though hearing, they do not hear." After his associates insisted relentlessly, Guénon decided to write a few articles about

---

[1] We may note that Saint Peter, even though Jesus told him in advance what would happen, did not believe Him, having more confidence in his ego than in the immortal Christ.

Christianity, yet later on, some of the same associates, joined by the so-called "Guénonians,"[1] started to criticize, since Guénon's writings did not match their illusions. Those who attacked René Guénon felt deeply insulted because he denied the existence of an esoteric and initiatory domain to Christianity. Some of them, as reply, attempted to prove the survival and permanency of an esotericism within the Christian religion, not as a separate domain, but integrated within it. Even though this episode might appear anecdotic and would perhaps fit better in a monograph about Guénon, actually it is aimed at our modern world. First of all, it is clear that, without Guénon, nobody would have heeded these individuals; secondly, no modern Catholics would have thought to talk about initiation and esotericism with regard to the Christian Church, prior to René Guénon. On the contrary, they would have rejected esotericism as something related to the occult and magic.[2] Thirdly, the fact that they felt insulted is out of order, since Guénon clearly stated the importance of exotericism and so, of the Christian religion, which, as we showed, is (or should be) a sacred domain; also, René Guénon indicated that in the frame of the Christian religion it is possible to achieve salvation, which means, in the ideal case, to enter the Earthly Paradise, and for our days such a realization is not little or negligible. Paraphrasing Ramana Maharshi, maybe it would be more useful for those detractors to focus on their own salvation and only then to be worried about esotericism and initiation. Guénon wrote: "We are afraid that for many the reason for which they would like to convince themselves about the initiatory value of the Christian rites is to dispense themselves from a regular attachment to an initiatory organization and to pretend that,

---

[1] The label "Guénonian" is absurd, and all those who are so proud of it should perhaps be labeled as "anti-Guénonians." Those who use this appellation, "Guénonian," for classification or for denigration, have no idea what it is all about.
[2] René Guénon noticed in his article already quoted, **Nouvelles confusions**, how the individuals belonging to religious circles were forced (due mainly to his writings) to admit the existence of esotericism.

even so, they obtained initiatory results" (Guénon, **Ésot. Chrét.**, p. 36).[1]

René Guénon doesn't deny the survival of an initiatory kernel. He wrote: "However, if Christianity as such ceased to be initiatory, there still remained the possibility to subsist, within it, an initiation, specifically Christian, for an elite" (Guénon, **Ésot. Chrét.**, p. 29). And he added:

All over where there are initiations belonging to a determined traditional form and taking exotericism as its basis, the exoteric rites can somehow, for those who received such an initiation, be transposed into another order, being used as support for an initiatory operation, and consequently, for these, the effects will not be limited to the exoteric order, as happens for the majority of the adherents of that traditional form. Nonetheless, far from replacing a regular initiation, this initiatory use of the exoteric rites requires, on the contrary, such an initiation, as an essential and necessary condition in order to use these rites (any other qualification, regardless of how outstanding it could be, cannot substitute this condition); otherwise, everything remains at the mystical level, that is, at the level of religious exotericism. It is now easy to understand the real nature of those who, in the Middle Ages, issued writings of obvious initiatory inspiration, erroneously considered today as «mystical.» We are not talking here about some cases of «spontaneous» initiation, or about exceptional cases where a virtual initiation, held attached to the Holy Sacraments, could become effective, when there was the chance of a normal attachment to one of the regular initiatory organizations that still existed in those times, often under the cover of the religious orders and within them, though not to be confounded with them. (Guénon, **Ésot. Chrét.**, pp. 37-38)

There is no doubt, unless perhaps for those who, like the Corinthians, declare: «I follow Paul»; «I follow Apollos»; «I follow

---

[1] It is deplorable how recklessly everybody talks about initiation. The Eleusinian Mysteries, for example, remained unveiled, and nobody knows what they really were; they remained, indeed, mysteries, and the Eleusinian initiation contained something ineffable. An initiation about which everybody talks loudly, or which could be described, is not a genuine initiation! And even if some traitors had unveiled parts of the initiatory ritual, the common people, hearing or reading about it, wouldn't have been initiated or illuminated.

Cephas»; «I follow Christ,» that the divine commandment was the foundation of an exoteric tradition for the nations (for the many and not for the few), in order to bring *salvation* (and not Liberation, *moksha* of the Hindu tradition).

When the Jews saw the crowds, they were filled with jealousy and talked abusively against what Paul was saying. Then Paul and Barnabas answered them boldly: «We had to speak the word of God to you first. Since you reject it and do not consider yourselves worthy of eternal life, we now turn to the Gentiles. For this is what the Lord has commanded us: I have made you a light for the Gentiles, that you may bring *salvation* to the ends of the earth.» (**Acts** 13:45-47)

It is obvious that, if it had remained a regular initiatory domain, all the initiatory organizations, which came from outside to reach their apogees in the Middle Ages, would not have been needed; it would have been an impossibility, like the absurd theory of reincarnation. If there had existed within the Christian skin an active esoteric core, with initiatory rites and transmissible divine teachings, which would have permitted the conquering of Heavenly Paradise and even the passage beyond it, it would have been impossible for some initiatory currents, like Hermetism, to be grafted from outside. If the religious rites would have permitted the initiation, as some erroneously pretend, it is even more difficult to explain the existence of these initiatory organizations, which formed at one moment an operative and effective Christian esotericism (Guénon, **Ésot. Chrét.**, p. 36). That is why, for the modern Western world, the Christian religion remains an exoteric way, having *salvation* as its objective.

We know that already in Saint Paul's times the distinction was made between the "worldly man" and the "spiritual man," as a reflection of the difference between esotericism and exotericism. What could we say today, in the modern world, about the "spiritual man" or about *salvation*? If an effective Western initiation were impossible to envisage today, thanks to the profanation of modern society, would it be possible to still have access to *salvation*? René Guénon wrote:

Initiation and Salvation

Exotericism, considered in its largest sense, that is, as the part of tradition open indistinctly to all, cannot provide but a goal of purely individual order, since anything other would be inaccessible to the majority of the adherents of that tradition, and this goal precisely constitutes salvation. There is no way we can even closely talk about an effective realization of a super-individual [angelic] state, much less about Liberation [beyond any conditioned state]. If «Paradise is a prison» for some, that is precisely because the being who attained the paradisiacal state (explicitly, the one who reached salvation), is still chained (and nor for a finite but indefinite period of time) by the limits that define the human individuality. (Guénon, **Initiation**, pp. 78-79)

Salvation, in the common sense of the word, cannot be obtained while alive, as Liberation (*moksha*) can.[1] It doesn't go beyond the individual world and, in the best of the cases, reaches the peak of the Mount of Purgatory, but, by no means, an angelic state. The fact that some initiatory forms, belonging to Christian esotericism, especially permitted the passage through the *Lesser Mysteries*, suggests that the exoteric rites, in general, had a limited efficacy even with regard to salvation. How effective are they today, in a world embroiled in great disarray? And then, even if, exceptionally, somebody would obtain salvation, what good would it be if there were no possibility of surpassing the individual state?[2]

What would be the advantage for the human beings who exactly followed the traditional precepts of the exoteric order to stay in this state indefinitely? The fact of the matter is that the advantage would be considerable, since, anchored in the prolongations of the human state for so long as this state

---

[1] There are though exceptional cases, and Saint Symeon the New Theologian encouraged the Christian believers: "I beg you to strive to see Him and contemplate Him already in this life. If we endeavour to see Him already here, we will not die, «the death will not rule us»" (**Catechises** 3, 421-426). Yet Saint Symeon was an initiate.

[2] The religious process allows us to communicate with the angelic states but not to take them in possession. "With regard to the initiatory process, the simple communication with the superior states cannot be regarded as an end but only as a starting point; if this communication must be established first by the action of a spiritual influence, it is to allow next the taking in possession of these states, and not simply, as in the religious order, to make descend a «grace» that connects us to them in a certain way, but without allowing us to penetrate them" (Guénon, **Aperçus sur l'initiation**, pp. 26-7).

will subsist in the manifestation (which is equivalent to perpetuity), these human beings will not pass to another individual state [where they could lose their central position]. (Guénon, **Initiation**, pp. 78-79)

René Guénon also wrote: "The common individuals, who cannot now reach a super-individual state, could at least, if they get salvation, put an end to the human cycle... they will not lose the advantage of a human birth, but will keep it definitively, salvation bringing them closer to the final goal, Liberation" (Guénon, **Initiation**, p. 81).

Yet we should not deceive ourselves. Although there is such a distance between salvation and initiation, for the modern man even salvation is hardly accessible. Since:

Anyone can follow the Evangelic way, as much as not only his or her capacity allows, but also the given contingent circumstances, and that is, indeed, all that can be asked, in a reasonable mode, of those who endeavour to surpass the exoteric practice. This exoteric practice could be defined as a necessary and sufficient minimum to assure «salvation,» because that is the goal to which it is destined. (Guénon, **Ésot. Chrét.**, pp. 31-32)

As we have already said, these words inflamed the Christian circles against Guénon, yet, in fact, what we witness is only a burst of the human *ego*, something that happens so often nowadays. There is no competition, actually, between initiation and salvation, but we have to place each one at its proper level. And for these days, when profanity and ignorance are so intense, salvation would be a very good antidote, considering that no special qualifications are needed, as in the case of an initiation. However, we don't see around us anything similar to such a redemptive operation. Even salvation requires a special vocation, a spiritual one, in the sense of Saint Paul's words, and how many worldly men are capable of following "exactly the traditional precepts of the exoteric order"?

Some people challenged the idea of a "profound distinction" between esotericism and exotericism, suggesting a common "revelation" and consequently considering the Christian tradition as some kind of "esoteric exotericism." Yet nobody has contested the unity of the Christian Word. The passage from esotericism to exotericism

> did not touch or modify [Christ's teachings] in any mode, with respect to their «letter,» and the permanence of the Evangelic texts and of the New Testament's other writings, which evidently are from the early years of Christianity, constitute enough evidence; what changed was only the manner of understanding them, or, in other words, the perspective from which they are now seen, and their meaning; yet we cannot say that there is something false or illegitimate with this meaning, because the same truth can have applications in different domains, in conformity with the correspondence that exists in all the orders of Reality. (Guénon, **Ésot. Chrét.**, p. 31)

In other words, even today the mystery of Christian teachings is no less permanent and immutable. What has changed is human perception and that is why we observe rites modified by human intervention. As René Guénon wrote, "actually, there is no profane domain to which some things belong by their nature; there is only a profane point of view, which is just the product of a spiritual decline of humankind, and so, it is completely illegitimate [*adharma*]" (Guénon, **Initiation**, p. 75).[1]

And so, this way we can explain why those, who think that the exoteric rites are also initiatory, are under the spell of an illusion; more than that, we can say that the exoteric rites themselves don't have anymore the power they had in the past, because of the profane perspective, which has invaded modern mentality.

Guénon considered that the spiritual influence has various effects in various orders of Existence. In all orthodox traditions, spiritual influence or divine blessing, transmitted usually through rites, is regarded, together with personal effort, as indispensable for a spiritual realization. The nature of the spiritual influence is, of course, transcendental; otherwise, it would be just psychical "force" acting only in the individual domain. But if the lesser cannot contain the

---

[1] René Guénon wrote also, in another work: "The fact of the matter is that, actually, there is no such thing as a «profane domain» that opposes a «sacred domain»; there is only a «profane point of view,» which is nothing else than the point of view of ignorance" (Guénon, **Crise**, p. 87).

greater, and the particular cannot contain the general, then, the psychical influence cannot activate in the super-individual domain; the spiritual influence, on the other hand, has access to all Three Worlds, where it operates accordingly with each level of existence. As the eye sees the light because it contains a luminous principle in its essence, so the angelic states cannot be reached unless something angelic is within us, and Dante demonstrated it. The spiritual influence intervenes, Guénon said, both in the exoteric rites (which still are sacred) and in the esoteric rites, but the effects are different. When the spiritual influence restricted itself to the exoteric domain, "its effects were limited to some possibilities of the individual order exclusively, having «salvation» as a goal, even though the same Christian ritual supports are used and without which we cannot talk about a truly Christian tradition" (Guénon, **Ésot. Chrét.**, pp. 25-26). It goes without saying that in the case of some rites or ceremonies invented by individuals, as they wished, there is no spiritual influence; similarly, if some individuals alter the authentic rites, the effects of the spiritual influence will be altered consequently.[1]

Of course, we must ask a question, essential to modern man: how does the spiritual influence know if the rite is initiatory, exoteric or profane? Guénon wrote that "there are some precepts which, aimed especially at those who followed an initiatory path, and, consequently, applicable only in a restricted and qualitatively homogenous area, become impracticable if they are extended to the whole assembly of human society" (Guénon, **Ésot. Chrét.**, p. 31), and: "Today all the Christian rites are public, which is inadmissible if they were initiatory rites" (Guénon, **Ésot. Chrét.**, p. 33). In other words, the sun doesn't shine more strongly or weakly only for some people and not for others; but, those who receive the rays are in a better or worse position from a spiritual perspective. Apuleius, speaking about the Mysteries of Isis, alluded to the initiate who sees the Midnight Sun. To see the Midnight Sun, the "eye of the heart"

---

[1] That is why those who want to shorten the funeral rites, as has occurred in the Christian Orthodox Church for example, perpetrate a sacrilege, depriving the deceased of the important effects of these rites.

has to be open, yet few are elected and "small is the gate and narrow the road that leads to life, and only a few find it" (**Matthew** 7:14).

Even Christ, though He urged the spreading of the divine Word,[1] suggested also that from many only few are chosen.[2] At the very moment when we pass from few to many, spiritual influence no longer has the same effects; and this, not so much because of the quantity, but especially because of the quality of the crowd. At the beginning of present humanity, all people, many, few, no matter how numerous they were, had free and direct access to this spiritual influence. Today, nothing like that is possible anymore. The problem is not only that, having become public, the initiatory rites are diluted by passing from few to many, but mainly that this crowd, without cohesion and homogeneity, acts in different directions, scattering and reducing, even rejecting the spiritual influence.

We can very well apply the parable of the sower to spiritual influence (**Matthew** 13:3-8, 18-23). Like the seed, spiritual influence descends into the world, but to produce a crop it needs good soil, and even after that, the plant has to be nursed, weeded, watered, etc. The barren soil is like the "callous" heart, a dry, solidified soil, full of weeds or a desert. The ignorant are those deprived of this divine blessing.[3]

---

[1] "What I tell you in the dark, speak in the daylight; what is whispered in your ear, proclaim from the roofs" (**Matthew** 10:27).

[2] It is interesting that "the many" are related to the "outside darkness": "Then the king told the attendants: Tie him hand and foot, and throw him outside, into the darkness, where there will be weeping and gnashing of teeth. For many are invited, but few are chosen" (**Matthew** 22:13-14). We note the ambiguity, because the chosen ones can follow either salvation or the initiatory way.

[3] The unfruitful, arid soil could be also a symbol of human decadence in this "Iron Age," hence the need for an intense rain. Rain in different traditions is the symbol of the spiritual influences and therefore, an intense rain means the necessity of an initiatory organization, which is able to concentrate spiritual influence. The birds, eating the seeds and representing the evil one that comes and snatches away what was sown in the man's heart, symbolize from an initiatory perspective the spiritual influence that left the world; related to this, Saint Symeon the New Theologian said that those who receive something after "the second baptism" and don't comprehend it, don't participate in the divine virtue and in the power of the Holy Spirit, because the grace has left them; the same thing happens with those who are baptized with water and after that they start to do evil things (Vâlsan, **Initiation**, p. 174). For this

Therefore, an initiatory organization has to be very careful when it receives new members, since anyone unqualified or ignorant will do nothing less than diminish the effects of the spiritual influence transmitted through the rites of this organization. It is interesting that Guénon referred in a short paragraph to the symbolism of the seed. He wrote:

> In the present situation, we cannot harvest without sowing [in contrast with the «spontaneous generation» at the beginning of the cycle], and that is true both spiritually and materially; the seed which has to be sown in the being in order to make possible future spiritual development, is exactly the influence which, in a virtual condition and a state of «complication» [in the sense of the word used by Nicholas of Cusa] perfectly compatible with that of the seed, is communicated to the being through initiation. And it is not because spiritual influence itself could be for a moment in a state of potentiality, but the neophyte receives it somehow in a proportional manner to his own condition. (Guénon, **Initiation**, p. 54)

In the same proportional manner, the spiritual influence operates in both the esoteric and exoteric domains. For this reason, religious rites do not have initiatory power. Guénon alluded also to the wheat grain of the Eleusinian Mysteries, which refers to the same symbolism, and reminds us that the neophyte, namely the one who is initiated, bears a name which signifies "new plant." Dionysius the Areopagite transmitted another fundamental parable:

> Imagine a great shining [super-luminous] chain hanging downward from the heights of heaven to the world below. We grab hold of it with one hand and then another, and we seem to be pulling it down toward us. Actually it is already there in the heights and down below and instead of pulling it to us we are being lifted upward to that brilliance above, to the dazzling light of those beams. Or picture ourselves aboard a boat. There are hawsers joining it to some rock. We take hold of them and pull on them, and it is as if we were dragging the rock to us when in fact we are hauling ourselves and our boat toward that rock. And, from another point of view, when someone on

---

reason (as René Guénon also said), the Christian baptism, which is given to all new born children cannot represent an initiatory rite, since a child can anytime later become preoccupied with things incompatible with the goal of initiation.

the boat pushes away from the rock which is on the shore he will have no effect on the rock, which stands immovable, but will make a space between it and himself, and the more he pushes the greater the space will be.¹

We may say that the golden chain is the spiritual influence. We see that, without a personal effort, without pulling ourselves, yet using the chain or the hawser, nothing will be accomplished. We understand now that personal effort on the initiatory way, which from an individual point of view means to try to pull Divinity to us into our heart, actually represents our rise. Eventually, if the boat is stuck or "solidified," or if the sailors are ignorant and clumsy and do not understand the function of the hawser, the boat will not come closer to the rock, and in some cases the space between the rock and the boat will even increase. And if the hawser (golden chain) misses, the boat will drift toward the "outside darkness."² We should remember that Dante, even though he belonged to Christian exotericism which, in his times, constituted a still strong traditional society, needed an initiatory way and guides of Vergil's and Beatrice's caliber, to travel through the *Lesser* and *Greater Mysteries*. If Dante needed an initiation in those times, how can we think that today it is easier and exoteric rites are enough to surpass the individual state?³

---

¹ **The Divine Names**, III, 1. See Pseudo-Dionysius, **The Complete Works**, Paulist Press, 1987, p. 68. A deep silence reigned upon Dionysius' works in the first five centuries, and then it couldn't be decided who the author was. That is why sometimes he is called Pseudo-Dionysius (Vladimir Lossky, **Essai sur la Théologie Mystique de L'Église d'Orient**, Aubier, 1944, pp. 21-22). We may wonder if, under this name, hid an initiatory elite. "A few men became followers of Paul and believed. Among them was Dionysius, a member of the Areopagus" (**Acts** 17:34).
² It is what Guénon wrote about the initiatory realization, which he defined as a "conquest," implying essentially individual initiative; but, obviously this individual cannot by himself reach what it is beyond him, and therefore, necessarily the intervention of super-individual elements are required as a response to individual aspiration (letter to Vasile Lovinescu, May 1936).
³ We can give two examples from more recent days. Joseph de Maistre wrote before the outbreak of the French Revolution: "Everything is mystery in the two Testaments, and the chosen ones of the one and the other Law were nothing else but initiates. And we have to question this respectful Antiquity and ask how it understands the sacred allegories. ... This word mystery doesn't signify, *principially*, anything but the truth hidden within the letter by those who possessed it (Joseph de

To end this chapter we might mention Michel Vâlsan who, in 1965, made efforts, in response to the attacks of some of René Guénon's "associates," to demonstrate the unambiguous difference that exists between the exoteric and esoteric domains, as well as the initiatory characteristic of esotericism, with regard to the Christian tradition. Maybe some readers will think that this persistence in stressing the distinction between exoteric and esoteric is exaggerated, but actually it is fundamental considering the deep disarray which reigns today in the world, when the most bizarre things are labeled as esoteric, occult or Gnostic.

Maistre, **La Franc-Maçonnerie**, Éd. D'Aujourd'hui, 1980, p. 106). Referring to this text, Guénon wrote: "Is it possible to affirm more clearly and more explicitly the existence of esotericism, in general, and of Christian esotericism in particular?" (Guénon, **Franc-Maçonnerie**, I, p. 27). Beside Joseph de Maistre, Martinez de Pasqually, from the same period, deserves to be mentioned. He tried, without success, to found an initiatory Order. Martinez de Pasqually's mission failed, not only because he died before finalizing the organization of the Order, and his disciples, barely qualified, lamentably deviated, but also because the use of "phenomena" and "passes," and auditory and luminous transient apparitions, especially at equinox, did not go beyond the individual world. A real regeneration, in those particular cyclic circumstances, would have required a very powerful capital of spiritual energies from the Most High, and not some magical phenomena of random value. The hidden organization that initiated Martinez into the ceremonial magic (Martinez possessed genuine "powers" and knowledge in this domain) used insufficiently strong weapons to match the unfavorable cyclic moment in which the Occident was at this time. The spiritual influence was more probably an influence of a cosmologic and subtle order, which could not be transmitted to Martinez's disciples; the qualifications of modern people were often inexistent, and for this reason it was impossible for the spiritual influence to operate. It seems clear that Martinez de Pasqually was in not a very good situation for his mission; the people were too worldly, and Martinez, sincere and naïve (a "veritable man," as he himself declared), had a lot of deceptions; he insisted that *la Chose* ("the thing") did not come directly from him, but from above, and so, each one proportionally to his qualifications, would obtain results accordingly. About Martinez's life see Gérard van Rijnberk, **Un thaumaturge au XVIIIe, Martines de Pasqually**, Éd. D'Aujourd'hui, 1980; in this monograph is reproduced a letter of Rudolf Salzman, who wrote: "This divine force activates as it pleases and produces various effects. Saint Paul indicated it in some paragraphs of his letters; some are the apostles, he says, others the prophets, others have the gift of explaining the prophets, of instructing, of producing miracles, of speaking foreign languages, etc. Yet it is the same spirit that operates, and there, where the divine spirit does not operate, the whole of human teaching remains fruitless" (I, p. 142).

Initiation and Salvation

Michel Vâlsan preferred to let the Fathers of the Church speak for themselves and Clement of Alexandria was the first one, not only because he belongs to primitive Christianity, but also for his wisdom. We have reproduced here some paragraphs quoted by Vâlsan, but we have extended them for better understanding (Vâlsan, **Initiation**, pp. 163-164).

For many reasons, then, the Scriptures hide the sense [the sacred meaning]. First, that we may become inquisitive, and be ever on the watch for the discovery of the words of salvation. Then it was not suitable for all to understand, so that they might not receive harm in consequence of talking in another sense about the things declared for salvation by the Holy Spirit. Wherefore the holy mysteries of the prophecies are veiled in the parables – preserved for chosen men, selected for knowledge as a consequence of their faith [to pass from faith to knowledge]; for the style of the Scriptures is parabolic. (Clement VI, 15)[1]

Clement of Alexandria, Vâlsan stressed, showed this initiatory tradition as an oral one, a way of the chosen ones with roots in Christ:

Thus the Lord did not hinder [us] from doing good while keeping the Sabbath; but allowed us to communicate concerning those divine mysteries, and of that holy light, to those who are able to receive them. He did not certainly disclose to the many what did not belong to the many; but to the few to whom He knew that they belonged, who were capable of receiving and being moulded according to them. But secret things are entrusted to speech, not to writings, as is the case with God. And if one says that it is written, «There is nothing secret which shall not be revealed, nor hidden which shall not be disclosed» [**Luke** 8:17], let him also hear from us, that to him who hears secretly, even what is secret shall be manifested. This is what was predicted by this oracle. And to him who is able secretly to observe what is delivered to him, that which is veiled shall be disclosed as truth; and what is hidden to the many, shall appear manifest to the few. (Clement I, 1)[2]

---

[1] Vol. II, p. 378.
[2] Vol. I, p. 356.

And it is important to note, Vâlsan insisted, that only an initiatory generation separated Clement of Alexandria from the Apostles. Those who transmitted the tradition received it from the Apostles Peter, James, John and Paul, the way the son receives it from the father, and the "blessed doctrine came by God's will to us [to Clement] also to deposit those ancestral and apostolic seeds" (Clement I, 1).[1] Vâlsan suggested that the initiatory transmission followed a way indicated in the early writings of the Church: "After Christ's resurrection, the Lord transmitted to the other Apostles and the other Apostles to the seventy, among whom was also Barnabas" (Vâlsan, **Initiation**, p. 165).[2]

The number seventy is first of all symbolic and it appears in the **Old Testament** where it is said: "The descendants of Jacob numbered seventy in all; Joseph was already in Egypt" (**Exodus** 1:5); and: "Then he said to Moses, «Come up to the Lord, you and Aaron, Nadab and Abihu, and seventy of the elders of Israel»" (**Exodus** 24:1); eventually, the posterity of Noah and his sons, mentioned in the **Bible**, was seventy (**Genesis** 10). Some scholars considered that the Jerusalem Church, shepherded by James, "brother of Jesus," was an *Ecclesia* composed of seventy members, but in the Judaic tradition the number seventy is a symbolic number designating, as does the "ten thousands" of the Far-Eastern tradition, all the living beings, that is, the entire population, which after the Tower of Babel episode, was scattered into the world. However, in the Christian tradition, seventy acquires a special value, even an initiatory one, since Eusebius, the bishop of Caesarea and the Emperor Constantine's close associate at the Council of Nicaea, wrote in his **History** that the Apostle Matthew, who replaced Judas Iscariot, was also part of the seventy. And these seventy were instituted by Jesus Christ: "After this the Lord appointed seventy others and sent them two by two ahead of him to every town and place where he was about to go" (**Luke** 10:1); the phrase is

---

[1] Vol. I, p. 355.
[2] The quotation is from **Hypotyposes** of Clement of Alexandria, quoted by Eusebius in his **History of the Church** (II, 1, 4).

enigmatic, yet we may find a key about the mission which was incumbent on the seventy, directly from Jesus: "When you enter a house, first say, «Peace to this house.» If a man [son] of peace is there, your peace will rest on him; if not, it will return to you" (**Luke** 10:5-6). These lines, as well as the next ones, are very rich in spiritual meaning. We have already mentioned Guénon's explanation that "peace" is an attribute of the spiritual center, with regard to the world, and Jesus said, "My peace I give you. I do not give to you as the world gives" (**John** 14:27), which suggests that this "peace" is the spiritual influence derived from the center, an equivalent to *hesychia* (the "stillness" or "quietness") and opposite to worldly wrath. It seems pretty clear that "peace" is received only by the "man of peace" (or the "son of peace"), the same way the Light is seen only by the "son of light," that is, only by the capable one, the chosen one, or the qualified one, by the one who is attracted to "peace," while to the unqualified one peace will be withdrawn.[1]

Eventually, Michel Vâlsan affirmed that another proof that an initiatory domain existed in Christianity, distinctly from the exoteric

---

[1] We should keep in mind that the number seventy has also an esoteric sense, both in the Judaic and Islamic tradition. It is said in the former: "On this day the Torah crowns herself with all beauty, with all those commandments, with all those decrees and punishments for transgressions – in seventy branches of light which radiate on every hand" (**Zohar** II, 89 a, vol. III, p. 272). And a famous *hadîth* of the Prophet says: "Allâh has seventy veils of light and darkness; if He removes them, the brilliant glory of His Face would consume anybody touched by His Look." We could risk a comparison and say that the seventy of the primitive Christian Church were these veils hiding the esoteric domain. We may consider, together with Vâlsan, that Christianity, in its early years, had an initiatory and esoteric position inside Judaism (Michel Vâlsan, **Mise au point**, Ét. Trad., no. 406-407-408, 1968, p. 144), and later, when it became a religion, the initiatory elite was named the "New Israel"; therefore, the seventy are this "Israel." Saint Paul wrote: "For not all who are descended from Israel are Israel" (**Romans** 9:6); and Guénon specified the same thing when asking: "The name «Israel» has not often been used to designate the assembly of the initiates?" (Guénon, **Ésot. Chrét.**, p. 85). We note that in Hebrew, the words *iain*, "wine," and *sod*, "mystery," each equals seventy (Guénon, **Roi**, p. 46); Guénon also mentioned that Noah was the one who planted the vineyard (**Genesis** 9:20), which would connect him to the initiatory and esoteric characteristic of the wine (Guénon, **Roi**, p. 91). This episode, as well as everything related to Noah, contains a, we should say, mysterious ambiguity.

one, is the work of Saint Symeon the New Theologian, "master" of the Hesychasm inside the Orthodox Church (Vâlsan, **Initiation**, p. 168).[1] Saint Symeon stated that "the divine grace descends upon some people, yet their number is very small, two or three maybe, and the rarity does not constitute the law" (Vâlsan, **Initiation**, p. 171). Saint Symeon also said:

> We must watch that the Wrath of God does not come upon us, when some individuals, who are outside this commandment [that is, outside the «wall,» outside the order of spiritual Gnosis, without grace], fill sacerdotal positions, as bishops or priests and masters of souls, and we have to see that no ignorant person teaches and abuses the divine things, because these are beyond human understanding. ... Therefore, many savants of the words proved to be the founders of heretic doctrines.[2]

They should look for support from "meditation and from the grace given by the administrators of the great mystery and by those instructed in the sacred Gnosis" (Vâlsan, **Initiation**, p. 172). Who are these keepers of the great mystery, these Gnostics whom the exoteric priesthood should obey? Vâlsan considered that the Orthodox Church maintained an initiatory way through the Hesychasm, to which belonged these administrators of the great mystery and Saint Symeon himself.[3]

Even though we restrained ourselves from mentioning too many individual names, we have to mention here Marco Pallis, about

---

[1] Vâlsan showed that Saint Symeon the New Theologian, who lived during the change between the Millenniums, was considered within the Church to have a prophetic and apostolic function.
[2] We remark the similarity with the "savants of the words" from nowadays, the so-called "philosophers" and "erudite" that invaded even the traditional domain. That was one of the biggest problems of the Occident, the discrepancy between the function and the individual who filled it; for this reason Dante threw Popes into Hell. In a perfect world, those who detained the sacerdotal (papacy) and imperial (royal) functions should have followed a spiritual realization, an effective initiation. As Clement of Alexandria showed, the Egyptians entrusted their mysteries only to the priests and kings.
[3] Guénon considered Saint Bernard, who was born seventy years after Saint Symeon's death, an initiate.

whom we have already written.[1] As he concluded that there is no Agarttha and no Lord of the World, because nobody confessed to him when he wandered in Asia, so this same Pallis denied the existence of a Hesychastic initiation, saying that all those who looked for such a rite wasted their time.[2] It is not our task to argue and start polemics, but we know, and not only theoretically, that even today there are sacred places within Orthodoxy where no stranger has access and probably, as the Hindus and Tibetans avoided Pallis, so the Hesychastic monks stay away from outsiders (exoteric people), and much the more from profane individuals. And Pallis was right when he said that it is a waste of time; yet it is so not because there is no esoteric kernel or a subterranean spiritual center, but because those who ask for them are unqualified and worldly.

As we are going to see in another chapter, usually when we say Occident we envisage Western and Central Europe and North America. When we talk about the Orient, Near, Middle or Far, we have in mind mainly Islamic countries, India and China. Almost nothing is known or is told about the Near-Occident or the Near-West that comprises Orthodoxy. There were an old division and wrath between Catholics and the Orthodox, and in some moments of world history, these were much stronger than those between Orthodoxy and Islam. Here we can insert the famous dispute between the Catholic monk Barlaam and Saint Gregory Palamas, the defender of Hesychasm, yet also here we might place the attacks of the Catholic "traditionalists" against Guénon, insulted by his words:

What we say here [about the lack of initiation] applies, however, only to the Latin Church, and it is remarkable that, in the Oriental Church there was no mysticism in the sense Western Christianity, after the 14th century, understood it; this makes us think that a specific initiation, similar to the one we alluded to earlier [an initiation under the cover of the religious orders] should have persisted in these [Orthodox] churches; and, something exactly like this exists in Hesychasm, which had (seems undoubtedly), an initiatory characteristic, even though, as in so many other cases in modern times this

---

[1] See our work, **Agarttha, the Invisible Center**, Rose-Cross Books, 2003.
[2] Marco Pallis, **La Voile du Temple**, Études Traditionnelles, no. 386, 1964, p. 267.

characteristic weakens more or less, as a natural consequence of the general circumstances of the epoch; only some initiations, very exclusive and «closed» would escape these circumstances. (Guénon, **Ésot. Chrét.**, p. 38)

CHAPTER V

INITIATION AND HESYCHASM

HESYCHASM, AS ANY OTHER ESOTERIC way, cannot be restricted by chronology or geography, and it is safe to assume that it appeared at the same time with the Christian tradition, even if modern scholars consider Hesychasm a mystical movement developed mainly on Mount Athos and promoted in the 14th century by St. Gregory Palamas. It is true that St. Gregory Palamas, in his controversy with Barlaam, unveiled the theoretical essence of Hesychasm, yet the effective realization and spiritual initiation remained further hidden and protected.

The Hesychastic doctrine is in full accordance with all the other great world traditions and has as goal the Supreme Identity, the Liberation, expressed as a direct and immediate vision of the Super-luminous Night, that is, of the non-manifestation or of *Brahma nirguna*. The Hesychastic initiate is a seer who follows *jnâna-mârga*, "the way of knowledge," a knowledge identical with the divine vision of the "tenebrous light." And the physical eye is not the instrument of this vision, but the "eye of the heart," like in Sufism. Guénon wrote:

On the part of the Orthodox Church, there is Hesychasm, which apparently has preserved all the characteristics of a real initiation, but, in fact, this initiation is almost inaccessible, since it is extremely difficult to find a qualified guide; for that, you have to go to Mount Athos, which is its center, and be admitted to live there for a time, and gain the monks' trust to obtain from one of them the transmission and the technical instructions.[1]

And René Guénon was right. If we expect to find manuals regarding the Hesychastic initiation or Hesychastic schools with the gates open to everybody, we will be greatly disappointed. For modern man, the hardest thing to understand is the prohibition on "the right to be informed," a slogan widely spread by reporters and other forms of medias. "The public has a right to know," is uttered emphatically. Yet the esoteric domain doesn't follow this rule; we gave sufficient examples to illustrate that true Gnosis is out of reach for the public. We have already said that the Eleusinian Mysteries, for instance, remained mysteries and in all these thousands of years they were not betrayed in any way, so today we know almost nothing "technical" about them. Similarly, the Hesychastic initiation continued to stay hidden, and even if some individuals, like Marco Pallis, could not understand how it survived so many years without betrayal (considering rather that, purely and simply, it does not exist[2]), the Hesychastic initiation remained an unbreakable mystery.

Michel Vâlsan strove to gather "evidence" regarding the Hesychastic initiation, to answer Marco Pallis' criticism. At the beginning of his article he mentioned Father John the Stranger (or John the Pilgrim) who came from Russia and revivified the Hesychastic tradition in Romania, during World War II.[3] **The Orthodox Work**, a Californian journal,[4] mentions another Father John: the Hesychastic monk, John the Desert-Dweller, who in approximately the same period of time wandered in the Agapia Mountains of Moldavia.[5] Yet before continuing to see how

---

[1] **René Guénon**, Le Dossiers H, L'Age d'Homme, 1997, p. 283.
[2] Which, by the way, is exactly what the Hesychasts want.
[3] Michel Vâlsan, **Études et documents d'Hésychasme**, Ét. Trad., no. 406-407-408, 1968.
[4] **The Orthodox Work**, St. Herman Press, no. 162, 1992. We owe this information to Alvin Moore Jr.
[5] About Moldavia and its perception in the West, see **Agarttha, the Invisible Center**.

Hesychasm fits into the modern world, let us try to catch a glimpse of the Hesychastic doctrine.

The word "hesychasm" derives from Greek and means "stillness," "quietness" (Gr. *esychia*). In this way the Orthodox esoteric doctrine is related to the other great traditions that all speak about Peace, Silence and Quietness. The "quietness" aimed at by Hesychasm is, evidently, the stillness of the Void, of the Silence, of the super-luminous Night, corresponding to "the straightening of the mountains and valleys" through which, in the microcosmic order, the mental swirls and the waves of the mind are tamed, and a calm and pacific ocean is obtained; this doctrine, going beyond the religious and theological level, touches metaphysics. Hesychasm, as any other esoteric kernel, was not restricted by chronology or geography, being born together with Christianity; there are plenty of examples concerning saints who perfected themselves through Hesychasm, and there is no need to dwell upon them. The fact that the scholars considered Hesychasm a mystical movement, developed mainly on Mount Athos and promoted in the 14th century by St. Gregory Palamas, is nothing else than a registration of its "public exposure," exposure related to Palamas' writings. One of Palamas' contemporaries, Saint Gregory of Sinai, a Hesychastic master, lived a hidden life, rejecting any "publicity" and, it seems, even asking Palamas that he not be mentioned in the dispute with Catholic "rationalism," which allow us to understand how absurd is any attempt to date such an esoteric doctrine; even today the *sihastrii* (a word derived from *esychia* meaning the more or less Hesychastic monks living in solitude) are hostile to any mode of communication and exposure.

Hesychasm came into the public eye due to the dispute between Saint Gregory Palamas and the Western monk Barlaam, an unequal dispute, since the former was talking from a metaphysical perspective, that of the Light of the super-luminous Darkness, and the latter proved to be the exponent of the rational light, and therefore limited to the individual domain; and despite how much the Catholic historians blamed Saint Gregory Palamas up to the present time, it is obvious that the doctrine he defended was the doctrine of the absolute Truth.

Hesychasm is, first of all, an initiatory way of seeing the super-luminous Light,[1] a way of perfection, awakening and illumination, the eye of the heart being the spiritual instrument with which divine Knowledge is realized, and the "prayer of the heart" is the method of opening this eye. The Prayer of the Heart allows the concentration of the individuality and the ego in the center of the being, in the heart, and establishes a beginning (*initio*) to the awakening of the spiritual eye, relating this meditation with the control of the vital "spirit" – the breath.[2] Nikephor the Solitary advised that, at the same time with inspiration (breathing in) we should pronounce "Lord Jesus Christ, the Son of God," and with expiration, "have mercy of me, the sinner"; in this way, the "uninterrupted prayer" (and this one has to be indeed uninterrupted) is accompanied by a respiratory procedure, comparable to *prânayama*, a well-known Hindu "technique," which has the double spiral as symbolic support.[3]

The vision of the Light in the Heart is similar to the Supreme Identity of Sufism, and Saint Gregory Palamas stressed that this vision of the super-intelligible Light implies a union with God. Spiritual realization means, in Hesychasm, a "unifying perfection" and a "divine communion of One" as a spiritual vision (in the sense of "seeing" as a seer) with the inner spiritual Eye, that is, with the "eye of the heart."[4] In the Hindu tradition, liberating Knowledge means an absolute identity of the knower, what is known and the act of knowing. Accordingly, the Hesychast who has surpassed individuality reaching the super-luminous Night and realizing the

---

[1] This "seeing" as "vision" should be related to the meaning of the English "seer."
[2] It is difficult to translate into English some of the Hesychastic subtleties, but we may say as an example that in Latin *spiritus* means both "breath" and "spirit"; similarly, in Romanian, *suflu* = breath and *suflet* = soul.
[3] The word "spiral" is related to "spirit," "inspiration," and "expiration."
[4] Nicholas of Cusa, who had links with some Hesychastic circles, wrote a famous book, **The Vision of God**, in which he said that we see God "not with the corporeal eyes, but with intellectual eyes, the eyes of understanding" (Cusa, **Vision**, p. 23).

unconceivable union with God – Saint Gregory Palamas says – is himself light and sees light with light. If the Hesychastic initiate looks to himself, he sees light; if he looks at an object of his vision, he also sees light; and the instrument of his vision is the light. That is the perfect union and vision.[1]

The spiritual influence, which Guénon compared to the seed sown in the center of the being, is not enough to accomplish a spiritual realization. Like the seed, it is only an *initium*. For the "new plant" (the *neophyte*) to become perfect, an intense effort is necessary, and it also needs authorized initiatory supports and guides that will be abandoned along the ascension. For this reason Dante, when he passed beyond Purgatory, ascending to Heaven (the super-individual spheres), got another guide, Beatrice (Buddhi, Shekinah), who replaced Vergil (spiritual influence operating only in the individual domain); and then, to see the eternal Light, Dante left Beatrice (the intellectual ray), passing beyond her and getting a new guide, Saint Bernard (the spiritual master of the Templars), and, even more, getting as absolute guide the Blessed Virgin, as only Saint Mary was capable of unveiling to him the Light of the Principle, the "vision" of the absolute Light being immediately (and not mediated). That is why even the intellectual ray as instrument, as an intermediary, had to be abandoned in order to realize direct "contact" with the Principle.[2]

This is what not too many understood: I don't see, in fact, Brahma with *Buddhi*, but Brahma sees Brahma with Brahma; this is what some theologians did not understand, after the collapse of the Christian traditional society (marked by the Templars' trial). And this is what started the polemic between the Catholic monk Barlaam and Saint Gregory Palamas (a few years after the Templars' trial). Saint Gregory Palamas' tough reaction in order to defend Hesychasm was, actually, the last attempt in the Christian tradition to save esotericism

---

[1] John Meyendorff, **Byzantine Hesychasm**, Variorum Reprints, London, 1974, p. 202.
[2] Regarding Saint Bernard, it is interesting to note that René Guénon, in a letter of November 1936, confessed to Ananda K. Coomaraswamy: "for me, this character is indeed an initiate and not only a simple mystic."

from a more and more obtuse exotericism, an attempt to maintain a somehow "official" initiatory way, which after that will hide deeper and deeper. This way, in a few words and following Saint Palamas' teachings, is[1]: the knowledge of the Light of God comprises three steps. The first step is the knowledge of the divine reasons in the world and in the beings, through which God is known indirectly (and analytically), as cause and support of the universal manifestation; it is more a knowledge of erudition, not rejected by Saint Palamas, but who says: "And Saint Gregory of Nyssa teaches that the wisdom from outside is barren and imperfect and he asks us to reject immediately this stepmother"; it is a knowledge of an affirmative type. The second step is the knowledge of God through negation, that is, the *apophatic* theology, but the light of the negative theology is after all also a reasoning in which the mind (as Father Stăniloae stressed, in his commentary of Palamas' work) unfolds, denying one after another the various attributes wrongly ascribed to God. Eventually, the third step is the vision of God in the super-luminous Darkness. The Hesychasts see, when they operate the Prayer of the Heart, this super-light and not a corporeal, material light; it is a Light beyond the corporeal and individual light, a super-individual and so, an intelligible light, yet, in fact, it is a super-intelligible Light.

The Hesychasts, Saint Gregory Palamas explained, considers the light of grace as intelligible, but not even this in a proper sense, because they define it as being beyond the mind, and descending into the mind only through the power of the Spirit, when any other work of the mind ceases. To say [like Barlaam] about the Hesychasts, who declare this light not only beyond the senses, but also beyond the mind, that they consider this light as corporeal and visible, is it not more than a calumny? It is, indeed, more than a calumny, since God is not only above the Existence, but He is Super-god (*hyper-theos*); and the height of That who is beyond and surpasses the whole

---

[1] We follow closely Saint Gregory Palamas' teachings, such as they were registered in the Romanian Philocaly (**Filocalia**, vol. VII, Ed. Instit. Biblic și de Misiune al Bisericii Ortodoxe Române, 1977, trad. și note de Dumitru Stăniloae).

height which can be conceived with the mind is not only above any affirmation, but also above any negation. It is a light and a grace non-corporeal and divine, a light seen in an unseen way and known in an unknown way.

The Being of God, Father Stăniloae explained, is not only invisible and inaccessible to our senses, but It is above this invisibility and inaccessibility. It is a peak beyond all the sensitive and rational peaks. It is not only beyond all the affirmative sayings, but also beyond all the negative sayings about It. It is above the meaning of the words: being, existence, and goodness, but also above the meaning of the opposite words. It is neither being nor non-being; It is beyond any word.[1]

In Hesychasm, spiritual realization is "seeing without words" the super-luminous Darkness; the Hesychast knows and realizes within (in the heart) God through a true vision and above all beings. Because That, Saint Gregory Palamas stressed, is always together with Its eternal glory. Therefore, this vision is not knowledge (in a discursive mode, a conceptive knowledge) and so, not only do we not have to consider the "ineffable vision" a partial knowledge, but also we have to consider it much more above any knowledge and any vision through knowledge. We obtain the divine, receiving and seeing within us the glory and the Light of God.[2]

Saint Gregory Palamas is in complete concordance with primitive Christianity, since Saint Paul wrote: "Now we see but a poor reflection as in a mirror [in a discursive mode and also in an obscure and ignorant mode]; then we shall see face to face [the effective spiritual realization]. Now I know in part [analytically]; then I shall know fully [synthetically, globally, integrally], even as I am fully known" (**1 Corinthians** 13:12).

This was equally supported by Dionysius the Areopagite who also, according to Saint Palamas, never declared the vision of the eternal light a subject of the senses when he said that it could be seen, because he said that it could be seen only by those similar to

---

[1] p. 273.
[2] pp. 284-5.

Christ. The vision of God is not only above the senses, but also above the mind and discursive knowledge.[1] The seers of this vision don't reason about God because they don't see God like the ones who think about God through negation, but they see with the vision ("the seeing") itself what is beyond seeing, not rationalizing but suffering the surpassing of everything.[2]

The speculative theology, Father Stăniloae said, either affirmative or negative, is not a theology of the seeing or of the vision. It is born precisely from the not-seeing of God. Those who see God don't need a speculative theology. They also follow an *apophatic* theology (or even better, a theology of not-speaking), but this one is generated not due to the fact that they don't see God, but because through this seeing they know that God is beyond seeing and any word. The vision of God is superior to rational theology, affirmative or negative. It is the "passion" of the divine reality, not its invention or assumption with the rational mind, with the imagination, with the fantasy. It is superior to negative theology because the vanishing of everything is not compulsorily produced by the rational mind, but because all creation, beings and its ideas, are overwhelmed and covered by the real vision of the supernatural light. This *apophatic* is an endless plus, not a minus with regard to the things known by senses and reason. The non-seeing is not purely and simply non-seeing. The non-seeing is seeing; the not-knowing and not-understanding are "experienced" more intensely than the seeing and knowing in the order of creation. It means that only those who have reached the union with God acquire this vision. People who have heard about it from those who possess it, but have not accomplished the union, might reach the knowledge of God through affirmative theology or through rational negation.[3]

In Hesychasm, the vision of God is at the same time union with God. We must be careful regarding the meaning of this "union."

---

[1] p. 295.
[2] Here the "suffering" has to be understood as Christian "passion." The word "passion" derives from the Greek *pascho*, and Latin *patior*, "to suffer."
[3] pp. 296-297.

Initiation and Hesychasm

Various traditional doctrines use the term in a purely initiatory sense. In Sufism, the perfect spiritual realization, namely, the completion both of the *Lesser* and *Greater Mysteries*, is called the Supreme Identity. In the Hindu tradition, Yoga, that is, the "Union," refers to Liberation, which, we saw, means the accomplishment of a total initiatory way, including the super-individual states. The Christian mystics often mentioned "union" with God, but in many cases it was about a partial and transitory union, achieved in ecstasy[1]; in other words, this "union" was not always effectively realized. It is interesting that usually Hesychasm is considered to be related to the *apophatic* knowledge, which, in its turn, is compared to the Hindu doctrine of negation (*neti, neti*). Yet, in conformity with Saint Gregory Palamas, negating and eliminating what God is not is not sufficient to realize the unification. The *apophatic* doctrine is, after the example of the divine Dionysius the Areopagite, the removal, from the marble block, of those pieces that hide the statue. And Meister Eckhart said: "When a craftsman carves an image in wood or stone, he does not introduce the image into the wood, but removes the chips that hid and covered the image, he removes the slag; then shines what was hidden within." Yet to Saint Palamas the union is beyond any affirmation and negation.[2]

---

[1] For the Hesychasts, the vision of the uncreated Light is not a transitory religious ecstasy, but a "consciously life into the light."

[2] For the Hesychasts, *The Prayer of the Heart* is the way allowing to "reunite what was scattered," an expression used also by the Masons and by other traditional forms; *The Prayer of the Heart* is aiming at the Center (*Brahmapura*), and represents the highest spiritual science, through which the scattered mind is reunited in the heart, and, in the end, the status of the second Adam is reached (for the Hesychasts, through *The Prayer of the Heart*, man reaches a level superior to the one from where Adam fell). The Hesychasts consider that for the first Adam, the *Prayer* was a natural component, but now it implies a lot of effort, because the "fall" represented a separation (in the beginning, Eve was part of Adam: "And Adam said, This is now bone of my bones, and flesh of my flesh: she shall be called Woman, because she was taken out of Man," **Genesis** 2:23; but then, with the "original sin," it occurred a separation, the birth of duality), and, by an uninterrupted *Prayer*, it is possible to reunite what was parted. Christ, extending his hands, united what was divided, and this union, for the Hesychasts, means, at the same time, the union of the mind in the heart, the union of Adam and Eve, the union of man with heaven and the mysterious union of the Holy Trinity. However, it is not possible to discuss *The Prayer of the Heart* and its degrees

Those who learn from those who see, Palamas said,[1] are in communion only with the light's mental gift and might ascend to the knowledge of God through negation; but to obtain such a vision, and through it and with it to see the non-seeing of God, is impossible if they do not achieve also the supernatural unification, a spiritual and super-rational union, since the light cannot be seen, says the prophet, by the one who does not look from inside the light.

No one has ever seen God (**John** 1:18),[2] and nobody will ever see Him; neither man nor angel. But this is only because this *nemo*, this "nobody" is an angel or man who sees either sensitively or intelligibly, Saint Palamas argued. When *nemo* becomes spirit and sees into Spirit, how is it possible for him not to see the similar with the similar? Yet even for this seeing into Spirit, the Light of God that is situated beyond everything appears to be hidden because through the communion with the Most High the Hesychasts transform themselves (shifting towards what is the most high) and annihilate any operation of the body and soul, in such a way that through them cannot be seen anything else but That; "so that God may be all in all" (**1 Corinthians** 15:28).[3]

The great Dionysius said: "Since the union of divinized minds with the Light beyond all deity occurs in the cessation of all intelligent activity, the godlike unified minds who imitate these angels as far as possible praise it most appropriately through the denial of all beings."[4] Yet they learn, not through denial, but through unification, which is supernaturally beyond all, Palamas stressed. Consequently, through this unification with the Light, that is beyond all beings and surpasses everything, those who have realized the union understand how the Light is beyond or surpasses all beings; and, not by the

---

since that would involve the use of the mind, and the mind (scattered) is incapable of describing the *Prayer.*
[1] pp. 297-8.
[2] *Nemo Deum vidit.* See about the ambiguity of *Nemo*, **The Everlasting Sacred Kernel**, p. 129.
[3] pp. 303-304.
[4] Pseudo-Dionysus, **The Divine Names**, I, 5, p. 54.

denial of all beings but through union, they see that all are denied and removed. Also this union is beyond and outside of all.[1]

And the one who sees, Saint Gregory Palamas continued, if he does not act in any other way,[2] being outside or without all other things, becomes entirely light, and becomes similar to what he sees; better said, he unites in an unmixed way, being light and seeing light with light. If he looks at himself, he sees light; if he looks to what he sees, that is also light; if he looks toward the instrument of seeing, this is also light.[3] This is the unification: to be all in one, without any possibility of distinction between the seer and what is seen and what the seer sees with; but he knows only that there is a light and he sees a light, different from that of the all beings. That is why the great Paul, Palamas added, says: "I know a man in Christ who fourteen years ago was caught up to the third heaven. Whether it was in the body or out of the body I do not know – God knows" (**2 Corinthians** 12:2). Saint Paul looked at himself. But how? Sensitively, rationally or intellectually? Yet being caught up, he was without these powers. Therefore, he saw himself through the Spirit, which caught him up. And what was he, if no natural power could encompass him, or, better, if he was freed of any natural power? No doubt, he was that thing he united with, and through which he knew himself and for which he left everything. It was a union with the Light, which even the angels could not reach if they would not surpass themselves through the unifying grace. This Light is the only true Light, eternal, unchangeable, without shadow, permanent, a Light through which we become light and the sons of the perfect light.[4]

---

[1] p. 305.
[2] This non-acting corresponds to *wu-wei* of the Far-Eastern tradition, representing, as the non-speaking, an expression of non-manifestation.
[3] Saint Symeon the New Theologian said: "God is Light and those considered by Him worthy to see Him will see Him as Light; those who received Him, they received Him as Light"; Saint Symeon declared that he is not talking about something he does not know, but about something he himself found out (Lossky 216). We could assume that, like Saint Bernard, Saint Symeon was a genuine initiate.
[4] pp. 311, 313. We should heed the expression "the sons of light." "Put your trust in the light while you have it, so that you may become sons of light," Jesus said (**John**

Saint Dionysius the Areopagite, taken by Saint Palamas as a traditional authority, said in the Fifth Letter:

The divine darkness is that «unapproachable light» where God is said to live.[1] And if it is invisible because of a superabundant clarity [the super-luminous Darkness, the supernal Night], if it cannot be approached because of the outpouring of its transcendent gift of light, yet it is here that is found everyone worthy to know God and to look upon Him. And such a one, precisely because he neither sees Him nor knows Him, truly arrives at that which is beyond all seeing and all knowledge.[2]

Yet only Moses, and those similar to him, could enter the super-luminous and super-divine darkness. The negative theology is for anybody who loves God. Yet this light and this divine darkness, Saint Gregory Palamas concluded, are something else than the negative theology and surpass it in an incommensurable mode; we should say that in the same way as Moses surpassed in his vision of God the many.[3]

It is not our purpose to intervene in doctrinal disputes like the one between Palamas and Barlaam, regarding the nature of the

---

12:36). And Saint Paul stressed: "You are all sons of the light and sons of the day. We do not belong to the night or to the darkness" (**1 Thessalonians** 5:5). It is interesting that Saint Paul opposed light to wrath: "But since we belong to the day, let us be self-controlled, putting on faith and love as a breastplate, and the hope of salvation as a helmet [the three theologian virtues]. For God did not appoint us to suffer wrath but to receive salvation through our Lord Jesus Christ" (**1 Thessalonians** 5:8-9). The expression "the sons of light" is present in the Qumran manuscripts and it will take a "Gnostic" garment, but the great danger is to get stuck in an irreconcilable dualism "light-darkness," inadmissible from a metaphysical point of view. Saint Symeon the New Theologian said: "for those who became the sons of light and the sons of the last day, for those who walk permanently into the light, the Day of God will never come, since they are always with God and into God" (Lossky 231).
[1] "Who alone is immortal and who lives in unapproachable light," Saint Paul wrote (**1 Timothy** 6:16).
[2] About the super-luminous Darkness and the apophatic theology in Saint Dionysius' writings see Lossky, pp. 23 ff.
[3] p. 329. Father Stăniloae added: "Palamas declares that there is a rational knowledge of God, which belongs to the affirmative theology of the beings; and one above the mind, negating all the beings. Eventually, there is a third one, superior, through union."

divine Light; but, we must ask ourselves if there is any glimpse of an initiatory light in the texts quoted previously, even though we should not expect public revelations. The question is that, as a lot of terms and words, carrying nothing of what they should mean, are used (and abused) today, the same the exoteric domain uses notions that have a much more limited significance than the one they have in the esoteric domain. "Union," "light," "vision," "liberation," "beyond" and others are often deceiving words. Similarly the various mystical or so-called spiritual "experiences" of various traditions could be deceiving.

René Guénon has heeded Light when he referred to the triad *Verbum, Lux, Vita* (Guénon, **Aperç. sur l'Init.**, pp. 294 ff.). The Word's act produces the "illumination" that is the origin of the universal manifestation, and the beginning of Saint John's Gospel, "In the beginning was the Word," alludes in fact to *In principio erat Verbum*, that is, the Word is the principle of any manifestation. In **Genesis**, the uttered Word was *Fiat Lux*, which links the sound to light, the hearing to seeing; in the Hindu tradition, **Vêda** was heard, yet the word *vêda* derives from a radical meaning "to see." In the Islamic tradition, Guénon showed, the first creation was that of Light (*En-Nûr*), directly generated by the divine commandment.

In Hesychasm, the Light of which Saint Palamas has spoken is an uncreated light, that is, it has its origins beyond the creatures, beyond the manifestation, and it is *in principio*, and even though it overflows "upon the world" it "is" not. In the Hindu tradition, an initiate that accomplished the spiritual realization is a *jîvan-mukti*, a "liberated while alive." It is very difficult to understand how a human being can, at the same time, be united with Brahma (be identical, in fact, with Brahma), and continue to exist as an individual. If for a *jîvan-mukti* this problem does not exist anymore, for a neophyte it remains a perplexity. For this reason, Hesychasm solved the problem at a doctrinal level, considering that a union with God's essence is impossible (since then the individual would not exist anymore as such, and would be God); instead, a union takes place with God which is expressed as an identification with His uncreated Light.[1] The uncreated energies, among which is Light, solved also another serious problem, that of One and multiple. Obviously, this whole doctrinal exposé is only for our benefit as individuals, to understand, to some extent, the "not-understandable," the unfathomable. One generates the multiple with the help of its divine rays that spread into the world starting from the center, these rays being precisely the uncreated energies.[2]

As the Hindu tradition introduced Shakti as Brahma's partner, to reconcile the Principle's immutability with its activity, likewise Hesychasm introduced the uncreated energies, comparing them to the solar rays.[3] The uncreated Light is the celestial Ray that, by uttering the Word, generates the whole manifestation, all the beings, yet this Light is also the Hesychastic way to become reunited with God.[4]

We see this Hesychastic way, which Guénon and Vâlsan called "initiatory," exposed by Saint Gregory Palamas as a doctrine. Yet what interests us most is not the doctrine, but the effective realization, the "technical" part. Or, better yet, we are looking for an answer to the question: Does Hesychasm offer modern man a possibility of initiation?

We have shown that Vâlsan wrote about a John the Stranger, who during World War II came to Romania, revivifying the Hesychastic method.[5] Another source mentioned John the Desert-

---

[1] This is different from the Western *visio beatifica* (see Paul Evdokimov, **L'Orthodoxie**, Desclée de Brouwer, 1979, p. 27).
[2] About the uncreated energies see Lossky, pp. 65 ff. Lossky showed that the Fathers of the Church, previous to the Council of Nicaea, called the Word (*Logos*) either "force" or divine "energy" manifested into creation (p. 69). Saint Dionysius named the uncreated energies "divine rays," and Saint Palamas "uncreated light."
[3] It doesn't matter if the creatures exist or not, God manifests "outwards" through the uncreated energies, in the same way the sun manifests through its rays, even if there are or not beings to receive them (Lossky 72).
[4] About the celestial Ray see Guénon, **Croix**, pp. 125 ff.
[5] The work of John the Stranger is related to the Cernica and Antim Monasteries (see André Scrima, **Timpul Rugului Aprins. Maestrul spiritual în tradiţia răsăriteană**, Humanitas, 1996, pp. 158-160, in Romanian; about Cernica see also **Agarttha, the Invisible Center**, p. 57).

Initiation and Hesychasm

Dweller, who came from Tighina to the Agapia Mountains, being noticed around the year 1930 as a saintly Hesychast, wandering through the woods followed by one disciple.[1] There is no doubt that the two Johns are very close from a spiritual point of view. What is remarkable in father confessor's description is the elusive characteristic of John the Desert-Dweller, the difficulty of placing him in one location or of talking to him, and his final retreat to the Sihla Monastery. We are able to assert that in those days, when the interview was given, thirty years after Father John's disappearance (1946), Sihla was still a tightly closed monastery, where no outsider had any access, and the monks, when they saw you coming near, ran away and hid. What we want to say is that, if we can have access to the Hesychastic doctrine, to the theoretical knowledge, this is not the same as having access to effective initiation. It is almost impossible to make contact with genuine Hesychasts, and no one will unveil anything about the Hesychastic initiation; on the contrary, they will declare with innocence that Hesychasm does not exist and everything is just fantasy. And this is valid not only for the profane or outsiders, but even for the official exoteric people (priests), because generally even the exoteric priests are not admitted into the Hesychastic mystery, being unqualified. For this reason, some of the priests today consider that Hesychasm is just a memory and they could be right, partially at least, considering the exclusive characteristic and the difficulty of transmitting the Hesychastic initiation (due to the lack of qualified disciples).

We must add another important observation. Remembering the turbulent history of the foundation of the Christian Church and its struggle against division and sectarianism, the Orthodox (exoteric) Church never agreed with an esoteric initiation in its ranks. Therefore, Saint Gregory Palamas, even if he followed a Hesychastic initiatory line, kept it hidden not only from the public eye, but also from the eyes of the Church. Today, as yesterday, a genuine Hesychast will never talk about his initiation; quite the opposite, he

---

[1] We refer to the father confessor of the Monastery Agapia, whose interview published in Romania was reprinted in **The Orthodox Work**.

will strongly deny the existence of any initiation, and so, it is impossible to know for sure, from outside, the real situation of the Hesychastic initiation.

On the other hand, we witness today an explosion of pseudo-Hesychasm in the profane world. It started in the Far and Middle-West, when in the Near-West the atheistic doctrine officially ruled; yet now it is everywhere.

In modern times, the antitraditional world and what Guénon would have called "the counter-initiatory forces" strove to undermine the authentic traditional doctrines, adopting them in a profanatory mode. One after another, Yoga, Zen and Sufism were commercialized in the Occident. Many dubious books and articles were written on this subject, these spiritual orthodox ways being altered and contaminated with modernism and scientism, and presented to the public as some sort of "psycho-physical" experiences. Hesychasm was the target of a similar attack. It started to be unveiled to the profane world, to be distributed throughout the Occident, to be analyzed, to attract disciples who were converted to Orthodoxy for the sake of novelty and the mirage of a facile Hesychastic initiation.[1] As we indicated above, genuine Hesychasm is so exclusive that any attempt at popularization and vulgarization is impossible. What is scattered in the modern world is a pseudo-Hesychasm which gives many the illusion that they obtain an initiation by repeating the Prayer of the Heart or practicing other techniques made public.[2]

The Near-West is in no better position. After the pseudo-Hesychasm was embraced by the Far and Middle-West, and Hesychastic texts were published, a "hesychastic" explosion happened in Eastern Europe when the regime change took place. The term "hesychasm" became a fashion and it was extremely

---

[1] Of course, we don't have in mind here the honest believer who is attached to the Greek-Orthodox Church.
[2] Ferdinand Ossendowski registered in one of his books a technique for the "Jesus' Prayer," practiced by an Orthodox Russian and which is considered by Michel Vâlsan as having an initiatory characteristic. (Michel Vâlsan, **Notes diverses**, Ét. Traditionnelles, no. 411, 1969, p. 29).

abused. Conferences were held with "hesychastic" subjects and a dangerous syncretism between the Hesychastic prayer and some Oriental techniques was recommended; also, there are now a lot of modern works about Hesychasm. We see a desecration and a counterfeit, not exactly of the Hesychastic doctrine, but of the Hesychastic spiritual realization. Even if some of the published texts are valid and orthodox, they cannot replace the effective Hesychastic initiation. And this initiation is undercover more than ever. In fact, those who write about it, in the majority of the cases have no idea what they are talking about, and many have an antitraditional mentality. From what we know, if there still are true Hesychasts, these, due to the present situation of the modern world, reject any contact with this world. We may say, symbolically, that they withdrew within the immutable "Oriental" core of Hesychasm. And the conclusion we can draw is that, for the moment, the Hesychastic initiation doesn't seem to be the way to straighten and revivify the Occident which is in need; it could be an Ark, but this is beyond our subject.[1]

---

[1] Charles-André Gilis, in his recent work **La papauté contre l'islam** (Le Turban Noir, 2007, p. 27), draws the conclusion, by comparing Vatican's architecture with that of Hagia Sophia basilica, that the Renaissance style and Michelangelo's frescos are not trustful supports for spiritual influences, while Hagia Sophia is the only Christian edifice that deserves the name of "basilica." "Hagia Sophia, which the Turks tried in vain to imitate," says Gilis, "was the object of all degradations, humilities and profanations, without forgetting the outrage of a hooliganic «islamization»." Gilis concludes: "if Europe had kept a minimum of traditional sense, it would have asked Turkey to give back Hagia Sophia (geographically located in Europe) to the Orthodox Church." Gilis' position is more understandable if we say that he is Michel Vâlsan's disciple (Vâlsan wrote in the West about Hesychasm, advancing the idea that it has an initiatory kernel), and that Turkey, as René Guénon wrote, became, when Atatürk's reforms occurred, a modern state, which had divorced the traditional life, even though there is today a "religious" reaction, facilitated by the confused and bloody movements we have witnessed for some time. Moreover, Gilis' position is part of a strong campaign started by the author against the Pope and Catholicism, and to support Islam. For this reason, Gilis accuses the Papacy of failing in asking Turkey to return Hagia Sophia to Christianity, the basilica being the adequate architectural image of the divine wisdom and power, since Orthodoxy remained under the protection of the Christian initiatory organizations derived from Hesychasm, while the San Pietro basilica bears the stigma of a pretentious and profane grandeur. It is, of course, true what Charles-André Gilis says about the

Orthodox Church, which cannot stand the Papacy too, yet, we have our doubts that we can talk so lightly about Hesychastic "initiatory organizations." With regard to "handing back" the Hagia Sophia basilica, normally, that is, traditionally, this cannot happen at the profane level of modern politics, since a divine mandate is needed, which means that there should be an army of genuine crusaders to conquer Constantinople, but the crusaders are long gone (and so are the Hesychastic "initiatory organizations"). Charles-André Gilis rightly accuses the Catholic Church of being hostile to any esotericism (**La papauté**, pp. 23, 33); yet, concomitantly, the Orthodox Church has the same unwise attitude and also the Islam is not very indulgent with its own esotericism. Gilis points out the hate of some Muslim exoterists against Ibn Arabî's work, and gives by way of example the Wahhabits. In Arabia, René Guénon's work is almost unknown, but also the Maghrebiens do not accept Guénon's work and are hostile to the "guénonists" converted to Islam. These exoterists are surprised to see that in René Guénon's writings the Islamic tradition has the same rank as the Hindu and Chinese traditions (Abd Ar-Razzâq Yahyâ (Charles-André Gilis), **Tawhîd et Ikhlâs**, Le Turban Noir, 2006, pp. 65-66, 68). The idea we advanced with regard to the "conquest of Constantinople" belongs to the traditional concept of "the battle for the Center," found in all the sacred texts; therefore, it has nothing to do with the present situation, when, due to the world's decadence, such a battle is out of the question, taking into account that its profound significance is not the external war, but the spiritual realization, the initiatory journey aimed at reaching the Center, which was occupied by forces of the inferior psychism, by the devils (like the city of Dis in the **Divine Comedy**), such a significance being also hidden in the story regarding "the conquest of Troy." A similar hidden symbolism is found in "the conquest of Jerusalem" by the Western crusaders. It is interesting that the conquest of Constantinople was equally important for the crusaders' journey, since the Byzantine capital represented the legitimate and true abode of the Emperor, a fabulous city, with mythical riches, another world, the center that, in comparison to Rome or any other Western city, was a legendary place. We should not be surprised that the Turks had the same desire to conquer Constantinople (Mehmet redefined himself as the inheritor of Byzantium; see André Gerolymatos, **The Balkan Wars**, Stoddart, 2001, p. 76), and we should mention that the crusaders, at one moment, forgetting Jerusalem, have occupied the Byzantine capital. On the other hand, we could ask ourselves why the Orthodox Christians did not try to conquer Jerusalem, not in a superficial way, but energized by an immense desire for the Center, as the Catholic crusaders did, and one of the reasons is precisely the existence of Hagia Sophia and of Constantinople itself, which had all the characteristics of a spiritual center. But is Constantinople even now a spiritual center? The answer cannot be but negative, because as the crusaders have disappeared, this center has gradually dried out, beginning with its change into Istanbul, albeit, despite the Christian historians' opinion, we could not blame the Turks entirely for its profanation. During the Ottoman occupation, the Patriarch of Constantinople remained the absolute head of the Christians living in the Turkish Empire, the Turks having no desire to intervene into the Christians' affairs, as long as these continued to pay their taxes promptly. Mehmet, following the Roman emperors' ritual, invested the Patriarch with the staff and the cross, granting the Orthodox Church greater powers and privileges than it had had under the Byzantine rule. Obviously, Mehmet granted also religious freedom to the Orthodox Christians and guaranteed that the Patriarch is untaxable and irremovable. The Patriarch became not only the head of the Church, but also of the Christian society in general. Thus, the Serbian and Bulgarian Orthodox Churches, which previously were independent, became the Patriarch of Constantinople's vassals, in the end, a united Orthodox society developing, under the Ottoman protection, where the Orthodox Church not only maintained a distinct position regarding its control over the Orthodox world, but extended its authority over all Christians of the Ottoman Empire. We must underline the genuine spiritual aspect kept by the Orthodox Church, a fact illustrated by its anti-Western attitude and the rejection of the Renaissance messengers, the Orthodox Church being appalled by the "exaltation of reason in place of dogma, the turn to Greek antiquity" (Gerolymatos, p. 77). The Orthodoxy repelled the West, not so much because it was heretical, but because it became modern, and the Turks were the handy shield to keep the Westerners far from the Christian Orthodox tradition. Thus, another modern "myth" was born in the 19th century, that is, the dark and oppressive Ottoman domination (Gerolymatos, p. 78).

CHAPTER VI

RENÉ GUÉNON AND INITIATION

RENÉ GUÉNON WAS RETICENT to write about initiation, not only because he did not perform the function of a spiritual master and did not accept disciples, but also because it is almost impossible to write in general terms about spiritual realization, when this one is very real and "positive," containing a great number of specific initiatory ways, in accordance with the human diversity.[1] Nevertheless, Guénon considered, at one moment, that it was important to write a series of articles having spiritual realization and initiation as subjects; our present chapter is dedicated to these written teachings. Of course, anybody can challenge the validity of what René Guénon transmitted, and there were such antagonists. Yet we have not seen up to the present even one of these opponents provide a different teaching about initiation, or a coherent one, or a better and essentially richer one. That is because what René Guénon transmitted are not his individual inventions, but traditional and ineffable data that he reformulated in an understandable language.

---

[1] Guénon wrote in a letter to Vasile Lovinescu (August 1934, in French): "Quant à indiquer à quiconque une voie de «réalisation,» c'est là une chose que je dois m'interdire rigoureusement; je ne puis accepter de «diriger» personne ni même de donner de simples conseils particuliers, cela étant entièrement en dehors du rôle auquel je dois me tenir. ... Je ne pourrais mettre personne en relation directe avec des organisations initiatiques, ni en ayant point reçu la charge; j'avoue d'ailleurs que je suis fort loin de souhaiter que cela m'arrive jamais, pour de multiples raisons..."

The Islamic tradition affirms that the number of initiatory ways (*turuq*), which aim towards the spiritual center, is indefinite, each human being following a suitable liberating way called *tarîqah*.[1] The center is unique, but the points on the circumference are multiple, and therefore the ways connecting these points to the center are multiple, adapting themselves to the diversity of individual conditions (Guénon, **Initiation**, p. 136). In Islam there is this saying: "each shaikh has its own tarîqah," which makes the multiplicity of the Islamic ways (*turuq*) correspond to the multiplicity of yogas from the Hindu tradition (Sri Aurobindo spoke of "his yoga," even though Yoga is one-and-only, and only the methods are different). Using Ibn 'Arabî's expressions, we may say that the circumference of the circle is the skin of the fruit (*el-qishr*), that is, *sharîyah*, the religious law or exotericism, addressed to all, comparable (and only from a specific point of view) to the Christian baptism with water (*via lata*, "the wide way," *pitri-yana* of the Hindu tradition); while the center of the circle is the kernel (*el-lobb*), Rabelais' marrow (*la substantifique moelle*), the essence, esotericism, *haqîqah* (the truth, the essential reality), reserved for an elite, and comparable to the Christian baptism with fire or Holy Spirit for the chosen ones, the spiritual men (*via arcta*, "the narrow way," *dêva-yana*). *Sharîyah* is the "body" (*el-jism*), and *haqîqah* is the marrow (*el-mukh*), the former protecting and hiding the latter like a hide or a cloak, and reflecting it outwards (Guénon, **L'ésot. islam.**, p. 29).

The passage from skin to kernel occurs following a radius of the circle, that is, a "way," a *tarîqah*, a narrow way like the sword's blade, and there are few daring enough to embark on this road; "For many are invited, but few are chosen" (**Matthew** 22:14). The word *initiatio* derives from *in-ire*, "to enter" a gate or a way (Guénon, **Symboles**, p. 149), hence initiation means to penetrate the skin and enter within the fruit,[2] to embark on a spiritual way, to enter the gate of gods, to

---

[1] René Guénon, **Aperçus sur l'ésotérisme islamique et le Taoisme**, Gallimard, 1973, p. 32.

[2] To penetrate inside the fruit, there must first be a skin as a starting point; in other words, to aspire to initiation, an attachment to a traditional form is first needed (Guénon, **Initiation**, p. 73).

"begin" a spiritual journey aiming at the Truth, that is, the Center, where the initiate will surpass the particular ways, reaching beyond any differentiation. In the center, the neophyte suffers a "conversion" or an "intellectual metamorphosis" (as Ananda K. Coomaraswamy wrote, see Guénon, **Initiation**, p. 101).[1] In consequence, the initiatory process is, essentially, a purely inner process; on the other hand, spiritual realization imposes a specific way on the initiate, that is, an adequately traditional form and in accordance with his or her nature and possibilities. For this reason an exoteric "conversion" could (and should) sometimes occur, through which the being passes to a more adequate traditional form (especially if the former one does not possess an initiatory possibility anymore). Yet any "conversion" due to some sort of proselytism would be a mistake and a misunderstanding of the intimate concordance, which has to be between the individual nature and the traditional form; without this concordance the "converted" one could wander to sectarianism and other deviations, even to a lack of sincerity.[2] Therefore, there has to be a strict distinction between the conversion due to esoteric and initiatory reasons (imposed by *Kali-yuga*'s conditions and disarray), and the one as a result of contingent and exoteric motives.

The initiate, the one who "enters" a way or "begins" a spiritual voyage, has his status transformed in the center, from a "chosen" one to a perfect and accomplished Chosen, that is, *El-Mustafâ* of the Islamic tradition; though, he is from the beginning the "chosen" one, possessing some "initiatory qualifications" previously proved in order to be accepted as an initiate. The initiatory qualifications are part of his own possibilities and refer to the individual domain (the mortal ego), since from the point of view of the "personality" (the immortal Self), all beings are "qualified." Amid the qualifications we

---

[1] We have in mind here the original sense of the Greek word *metanoia* (the change of *nous*); this inner transformation or conversion (lat. *cum-vertere*) implies a "reassembling" of the being's energies in the center, a passage "from the human reasoning to divine comprehension," when the being rediscovers its Self.

[2] That is why, the "conversion" to Orthodoxy or to Islam should not be just a fashion or even a "try" (let's see what it is all about).

should mention first the intellectual possibility that makes the intervention of the spiritual influence possible, and then the "aspiration" or "intention" (spiritual will or vocation), a tendency toward Truth, toward the Center, without which we cannot talk about initiation; there are also the qualifications regarding the whole individuality, they are all defining the "chosen" one (Guénon, **Aperç. sur l'Init.**, p. 283).

It is true that in a society in which many individuals fill functions and positions that are in disaccord with their individual nature and in which the traditional sciences do not exist anymore, the finding of those qualified for initiation is much more difficult, almost impossible, the initiatory organizations admitting, in consequence, by mistake, profane elements, which desecrate and produce decadence in those organizations (as has occurred in Masonry[1]). The initiatory qualifications constitute the first condition of the initiation; the second one, very important for the present situation of humankind, is the attachment to an authentic and regular initiatory organization.

There are ignorant people who imagine that they can "initiate" themselves, by simply reading some books or imitating some rites, or who think that they can be "initiated" through the Internet ("on line"). The word *initium* means, as we showed, "entrance," "beginning," that is, "a second birth," yet how could somebody give birth to himself? (Guénon, **Aperç. sur l'Init.**, p. 31). There are, it is true, exceptions, human beings who are born seers from the beginning and who are exempted from the difficult effort or the initiatory work under the *guru*'s supervision, but even these, in our dark age, must be initiated in a specific traditional form to actualize their supernal possibilities; Ramana Maharshi is the most known example, yet we should not forget that Jesus also accepted the need to obey the regular rules, being baptized by Saint John the Baptist.[2] Actually, everybody has to respect the laws that govern the world

---

[1] The "Morgan case" is a good example.
[2] In the Islamic tradition, there are the *Afrâds* ("the solitaires") who follow an initiatory realization outside the regular ways (see, for example, Charles-André Gilis, **Introduction à l'enseignement et au mystère de René Guénon**, Les Éditions de l'Oeuvre, 1985, p. 25).

and to obey the temporal conditions of the world, and as children are born from corporeal parents,[1] so initiation and the entrance into an initiatory organization are necessary conditions. On the contrary, at the beginning of the cycle the initiation wasn't required, since primordial man spontaneously obtained the perfection of his (her) individuality (Guénon, **Initiation**, pp. 46 ff., Guénon, **Aperç. sur l'Init.**, p. 32).

Yet entrance into an initiatory organization cannot replace active and personal effort, the inner effort of the chosen one, without which spiritual realization wouldn't be possible, but would remain only in the "initial" phase. There are, consequently, three fundamental initiatory conditions, in accordance with the triad potential – virtual – actual: the "qualification," composed of some inherent possibilities in the individual nature; the "transmission" of a spiritual influence (inside a traditional organization to which the neophyte has to belong), representing the "illumination" that awakens the dormant possibilities; the "inner work" through which, and with the help of some external "supports," the being passes from degree to degree, along the initiatory hierarchy, reaching at the end Liberation or the Supreme Identity (Guénon, **Aperç. sur l'Init.**, p. 34).

In fact, the attachment to an initiatory organization is not only a necessary condition, but defines precisely the initiation, in its strict etymological sense, and this attachment must be real and effective, since a spiritual influence (a divine blessing) has to be transmitted. As we said, it is not enough that an individual wants to enter an initiatory organization; he also has to be accepted, due to his initiatory qualifications, as "chosen," and, in addition, the initiatory

---

[1] That is, human beings are born today through an intermediary and not spontaneously from subtle seeds (seeds sheltered in the World Egg from the beginning, as possibilities of manifestation), as they could very well do (and that is how it probably occurred at the beginning of the cycle, since otherwise nothing could have started). We know the old dilemma: which came first, the chicken or the egg? The discussion of this dilemma can be found in Macrobius' **Saturnalia** VII, 16. In fact, from a *principial* point of view, the rooster was at the beginning; from a worldly point of view, it was the egg.

organization must be authentic and effectively possess a spiritual influence. The spiritual influence is transmitted within an initiatory organization through rites, yet we ought to underline that, on the one hand, the initiatory rites (in fact, all rites in general) have their own efficacy (if they are distorted, for example, no effective result is obtained anymore), and on the other hand, the rites can be operated only by qualified personnel (for example, in the religious domain, only by those who have been consecrated as priests, the consecration being the modality through which the spiritual influence is transmitted[1]).

The word "rite" derives from Sanskrit *rita*, meaning "in accordance to order." In a traditional society, the sacred represented the normal situation and all the daily activities were in accordance to order, that is, were pursued in a ritual mode, yet we have to keep in mind that the rites also respect a hierarchy with regard to their domain of operation. The initiatory rites aim at an elite, characterized by special qualifications, while the exoteric rites are public, intended for a community, without discrimination (the spiritual influence using the "psyche" to descend upon that community); the exoteric rites are destined exclusively to the individual domain, the Christian religion, for example, having as its unique goal salvation, that is, the Eden-like state, a state which represents the quintessence of the individual order. Any rite is an assembly of symbols, both the rite and the symbol being of non-human origin: the gestures, the words uttered in a specific mode, the graphical figures, the objects, the place, all the rite's elements are symbolic, rites therefore being "working" symbols (Guénon, **Aperç. sur l'Init.**, p 118).

Since both language and human reason are by definition discursive, the "ritual" transmission of the initiatory teachings can be

---

[1] It seems obvious (even if some people don't want to recognize or don't care) that if the chain of consecration is interrupted, the spiritual influence is lost. In consequence, the priests who don't have a regular consecration, which should be unbrokenly linked to Christ and his Apostles, are without real sacred power and will deceive their community. We should add that "consecration" does not mean some profane, formal gesture, as we can see today when profane individuals are allowed to perform marriages.

done only through symbolism, the only adequate "language" for the intellectual intuition and super-rational (with roots beyond the beginning of the world and time); the symbols, due to their universal characteristic are the only ones capable of "translating" the inexpressible into an "intuitive" mode, the true foundation of the symbolism being the correspondence existing between all the levels of Reality (for this reason the whole of Nature is nothing else than a symbol, namely, a support helping us to reach the knowledge of the supernatural and metaphysical realities: that is precisely the essential function of the symbolism and the profound reason why the traditional sciences exist). The myth is a special type of symbol, and represents symbolical tales, these myths being integrated in rites, as has happened in Masonry. The myth, like the fairy tale, is far from being a product of individual fantasy; it has a non-human origin, and only cyclic decadence has caused its real significance and its function to be forgotten.[1] In the Western Middle Ages, various symbolic tales accompanied the pilgrims, helping them on their spiritual voyage; the fairy tales are vestiges of such initiatory symbols. The Greek word *mythos* derives from the radical *mu*, which indicates silence (Latin *mutus*); indeed, the myth, similar to other symbols, is an initiatory teaching instrument, teaching that operates first of all through silence; the myth transmits the incommunicable essence, translating the silence into human language as an allegory (Guénon, **Aperç. sur l'Init.**, pp. 122 ff.).

One of the serious errors of the modern world is the desecration of the myths and fairy tales. Today all types of "tales" and "legends" are elaborated by individual fantasy and imagination, which makes them just some parodies, often noxious and generating mental disarray. Yet there is little else we can expect in a profane world, that is, in a world totally opposed to any authentic rite (and genuine "order"), where the mystic is considered an ecstatic religious character, the fairy tale is a human invention for children, and the

---

[1] In the Occident, the Greeks were those who started to desecrate their myths, in the same way they desecrated art and changed the sacred "love for wisdom," *philo-sophia*, into profane philosophy.

rites are replaced by ceremonies and glamorous festivities of individual origins, destined to substitute for the essence of the traditional life.

It is not useless to remind ourselves that the word "tradition" means "transmission," a transmission of sacred elements; consequently, the initiatory organizations are the most justified to be called traditional, when we think of the quality of the influences transmitted within their bosom. These influences were obtained through a regular way, through a regular transmission, from a secondary spiritual center linked, in its turn, to the supreme center, the keeper of the primordial Tradition. The entrance into an initiatory organization, through the transmission of spiritual influences, represents the attachment to the tradition of a spiritual center, in the most profound possible mode; this constitutes the virtual initiation, while the inner work that follows represents the effective initiation (when the possibilities marked by the virtual initiation are developed in "act").

The initiation means the transmission not only of a spiritual influence, but also of an initiatory teaching, the latter being an outer "support" for the inner work, helping and guiding the neophyte as much as possible. Initiatory instruction can only prepare the human being in view of assimilating genuine initiatory knowledge as a result of personal work. It can indicate the way to follow, and create a mental and intellectual attitude needed to achieve the effective and not just theoretical comprehension. It can assist and guide the neophyte, controlling his work, yet not even the most perfect spiritual master can realize the inner work in his place, because nobody from outside can communicate what he himself must obtain, namely, the initiatory secret.

"Gods love secret things," **Aitareya Upanishad** says. The initiatory secret is the inexpressible and uncommunicable Truth,[1] and for this reason it is impossible for it to be betrayed, being

---

[1] We understand very well that for some common people, too disappointed by politics, words like "truth" do not mean much. Yet, from a traditional perspective the Truth means everything.

inaccessible to the profane world, its comprehension being realized only through initiation. Initiatory instruction uses symbols and rites as the only possible instruments to express the inexpressible, yet only the inner work permits the uncovering of the Truth. On the other hand, the initiatory organizations are tightly closed and secretive in order to protect themselves against external pernicious infiltrations and especially against counter-initiatory forces; also, they try to prevent the danger that would be generated if some "secrets" were exposed outwardly and used by unqualified people. More than that, the "discipline of secretiveness" is an exercise, a method of training, reflecting the "discipline of silence" (as in the case of the Pythagoreans); in India, the *sannyasins* hidden in the caves of the mountains, following Yoga, favoured silence. The early Christianity contained *disciplina arcani* or *disciplina secreti*; the word "discipline" primary meant "instruction," and so appeared the word "disciple." The obligation to keep silent, not to talk at all, or to keep some teachings secret, refers exactly to the act of disciplining the disciples; the one embarked upon the initiatory journey needed all available energies in order to succeed in his inner transformation, and silence was a very efficient way to make sure that his powers were not wasted outwardly (Guénon, **Aperç. sur l'Init.**, pp. 90 ff.). More than that, the silence was a sort of "preview" of the non-manifestation, of the super-luminous darkness.[1]

---

[1] We are amazed how much talking occurs in our days. The lack of discipline in this sense (a child or a student thinks that he or she should feel insulted if the teacher or parent utters the magic words "shut up") is exactly the opposite of initiatory discipline. Yet what is worse is that everybody talks but nobody has the time and patience to listen. On the other hand, in any traditional society silence played an important role, both in the exoteric and esoteric domain. René Guénon wrote in 1949 an article called **Silence and solitude**, in which he stressed the importance of silence in connection with the initiatory rites. It is interesting that Guénon composed this particular article inspired by the traditional life of the North American "Indians" or, as they are called today, "native people." René Guénon stressed that the "Indians" had two types of rites, exoteric and esoteric (or initiatory), the latter being something totally different from the "rites of passage" considered by ethnologists. The "Indians" practiced a silent and solitary adoration of the "Grand Mystery," identified by Guénon with the supreme Principle. The communication with the "Grand Mystery" could be obtained only through silence, and the silence itself is the "Grand Mystery,"

The first steps of the inner work, though, require initiatory instruction and the presence of a spiritual master and guide. Sri Aurobindo wrote: "In the process of the descent [of the divine influence] and of the [inner] work, it is extremely important to count not only on yourself, but to accept the guidance of a guru and to let him judge your work and make decisions. Since it often occurs that the inferior forces will be stimulated and excited by the descent, and will try to intervene and hijack it in their favour."[1] Submission to a spiritual master is the mirror of genuine "humility," humility (the only one truly valid) with regard to the Principle, this status of vassalage, of servitude ("God's servant"), representing the inner opening of the being for Divinity and for divine grace, which does not mean that submission implies passivity in the inner work.

The initiatory work is an active process and truly within, the supreme and authentic goal of the effective initiation being the Supreme Identity, the realization of the Universal Man, the integral of the individual and super-individual states. There is a fundamental qualitative and hierarchic difference between the goal of the

---

since this Mystery is the non-manifestation and the silence is a state of non-manifestation. Silence is the Word unuttered, that is why "the sacred silence is the voice of the Grand Mystery" (René Guénon, **Mélanges**, Gallimard, 1976, pp. 42-46). There is in Romania a traditional rite, named *Căluş*, and performed on Pentecost (about this rite see Gail Kligman, **Căluş. Symbolic Transformation in Romanian Ritual**, Univ. Chicago Press, 1981). Even if connected to a Christian feast, the rite is probably older. This is not the place to elaborate about the ritual, but we must stress its sacred and absolute traditional nature, and also the similarity with some of the North American "natives'" rites. There are two elements of the rite which will help us here. First, some parts of the ritual were performed in total silence, and a member of the *Căluş* is called "the Mute"; he is a very important sacred character and represents the Silence we were talking about. Second, there is another type of silence, related to the *disciplina secreti*. The members of the *Căluş* (which have to be an odd number, that is, a celestial number) are forced to secrecy by a special oath and the leader could transmit (orally) the secrets only to the next leader and not to his son or others. Even if the *Căluş* became dormant, the leader still had to transmit his secret learning to a chosen new leader, when the time came. Many tried to find out their secrets, but still recently when some old member was interviewed, he played the ignorant and preferred to lie (he said that only the leader knows the secrets, yet he was in fact their leader). This is a common practice, and we know how Pallis was deceived in his research for Agarttha, confusing secrecy with ignorance.

[1] Shri Aurobindo, **Le guide de Yoga**, Albin Michel, 1970, p. 168.

Christian religion and that of the initiation: the former aims at salvation, the latter at Liberation. Liberation targets the spiritual domain and the states of the pure intellect; salvation deals with the subtle domain, that is, the individual one. In the best of cases, religion leads the individual to the Earthly Paradise, yet "Paradise is a prison," because the one who has obtained salvation is still chained by human individuality for an indefinite period, and only the Heavenly Paradise, the goal of effective initiation, allows a real and complete "liberation."

Of course, we might ask the questions: why do we need an initiation and an inner effort if, in fact, nothing is different from the Principle, and the individual being is the same as the Universal Man? Why do we need an initiatory attachment if, actually, everything is tied to the Principle? There are, always, multiple points of view, yet two are fundamental: the *principial* point of view and the worldly one; the questions refer to the former, the *principial* one; but for the human individual, the latter is the normal one, and therefore inner work is needed to make the individual become effectively conscious (not only theoretically) of the *principial* unity; "liberation" (*moksha*) regards the ego and dissipates the illusion that ego is different from the Self. If for primordial man initiation made no sense, for the decadent man of *Kali-yuga* it becomes indispensable in the endeavour to remove the thick curtains of ignorance and illusion.

CHAPTER VII

RENÉ GUÉNON AND TRADITION

THE PRESENT VOLUME IS BASED upon the authority of René Guénon's work and we cannot go further without saying a few words about Guénon and the Tradition he served so well.[1] First, we should explain what we call Tradition, as it appears in René Guénon's works.[2]

---

[1] Those who disagree with Guénon's work should try to understand, following Ramana Maharshi's teachings (a spiritual master whom nobody contests), "who is the one who disagrees?" When somebody says: "I disagree," who is this "I"? An honest attempt to comprehend this will lead to the surprising discovery that only the ego, the individual side, could be in disagreement with Guénon's work and the Tradition. The more we disagree, the more we are controlled by the ephemeral ego. As Coomaraswamy said, we'd better try to understand the traditional texts than spend so much energy disagreeing and criticizing.

[2] "Guénon succeeded to unify the various particular traditions, to pacify the apparent contrarieties, to restore the «ideal model» of what would have been the primordial Tradition" (**Agarttha**, p. 6), in accordance with René Guénon's sayings: "It is strange that, when we affirm the fundamental unity of all the traditional doctrines, some could understand that we are talking about a «fusion» of different traditions" (René Guénon, **Orient et Occident**, Guy Trédaniel, 1987, p. 192). We should not confuse Guénon's synthetically and integrative perspective with that of a "one-and-only religion" (as Schuon's followers promoted, using his expression "unité transcendante des religions") or, much worse, with that antitraditional syncretism of the occultists. On the other hand, if others use the same expressions, that should not stop us to employ them. Guénon wrote: "Because the occultists, these counterfeiters of esotericism, took possession of some elements that do not belong to them, almost always altering them, should we abandon and stop talking about them, risking to be qualified as «occultist»?" (**Comptes rendus**, Éd. Traditionnelles, 1973, p. 130).

In contrast with a profane society (like the modern one), based not on super-human principles, but on conventional rules, of an individual order (being, therefore, a "drifting" society, threatened by chaos since the link with the Principle was broken), a traditional society means a homogenous human group, not from the point of view of nations or race, but from the point of view of mentality and spirituality. It means that all the individuals of the specific group obey the same doctrinal form, think and act, spiritually and ritually, inside a one-and-only metaphysical doctrine, behave in the social life in accordance with the laws derived as contingent applications from the divine principles, and in fact, respect completely the celestial archetypes that were used as models for earthly traditional civilizations. The traditional doctrine, conferred on a specific society, is of super-human origin, derived from the primordial Tradition, and a traditional society allows the unaltered transmission, usually in an oral form, of the doctrinal elements, with the essence remaining the same, only the envelope changing as it is influenced by historical circumstances. We must not confuse tradition with "traditionalism"; the latter has no spiritual connection with the Principle, and is limited to a summation of habits and customs, more or less ancient, with their true significance lost in time, as well as the principles that used to activate them. Even though the tradition was oral at its origin, we have to accept that it can also be written, as with the "traditional scriptures," which are of great importance today. We should add that, etymologically, *tradition* means "what is transmitted" under one or another mode (Guénon, **Introd.**, p. 67), yet we are talking here about the transmission of sacred elements, operated without interruption, and using a regular and continuous channel, with the origin of these elements being beyond the cycle of present humanity, that is, having a "non-human" origin.

In a traditional society, everything had a sacred essence, each member providing in a ritual mode an activity learned through a regulated transmission, that is, through tradition, imitating, in a way, what gods did at the beginning of time. Only with cyclic decadence, when the profane perspective gained more and more terrain, was the chain of regular transmission broken; the communication with the principles' order was lost and for modern man, any vulgar and common habit or individual invention became something "traditional." Tradition, due to its non-human and transcendent characteristics, has a permanent essence, reflecting the Principle's immutability, which is, actually, the origin of any orthodox transmission, while for modern man all the "traditional customs" are in an incessant state of change, following the caprices of fashion and belonging therefore to the profane domain. The Way (*Dao* in the Far-Eastern tradition) of Heaven and Earth, as recorded in **Yi Jing** in connection with the hexagram *Heng* (number 32), is permanence. Also in **Yi Jing** there is a hexagram, *Li* (number 30), composed of *Li* (fire) up and *Li* (fire) down, about which the commentary says that it expresses the inner void as luminosity and clarity, and adds: "The great man watches the symbolic image of clarity in a reciprocal sequence, and applies this concept to the transmission of intelligence from generation to generation; by perpetuating this brightness he illumines the four quarters of the world." Tradition might be considered such a Light, such a Fire transmitted from generation to generation, governing the four cardinal points, hence, the whole manifestation.

The primordial Tradition manifested on earth at the same time as the beginning of the human cycle and, without confusing it with the revelation conferred on some individuals by God, in a religious sense, Tradition can be identified with the Principle in manifestation, constituting a super-human "treasure" of metaphysical knowledge offered to humanity when it was produced by the same Principle, and assimilated through direct inspiration (*Shruti* in the Hindu tradition). Tradition has, therefore, a permanent and infallible nature. Thus, any traditional doctrine participates to the *principial* essence of the Truth being, in its turn, infallible and, specifically for this reason, the exponents of some traditional forms, invested in exposing the doctrines, are infallible, not as human individuals but as instruments of those traditions. Having a super-human origin and being absolutely true, the traditional doctrine represents, beside the spiritual master or *guru*, the infallible guide; hence, the condition of *çraddhâ* (total faith) for the neophyte.[1] What is fallible is the so-called "human factor" or "individual factor."

The primordial Tradition is identical in its essence to the "doctrine of non-duality" (*adwaita-vada*), a pure metaphysical doctrine, which comprises the "vision," the "science" (*vidya*) about the supreme Principle, *Brahma nirguna*. That which is beyond the duality of the manifestation, but also beyond One. *Adwaita-vada* is the only doctrine that mirrors the universality of metaphysics. Metaphysics cannot be limited in any mode and represents the sum of the spiritual principles and of all the data of an intellectual order, which constitute the reality of the entire manifestation, without actually being dependent on this one. If the form used to express the metaphysical knowledge is influenced by elements of contingent order, its essence remains immutable and above any human activity, since the traditional doctrines are specifications of metaphysics for the specific conditions of some particular civilizations.[2] Metaphysics, delving into the order of pure intellectuality and pure spiritual principles, represents the kernel of primordial Tradition; all traditions, and traditional societies respectively, depend on and listen to a doctrine of an intellectual order; yet, only in the case of the pure intellectuality we can talk about a traditional doctrine indeed metaphysical (Guénon, **Introd.**, pp. 87 ff.).

Islam, Guénon showed, represents a tradition having two distinct aspects: a religious one, which refers to the assembly of the social institutions, and a purely *oriental* one, that is, one indeed metaphysical (in this latter aspect, Sufism plays a major intellectual role).[3] In the Middle Ages, there was something similar in the Occident. This was the Scholastic doctrine containing a metaphysical kernel, which was unfortunately insufficiently detached from theology, since Western mentality, the heir of Greek and Judaic mentalities, was more apt for the religious aspect, and the assimilated metaphysics was incomplete

---

[1] The condition of *sraddhâ* implies the absence of a conceited ego, eager to criticize everything, including the master.
[2] Milk is white, regardless of the colour of the cow. Ether is the same; the form of the containers, which apparently contain it, doesn't matter.
[3] Hesychasm, we can say, also has such an *oriental* kernel.

and limited (Guénon, **Introd.**, p. 69). Today it is hard to find any trace of genuine metaphysics in modern thoughts. We might hope that Orthodox Christianity still hides a metaphysical kernel; yet, from what we said previously, there are slim chances that, even if it is true, this kernel will flourish again.

Immediately after World War II, René Guénon published a book called **Le Régne de la quantité et les signes des temps**, in which he introduced a chapter called *Tradition and traditionalism*. In reviewing this chapter for the present work, we realized again that all we can do is to repeat Guénon's sayings. It is a good opportunity for us to join the advice of some traditional *pilgrims*, and declare that, regardless of how many contemporary works we read of a more or less traditional nature, we must always return to Guénon's works if we do not want to wander. However, due to René Guénon's function in the Occident, it is impossible to write about Tradition and traditional doctrines without referring to Guénon; therefore, everything written in the Occident in connection with traditional studies repeats, willy-nilly, in a better or worse mode, the teachings found in his works.

Many biographies were written about Guénon and some people still await an even better one; which means that he continues to be misunderstood, and that there is little comprehension regarding who and what he was, since many individuals, even though they read Guénon, cannot or don't want to understand. René Guénon, knowing how easily the ego and individual elements intervene in the traditional domain, not to talk about other suspect forces, repeated the same statements many times, considering that for some people this repetition "will be never enough." One of the important statements is that we should not heed his individuality, since the individual René Guénon is a private matter, and there is no reason why should anybody be interested in this; the only thing that counts is his work, the work signed with the name René Guénon, and not the articles signed with nicknames, not his personal letters, not the notes he made with regard to his social life, not his family life.[1]

Of course, there is a natural justification for those who did not listen to Guénon's sayings. There are some who purely and simply are incapable of matching the challenge of his work and therefore, it is much easier to lower Guénon to their profane and worldly level, which means a special interest in everything related to his individuality. It is something we see around us every day: the intense attraction for gossip, for all sorts of intimacies, for scandal and dirt. Others, erudite and academic people, even if they have the capacity to read Guénon's works, do this considering him another "philosopher," "orientalist," or "thinker,"[2] and the only natural desire of their ego is to criticize and to contest Guénon, to find errors in his work, to show that they also can think and even better than him.[3]

There is a proverb saying, "The truth bothers man." When we first had one of Guénon's books in our hands, the ego revolted against the inexorability, the self-confidence and the air of "all-knowing" the book transmitted. We understand why those who are the servants of their ego are so upset with René Guénon; hence their obsession with his individuality, since any weakness, error or scandal, would make those full of ego feel better, allowing them to say: "He

---

[1] Guénon wrote: "Sometimes, individualism, in the most common and low sense of the word, manifests in an even more obvious mode: don't we see everywhere individuals who want to judge the work of somebody by delving into his or her private life, as if it would be possible to make a connection between these two?" (Guénon, **Crise**, p. 108). Did those who pretend to be "Guénonians" and interested in René Guénon's life, not really read these lines? Guénon added: "From the same tendency, joined with an obsession for details, also derives the interest for the smallest particularities of «great men»'s lives and the illusion that everything they did can be explained through a kind or «psycho-physiological» analysis" (Guénon, **Crise**, p. 108).
[2] Guénon wrote: "We categorically refuse any Western label, because there is not one that could be applied to fit us" (Guénon, **Crise**, p. 180).
[3] To give just one example: a "Christian Guénonian," who spent a lot of energy in combating Guénon's sayings about Christianity, at one point had to admit that René Guénon stated very clearly the correlation between exotericism and esotericism. Yet for him this meant nothing and he started immediately to criticize as if there were an irreconcilable opposition between the two domains!

is not better than us." It is an old tactic, belonging to the profane world, and we see the same thing occurring today with Jesus, who is reduced to the level of some individual.[1] Guénon wrote: "What we could call «individualism» is identical to the antitraditional spirit, and its multiple manifestations, in all domains, constitute one of the important factors of modern disarray" (Guénon, **Crise**, p. 88).

What counts is not René Guénon's individuality, but his function and his work as a consequence of this function.[2] That is why when some people called themselves Guénon's "heirs" or his "successors" or even "Guénonians" we could not be more amazed. It is known beyond any doubt that René Guénon did not delegate his function to anybody. Is there somebody who can now claim to possess Guénon's function as a "heritage" from René Guénon? Any one who has any doubts just has to reread Guénon's works; he will understand immediately that the appellation "Guénonian" is improper, as well as that of "Guénonian doctrine," that his function was unique for the Occident and non-transmissible.[3] Similarly illusory is the endeavour to discover René Guénon's "sources," his spiritual masters, his initiatory status; if Guénon would have considered it somebody's business, he would have shared all this information.

Regarding the "sources," we want to refer to the lack of references in Guénon's work, which frustrated the erudite and academic persons, who were used to tons of bibliographic titles.

---

[1] We must stress that we don't compare Guénon with Jesus, far from it, even if there are some traditionalists who consider Guénon a sort of god, forgetting too that his individuality does not count.

[2] We presented Guénon's function in our *Introduction* to **Agarttha, the Invisible Center**. With even more profit one can consult Michel Vâlsan's articles about René Guénon's function, and also the works of Charles-André Gilis. Many other publications need vigilance and extreme circumspection. However, in a recent work, we find the declaration (to motivate why it was written) that it is impossible to separate Guénon's work from his life (considered saintly and holy) and from his letters; the declaration is insulting with respect to Guénon, who insisted upon exactly the opposite, warning that his life is a personal matter and nobody has a right to delve into it, and that his work has nothing to do with his individuality, sacred or not.

[3] We recently saw the barbarism "Guénonianism" used, and somebody suggested a "Guénonian esotericism" and was asking to which exotericism it would correspond.

Considering René Guénon's function, the problem is not one of believing what he wrote, and having the possibility of checking his sayings by confronting his writings with various sources, but of comprehending what he wrote and of making use of available parallel traditional authorities. Yet today, when some people accuse Saint Paul of duplicity or consider Shankarâchârya biased with regard to Buddhism, we cannot expect anything else.

The problem of the "sources" is connected to the error of considering Guénon just another "thinker" or "philosopher" or even a "cultivated man," since some individuals read Guénon only to cultivate themselves, as an act of erudition or even to try to follow literary fashion. A Romanian Orientalist, in vogue two decades ago, referred to René Guénon's doctrine as "close to ancient Gnosticism"; and recently we found this inanity again, where Guénon was labeled a Neoplatonian Gnostic.[1] It is most ridiculous that there are men of letters who chose Guénon as a subject for their thesis, similar how others have chosen Mark Twain or Balzac, and they call René Guénon "notre ami" ("our friend"), or "notre penseur" ("our thinker")! Eventually we saw with stupor a "Guénon dictionary" being published; the "dictionary," representing the result of the author's mental operations with regard to Guénon' work, obviously disappoints. It seems rich and it is not; it seems a "Guénon dictionary" and it is not. Yet, in fact, the idea of such a "dictionary" is incompatible with the idea of "Guénon." Those who have studied and comprehended Guénon's works, do not need this dictionary; those who have studied and did not really understand Guénon's works, will not be helped by this dictionary; and those who have not studied Guénon, will only be confused by the dictionary, for the reason that René Guénon's works are indissolubly related to his function, hence its special quality and the absurdity of it being treated as a philosophical or literary *Corpus*.

It is interesting to notice in these cases of abuse regarding Guénon's work that the tactics are the same, regardless of the time

---

[1] René Guénon received this accusation even when he was still alive, more than fifty years ago, and he gave a response, but it seems nobody listened to it.

period (today or fifty years ago), which represents one of the typical signs betraying the *tamasic* influences involved. For example, in 1946, the first attempt was made to publish a work about René Guénon; the occultist Jacques Marcireau wrote a book called **René Guénon et son oeuvre**,[1] which is in fact a "Guénon dictionary." It is an unintelligent book. Since it was published while Guénon was still alive, he was able to reply to such an insult:

[Mr. paul le cour] felt the need, with this occasion, to recommend to his readers a booklet called **René Guénon et son oeuvre**, by Mr. Jacques Marcireau, which he declares «very well written,» when we, from our part, have exactly an opposite opinion; we hope he will admit that we are better qualified to judge it. The book, which was published with us being unaware of it (and we cannot approve its publication), is nothing more than a simple compilation of extracts taken out from our works and articles, from here and there; there are a good number of phrases detached from their context and consequently, incomprehensible, sometimes truncated or altered; and everything is put together in an artificial way, we should say in an arbitrary mode, in paragraphs having titles which are the only thing belonging to the author. (Guénon, **Comptes rendus**, pp. 180-181)

It seems that the modern author of the "Guénon dictionary," by some strange inspiration, felt that his book did not exactly match Guénon's words quoted above, and he has now published (2004) what he calls a "complement" to the Dictionary, a sort of book named **La Métaphysique de René Guénon**; this "complement" is precisely the type of work Guénon would vehemently reject.[2]

---

[1] Jacques Marcireau, Éditeur, Poitiers (Vienne), France.
[2] To see how such individuals operate, we should note that the title "René Guénon's Metaphysics" is improper, of course, since Metaphysics is universal and doesn't belong to an individual. The author, knowing very well this simple truth, tackles it in his *Introduction*, and even though he admits is inaccurate, he justifies the title as "une nécessaire commodité de language et clarté d'énonciation à l'intention d'un large public" (a necessary convenience of language and clarity of enunciation for the general public). What he is saying makes no sense and we hope that only the author's ignorance is involved here; it is obvious that Metaphysics has nothing to do with a general public and so a "convenience of language" is not only futile but also misleading. Yet this author is not an isolated case and we would like to give another example. In 1988, Elie Lemoine published in *Études Traditionnelles* a review regarding

The abuse and detour of René Guénon's work seems to have no limits today and we recently encountered the expression "Guénonian traditionalism," as well as the attempt to classify the "traditionalists" into groups and individuals, starting with the "Guénonians." The idea of classifying and systematizing the traditional domain is so profane and anti-metaphysical, that its effect is not a clarification, but an increase of disarray. Beside this, the term "traditionalist" accentuates the same disarray too.

Guénon underlined the difference between Tradition and "traditionalism." Warning about language abuse and the detour of some keywords' meanings occurring as part of the Great Disarray which rules today, he showed that in the modern world "tradition" represents all kinds of profane things that don't have anything in common with genuine Tradition (Guénon, **Le règne**, pp. 277-8); "the idea of tradition was so much damaged that those who strive to find it don't know where to go" (Guénon, **Le règne**, p. 279). Any abuse of the word "tradition," such as considering tradition a simple "habit" or "custom," or talking about a "revolutionary tradition," only amplifies the disarray (Guénon, **Le règne**, pp. 281, 283); all these abuses have in common the fact that they consider tradition something purely human, a human invention.

Regarding the "traditionalists," they are the ones "who have only a tendency or a kind of aspiration toward tradition, without really possessing any authentic knowledge about it; we can measure through this the distance which separates the «traditionalist» spirit from the true traditional spirit. ... In conclusion, the «traditionalist» is only a simple «researcher» [or «searcher»], and for this reason he is always in danger of waywardness" (Guénon, **Le règne**, p. 280).[1]

Antoine Faivre's article, **René Guénon**. Lemoine highlighted Faivre's erroneous expressions "Guénonian metaphysics" and "Guénon's doctrine of Supreme Identity" (see Elie Lemoine, **Theologia sine metaphysica nihil**, Éd. Traditionnelles, 1991, p. 106; the book is a gathering of Lemoine's articles published in the *Études Traditionnelles* Journal).

[1] Normally, the "traditionalist" should oppose the "modernist" (of course, understood as antitraditional and profane), yet the danger is that the "traditionalist" himself is affected by modern ideas, as actually happens in some cases, some who

The irony is that, after René Guénon clearly established the difference between Tradition and "traditionalism," he was labeled as "traditionalist"! A recent work,[1] which wants to be a history of "traditionalism," talks about the "traditionalist philosophy," abusing the sense of the word philosophy, and about the "traditionalist movement," in which Guénon is placed too.[2]

---

criticize aspects of the profane point of view, being conquered by other aspects, no less antitraditional (Guénon, **Le règne**, p. 284).

[1] Mark Sedgwick, **Against the Modern World**, Oxford Univ. Press, 2004.

[2] What makes it more ridiculous is that Guénon himself exposed the expression "traditionalist philosophy" as a wrong one (Guénon, **Crise**, p. 49). There are also other labels such as "political traditionalism," applied to a "group of Romanian traditionalists," containing Michel Vâlsan and Mircea Eliade, the latter being considered the exponent of a "soft" traditionalism.

The author starts his book with this line: "The book is a biography of René Guénon and a history of the Traditionalism movement that he founded…" Nothing is true in this first line, which wants to specify the objective of the book. We would assume that an author, writing "a biography of René Guénon and a history of the Traditionalism movement that he founded," has read Guénon's work, but this author shows that he has no idea about it. First of all, the book is not a biography of Guénon; in fact, there have already been so many biographies written that another one would be just a non-sense. And Guénon stressed that his individuality does not count, so his biography means nothing. Second, René Guénon did not found any movement, even less traditionalism. For this reason, we cannot talk about "Guénonianism" and so on. We can ask ourselves: is René Guénon the creator of a new doctrine? No, absolutely not! In the Foreword of his book **Le Symbolisme de la Croix**, Guénon confessed that he wanted either to expose directly some aspects of the Oriental metaphysical doctrines, or to adapt these doctrines to our mentality, preserving their spirit. Guénon dressed in essential clothes the traditional data, presenting a unitive doctrine about Unity, which brightly illustrates his providential function. Guénon explained that he doesn't want to be limited by the frame of a specific doctrine, especially when someone is aware of the essential unity of all these doctrines, the various forms being just garments of the same truth.

The expression "traditionalism" the author used across his entire book is wrong and meaningless, especially in connection with René Guénon. In fact, "traditionalism" does not exist, and if we refer to Tradition, that is something totally different. The author also considered that Guénon developed the "traditionalist philosophy" having occultism as source. It is well-known that René Guénon exposed occultism as antitraditional and pseudo-spiritual. The book ends as it started. The last chapter begins with the insulting statement: "In the years before the 1927 publication of his **Crise du monde moderne**, René Guénon constructed an anti-modernist philosophy, Traditionalism." We must repeat, René Guénon did not construct anything, tradition has nothing to do with philosophy (a modern term) and there is no such thing as "Guénon's philosophy." René Guénon was traditional and not "anti-modernist." He was against fascism and any sort of extremism. He was not against the West, but he fought against the modern mentality as antitraditional and pseudo-spiritual, as an "anti-God" mentality. And all his work was directed to the Western people to help them recover from the disaster induced by the profane mentality. This mentality has no location.

CHAPTER VIII

THE WRATH OF TRADITIONALISTS

WE PURPOSELY INTRODUCED, in the title of this chapter, the label "traditionalist." As a reaction to the modern world where everybody talks about occultists, esotericists, theosophists, etc., the term "traditionalist" tries to delineate itself from the other appellations, and to define those who are more or less sincerely interested in traditional studies and doctrines. Yet we have already seen how Guénon defined the "traditionalist." For this reason the label "traditionalist" is also in disaccord with traditional teachings; it should be used in connection with Tradition only if we want to indicate those who wander around it, without finding the gate to it.

The philosophers (in the modern sense of the word), who invented systems after systems, are fond of labels, which give them a feeling of order in the flood of words and complicated ideas composing their philosophies. There are today categories such as "Guénonian," "Schuonian," "Evolian," etc. in the ambiance of people attracted to traditional doctrines. We have nothing against seeing those with a philosophical background of an academic type interested in traditional doctrines; on the contrary, we think that philosophy could be useful, the same way mathematics are more than necessary in the individual endeavour to assimilate metaphysical knowledge.[1] The difference between mathematics and philosophy is

---

[1] "Nobody crosses the threshold without mathematics" (Ioan Tzetzes, **Chiliades**, VIII, 973). Agrippa, in his turn, declared that without mathematics it is impossible to

that the first one forces us to limit our flood of words, often so shallow, while philosophy encourages it.

Labeling some as "Guénonians" even if it seems an easier mode of communicating does not reflect the truth but only the fact that in the mind of the "traditionalists" the division is implicit. Taking into account that René Guénon did not established his own doctrine, the label "Guénonian" is nonsense and expressions like "Guénonian esotericism" are absurd. As much as it is comfortable to imitate the philosophers' model regarding their systems and categories, we have no right to falsify the truth. Reading and agreeing with Guénon's books doesn't make us "Guénonians," even if the modern world adores labels, tags and acronyms.[1]

"The consequence of incantation (*dhikr*)[2] is inseparable from the total and perfect fraternity amid the initiates," Shaikh Tâdîlî said, and

---

study the science of magic (Henry Cornelius Agrippa, **Three Books of Occult Philosophy**, Llewellyn Publications, 1998, p. 233). Nicholas of Cusa wrote: "Mathematics represents the scientific domain that offers the most numerous similarities with metaphysics," and added: *Nihil certi habemus in nostra scientia, nisi nostram mathematicam*, stressing that from Pythagoras and Plato to Saint Augustine and Boethius, the philosophers stated that nobody can reach the knowledge of the divine order without learning mathematics. "On this path," concluded Cusa, "we will follow them, and, because there is no other way to lead to the divine order but that of the symbols, we affirm that we may select the mathematical signs, which contain an incorruptible certitude" (Nicolas de Cusa, **De la docte Ignorance**, Guy Trédaniel, 1979, p. 58).

[1] Michel Vâlsan used the epithet "Guénonian," but only in a given context and with reservation: "we normally trust the data we receive from individuals having indeed a traditional mentality and, if it is the case (and we have to say the word), of a «Guénonian» doctrinal formation" (**L'Initiation Chrétienne**, p. 178). Gilis followed Vâlsan in this respect: "Only, indeed, the veritable «Guénonians»" those who, using Michel Vâlsan's expression, presented «a perfect fidelity with regard to the teachings» of their grand predecessor, have taken up and developed this aspect of his doctrine..." (Gilis, **Introd. Guénon**, p. 17); yet Gilis stressed also that, "Guénon does not lead to Guénon, and it would be the worst insult to his memory of wanting to change the *Traditional Studies* into «Guénonian Studies»" (p. 105). On the other hand, labels like "Schuonian" and "Evolian," even if we disapprove of them because of the division they endorse, are, at least partially, understandable, considering that both Schuon and Evola have been marked by their powerful individuality.

[2] In the Islamic tradition, *dhikr* is an initiatory rite (Guénon, **Aperç. sur l'Init.**, p. 170).

warned: "Beware of a science where is found your and our salvation: do not divide the groups (*tawâif*) of initiates (*mansûb*), even if they do this themselves! Because division is an error which facilitates the heterodoxic innovations that divide the hearts."[1] It is exactly what Saint Paul cautioned: "My brothers, some from Chloe's household have informed me that there are quarrels among you. What I mean is this: One of you says, «I follow Paul»; another, «I follow Apollos»; another, «I follow Cephas»; still another, «I follow Christ.» Is Christ divided?" It is exactly what happened to those who have been in a direct relation with René Guénon,[2] but also to others who came later.

Of course, it is "human" for differences and different opinions to exist, and hence it was expected that, after Guénon's corporeal disappearance, various "traditional[istic] groups" would appear. The problems begin when the "human" becomes too human and much less traditional. Michel Vâlsan narrated how he was denigrated in front of Guénon's widow, who thought that he is the most acerbic enemy of René Guénon.[3] Almost immediately after René Guénon's death diverse "groups" were born, which, forgetting sometimes why they came to life, focused more on the worldly aspects, like for example the battle for leadership with regard to the "Guénonian

---

[1] Sheikh-Tâdîlî, **La vie traditionnelle c'est la sincérité**, Edizioni Studi Tradizionali, pp. 23-24.

[2] We understand "direct relation" either as "face to face" or through letters.

[3] Look at what kind of individuals, he complained, "are the exponents of Guénon's family's interests, and therefore, of «Guénon's work»"; see Michel Vâlsan, **Rumeurs, médisances et vérités**, Études Traditionnelles, no. 423, 1971, p. 30. Related to Vâlsan, we note his polemic with Marco Pallis on the subject of Christian initiation and the extremely instructive fact that no one, after their long duel, has changed his opinion. We do not want to take Vâlsan's side, even if we are in complete disaccord with Pallis, but we must underline the "callousness" of the hearts of those who undertake such polemics from a human and worldly perspective. Over many years we have witnessed a lot of disputes among the "traditionalists" and very rarely was an accord reached; usually, energies were concentrated on a better and stronger response, than on listening and understanding, and eventually, when no arguments were left, the personal attacks started.

heritage."[1] It was and still is possible to watch an aggressive polemic between groups and individuals, each one imagining they are the only genuine defenders of Tradition, hence the labels "Guénonian," "Schuonian," "Evolian," etc.[2]

Guénon wrote about polemic: "Those who are qualified to speak in the name of a traditional doctrine should not discuss with the «profane» ones and should not be involved in «polemics»; they must only transmit the doctrine as it is, for those who can understand it, and, at the same time, denounce the errors where they show up" (Guénon, **Crise**, p. 109); and: "we decided to stay out of any kind of polemic, of any kind of dispute between schools or parties" (Guénon, **Crise**, p. 180).[3]

Sure, the present division is caused, among other reasons, by the ego's powerful position in our modern world.[4] There is, even in the

---

[1] It is true that a member of such a group, more than twenty years ago declared that, what seems to be from an individual point of view a quarrel among "traditionalists" or "Guénonians," hides in fact a much more important stake and of a completely different nature.

[2] Marco Pallis used the bizarre expression "Christian Guénonians" and argued that those who were influenced by Guénon can nevertheless have opposite opinions, as an apropos to the problem of Christian initiation. Yet, Pallis should have decided: or these ones are "Christian Guénonians" and follow Guénon with respect to Christianity; or they are against what Guénon stated and then they are no longer "Guénonians"! It is not the first time Pallis contradicted himself. For example, at one point he suggested that even an atheist could receive an initiation, as if somebody would strive with all the energies and with all the sacrifices to reach something that he is convinced does not exist. One of Pallis' "successors" recently stated his worries about a "guénonization" of Christianity; he spoke about a "Guénonian doctrine," yet his work is of poor quality.

[3] No doubt, there are alarming signals with regard to division, and we should mention Jonas' article **Pour en finir avec René Guénon** published in the journal *Vers la Tradition*, no. 83-84, 2001, in which we are reminded of the confrontations among diverse "groups" composed of "guénonians, anti-guénonians and guénolatries" (p. 234). "The majority of criticism against René Guénon comes from pharisee, «phony esotericists,» scholars or intellectuals... whose thoughts make you smile" (p. 236). We should mention also, in the same journal, Abdellah Penot's article, **Guénon et les «Guénoniens,»** where are listed, not by name, some of the modern "guénonians" and their errors.

[4] Schuon said: "According to some Sufis, the devil was the first being that uttered the word «I»" (Frithjof Schuon, **Forme et substance dans les religions**, Dervy, 1975, p. 39).

case of good people, a significant activity of the ego, which wants to be noticed and appreciated; this ego has a tremendous appetite to criticize, yet does not accept any criticism; this ego today is extremely aggressive[1] and has a "wrath" that makes the individual have no patience to listen to somebody else, and to want just to expose his own point of view. As we have already seen, Guénon considered that "individualism" is the main factor of the present disarray. René Guénon wrote: "What we understand through «individualism» is the denial of any principle superior to individuality and, consequently, the limitation of civilization, in all fields, at its purely human elements... and this defines what we called «the profane point of view»" (Guénon, **Crise**, p. 90); and "who says individualism says necessarily division" (125).

"Individualism," Guénon continued, "introduces everywhere the addiction to discussions. It is very difficult to make your contemporaries understand that some things, because of their nature, cannot be discussed; modern man instead of trying to ascend at the level of truth, imagines to bring it down, to his level" (Guénon, **Crise**, p. 107). And Guénon wrote too:

In the domain of individual opinions discussions are always possible, because they are not beyond the rational order and, without considering any superior principle, various arguments more or less valid can be found to support the «pro» and the «counter»; it is even possible, in many cases, to continue the discussion indefinitely without reaching an agreement... and the most common result is that, each one, striving to convince the opponent, becomes more and more acerbic attached to his own opinion and locks himself even more exclusively. (Guénon, **Crise**, pp. 107-108)

Today, some of the "traditionalists" (we must use this word) behave in the same way as the "opponents" against whom Guénon fought in the past. This is very alarming. In the name of tradition, some people believe that insults can replace arguments, that personal attacks can substitute for doctrinal opinions, and polemics do not need an urban language and a minimum of civility. They imagine

---

[1] "God does not love those who are aggressive" (**Qur'ân** 7:55).

they are intransigents and, with wrath, they defend the traditional doctrines, as seemingly René Guénon did. Yet René Guénon, even if inexorable with regard to the Truth, admitting no compromises or concessions, without mercy in his task of denouncing pseudo-esotericism, pseudo- and antitradition, counter-initiation, and the profane point of view, never lowered himself to the level of personal attacks, never used boorish and uncivil language, never used ill-famed words, never trespassed the limits of politeness. As ruthless as Guénon appeared to be, he never attacked individuals as such, but only wrong ideas, pseudo-doctrines and conceptual errors.

The same thing cannot be said about some of his opponents and here we would like to give an example.[1] This is what an individual wrote to René Guénon in 1949: "Between us, face to face, I am telling you: «Guénon, my boy, you are a humbug»[2]... If you would have been indeed a jîvan-mukhta, you would not lie or falsify texts, you would not make assumptions worthy of Abbot Barbier or of brave Delassus, you would totally avoid attributing without justification intentions to the opponents."[3] Guénon replied: "And we, to this individual who for sure is much younger than us and to whom one tongue is not enough to exhale his wrath, we answer: «you are a boor!»"[4]; Guénon added that he never pretended to be a jîvan-mukhta and "our individuality, which pleasant or not, does not matter and has nothing to do with what we are writing."[5] As a reply to a new attack, René Guénon wrote: "It is impossible for us to answer such profanities and sarcasm. And this one [Dr. G. Mariani] claims that he «never attacks individuals»; yet what else does he do?" (Guénon, **Franc-Maçonnerie**, I, p. 191). Eventually, on another

---

[1] Vâlsan wrote: Guénon, "fulfilling his mission, consciously accepted the misunderstanding, the hostility, the attacks and disapproval of the academic generation (Orientalists, theologians, philosophers) and of the pseudo-spiritualists (theosophists, occultists), not to talk about other groups" (Vâlsan, **Hésychasme**, p. 178).
[2] In English, in original.
[3] René Guénon, **Comptes rendus**, pp. 211-212.
[4] It is the "strongest" word ever used by Guénon.
[5] Many times Guénon underlined that his individuality does not count, but only his work (see, for example, Guénon, **Franc-Maçonnerie**, I, p. 182).

occasion, René Guénon responded: "We are nobody's «servant» [either group or individual], but of the Truth" (Guénon, **Franc-Maçonnerie**, I, p. 197).

We presented these quotations since such a wrath and aggressive attitude can be encountered today in some of the so-called defenders of Tradition: the same old personal attacks, the same old comparisons with who knows what individuals, the same old accusations of servility. Sure, we can find explanations for such a bizarre attitude. Some people think that if they imitate Guénon's intransigence, they will come closer to the level of his work. Yet, more probably, our modern world sows in the individual an extreme aggressiveness. As Plutarch wrote, wrath (gr. *orge*[1]) replaces intelligence, producing mental chaos[2]; but all the traditional doctrines stress that worldly anger is one of the strongest obstacles on the spiritual journey, the opposite of peace and quietness.

We should not confuse anger with rigor though. The Wrath of the Gods refers to Justice and Rigor; worldly wrath is nothing of this kind. And it should be remembered that in the Islamic tradition the highest name of Allâh is "the Merciful," while human anger is a characteristic of great disarray, the wrath of traditionalists being nothing else than another "sign of the times." Like individual manifestations, worldly wrath cannot be cured otherwise than through knowledge, being a type of ignorance. Guénon was accused of writing his work without optimism or joy (Guénon, **Initiation**, p. 129); sadness, joy, anger and calmness, understood as individual elements have nothing in common with the traditional doctrines and their comprehension.[3]

Conversely, during all these years there were also valid interventions coming from various traditional[ist] groups, and justly criticizing the abuse and profanation of Guénon's work, or warning about the "wrath of traditionalists" (even if they did not called it so)

---

[1] We must not confuse *orge* with *orgia*, the initiatory rites in the Eleusinian Mysteries.
[2] Plutarch, **Essays**, Penguin books, 1992, pp. 176 ff.
[3] That is why the traditional writings do not have to produce joy, love for life, or sadness, anguish; if they do this, either the text is at a psychical level, or the reader cannot surpass the ego.

and about the "fights" among the "guénonians" and / or "traditionalists." These legitimate interventions exposed those who claimed to be knowledgeable about Tradition yet had an antitraditional mentality, if not worse. The Evangelic question, "Why do you look at the speck of sawdust in your brother's eye and pay no attention to the plank in your own eye?" (**Matthew** 7:3) rises by itself, since each human intervention is biased.[1] There are a small visible number of "sons of Tradition" (there are others, invisible) who activate in this world and their intervention has nothing to do with "the wrath of traditionalists."[2] They are the guardians of the Truth, they do not take sides, and their "criticism" aims not so much at individuals but at the doctrinal errors[3]; the less their words contain worldly anger, the more we know that they are close to Knowledge and Truth.

Coming back to the "boor" who attacked Guénon, there is an element which is worthy of mention. The individual accused René Guénon of having an attitude "opposite to the Christian spirit": "After the rightful expulsion of the Gnostics, after throwing the

---

[1] Since we mentioned Michel Vâlsan, we may note that some of Guénon's "associates," belonging to another "group," rightly criticizing dubious authors, who wrote without any discrimination about René Guénon, also blamed Vâlsan for being quoted by those individuals; they even insinuated that Vâlsan was open to some deviated psychical influences. In fact, what the critics could not stand was the opinion of some who considered Michel Vâlsan "the most authoritative commentator of Guénon's work." It is difficult to understand that even today, after only fifty years since Guénon's corporeal disappearance, somebody could think that there exists a commentator more authoritative than René Guénon himself. Guénon obsessively tried to preempt any error of interpretation and he tirelessly repeated his comments; the study of his work should be totally sufficient (and necessary) to understand Tradition, and any commentator of Guénon is usually an unwanted intermediary who could bring the errors of his own individuality.

[2] There are very few in the Occident interested in traditional studies. In 1935 already, Guénon, commenting on the Romanian traditional journal, *Memra*, which was just published, said that the journal had many difficulties to be printed, "which is not surprising, since in our days that is what occurs to everything related to the traditional studies" (René Guénon, **Articles et Comptes Rendus I**, Éd. Traditionnelles, 2002, p. 215).

[3] Of course, that does not mean to weaken the rigor and forgive the individuals who are a danger to Tradition.

Paulicians, Bogomils, Cathars and Patarins into the outside darkness, the Christian *orbis terrarum* clearly showed that it rejects esotericism. Yet, you [Guénon] stand in Gnosticism's wake." René Guénon replied: "It is really a pity for Mr. M. F.-D.'s «erudition» that Gnosticism under its many forms (which, anyway, was not esotericism, but the product of some confusions between esotericism and exotericism, therefore its «heretical» characteristic[1]) does not interest us at all, and everything that we know came from sources without any connection to this one" (Guénon, **Comptes rendus**, p. 205).

A similar accusation came from the part of a Catholic philosopher, Jacques Maritain, who assumed that René Guénon wanted a renovation of the old Gnosis, the mother of all heresies. René Guénon answered this aberration in a letter of 1921:

If you take the word «Gnosis» in its true sense, that of «pure knowledge,» in the same way I always do when I use it (and this is the sense under which it is found, for example, in the texts of some Fathers of the Church), I would say nothing against the intention «to renovate knowledge» with the help of the Hindu doctrines, even if I am probably not qualified enough to aim at such a goal; yet the rest of the phrase clearly shows that this is not what you meant. First, Gnosis, thus understood (and I refuse to understand it otherwise) cannot be called «the mother of all heresies»; that would be like saying that the truth is the mother of all errors; if there are human beings who do not understand the truth, and consequently errors are generated because of that, the truth is not responsible for this. You confuse purely and simply «Gnosis» with «Gnosticism.» [2]

Yet, even today, the wrath against Guénon is present, and we witness the same old tactics, the same accusations, the same calumnies, which are vivid proof that Guénon's work is timeless and a continuous danger for the adversary. For example, a Catholic website declared war against Guénon and Tradition, calling him an

---

[1] The same "heretical" confusion can be noticed to those who suggest an esoteric exotericism in Christian tradition.
[2] **René Guénon et l'actualité de la pensée traditionnelle**, Actes du colloque international de Cerisy-La-Salle, Archè, 1980, pp. 36-37.

anti-Christian, who supposedly wanted to destroy Christianity! René Guénon died in 1951, more than half a century ago, and Christianity still exists; so, why should somebody be so concerned today?[1] The Catholic Church has many problems and it needs all its energies to fight its own anti-Christian attitudes, its own anti-traditional gestures, the lack of vocation of some of its priests, the emptiness of its churches, the influence of the profane and modern mentality that invaded it, and so on. All the Church's problems are not a consequence of Guénon's work, on the contrary.[2]

Another one of René Guénon's modern foes is Jean-Marc Vivenza. For the English-speaking reader, this name probably means nothing and that is a good thing. Our work tries to show how even now the "hate" for Guénon remained intact, a phenomenon clearly suggesting that today, more than ever, Guénon's work must be studied and, if possible, assimilated; therefore, it is necessary to list some of the contemporary authors that participate in the above mentioned phenomenon, and Vivenza is one of them.

---

[1] The answer to this question is obvious: René Guénon's work is an incessant danger for the adversary.

[2] The same site hosted another article called "René Guénon: an anti-Christian esoterist, or the tenebrous and corruptive nature of the Guénonian Gnosis." How can someone be an "anti-Christian esoterist"? And where did the author find a "Guénonian Gnosis"? The article considers René Guénon as one of the most dangerous enemies of the Church and Christianity, while his teachings about a primordial Tradition are labelled as fantasy and as an occultist gnosis; to support his attacks, the author refers to a Canadian author, Marie-France James, whose contribution to the study of René Guénon's work and life is so misleading that her book doesn't deserve to be read. The author feels insulted that Guénon considered Christianity a religion and not an initiatory way. Now, is not Christianity a religion? Is not the Church against initiatory organisations? Shouldn't the author be happy that René Guénon considers Christianity a religion and not something else? The author is so limited, and the fact that others, belonging to other traditional forms, are also, does not excuse his ignorance. He cannot accept the existence of a primordial Tradition and the diversity of secondary traditions, in this way limiting God and the Holy Spirit to a particular traditional form. We know that in the Greek-Orthodox Church there is the tendency to limit God to a particular country or nation, and we know that other traditional forms have similar problems. There is no surprise here, because this is the consequence of the multiplicity and of the law of the cycles.

Today, there are various methods used to divert people from Guénon; one of them, which we already mentioned, consists of publishing dictionaries regarding Guénon. Vivenza published, in 2002, **Le Dictionnaire de René Guénon** (Le Mercure Dauphinois), and later, in 2008, Graham Rooth published his **Prophet for a Dark Age, A Companion to the Works of René Guénon** (Sussex Academic Press).[1] We see the mischievous scheme: why study Guénon and spend precious time, when there is a "Guénon Dictionary," with everything you need? First, a dictionary in itself suggests "erudition," and so, the reader will consider Guénon just as a common scholar; second, a dictionary about metaphysics and Tradition is an insult, diverting the reader from the meaning of traditional studies and initiatory knowledge.

In 2004, Vivenza insisted with his antitraditional campaign, by publishing, as we previously indicated, a new book, **La Métaphysique de René Guénon**, which had two purposes: first, to suggest that there is a "Guénonian" doctrine, or "Guénonian" metaphysics, invented by René Guénon, similar to the inventions of the philosophers; second, to suggest that the author is an authority with respect to Guénon's works, preparing the public at large to accept his opinions about Guénon.

In 2007, Vivenza decided that enough is enough and the time had come to give up the subtleties, which anyway were not his strength, and therefore he published a new book, **René Guénon et le Rite Ecossais Rectifié** (Les Éditions du Simorgh). On the front cover, the title is explained, to make sure that everybody can see and understand what is the book about: "clarification regarding Guénon's mistakes and misunderstandings with respect to the doctrine of Elus Coëns, the order *Ordre des Chevaliers Bienfesants de la Cité Sainte*, and the theosophy of Louis-Claude de Saint-Martin." The fact that Vivenza, the author of a dictionary about Guénon, in which he presents (sympathetically) Guénon's views about Masonry, and of

---

[1] We may notice that the *Foreword* was written by an antitraditional individual, Mark Sedgwick, whose devious book **Against the Modern World** was considered by Rooth as "an excellent account…"

a book trying to explain "Guénon's metaphysics," becomes his open enemy, represents nothing else but a natural development of an individual, who from the beginning was antitraditional and probably worse.

Vivenza's case is interesting because it is a good illustration of what individuals like "Louis de Maistre" and others hide. In his new book **René Guénon et le Rite Ecossais Rectifié**, Vivenza is happy to get rid of Guénon's teachings. Of course, he has to mention the *Ordre du Temple rénové*, which, curiously enough, he calls it "Ordre rénové du Temple," and considers that its creation took place in "circonstances rocambolesques (?!)" (p. 23).

Before adding a few more words about this book, let us stress what happened to Vivenza: he considered that the time had come to affirm that his master is Robert Amadou. Again, for many this name means nothing, but Amadou was one of those who could not accept René Guénon's direct way of unveiling the inconsistency, the masquerade and pseudo-spirituality of various occultist orders. As a result of this connection with Amadou, Vivenza becomes immediately a completely uninteresting character, and his grand words (*remarquable, merveilleux, grand valeur, essence du sacerdoce primitive, elements fondamentaux, grandes et profondes vérités, enjeux initiatiques*[1]), praising Occultism, makes him a demagogic figure under the influence of adverse forces. He also uses grand words against Guénon: *une stupéfiante ignorance, complète méconnaissance, absolue ignorance, la "cause" guénonienne,*[2] *l'absurdité de la plupart de ses* [Guénon's] *assertions*.[3] At the end of his book, Vivenza affirms that he has demonstrated Guénon's *incroyable mauvaise fois ou insondable ignorance* regarding *la perspective saint-martinienne*, but, of course, he did not prove anything, he talked to himself in a sort of frenzy, uttering with arrogance that Robert Amadou and Vivenza know better what Martinez de Pasqually wanted to express, much better than Martinez himself!

---

[1] Jean-Pierre Laurant's last book about Guénon has this title: **René Guénon, Les enjeux d'une lecture**.
[2] La "cause" guénonienne? Soon we will hear about a "Guénonian conspiracy."
[3] After writing a "Guénon Dictionary," now Vivenza scolds and gives lectures to Guénon! Obviously, he belongs to Kubin's "Dream Land" (see the next chapters).

The Wrath of Traditionalists

Vivenza dares to say (and why not?) that "the author of **Aperçus sur l'initiation** sensed, even though in a confused way, that in the works of Martinès and his disciples resides a mystery of superior nature" (p. 55). And Vivenza considers that he is doing a charitable work not mentioning the uncertainty regarding Guénon's orthodoxy, which he mentions anyway; indeed, the charitable intention is not so charitable after all, since Vivenza lists pell-mell Guénon's wrong doings: his theory of the cycles,[1] his belief (?!) in the existence of a "Lord of the World," his idea that Christ was only (?) an *avatâra* (p. 60). And he calls René Guénon either l'*occupant de la villa Duqqi au Cairo*, or the Master of Cairo (sometimes the master of Cairo). Not to say that Vivenza ascribes to Guénon all the truths found in the sacred texts; maybe he does not know, for example, that René Guénon did not write the **Upanishads**.

We could characterize Vivenza with his own words: *une stupéfiante ignorance, complète méconnaissance, absolue ignorance, incroyable mauvaise foi ou insondable ignorance, incapable de comprendre*, but these words are rather inaccurate.

The "OTR affair" separated Guénon from Papus, who was the inventor of the so-called Martinist Order, and it is well known that Guénon considered Papus, the Martinist Order, and the whole occultist movement, a fraud, antitraditional and even worse. In 1968, Philippe Encausse, Papus' son, created *L'Ordre Martiniste Belge*, having, among others, Maurice Warnon as member of the Supreme Council. In 1975, *L'Ordre Martiniste des Pays-Bas* was created and Maurice Warnon moved to this one, also as a member of the Supreme Council; the Order spread to France, England, Canada, and the USA. In 1979, Warnon immigrated to the USA and founded a counter-initiatory "center" called the "King's Garden" in the Hudson valley; the "King's Garden" was dedicated to the "Universal Brotherhood." However, in 2008, the "center" was moved to Belgium and its activities decayed.

---

[1] Yes, that is exactly what Vivenza said: the theory of the cosmic cycles is Guénon's theory!

One of its "products" was an on-line *Biographical Note* on René Guénon, which illustrates that the old hate has not died; the note is an amateurish fake, like the Martinist Order itself, but, as surprising as it may seem, it is a much "better" biography than all the others, because it is so dim-witted that it annihilates any notion of a "biography" on Guénon, which is in accord with Guénon's wish. Guénon is depicted as a racist, an anti-Semite, a sex maniac, a traitor, a skilful plagiarist, an arrogant and unscrupulous individual, faking his health problems, a spirit (inside the OTR), a false friend of Fabre d'Olivet,[1] a master of duplicity, a denigrator, a lover of Ivan Aguéli, hating the theosophists because they did not want to publish his work, a spy hired by England and then a double agent; and he died poisoned by the Egyptians. Each element of Guénon's known biography was distorted and contaminated[2] to such an extent that, after reading this *Note*, nobody would want to see any biography about Guénon and any hypotheses or opinions about his life.

---

[1] Fabre d'Olivet died in 1825. The author confuses this one with Fabre des Essarts.
[2] We may note that others, who belong to the "guénonist" camp, use a similar language and tactic on-line, ignoring the fact that the dirt always comes back, in strange ways, to the source.

CHAPTER IX

RENÉ GUÉNON AND HIS SOURCES

IN THE YEAR 2004, Archè – Milan published an obese work of 958 pages called **L'Énigme René Guénon et les "Supérieurs Inconnus," Contribution à l'étude de l'histoire mondiale "souterraine,"** written by Louis de Maistre, a pseudonym hiding more than one author. Since **L'Énigme René Guénon et les "Supérieurs Inconnus"** wants to be a "scientific" work of documentation and investigation, it is not clear why the "enigma" regarding the authors' names, the only reason we could think of being the authors' (unconscious) desire to feel important. **L'Énigme René Guénon et les "Supérieurs Inconnus"** unfortunately has no reason to be so voluminous, since the 958 pages could be concentrated in one sentence: "we, the authors, have no idea what really happened," its "contribution to the study of the underground worldwide history" being negligible.[1]

There is no doubt that "Louis de Maistre" considers Guénon as a common writer who dared to disobey the common rules of writing, who dared not to reveal his references; for "De Maistre," this sin is "gratuite et assez peu traditionnelle," as he declared at the beginning of his work, in *Avant-Propos* (p. 11), when, from a traditional point of view, nobody is concerned with chronology and sources (René Guénon explained it more than once). It is well known that René

---

[1] In 2006, L. Toth, the publisher, wrote a letter trying to defend the book, but his attempt is, like the book, unconvincing (see *La Règle d'Abraham*, no. 21, 2006, Archè).

Guénon's work is not a work of erudition, it does not comply with the rules of the profane educational institutions (like Universities).[1] It is typical for authors like "Louis de Maistre" not to touch Guénon's metaphysical writings where, as we know, the references are always there (and they are the sacred texts). "De Maistre" does not care about spirituality and metaphysics and spiritual realization, since these are domains he cannot reach; instead, he is interested in what suits his mentality, that is, gossip and underground stories, subjects for tabloids, "secrets" that are not secrets, which makes him a good companion of books like **The Da Vinci Code**.

"De Maistre" thinks that it is necessary to conduct a deeper study of the "problematic aspects of Guénon's activity" (*la nécessité d'approfondir les aspects problématiques de l'activité de Guénon*) (p. 12), without telling us for whom these aspects are problematic and why should we be interested in Guénon's "activity," an activity that, as René Guénon stated so many times, has nothing to do with his work. "De Maistre" is such a profane individual that he reproduces what happens today in the modern life, where all the journals are focusing on the "secret" lives and activities of so-called "celebrities"; we live now a horrible tenebrous age in which the heroes are these "celebrities," where the public at large is hypnotized by all the scandalous (problematic) activities.

"De Maistre" said from the beginning that he does not claim to definitely clarify the historical problems he tackled (*ce que nous exposerons n'a pas la prétention d'éclaircir de manière définitive les problèmes historiques abordés*), and that his work raises more questions than offers answers (*on trouvera dans cet ouvrage plus de questions que de réponses*)! (p. 13). In fact, the author gives for each problem an opinion and then he provides an opposite opinion, concluding that each hypothesis could be right.

The perversity of "De Maistre"'s method is obvious from the first page of the first chapter. He poses as the defender of "human rights" and with "proletarian anger" condemns Guénon's lack of

---

[1] Ananda K. Coomaraswamy was the one who tried to teach the University about Tradition, of course without results.

references, since knowing these references is the "fundamental right of any individual" (*un droit fondamental de tout individu intéressé par l'enseignement écrit et oral (sic) d'un quelconque auteur*) (p. 17). Now, René Guénon is not "any" author, and he explained from the beginning that he is not writing for the public at large, he doesn't do a work of vulgarization, on the contrary. There is no such "fundamental right" as the one claimed by "De Maistre" and, again, we notice his profane and antitraditional mentality, since the media's slogan "the public has the right to know" is very well known: it is abused and overused to hunt all sorts of gossip and intimacies and so-called "secrets," when, in fact, the information people need and have a right to know should be of a totally different nature. For the same reason, books like **The Da Vinci Code** were well received by the public at large (and then, quickly forgotten), and there is no big difference between Brown and "De Maistre," not only with respect to their mentality but also regarding their books, both promising to solve and reveal a lot of "secrets," but lamentably failing in the end.

"De Maistre" considers that Guénon's work, because of this lack of references, appears as a kind of "mystification" and the result of his imagination (p. 18). The hypocrisy of such a statement is evident: Guénon's work is taken as a whole, when, in fact, the lack of references regards the question of Agarttha mainly (in **Le Roi du Monde**) and, of course, the question of initiation; otherwise, all the references with respect to the sacred texts are there, but the sacred texts, they don't have references.

"De Maistre" cannot accept René Guénon's repeated declaration that his work has nothing to do with his individuality (*sa personnalité énigmatique*, "De Maistre" says, p. 18), since this is the only way the antitraditional forces could expect some success. The author talks about the greatness of Guénon's work (*la grandeur de cette oeuvre*) and about its weakness, which is, in his view, the fact that René Guénon "hid" his sources and, so, he could not be verified, this situation generating supplementary investigations (like this one, of course). In fact, from a traditional point of view, the purpose of René Guénon's work was to open the door to the capable ones to continue not with investigations but with serious studies of metaphysics, of the traditional doctrines and to try to find a spiritual path; and for this purpose, his work gave the reader all the necessary sources. Evidently, "De Maistre" does not refer to this aspect of Guénon's work, but to the "spicy" side, which includes the texts about Agarttha, even if only in "De Maistre"'s mind what René Guénon wrote about Agarttha was something occult and without references: the reality is that Guénon stated the equivalence between Agarttha, Salem and the Earthly Paradise; consequently, what specific references should we expect about the Paradise, when all the traditions witness it? But, of course, this is too much for the author(s) of **L'Énigme René Guénon**, because what he is after are the occultist gossip, the political intrigues and the "spicy" aspects, for which reason he is mainly interested in Guénon's youth[1] and his writings signed with a pseudonym (p. 20). Sure, "De Maistre" quotes René Guénon's letter in which this one affirms that only the texts signed "René Guénon" are designated for the public at large (p. 24), but who cares what Guénon wanted or explained, he is dead now, and "De Maistre" knows better what the public at large needs, since the people have a right to know, and "De Maistre," even if he cannot find the truth, he can stir up these "secrets" and suggest to the public at large all kinds of piquant hypotheses.

As expected, "Louis de Maistre" is concerned with Guénon's "enigmatic" activities[2] during the period 1909-1912, when he was involved with various publications and organizations; however, the author admits that he cannot offer anything else than mere hypotheses (*on ne peut formuler que de simples hypothèses*). "De Maistre" tries to understand, without success, how the "Mason René Guénon" (p. 31) could write in an anti-Masonic journal, forgetting that Guénon was also the "Muslim René Guénon" and the "Christian René Guénon," etc. "De Maistre" admits he cannot explain Guénon's collaboration to *La France Antimaçonnique* (p. 42), but at least what he can do is insinuate that this collaboration was

---

[1] Since in that period René Guénon had contacts with the various occultist organizations.
[2] He calls them "cultural activities"! (p. 26).

essential for Guénon's work (*cette collaboration, pourtant, a eu un poids énorme dans son oeuvre*), where "work" meant for "De Maistre" very little: the book about Theosophism and Guénon's few writings about the *Superiori Incogniti*. And after beating around the bush for 20 more pages, "De Maistre" concluded this first chapter by saying that René Guénon's activity at *La France Antimaçonnique* remains totally enigmatic. If we have to accept an *Énigme René Guénon*, we suggest this one: during this period (1906-1912), at one moment, René Guénon disappeared, and, when he appeared again, he was completely changed.

There is another reason why some individuals, like "Louis de Maistre," are concerned with an author's sources. More than once we have heard people say: "Oh, if I had had time to read so many books and study so many documents, I would have written myself works similar to these ones produced by René Guénon." The modern ideas of "equality" and "egalitarianism" are so strongly planted in the individual's mind that even those interested in traditional studies cannot escape their influence. They think that almost anybody (with some education) could write like Guénon if this anybody would have time and access to Guénon's sources. Consequently, one of the reasons for wanting to discover these sources is to please the ego and believe that anyone could be inspired by previous documents, the way René Guénon presumably was. This basic error, together with the idea that the public at large has a right to know, is part of the profane point of view that governs our world, a viewpoint that confuses metaphysics with fast food and the traditional studies with watching "breaking news" on TV.

However, the principal reason is tenebrous, since it aims at the obliteration of Guénon and what he represents. We know for sure that, if the source of René Guénon's initiation and the sources of his knowledge become public, an absurd hypothesis, the same authors, who vehemently demanded these sources, will start a campaign to demolish the sources, labeling them as fake, since their real objective is to annihilate René Guénon's influence.[1]

Before "Louis de Maistre," Jean-Pierre Laurant suggested that Guénon followed the example of Creuzer and De Rougemont to present the doctrine of the cosmic cycles. Now, this is not true, but such a subject represents a good opportunity to try and undermine Guénon's reputation. "Louis de Maistre" declares: "Even though he [Guénon] always kept the Hindu doctrines in high esteem, the writings of this «Western» school [Hermetic Brotherhood of Luxor] were the main source for his theoretical developments about the cosmic cycles."[2] "De Maistre" should be content: eventually he found one of Guénon's "sources"; moreover, the author considers that the Hermetic Brotherhood of Luxor was inspired by the work of Samson Arnold Mackey, which means that a second "source" was uncovered. If we remember how offended "De Maistre" was about Guénon's lack of references, we would expect now an astral commotion, changing everything. Now, we know! We have two palpable sources. Unfortunately, reality is more complicated. "De Maistre" found the information about Mackey in Godwin's **Arktos**,[3] where, as a committed theosophist, Godwin discussed the connection between Blavatsky and Mackey. He showed that Blavatsky called Mackey "the self-made adept of Norwich," and knew his work. Blavatsky, who was all her life a shrewd crook, used Mackey in the same way she used Csoma de Körös, and made him an "adept," because who cares about words? Godwin assumed that she discovered Mackey through the Hermetic Brotherhood of Luxor, which "taught Mackey's doctrine,"[4] without mentioning

---

[1] As expected, "Louis de Maistre" was not the only one who tried to discover René Guénon's sources. Jean-Pierre Laurant, for example, in his work **Le sens caché dans l'oeuvre de René Guénon**, L'Age d'Homme, 1975, suggested a few books that could have been at the origin of Guénon's ideas (*l'origine des idées qu'ils exposaient*), forgetting that Guénon was not a common erudite or writer.

[2] **L'Énigme René Guénon**, p. 731.

[3] Joscelyn Godwin, **Arktos, The Polar Myth**, Thames and Hudson, 1993, pp. 196-202.

[4] Probably we could say "Mackey's theory," but never "doctrine."

Mackey's name (he was called "an initiate of our Noble Order").[1] However, Godwin admits that Mackey's theory was changed and the traditional cyclical values replaced his profane ones,[2] which undermined Mackey's speculations; and in the journal of the Hermetic Brotherhood of Luxor, Mackey was presented as "the Neophyte of an Initiate of the H. B. of L.," and from this Initiate, Mackey "acquired his knowledge of the Ancient Astronomy." "Louis de Maistre" disregards this last part and prefers to consider Mackey an enigmatic genius who supplied René Guénon with the data about the cosmic cycles; he concludes: "the authority that is attributed to Guénon with respect to the doctrines of the cycles seems to need profound critical revisions. From now on, Guénon's judgment regarding the refutation of the astronomers' affirmation that the precession of the equinoxes lasts for 25,765 years, instead of the «real traditional duration» of 25,920 years, also becomes quite questionable."

"Profound critical revisions"? "De Maistre"'s verdict is more than ridiculous; but he is not alone. Jean-Pierre Laurant, researching some documents of the so-called *Ordre du Temple rénové* (year 1908), found some reviews regarding the cosmic cycles, where the precessional duration was 25,765 (as mentioned by "De Maistre"),[3] and even though Laurant did not say it, we are left to believe that Guénon, as the leader of the Order, would accept this number and other calculations existing in the document.[4] On the other hand, Marcel Clavelle (Jean Reyor), in his *Document confidentiel inédit*, affirmed that he saw some notebooks belonging to the OTR, where the "theory of the cosmic cycles was correctly restored."

The traditional doctrine of the cosmic cycles is based, obviously, on the cyclic numbers. If we consider the four lunar phases as

---

[1] Godwin 201.
[2] For the precession of the equinoxes, the traditional value of 25,920 years replaced Mackey's.
[3] **Le sens caché**, p. 48.
[4] Feydel, commenting on Laurant, says that everybody agrees not to consider the reviews "guénonian." See Pierre Feydel, **Aperçus historiques touchant à la function de René Guénon**, Archè, 2003, p. 30.

reflections of the four *yugas* and we multiply 4 by the number of *Nakshatras* asterisms,[1] we will have: 4 x 27 = 108, a fundamental cyclic number. If we multiply the number of *Nakshatras* asterisms by 16 (the parts of the lunar disc), we obtain: 27 x 16 = 432 (108 x 4 = 432), another fundamental cyclic number.

Symbolically, the four *yugas* last 4,000, 3,000, 2,000 and 1,000 years (we note the proportion 4 – 3 – 2 – 1). Each *yuga* is preceded and followed by a dawn and a dusk, which link the cycles together; therefore, the "Golden Age," *Krita-yuga*, is valued at 4,800 years (4,000 + 400 + 400), *Treta-yuga* at 3,600 years, *Dwapara-yuga* at 2,400 years, and *Kali-yuga* at 1,200 years. Consequently, a *Manvantara* or a *Mahâyuga* will be valued at 12,000 years. Because each divine Year lasts 360 terrestrial years, a Manu Age will last 4,320,000 years.[2] Now, 4,320 x 6 = 25,920,[3] which is the precessional duration.

Leonard Woolley's research produced a list of the antediluvian Chaldean kings, which specified the traditional duration of king A-lu-lim's reign – 28,000 years, of king A-lal-gar's reign – 36,800 years, and of king En-me-en-lu-an-na's reign – 43,200 years.[4] 28,000 + 36,800 = 64,800 years and this last value René Guénon considered to be the traditional duration of a *Manvantara*, composed of five Great Years (5 x 12,960).[5]

---

[1] With respect to the Vedic astronomical science (*jyotishavedanga*), there were 27 Nakshatras asterisms (half of the fundamental number 54), which made it possible to observe the variable positions of the sun, moon and planets, and to correlate the movements of the sun and moon.

[2] The cyclic numbers 10,800 and 432,000 are to be found also in other traditions. Censorin mentioned Heraclitus' *Great Year* of 10,800 years and the Babylonian Berossos pointed out a cosmic period of 432,000 years. Often, the ancient Greeks and Persians evaluated the *Great Year* as having 12,000 or 13,000 years (see René Guénon, **Formes traditionnelles et cycles cosmique**, Gallimard, 1980, p. 23). The **Satapatha Brahmana** stated that Prajâpati (the Principle of universal manifestation) is the Year, his Word, which produces the World, being collected by the **Vêda**, which is divided into 10,800 moments of the Year, as the **Rig-Vêda** contains 10,800 units of 40 syllables each, that is, 432,000 syllables in total.

[3] See Guénon, **Formes**, p. 22.

[4] C. W. Ceram, **Gods, Graves, & Scholars**, Alfred A. Knoph, 1968.

[5] Each Great Year values half of the precessional duration.

There is almost no "enigma" regarding the doctrine of the cosmic cycles and René Guénon's knowledge of it. That Guénon possessed traditional data, other than those from the Hindu tradition or from the Chaldean and Persian antiquity, it could also be possible, but it is more important to stress that he was very cautious in presenting these data, because there is no benefit for us, as all the traditional forms affirmed, to find out in more details when the end will come; therefore, with the exception of one article published in English, in 1937, in the *Journal of the Indian Society of Oriental Art*, he did not mention the values of the cycles directly. What we also have to point out is that, as René Guénon said, because perfection is not to be found in our world, the planets, like Earth, are not spheres, and their trajectories are not circles but ellipses.[1] Similarly, we cannot expect to find the cyclical numbers and the traditional value for the precession of the equinoxes in this world, especially now, at the end of the *Kali-yuga*.[2]

In addition, "Louis de Maistre" is very interested in the foundation of the *Ordre du Temple rénové* (OTR), since he thinks that René Guénon played "an enigmatic role in this unjustified episode on a traditional level" (p. 725), and could be compared to those experiences that gave birth to Neo-Gnostic, Martinist or para-Masonic movements, which all had an evil aspect ("De Maistre" even suggested a "counter-initiatory" activity). Since this subject was debated at large by others, "De Maistre" tried to temper his comments and play the "devil's advocate" criticizing Robert Amadou for his work **L'Erreur spirite de René Guénon**, in which the author accused Guénon of being a spiritualist.[3]

---

[1] Therefore the Sun is not in the center of a circle, but in one of the ellipse's focus. In Godwin's **Arktos**, all the diagrams show erroneously the Sun in the middle (center?) of the ellipse.

[2] Likewise, the number of days in a year is not 360. Another important thing would be to understand how the duration of the cycle harmonizes with the fact that a cycle is not a smooth continuous descending path and how the activity of an *avatâra* or of the sages could influence this duration.

[3] p. 723. However, for "De Maistre," the "OTR affair" is a somber one (p. 205).

"Louis de Maistre" considers that the episode of the *Ordre du Temple rénové* needs a radical clarification, since it was an enigmatic affair with René Guénon as its "profound heart" (*coeur profond*, p. 722). But, in fact, the author cannot offer a "radical clarification," for the simple reason that such episodes are not for the public at large, and the only one who could have clarified it would have been Guénon himself. Also, it is difficult to understand what kind of drastic explanation "De Maistre" wants, considering that many others already tried all sorts of elucidations.[1]

Immediately after René Guénon's death, in the special issue of the *Études Traditionnelles* (no. 293-294-295, 1951), Michel Vâlsan wrote an article called **La fonction de René Guénon et le sort de l'Occident**, in which he suggested that the birth of the OTR could be a result of the activity of the ancient retired center of the Western tradition, aiming at the restoration of a Western elite, with Guénon as initiatory pivot (p. 250). Then, Paul Chacornac, in 1956, wrote Guénon's first biography, where the spiritist modality used for the foundation of the OTR is described and the idea is advanced that René Guénon wanted to gather the most interesting elements from occultist organizations (p. 34); indeed, the apparition of the OTR caused a complete separation between Guénon and "his friends," on the one hand, and Papus and Teder (the leaders of the occultists), on the other hand, which would suggest that the OTR was a sort of Noah's Ark.

As Marcel Clavelle declared, he helped Chacornac with Guénon's biography.[2] In the unpublished *Document*, Clavelle said that he knew

---

[1] We should mention, as an illustration, the interminable discussions on the Internet regarding this topic, when a group tried in 2007 to write a biography on Guénon for French Wikipédia (see *http://fr.wikipedia.org*, Discussion: René Guénon/Archive 4). Various sources were indiscriminately taken into consideration and the members of the group spent a lot of time and energy weighing the sources, without understanding that these are just different authors' opinions on Guénon's activity and life, and that, in fact, the only conclusion the discussions should have drawn (since they clearly illustrated it) is that nobody knows anything about the OTR.

[2] See Jean Reyor, *De quelques énigmes dans l'œuvre de René Guénon*, Les Cahiers de L'Herne, **René Guénon**, 1985, p. 137. From this article, we deduce that Reyor knew almost nothing about René Guénon (therefore "quelques enigmes").

about the OTR from Patrice Genty, because Guénon did not talk about this subject; then, he gave his personal opinion trying to explain this episode: or Guénon influenced the medium's mind, or Guénon himself caused the spiritist phenomenon.[1] René Guénon exposed the "spiritist fallacy" in a work with this title, but he also carefully suggested that various phenomena could be produced by the subtle forces and, more so, by the spiritual forces.[2] The idea that René Guénon was involved in a spiritist activity is ridiculous; nonetheless, the fact that he and not somebody else was elected the leader of the OTR shows that, already at that time, his traditional status was well established, as confirmed by the OTR's documents (some of the subjects debated there were later part of Guénon's books[3]), and that the members of the OTR hoped to find a genuine spiritual path that the occultist organizations were incapable of providing; unfortunately, they could not break away from their old habits (because of lack of qualification) and so the OTR died.

Antonello Balestrieri, in an article called **A propos d'un "Document confidential inédit" (et de "apories" de son "auteur")**, May 2002, vehemently criticized Clavelle and refuted his explanation regarding the foundation of the OTR. But between Clavelle and "Louis de Maistre" there were many others interested in the "OTR affair." Jean-Pierre Laurant, quoting Paul Vulliaud, said that "Guénon presented himself as a reincarnated Templar," which is an absurd statement; and he continued, in relation to the OTR, to depict a René Guénon avid of power and ready to use treachery to obtain it.[4] We see here a standard portrait of the false prophets, and Laurant's dishonest way to present Guénon, similar to that of "De Maistre," has as objective to make him "one of them," and maybe

---

[1] However, Clavelle said that he had some doubts that the "OTR affair" was provoked by Guénon.
[2] René Guénon, **L'Erreur spirite**, Éd. Traditionnelles, 1984, pp. 41, 94, 103, 105, 108, 116-117, 120-121. See also René Guénon, **Symboles fondamentaux**, p. 56, about the subtle influences.
[3] For Gilis, the OTR was the privileged place where Guénon's work was born (Charles-André Gilis, **Introduction à l'enseignement et au mystère de René Guénon**, Éd. Trad., 2001, p. 60).
[4] **Le sens caché**, pp. 45-6.

both Laurant and "De Maistre" were mentally unable to go beyond this level. Jean Robin presented in his book the same data already published by the previous authors,[1] and, of course, he was unable to produce any clarification. Nonetheless, Charles-André Gilis who, as expected, embraced Vâlsan's hypothesis regarding the revival of an ancient center and considered the OTR a beneficiary of an authentic initiatory transmission, praised Robin for assimilating Vâlsan's teachings well.[2]

Feydel, starting from one of Balestrieri's affirmations, which regards the Hermetic Brotherhood of Luxor, assumed that it had to be a strong connection between this organization and the OTR.[3] After reviewing the data found in other published works, he launched his own hypothesis, considering the "inner circle" of the Hermetic Brotherhood of Luxor behind the OTR, and this "circle," aware of Guénon's strong personality, would have called him to become the leader (p. 38); we see how Feydel is in accord with "Louis de Maistre," who also considered this organization one of Guénon's "sources."

In fact, there is no solution to the "OTR affair" for the simple reason that René Guénon was not a writer, an occultist, a scholar, nor a philosopher; he was an initiate who transmitted in his work a traditional teaching that belonged to the primordial Tradition and its orthodox branches, and so, all the episodes of his life are of no importance and cannot influence what he transmitted, and we do not have to forget that he was not a spiritual master whose life would have then contained symbolical ingredients valuable for the disciples.

Also, we can see how the attacks against René Guénon, which started at the same time as his work, steadily continued after his

---

[1] Jean Robin, **René Guénon, Témoin de la Tradition**, Guy Trédaniel, 1986, pp. 50-64.
[2] Gilis, **Introduction**, p. 63. It is true that Robin considered the OTR genuine and a last attempt to restore the Western tradition (Robin 61, 198), but he also declared that Vâlsan did not receive any information from Guénon, and so, all the opinions regarding the OTR, pro and contra, could be valid.
[3] Feydel, **Aperçus historiques touchant à la fonction de René Guénon**, p. 23.

disappearance and even today these attacks burst out with a lot of hate. Even if, apparently, this is not good news, in fact it illustrates better than anything else that Guénon's work did not lose its influence, and still provokes strong reactions from the adverse forces. As expected, these reactions are much stronger on the Internet than in a printed book, since the Internet creates the illusion of safety and anonymity, which makes it possible to say anything about anything. In fact, the Internet in this respect is like a garbage bin, like the "subconscious mind," like a relief valve that allows anyone to unload their frustrations and anger. However, like anything else related to the computer and other modern inventions, it is just a way to waste energy and time, and we see a lot of polemics that, like "video games," lead to nothing but loss and confusion.[1]

"Louis de Maistre," in search of Guénon's "sources" with regard to the Lord of the World, mentions Gustav Meyrink and his novel **The Walpurgis Night**, where he alluded to the "Emperor of the World," and the reader is left with the impression that Meyrink was one of the "other" sources for Guénon's **Le Roi du Monde**.[2]

Gustav Meyrink makes good company with Jules Verne, Edgar Allan Poe and Mark Twain.[3] He also uses some traditional symbols, but it is obvious that his work is a "parody" of the genuine initiatory stories and creates a terrible confusion. Like Jules Verne in his works **The Carpathian Castle** and **Mathias Sandorf**, Gustav Meyrink uses (in fact, abuses) the symbolism of the center. Verne's and Meyrink's center is a pseudo-center, an "occultist" center, a caricature and a mockery, a suspect center influenced by the "counter-initiatory" forces, and we have to use our power of discrimination to understand Guénon's statement that the "«counter-initiation» derived from the unique source to which every initiation is attached," which indicates how dangerous such a pseudo-center could be.

---

[1] Modern "inventions" are designed to replace all traditional activities and to keep people busy. Modern individuals spend hours in front of their TV screens, computers, cell phones, and so on, and feel full of activity.
[2] **L'Énigme René Guénon**, p. 108.
[3] See our work, **The Everlasting Sacred Kernel**, Rose-Cross Books, 2002.

Mircea A. Tamas

In a letter to Julius Evola (from 1949), René Guénon wrote: "There are cases in which the influence of counter-initiation is clearly visible. Among these cases we must include those in which the traditional elements are presented in an intentionally «parodist» form; this is, in particular, the case of Meyrink, which, of course, does not mean that he was clearly aware of the influence which was exercised upon him. Therefore, I am surprised to learn that you seem to respect Meyrink."[1]

When Meyrink's last book, **Der Engel vom westlichen Fenster** (*The Angel of the West Window*), was translated into French, it was published with a *Foreword* by Julius Evola, and this *Preface* shows how such books can create confusion, even in the case of people like Evola, who knew Guénon's teachings well. However, Evola himself had his contribution to the general confusion, with his wrong ideas about initiation, Masonry and spiritual authority.[2] Even though Evola tried to highlight some of Meyrink's errors, the *Preface* remains dubious, especially at the end when Evola compares Agarttha from Guénon's **Le Roi du Monde** to Meyrink's Elsbethstein.[3] Meyrink's center is, in the best case, a pseudo-Agarttha; nonetheless, it is instructive to see how Meyrink abuses the traditional symbols. For example, in Evola's opinion (expressed in his *Foreword*[4]) the novel

---

[1] Julius Evola, **René Guénon, A Teacher for Modern Times**, Sure Fire Press, 1994, p. 33.

[2] Regarding Julius Evola's serious errors and his incompatibility with Guénon's work and with the traditional doctrines in general, see André Lefranc, **Julius Evola contre René Guénon**, *La Règle d'Abraham*, no. 21, 2006, Archè; the author concluded that "Evola is not a traditional man and even less a spiritual authority" and it is better not to read his work; often, his theories are antitraditional and he is more than a pseudo-Guénon, he is an anti-Guénon. About Evola's mistakes see also Andreas Brunnen, **L'influence de René Guénon dans les pays de langue allemande**, *Vers la Tradition*, no. 122, 2011.

[3] "[Meyrink] talks about a supreme center of the world (Elsbethstein, an analogue idea to that of Agarttha)" (Gustave Meyrink, **L'Ange à la fenêtre d'Occident**, La Colombe, 1962, p. 17). We should add that, without reason, Julius Evola considered Gustave Meyrink as expressing in his work some "magico-initiatory teachings" (Julius Evola, **Masques et visages du spiritualisme contemporain**, Les Éditions de l'homme, 1972, p. 271).

[4] See also **Masques et visages**, p. 288.

transmits a real teaching when, at the end, denounces the Angel to be just an echo, an illusion,[1] a spiritist error. What Evola could not see is that the title, which represents the quintessence of the work, is *The Angel of the West Window*, emphasizing the importance of this "Angel," and by negating the "angel" at the end, Meyrink negates the whole book. Not to say that the idea to use the term "angel" for this ghost is not only inadequate, but directly diabolical. And even if it seems that Meyrink eventually rejects the "Angel," his book extensively presents spiritist sessions.[2]

The Angel of the West Window continued the confusion created by Verne, Poe, and Twain, and influenced the modern antitraditional authors. We see from the beginning the importance of the "documents,"[3] a modern and profane idea, used by malevolent authors with regards to Masonry, Templars, and initiation. This is not only about the modern mentality, which cannot accept anything that is not "corporeal" and cannot understand that the genuine spirituality and initiation do not need "documents," but it is a result of the influence of the "counter-initiatory" forces. Meyrink introduces a character called Lipotine or Nitchevo (p. 9), a name similar to Verne's Nemo; in Russian, *nitchevo* means "nothing"; *nemo* comes from Latin and means "nobody." As in Twain's case, the (malefic) dream plays an important role (p. 11); but also the abyss, the Templars[4] and the Baphomet, which becomes a substitute for

---

[1] That is what Meyrink says at the end of his book (Gustav Meyrink, **L'ange de la fenêtre d'Occident**, Le Rocher, 1986, pp. 292, 312-313). We see here the same pattern that Twain used in **The Great Dark**, where the conclusion was that everything is illusion, but, in comparison with the sacred writings, there is nothing beyond this illusion. The Angel could be compared to Twain's "Superintendent of Dreams."

[2] **L'ange de la fenêtre d'Occident**, p. 138. Marcel Clavelle (Jean Reyor) published in 1932, in *Le Voile d'Isis*, un article about Meyrink, and it is sad to read that this collaborator of Guénon could say that Meyrink's *Green Face* offers practical guidance with respect to the initiatory process (Jean Reyor, **Études et recherches traditionnelles**, Éditions Traditionnelles, 1991, p. 179); however, this is another proof that Reyor's opinion cannot be trusted or at least that his opinions should be regarded with caution.

[3] **L'ange de la fenêtre d'Occident**, p. 7.

[4] "The Knights Templar of the New Grail," see *ibid.* p. 254.

the Principle, the head turned backward, the blood, Tula,[1] St. Patrick and St. Dunstan,[2] are elements participating at the general confusion (pp. 13-14). Meyrink makes of Bartlett Green a mock imitation of Christ.[3] Even though Evola tried to defend Meyrink, this one uses the erroneous theory of reincarnation (p. 70), and expressions like "the satanic astral body" (p. 102), "Golden Rose,"[4] "vampirism" (p. 233), "the Lodge of the West Window" (p. 257), and "the realization of Baphomet" (p. 158). We find in this work the same pattern used today in books like **The Da Vinci Code, Mysteries and Secrets of the Masons** and many others, where Alchemy, Rose-Cross, Masonry, Templars, etc. are mixed together in a horrible way. But **The Angel of the West Window** is more than a mixture; it is a sinister "parody"[5]; and even more, it transmits an upside down symbolism, which represents the actual "Satanism." In opposition to Solomon's Temple, where there are three windows / doors opened to three of the cardinal points, Meyrink describes a room of a castle having the East, South and North windows immured (p. 139). Alchemy is combined with Chemistry (pp. 147, 150), the Pentagram is abused (p. 140), the angels are ghosts, and the spiritual forces are magnetic forces (p. 173). At the end, it is said: "Brother, you have crossed the threshold of initiation with your face turned backwards" (p. 315). In fact, in a genuine spiritual realization, the neophyte must not look back, and all initiatory stories emphasize this rule.

Although the author builds the entire book around the Angel, he concludes that the Angel is an illusion. Similarly, the modern occultist books are built around the "Secret," which in the end

---

[1] And also Thule of Greenland, *ibid.* pp. 84-5.
[2] It is known that both St. Patrick and St. Dunstan were connected by some authors to Glastonbury. "St. Patrick's well," often used by Meyrink, is, in this case, similar to the abyss of Poe and Twain, or to Dumas' "le trou de l'enfer." *Ibid.* pp. 21, 30-31, 133.
[3] *Ibid.* pp. 60-61, 63 (Green is resurrected), 65 (he comes back to visit the main character of the book, but he is a ghost).
[4] *Ibid.* p. 114. Guénon described *Rose-Croix d'Or* as an imposture (**Aperçus sur l'initiation**, p. 246). Also, the symbol of the Rose-Cross is suggested by Meyrink on page 282.
[5] It presents a parody of initiation (see *ibid.* p. 175).

appears to be something very disappointing, a *nitchevo*. **L'Énigme René Guénon et les "Supérieurs Inconnus," Contribution à l'étude de l'histoire mondiale "souterraine,"** written by "Louis de Maistre," is not different in this respect; on the contrary, it is the best illustration, since the effort was a long one, covering a length of 1000 pages.[1]

"De Maistre" cannot develop his suggestion that Meyrink was one of the "other" sources for Guénon's **Le Roi du Monde**, since René Guénon clearly denounced Meyrink, so he tries to work out his scheme using another similar individual: Alfred Kubin, a friend of Meyrink. "Maistre" declares: "Kubin's book [**Die andere Seite**, "the other side"] ... has a superior load and visionary power in comparison to Gustav Meyrink's work, for example" (p. 139). In fact, the "superiority" of Kubin is "inferiority," since, in comparison to Meyrink, he is even more influenced by the "counter-initiatory" forces. For "Louis de Maistre," the almost 1,000 pages were not enough to clarify the "enigma Guénon," and another book was published under another pseudonym: Alexandre de Dánann, **Un envoyé de la Loge Blanche, Bô Yin Râ**,[2] where again Gustav Meyrink and Alfred Kubin were mentioned,[3] even though, this time, it is suggested a comparison between Bô Yin Râ's book, **The Book of the Living God**, and Guénon's **Le Roi du Monde**.[4]

Without any doubt, **Le Roi du Monde** was the most disputed and attacked work of Guénon, and the notion of Agarttha the most

---

[1] This is not new. When Baron Hund promised to reveal his great secret, everybody was thinking of something magical and miraculous, yet his secret was that every Mason is a Knight Templar. René Guénon was very explicit about what an initiatory secret really is. Today, many execrable books about Masonry abuse the word "secret" in their titles, but it is only a revival of the title of a book written at the end of the 18th century.

[2] Archè, Milano, 2004. **L'Énigme René Guénon** was also published in 2004, at Archè.

[3] **Un envoyé de la Loge Blanche, Bô Yin Râ**, pp. 22, 69, 93.

[4] *Ibid.* p. 26. Also, the author, ceaselessly in search for Guénon's "sources," advanced the hypothesis that maybe René Guénon's idea about the initiation and the counter-initiation came from the Hermetic Brotherhood of Luxor and Taychou Marou (*ibid.* p. 49).

criticized; a lot of energy, hate and malevolent suggestions were used to annihilate this notion. Also, as we already said, creating confusion was a very convenient scheme that could make Agarttha look like a fantasy and Guénon like an "occultist," no better than Bô Yin Râ or Meyrink. However, the hidden objective was not only to present Guénon as a common individual interested in all kinds of occultist subjects, but to suggest his connection to the "counter-initiation." Therefore, if we ask the question «why should "De Maistre" spend time writing about Alfred Kubin?,» the answer is obvious: his objective is, of course, to create confusion; but, moreover, his efforts are aimed at creating a parallel between Guénon and Kubin, not by comparing their works, but by suggesting similarities between their lives, and then, by implying that they had a similar mentality.

"Louis de Maistre" titles his chapter about Kubin "Alfred Kubin the «prophet» of Agarttha,"[1] which is a wretched and malevolent title, and suggests, of course, a resemblance between Guénon and Kubin. There were other elements taken into consideration, although not mentioned: Kubin had health problems when he was young and was very sensitive; and so was Guénon. Kubin was called "the hermit of Zwickledt"[2]; Guénon was called by "De Maistre"'s friends "the hermit of Duqqi."[3] In fact, if we must compare Kubin to someone, we should compare him to Evola.

For the reader interested in Kubin, "De Maistre"'s chapter does not help much; for the reader interested in Guénon, the chapter is out of place and futile. Hence, it seems that "De Maistre" wrote this chapter for the "traditionalists" (see Guénon's definition), occultists like "himself" and for the newcomers, aiming at corroding René Guénon's reputation; at the same time, the author(s)' main purpose was to weaken the concept of Agarttha. To name Kubin a "prophet" of Agarttha, even if the word prophet is put inside

---

[1] **L'Énigme René Guénon**, p. 133.
[2] Alfred Kubin, **L'Autre côté**, Jose Corti, 2007; see Laurent Évrard's *Une lecture de L'Autre côté*, p. 368.
[3] Xavier Accart, **L'Ermite de Duqqi**, Archè, 2001.

quotation marks, is such an enormity that you have to belong to Twain's "country of dreams" to do such a thing.

"De Maistre" is not embarrassed to declare that many of the themes developed by Kubin in his novel **The Other Side** were tackled later by Guénon in his **Le règne de la quantité et les signes des temps** (p. 135). Also, he says that some of **The Other Side**'s themes present, in detail, disturbing analogies with what Guénon and Ossendowski said about Agarttha (p. 139). As usually, "De Maistre," after making the calumnious affirmations, fakes objectivity, and adds that these are analogies and not assimilations, and there are fundamental differences between Guénon and Kubin. If there are fundamental differences, why then introduce Kubin in "Enigma René Guénon"?

Alfred Kubin, the so-called "prophet" of Agarttha, is a sad character. He has nothing to do with René Guénon, but "Louis de Maistre" tried to promote an illusory connection in order to, as we already stressed, degrade Guénon. In **My Life**,[1] Kubin describes a life that is interesting only because it illustrates pseudo-tradition, pseudo-initiation and "counter-initiatory" influences at work. One of Kubin's masters is no other than Schopenhauer, and it is well known how Guénon criticized his erroneous understanding of Buddhism.[2] The Buddhism Kubin discovered through Schopenhauer and Hermann Grimm, in a word, through the German school, is a pseudo-Buddhism, a deformed Buddhism, for the use of the Occident, and, as Kubin said, a "moral jolt"[3] made him turn to this Buddhism; there is no need to say that Kubin appears in a flagrant contrast with Guénon, his attitude is exactly what Guénon criticized without mercy.[4] Kubin describes his Buddhist "initiatory" practice, which, again, represents a vivid illustration of what Guénon told us not to do. However, Kubin's Buddhist practices without a guide

---

[1] Alfred Kubin, **Ma vie**, Allia, 2000.
[2] René Guénon, **Orient et Occident**, Guy Trédaniel, 1987, pp. 139-140. See Kubin, **L'Autre côté**, p. 318.
[3] Kubin, **Ma vie**, p. 92.
[4] Not to say that Kubin hated Mathematics (see **L'Autre côté**, p. 303).

kept him interested for only ten days[1]: after that, he forgot about Buddhism.[2]

If we turn now to his **The Other Side**, we do not find anything traditional, only a dark parody. Kubin's "center" is called the "Dream Empire" and the "Emperor" is someone called Claus Patera (p.11), and we see the same idea like in Mark Twain's case. The "Dream Empire," located in Asia, is isolated by an impenetrable wall, a parody of Cusanus' paradisiacal wall; it is a shelter, Kubin says, for all who are against the modern world and everything is organized with respect to the high spiritual life (p. 12). The author is invited to travel to this "Dream Land," a "secret" place, having as center a city called Pearl (pp. 21, 27). Of course, Patera's palace is in the center of Pearl. Yet, what seems to be just a parody of Agarttha, of a spiritual center, is, in fact, an anti-center, because here there is no sun or moon or stars, only a grey sky and a somber river called The Black (pp. 55-6). And there is no high spiritual life, on the contrary. Even though all the world religions were represented in this "Dream Land," there was a secret religion, a kind of Free-Masonry, and a secret Grand Temple (p. 124). Kubin introduces a strange race of people with blue eyes (p. 158), who, he suggested at the end, could have been the Master Puppeteer of this "Dream Land." Kubin also invented a false opponent of Patera, the "American," who founded a political society called "Lucifer" (p. 174), but the "American" denounced Patera as a sort of Satan (p. 180). And now Kubin uses his "imagination" to describe the agony and the end of the "Dream Land," crowned by the fight between Patera and the American.[3]

---

[1] **Ma vie**, pp. 94-96.
[2] Evola, at the age of 23, tried to commit suicide and he was saved by a Buddhist text (Julius Evola, **Le Chemin du Cinabre**, Archè-Arktos, 1983, pp. 13-14). We should add that Evola's perspective on Buddhism is not reliable.
[3] *Ibid.* p. 278. **The Other Side** is really boring. However, North-American schools would love to have it for their students, since the interesting works for school boards are those connected with mental illness (hence their favourite painter is Van Gogh, who cut his ear). They are not alone, of course. We should mention here a curious fact: the most famous ancient sculptures exposed in the Louvre Museum are Venus of Milo and the Victory of Samothrace. Why, when there are many other similar ancient Greek sculptures, these two became the most celebrated? The only reason is

We insisted on presenting **The Other Side** only to make sure that the reader understands how devious **L'Énigme René Guénon et les "Supérieurs Inconnus," Contribution à l'étude de l'histoire mondiale "souterraine"**, written by "Louis de Maistre," is. How can works like **L'Énigme René Guénon** be written and published?[1] The answer to this rather rhetorical question is the title of our first chapter: The Great Disarray; the hunt for René Guénon's sources is a striking illustration of how the "sources" of this Disarray work in our agonizing world.

---

that these two specific pieces have something special: Venus of Milo has no arms and the Victory of Samothrace has no head, and these kinds of mutilations are compatible with the modern mutilated mind.

[1] Let us mention here, as exemplification, one more title: **Mysteries and Secrets of the Masons**, by Lionel & Patricia Fanthorpe (The Dundurn Group, Toronto, 2006); this is a ridiculous book, yet it was published with the support of the Canada Council for the Arts and with the financial support of the Government of Canada!

CHAPTER X

RENÉ GUÉNON AND AGARTTHA

THE QUESTIONS ABOUT AGARTTHA emerged in minds infected by the modern and profane perspective, minds ready to admit any SF explanation or to look for sensational elements, minds that are incapable to accept God, even though they think they do, minds that are ready to encourage a "quest" for "Guénon's Agarttha," but no longer for the "Realm of Prester John."

Herodotus narrated:

For myself, I have been told by the Greeks who dwell beside the Hellespont and Pontus that this Zalmoxis was a man who was once a slave in Samos, his master being Pythagoras, son of Mnesarchus; presently, after being freed and gaining great wealth, he returned to his own country. Now the Thracians were a meanly-living and simple witted folk, but this Zalmoxis knew Ionian usages and a fuller way of life than the Thracian; for he had consorted with Greeks, and moreover with one of the greatest Greek teachers, Pythagoras; wherefore he made himself a hall, where he entertained and feasted the chief among his countrymen, and taught them that neither he nor his guests nor any of their descendants should ever die, but that they should go to a place where they would live for ever and have all good things. While he was doing as I have said and teaching this doctrine, he was all the while making him an underground chamber. When this was finished, he vanished from the sight of the Thracians, and descended into the underground chamber, where he lived for three years, the Thracians wishing him back and mourning him for dead; then in the fourth year he appeared to the Thracians, and thus they came to believe what Zalmoxis had told them. Such is the Greek story about him.[1]

The idea of finding Zalmoxis' cave is, of course, not a very good idea, but the modern mentality tried to relate his underground disappearance with the theory of reincarnation and spiritism, which illustrates again how any real understanding of the traditional symbolism is forbidden to the modern mind.

René Guénon mentioned Agarttha in his book **Le Roi du Monde**. He wrote many books, but this specific one was very convenient for the modern mentality, since it brought up something sensational indeed: an underground realm with a King reigning over the whole World; it represented something that the profane and corrupted mind could understand. And some individuals hurried to find this realm! Can you imagine Marco Pallis entering the underground territory and meeting the Lord of the World? Sensational! Such a discovery could have been so profitable. Travel agencies could have book trips and holidays to Agarttha, the Lord of the World could have been on a television show! And "Louis de Maistre" could have been their guide. We mention here that the Templars' treasure, the Masonic secrets and the Grail's mystery are all, together with the "Agarttha syndrome," part of the same diabolic plan aiming at creating Kubin's "Dream Land."

Reading **Le Roi du Monde** today is an interesting experience, but a very disappointing one for the modern reader. The first chapter[2] starts well: Guénon elaborates on Agarttha, as described by Saint-Yves and Ossendowski, and the modern reader is anxious to find in the following pages the secrets of the underground realm. The second chapter talks about the spiritual authority and temporal power, about the "Realm of Preaster John" (its mention should have been a clue for the "Agarttha hunters"), and not really about Agarttha. The third chapter is even worse, since it deals with the

---

[1] **Histories**, IV, 95.
[2] There are 12 short chapters composing **Le Roi du Monde**.

Jewish Kabbalah, with Shekinah and Metatron, with Mikael and Samael, and not a word about Agarttha.

The next chapter though, the fourth chapter, seems to be about Agarttha; however, it is not really about Agarttha, since Guénon used what Saint-Yves and Ossendowski recounted as an opportunity to develop the doctrine of the three supreme functions. You really have to be narrow minded and have a profane mindset to continue, after studying this chapter, to think that René Guénon blindly, or mischievously, or by pure ignorance, or by naivety, promoted Agarttha as an underground realm similar to the one described by Kubin, for example, or similar to a subway station. You have to be especially malevolent, and even diabolical, to suggest that the author of **L'Erreur spirite** (1923), of **Orient et Occident** (1924), of **L'Homme et son devenir selon le Védânta** (1925), became in 1927 blind and ignorant, forgetting his metaphysical lore, that he decided to advertise a sensational place, competing with James Hilton and his Shangri-La. What his detractors and enemies try to hide is that René Guénon was not a scholar, not a pundit, not a university professor, not a theosophist or an occultist, for whom initiation meant nothing more than a parody, not a political agent, with a tenebrous agenda; René Guénon was a veritable initiate whose function was to transmit the Truth. We are not sure that people can comprehend what a real initiate means in our days, when so many false prophets preach, when nobody listens and everybody talks, when to tell untruths is normal and when words have no meaning. However, René Guénon was an initiate and, as we said before, he must be measured with the compasses; could anybody draw a line using compasses, instead of the square? In Guénon's case, he could.

In the fourth chapter, René Guénon explained that the Lord of the World is not the modern minds' dream as seen in James Bond movies, he is not a political dictator reigning over mankind, and implicitly he is not *princeps hujus mundi*. The Lord of the World is the "Lord of the Three Worlds." This is what Guénon said at the beginning of this chapter. Maybe his detractors can imagine the Second World, but for sure they have no access, of any kind, to the

Third World, not to say that they could not think about the Fourth World. Modern people always look downwards, their eyes are glued to our insignificant earthly world.

René Guénon prepared his reader, in the previous chapters, explaining what the "real presence" (Shekinah) and the spiritual influences mean, how Shekinah is the synthesis of the right and left sephirotic pillars,[1] and how, in a similar way, the Center has two arms, the spiritual authority and the temporal power, Peace and Justice. In the fourth chapter, Guénon developed what he said in the previous ones, stressing some essential truths. Saint-Yves' hierarchy (and also Ossendowski's) represents in fact the hierarchy of the Three Worlds. This truth is a universal truth, found in the Hindu tradition, but also in any other genuine tradition. As we explained in other works,[2] spiritual influences descend by countless degrees and eventually reach the human being's state; correspondingly, Shekinah is present in all Three Worlds, but even more, she is present, similarly, in each world or degree of the Existence. Equally, Agarttha is present in each world, and, whereas the ignorant people hunt for it in the profane world, the seer's quest aims at a very sacred, very inaccessible Agarttha.

This fourth chapter of **Le Roi du Monde**, which apparently deals with Saint-Yves' Agarttha, is a real blow to Guénon's detractors, even though they did not seem to be aware of this. Presenting the traditional hierarchy, Guénon compared the three leaders of Agarttha to Ishwara, Hiranyagarbha and Virâj, who are respectively the lords of the Three Worlds, and to the Three Magi. This is enough to make us understand what Agarttha meant for Guénon. However, to further elucidate what he was transmitting, René Guénon wrote in 1929 (**Le Roi du Monde** was published in 1927) **Autorité spirituelle et pouvoir temporal**, where he developed the traditional significance of the three functions. Much

---

[1] In the Hindu tradition, there are three "channels," *sushumna, ida* and *pingala*. Since Guénon's detractors repeatedly mumbled that they could not find in India or Tibet any reference to what Guénon said in **Le Roi du Monde**, it is not futile to turn to the Hindu tradition, from time to time.

[2] **René Guénon et le Centre du Monde**, pp. 74-75.

later, in 1942, Ananda K. Coomaraswamy tackled the same subject in his **Spiritual Authority and Temporal Power in the Indian Theory of Government**,[1] and, for the benefit of Guénon's detractors, we will refer to Coomaraswamy's work to illustrate what René Guénon said in **Le Roi du Monde**.

Coomaraswamy illustrated the concept of the "Lord of the World," in the Hindu tradition, with "the Mixta Persona of Mitrâvarunau, Supreme Identity of Conjoint Principles, [that] is the same as that of «One Akshara that is both Agni the Sacerdotum [spiritual authority] and Indra the Regnum [temporal power].»"[2] Guénon stressed that, in the Agarttha's case, each of the three functions, Brahâtmâ, Mahâtmâ, and Mahânga, possesses in itself a dual authority, sacerdotal and temporal, even though the first corresponds to the Lord of the World, the second to the spiritual authority, and the third to the temporal power. Likewise, Agni is not only the spiritual authority,[3] Coomaraswamy said, but he is "the marriage of the two Agni, kshatra and brahma ... a union of mutually antagonistic principles, [that] reflects the natural opposition of Sacerdotium and Regnum" (p. 23; French p. 40). Moreover, Manu corresponds to the Lord of the World, and Yama, his brother, to the spiritual authority, and Yamî, his sister, to the temporal power (pp. 32, 34; French pp. 52, 55). And Agni, united to Indra, represents the Lord of the World: "In the same way in SB X.4.1.8, in connection with the union of Sacerdotium and Regnum, here represented by Indrâgni..." (p. 39; French p. 62).

Heinrich Zimmer described "the great Shiva-Trinity of Elephanta": "The middle head of the threefold image is a representation of the Absolute... Over the right shoulder of this presence, perpetually growing out of the central form, is the male profile of Shiva... Correspondingly, to the left of the central mask is

---

[1] Manshiram Manoharlai Publishers, 1978; French translation: **Autorité Spirituelle et Pouvoir Temporel**, Archè, 1985.
[2] **Spiritual Authority**, p. 6. **Autorité Spirituelle**, p. 16.
[3] "Agni and Indra, Sacerdotium and Regnum..." *Ibid.* p. 37 (French p. 58).

the profile of the female principle."¹ Even though Zimmer is just a scholar, his descriptions are good illustrations of Agarttha's symbolism in the Hindu tradition.

In terms of René Guénon's statement that Saint-Yves' hierarchy (and also Ossendowski's) represents in fact the hierarchy of the Three Worlds, we should quote Coomaraswamy again: "Agni, Vâyu and Âditya are the «Threefold Brahma» ... To this «Threefold Sovereign» correspond the «Threefold» World of Rig Vêda, the «Three Bright» Realms."² This three-partition found in Saint Yves' work is common in the Hindu tradition; "the Three Gandharvas or Lights, Agni, Vâyu, Âditya (the Persons of the Vedic «Trinity,» and the Universal Lights of the Fire-altar)" (*Ibid.* p. 42; French p. 67). "The King of Kings is thus the progenitive Solar Spirit, who takes the form of Agni, Vâyu and Âditya in relation to the triple Dominion or Three Dominions which are so often spoken as Dawn or Dawns, and are the Three Worlds" (*Ibid.* p. 43; French p. 68).

With respect to this three-partition, we should add that at the end of the universal manifestation, the Three Worlds will be invaded by "counter-initiatory" forces, by the demonic forces, in the same way Dante's Dis was a city invaded and occupied by the devils.³ "The story goes, that, once again in the course of history, the demons, titans, or anti-gods (*asura*), half-brothers and eternal rivals of the proper rulers of the world, had snatched to themselves the reigns of the government. As usual, they were led by an austere and crafty tyrant... Maya [Mayasura] was this tyrant's name... he constructed three mighty strongholds [as centers of the Three Worlds, these three cities being called *Tripura*]. By a feat of magic he then amalgamated his three fortresses into one – a prodigious center of demon-chaos and world-tyranny, practically unassailable."⁴

This unassailable *Tripura* is not Agarttha. We know that the modern and profane individuals are easily tempted by the devil. We

---

[1] Heinrich Zimmer, **Myths and Symbols in Indian Art and Civilization**, Harper, 1962, pp. 148-9.
[2] **Spiritual Authority**, p. 40; **Autorité Spirituelle**, p. 64.
[3] See our **The Everlasting Sacred Kernel**, p. 76.
[4] Zimmer, **Myths and Symbols in Indian Art and Civilization**, p. 185.

know that these people lack the power of discrimination, and, furthermore, they are manipulated to confuse Mikael with Samael, reality with illusion, Shiva with Mayasura.[1] This unassailable *Tripura* was built by Mayasura, who is a master of illusion. At the end of the universal manifestation, the real, true and inviolable *Tripura* disappeared "underground" and became hidden. In its place, Mayasura deployed his illusory *Tripura* that was not in fact unassailable, since Shiva could destroy it with an arrow. There is no doubt that authors like "Louis de Maistre" and others are completely under the power of Mâyâ. For example, the elephant is a sacred and divine symbol both in the Hindu and Buddhist traditions; but, because of Mâyâ, the elephant can also be a demon.[2]

As we said, Mâyâ has a peremptory role in confusing the modern minds, and we should give one more example. Mayasura is the king of the *Asuras*, *Daityas* and *Râkshasas*, representing the past cycles, the races that revolted,[3] and the "counter-initiatory" forces, which makes his symbolism complicated, since he appears also as the Lord of Tripura, the center of the Three Worlds (whose architect Mayasura is)[4]; but most of all, he symbolizes the "illusion." Yet here this "illusion" is aggressive and deceptive, belonging to the "counter-initiation," as attested by the **Râmâyana** episode of the "black cave," when Hanumân and the *Vânaras*, in quest for Sîtâ, entered a dark cave in the Vindhya mountains and discovered a paradise-like

---

[1] For this reason, "Louis de Maistre" shamelessly suggested that Agarttha is a parody or a "counter-initiatory" center, and, moreover, that René Guénon himself is malefic and connected to the "counter-initiation" (**L'Énigme René Guénon et les "Supérieurs Inconnus," Contribution à l'étude de l'histoire mondiale "souterraine,"** pp. 213, 214, 220, 231, 368).

[2] Zimmer, **Myths and Symbols in Indian Art and Civilization,** p. 192.

[3] To revolt against the normal hierarchy means to create disorder ("anti-Cosmos") and confusion (Guénon, **Autorité spirituelle,** p. 17). Normally, the *Dêvas* are associated with the "truth" (*satyam*) and the *Asuras* with "falsehood" and "disorder" (*anritam*) (Coomaraswamy, **La doctrine du sacrifice,** p. 169).

[4] In this case, Mayasura is comparable to Râvana, being described at the end of the cycle, when the unrighteousness reigned in Tripura and Shiva had to destroy the triple center. Nowadays, in India, the capital-city of the small province Tripura is Agartala.

center built by Mayasura.[1] It is a deceiving center,[2] which tempts the hero of the quest away from the straight route, like the many other temptations present in various initiatory stories[3]; it is an "illusory" center, but at the same time, from a higher perspective and obeying the *lîlâ* of Brahma, it appears like a subterranean, hidden, and inaccessible center, similar to Agarttha,[4] which is protected by a thick curtain of darkness,[5] and where Mayasura kept Hema captive.[6]

Coming back to Guénon's **Le Roi du Monde** and the other chapters, from five to twelve, we observe that all the other chapters are not about Agarttha at all; they clarify the Holy Grail's symbolism, the symbolism of Melki-Tsedeq, they expose the doctrine of the spiritual centers, insisting on the fact that at the end of the present cycle the spiritual center became hidden (that is, "subterranean").[7]

Agarttha, as discussed by Guénon's detractors, is just not there. For René Guénon, the works of Saint-Yves and Ossendowski were only an opportunity to reveal the symbolism of the center, and he could not care less about the materialistic view regarding the

---

[1] "Here the monkeys beheld choicest mansions everywhere made out of gold and silver, some with golden and some with silver domes, while some with golden and some with silver multi-stories, but all are studded with lapis gems with golden windows covered with laceworks of pearls. They have also seen everywhere flowered and fruited trees that are similar in shine to red corals and rubies, and golden honeybees, as well as honeys."
[2] In the Grail stories, this paradise-like center is the initiatory starting point, and illustrates the adage that the "Paradise is a prison." This paradise-like center was born at the same time with the need for initiation.
[3] The *Vânaras* decide to give up the quest and remain in the cave, which, as in the Grail stories, suggests how the "Paradise is a prison."
[4] At the beginning of the cycle, the spiritual center was situated on the top of the mountain; at the end, it hid in the cave (Guénon, **Symboles fondamentaux**, p. 223).
[5] This tenebrous curtain could be penetrated only because Hanumân chanted Râma's name as a *mantra*.
[6] We see the similarity with Râvana, who abducted Sîtâ; Hema is here the daughter of Mount Mêru.
[7] "Louis de Maistre" thoughtlessly declared: "Without their [Saint-Yves' and Ossendowski's] revelations about the effective presence of a subterranean world, **Le Roi du Monde** would have remained just a work containing general and interesting views about the symbolism of the «center,» but which in themselves are not at all sensational and upsetting" (**L'Énigme René Guénon**, p. 184); on the contrary, these views are fundamental and essential!

underground world. For Guénon, Agarttha was another name for the Center; from the beginning of the present cycle (the Earthly Paradise) to the end of the cycle (Heavenly Jerusalem), he said, the Center had various names like Tula, Luz, Salem or Agarttha.[1] Guénon also said: "We must point out that the word *Salem*, contrary to the common opinion, has never really designated a city, but, if we consider it as the symbolic name of *Melki-Tsedeq*'s residence, it can be viewed as an equivalent of the term Agarttha."[2]

There is no doubt that, from René Guénon's perspective, Agarttha was an equivalent of the Earthly Paradise. If we understand that, the "Agarttha-hunt," pursued by Pallis and others, becomes a ridiculous enterprise, if not worse. Anybody, with a normal, just, and traditional state of mind, when reading **Le Roi du Monde**, understands that this book is not about Agarttha at all; it is about the inaccessible, inviolable, and untouchable doctrine of the spiritual centers.[3] Why would someone, after reading the book, want to go to Asia and find the "underground realm"? Why would many others write books about Guénon and Agarttha? The answer is obvious.

The idea of an "underground center" must be correlated to two other ideas: that of the "lost center" and that of the "hidden center." In fact, the "underground" center illustrates the reality of the *Kali-yuga*, when the Tradition is lost and the center becomes hidden. Wolfram von Eschenbach's **Parzival and Titurel** ended with the same conclusion. After Perceval fought and made peace with his brother Feirefiz Angevin, they left Arthur's center together to acquire the Holy Grail. But only Repanse de Schoye could carry the Grail; she married Feirefiz and left the Occident, travelling to India, to the Realm of Prester John, which, as we know, represents the supreme center, *Oriens*, "near Paradise"; Munsalvaesche also left the West and was transported to the same *Oriens*.[4]

---

[1] Guénon, **Symboles fondamentaux**, pp. 108-109.
[2] Guénon, **Le Roi du Monde**, p. 49.
[3] The Hindu tradition says: "The knowledge of the Three Worlds and their Rulers is the «Triple Science»" (**Spiritual Authority**, p. 44, **Autorité Spirituelle**, p. 68).
[4] See Guénon, **Le Roi du Monde**, p. 11.

René Guénon explained at the beginning of the seventh chapter of his **Le Roi du Monde** how the cave can symbolize a "hidden" center. In the **Râmâyana**, at the end, it is said: "Then a heavenly throne rose up from within the earth, borne on the heads of mighty *nâgas*, decked in shining jewels; and the Earth stretched out her arms and welcomed Sîtâ and placed her on the throne, and the throne sank down again."[1] Sîtâ retreating underground symbolizes the lost Tradition and is equivalent to the lost Holy Grail. Sri Aurobindo also said: "The Martanda or eighth Surya is the black or dark, the lost, the hidden sun. The Titans have taken and concealed him in their cavern of darkness."[2]

Even today the idea of a "subterranean" center is alive in India. At Haridwâr, there is a *Shiva Lingam*, which naturally emerged, and which, with the evolvement of the cycle, progressively retracted underground. Today, you can just see its top, since it is the end of the *Kali-yuga* and the center is almost completely subterranean.

However, for the twisted minds of Guénon's detractors, all this is just a huge "manipulation." These individuals are so caught by their ridiculous game that they cannot see how absurd their affirmations are; they cannot see because, obviously, they are themselves manipulated.

In 1995, Marco Baistrocchi published the article **Agarttha: una manipolazione guénoniana?** This article was brought to our attention only after we published our **Agarttha, the Invisible Center**, and so, we could not comment on it. Nevertheless, Joscelyn Godwin translated Baistrocchi's article, which was recently published,[3] and the antitraditionalist Mark Sedgwick hurried to praise it.

---

[1] Ananda K. Coomaraswamy and Sister Nivedita, **Myths of the Hindus and Buddhists**, Dover, 1967, p. 114. There is another symbol of the throne that stresses how the absolute center is "underground." On the "Island of Jewels" (*mani-dwîpa*), a symbol of the center, there is a throne with the goddess Mâyâ, and she sits on Sakala Shiva, who is laying on Nishkala Shiva (Zimmer, **Myths and Symbols in Indian Art and Civilization**, p. 197 ff).
[2] Sri Aurobindo, **The Secret of the Veda**, Sri Aurobindo Ashram, 1971, p. 426.
[3] Marco Baistrocchi, **Agarttha: A Guénonian Manipulation?**, Theosophical History, 2010.

We must declare that Marco Baistrocchi cannot be trusted at all. As Jean-Marc Vivenza is a "neo-martinist," so Baistrocchi was a "neo-theosophist," and both hated René Guénon, since Guénon has torn apart the occultists and the theosophists. You need to have some qualities to be able to understand your errors and give up the arrogance, admitting that you have made a wrong choice, instead of using your energies to defend it because it's "your baby." But, of course, there are other reasons, more sinister, for Baistrocchi's article.

Joscelyn Godwin considers, in his *Introduction*, that "Baistrocchi's is the first attempt at a rational solution to the puzzle, supported by a formidable apparatus of erudition and documentation." Now, such a presentation kills any desire to read the article. To bring a "rational solution" to the doctrine of the spiritual centers, by using "erudition and documentation," is a futile and absurd endeavour. Yet Baistrocchi's endeavour was not so much about finding a "rational solution" as it was about fighting Guénon and praising Theosophism.

Baistrocchi's "formidable apparatus of erudition and documentation" is based on very unreliable sources. But Baistrocchi uses a shrewd technique, which is very efficient even though it is not original. At one point Baistrocchi declared: "Now that the origin of the legend of Agarttha has been clarified…" (p. 24); in fact, nothing was "clarified," but this is the technique: you confuse the reader with all kinds of elements and after a while you declare that everything is now solved, and after that, the reader is manipulated to think that, indeed, it is so. The same technique was used by "Louis de Maistre."

There is another technique. We do not have time to list here various examples, but there are many that illustrate how an author uses a reference without checking its validity, and then this author becomes a reference for another one, and now the error is not anymore an error. In Baistrocchi's case, using the works of Jean-Pierre Laurant and Marie-France James as references meant perpetuating an error. What happened is that, because Laurant and James published their works about Guénon many years ago (1975 and 1981), they became some sort of taboo references, and

Baistrocchi forgot to say that both Laurant and James wrote based on their own individual fantasies, and that they are not at all reliable sources.

For Baistrocchi, René Guénon was an "intellectual," a "scholar."[1] Also, you have to have a special kind of mind, indeed, to declare that "the Judeo-Christian documentation, which is Guénon's truly innovative contribution to the subject, rather than being a response to Saint-Yves is intended to furnish a sort of doctrinal basis and consistency to the new myth of Agarttha" (p. 10). Baistrocchi, as many others, is so totally contaminated by modern mentality, that he cannot (or does not want to) understand that a traditional writer, like Guénon (or a traditional painter, or a traditional architect), does not innovate and does not try to be original. Baistrocchi's hypothesis is that René Guénon manipulated his readers to reject India and the Theosophism in favour of the "Judeo-Christian" tradition or Islam, and that Guénon was an agent of the Jesuits and of the Jews (pp. 25, 28, 29, 31, 33, 34, 38).

Baistrocchi wrote about Theosophism: "The Theosophical Society's noteworthy contribution to reviving the metaphysical and religious traditions of India was recognized ... by the most authoritative Western scholars of Indian spiritual traditions" (pp. 27-28). As Alvin Moore Jr. said, "Blavatsky was not a mere vulgar adventuress, she was a high skilled impostor." Blavatsky was, no doubt about it, a crook. And Theosophism is an invention, not because René Guénon said so, but because that is how it was built. Baistrocchi's above declaration is so foolish, when talking about Western scholars recognizing how the Theosophism revived the Hindu and Buddhist traditions, that we must accept that it is the end of the *Kali-yuga*. Baistrocchi complained that people considered his article to be "impious"; it is not "impious", it is pure and simple unintelligent.

However, we mention here that he attacked Guénon for his "baseless ... anti-reincarnationist statements" and for his "study of

---

[1] Ridiculous and insulting is also Baistrocchi's affirmation that Michel Vâlsan was a "scholar" (p. 66).

cycles, in which he seems basically ignorant of the Hindu doctrine of cosmic cycles" (p. 40). Both these subjects are fundamental parts of Theosophism, and, of course, Baistrocchi cannot accept René Guénon's "statements." Regarding the doctrine of the cosmic cycles, the numerous zeros composing the cyclical numbers, so dear to Baistrocchi, are, evidently, just a "cover," and there is no need for a lot of elaborated and bright studies to understand that.

Regarding the theory of reincarnation, this one is antimetaphysical and a modern invention. Ananda K. Coomaraswamy said that "The notion of «reincarnation» in the ordinary sense of a rebirth on Earth of departed individuals, represents only an error of understanding of the doctrines of heredity, of transmigration and of regeneration."[1] If transmigration means the passing from one state of being to another, metempsychosis represents, as René Guénon said, "the transmission of certain psychic elements from an individuality to another" and only this metempsychosis could be somehow confused with reincarnation.

As Coomaraswamy stated, the only one transmigrant is the Self, *Âtmâ*. And this Self is the One that gives reality to any "incarnation," which is called *jîvâtmâ*. The body and the soul, *Corpus* and *Anima*, they have no existence without *Âtmâ*, and therefore they cannot "reincarnate" by themselves. If we understand the Chinese concept of the "current of forms," illustrated by the river, with its ever changing waters, we will comprehend that the body and the soul will be disintegrated and their components will reintegrate in other combinations. *Âtmâ*, because is not different from Brahma, is Infinite, and we have to conceive the universal manifestation not from a temporal perspective (as succession), but as a sum of simultaneous events, like an infinite (in fact, indefinite) canvas, a canvas weaved by the "incarnations" of *Âtmâ*, and where there is no place for "reincarnation."

The modern mind and the sentimentalism and arrogance of profane people cannot accept that death is a change of state and

---

[1] **Hindouisme et Bouddhisme**, Gallimard, 1980, p. 14.

everything belonging to this state will remain in this state. There is transmigration, but never reincarnation. Theosophism enthusiastically helped to spread this inanity regarding reincarnation in the Western world, and hence Baistrocchi's foolish reaction.

Before ending this chapter, let us mention one last element from Baistrocchi's article. Baistrocchi quoted René Guénon on his comparison of the Hindu and Islamic traditions, and he interpreted Guénon's words as suggesting that, today, salvation can only come from Islam (p. 36). It is strange that Baistrocchi, with his conclusion, is in concert with Charles-André Gilis, who in his recent works, and especially in his **L'héritage doctrinal de Michel Vâlsan**,[1] declared the same thing.

Guénon wrote:

the accomplishment of the cycle must have some correlation, in the historic order, with the encounter of two traditional forms that correspond to its beginning and to its end, and which have Sanskrit and Arabic as sacred languages: the Hindu tradition, which represents the most direct heritage of the primordial Tradition, and the Islamic tradition, insofar as it is the «seal of Prophecy» and consequently the ultimate form of traditional orthodoxy for the present cycle.[2]

Using this text, Charles-André Gilis tried to demonstrate that the Islamic tradition is destined to engulf the whole world, to save it from profanation, and to bring it under the Islamic law. Gilis, who wrote many good things in the past, but who became at the end of his life obsessed with the task of "Islamizing" Guénon, made a fundamental mistake, because he did not want to accept two traditional truths. First, René Guénon did not say that the Hindu tradition *is* the primordial Tradition and the unique tradition; he only said that the Hindu tradition is the most direct heir of the primordial Tradition, and, therefore, other orthodox traditions have coexisted with the Hindu tradition; similarly, the Islamic tradition *is not* the primordial Tradition and the unique tradition, but the last revealed

---

[1] Le Turban Noir, 2009.
[2] **Symboles fondamentaux**, p. 176.

tradition, which will coexist with other orthodox traditions until the end of times. Second, the revival Gilis dreams of, and which means that the whole world will embrace Islam, is too similar to the New Age fantasies, where it is said that the return of the "Golden Age" will occur in this present cycle. In fact, the "reversal of the poles" happens *outside* this cycle, and the only event that we can expect inside the cycle is its end. The revival Gilis talks about already happened when Islam was revealed.

Today, we are in the last phase of *Manvantara*, and nobody should assume that the people of Agarttha will surface to recreate a "Golden Age" for this cycle.

CHAPTER XI

GNOSIS AND GNOSTICISM

THE GNOSTIC LABEL THAT SO PERSISTENTLY was attached to René Guénon, forces us to delve into this particular aspect. Here are two reasons that convinced us to dedicate two chapters to this problem. First, for half a century, repeatedly (and even today), René Guénon was categorized as "Gnostic," which suggests a mysterious face of Gnosticism in the eyes of the outsiders; second, even in the present days, some are under the illusion that Gnosticism offers a spiritual and initiatory way.

Studies about Gnosticism abounded. Thousands of volumes were published, and the discovery of the Coptic manuscripts at Nag Hammadi soon after World War II rekindled an interest for the Gnostic doctrines. It is not our task to add something to the rich materials written by historians, sociologists, psychologists, historians of religions, etc. Our point of view is strictly traditional and what interests us is if Gnosticism, about which some are preoccupied from curiosity or with a precise objective, can offer a ray of light to the modern world. Even before going further we must say that the answer is obviously negative: Gnosticism cannot supply any initiation or spiritual method, nor a solution to regenerate the world, and those who are attracted to the Gnostic texts hoping for a "Gnostic" realization are in deep error. More than that, even the authentic Gnosticism, which operated in the early years of Christianity, was doomed due to its "individualistic" component. As we have already seen, Guénon identified "individualism" with antitraditional mentality and we might say that today, more than ever, "individualism" is the main characteristic of the modern world, conferring its profane aspect and making it without defense against adverse forces. The same "individualism" functioned two thousand years ago, when Christianity intervened to revivify the Occident, and it is responsible for many of the Gnostic errors; it goes without saying that what we call usually Gnosticism means a wide range of so-called Gnostic "sects," sectarianism being another of its characteristics.[1]

There were endless discussions about Gnosticism's origins: was it Christian or did it derive from other traditions? As usually, various assumptions were made, taking into account, one after another, traditions like Hinduism, Judaism, and Zoroastrianism, but also other spiritual currents of the Roman Empire. It looks like Gnosticism is more a syncretism (and not a synthesis as some would think) of different traditional data, having mainly the Christian tradition as background. In fact, if Christianity had not made the sacrifice to come down from the esoteric domain to the exoteric one, we would not even have Gnosticism as a subject of discussion. The fundamental transformation suffered by the Christian tradition, passing from the few to the many, also produced significant turmoil, marked by sectarianism and individualism, by mental storms and quakes, by fights, all of these suggested by Saint Paul's letters. It is obvious that this "exteriorization" did not happen smoothly, or suddenly, the obscurity which covered the early years of Christianity being needed exactly to protect the success of such an operation. The esoteric and initiatory elements did not disappear purely and simply, and besides a hidden kernel that kept authentic spiritual data, a division and scattering occurred, associated with disarray typical for such critical situations. In this context, the Gnostic currents and sects appeared founded on some esoteric teachings saved during the "crisis" and precisely this fact made them dangerous.

---

[1] We remember that Saint Paul fought against sectarianism; yet some considered even Saint Paul "Gnostic" because of the confusion between Gnosis and Gnosticism.

It is not by chance that different traditions stressed the importance of the power of discrimination (*furqân* in the Islamic tradition, *viveka* in the Hindu tradition), that is, the capacity to distinguish between the wheat and the darnel (**Matthew** 13:24-30); yet the power of discrimination is acquired only with spiritual realization and a profane or even a neophyte could easily become overwhelmed by errors. That is also the problem with the heterodoxic doctrines or with the pseudo-doctrines. They present initiatory elements and genuine knowledge, a terminology related to that of the authentic doctrines, thus being situated on the border between truth and falsehood; for this reason it is very difficult to distinguish the error.[1] Yet even when the error is obvious, it is accepted as a truth because it is seen from a human perspective; the dualism and the existence of evil in the world are well-known examples, in this respect.

The error of dualism can be successful, gaining adherents, for the simple reason that the world in which we live is based on duality. By definition, the universal manifestation exists through duality, sheltering indefinite pairs of contraries, such as good-bad, beautiful-ugly, etc.; more than that, the human mind functions only in an environment based on duality and on pairs of contraries: any notion reasoned by the human mind generates automatically its opposite or complementary notion. That is why in Hesychasm the *apophatic* theology is highlighted, where through negation any attempt of creating dualities is stopped, while through affirmative theology there is a chance that saying "God is good" will give rise to the opposite idea, "God is bad," since God is All. Some Gnostic sects considered this problem, arguing that if there is evil in the world it cannot come from the good God, there has to be another God; that is, there are two "Gods," the Most High and another one, the creator or the demiurge of this world down-below (with the evil aspect).

---

[1] "A Hair perhaps divides the False and True;/ Yes; and a single Alif were the clue,/ Could you but find it, to the Treasure-house,/ And peradventure to the Master too" (Omar Khayyám).

Christian theology strove to demonstrate the existence of "free will" to explain the evil in the world produced by the Supreme Good, with Dante following the same track; yet we must say that, by its nature, the manifested world is built of dualities and therefore it contains the pair good-bad (beside an indefinite number of other pairs) as part of the primordial Unity; the theological problem, as well as the Gnostic one, can be solved only on a metaphysical level. In fact, from a metaphysical perspective, there is nothing else but the One, container and generator of multiplicity, and only from the worldly point of view does duality appear reflected in innumerable pairs as a unique reflection of the *principial* pair.[1] It is difficult for the human mind to understand the relation One-multiple, hence the intervention of individual reason which banished the One, replacing it with a dyad – origin of multiplicity or creating a pair composed by One and multiple.

When we refer to the manifestation, we cannot avoid the duality and, even though everything has its roots in the one-and-only Principle, for our mind the World has to be produced by a primordial pair, a Dyad that will multiply into an indefinite multitude of couples of contrarieties, couples weaving the universal manifestation. Yet highlighting the primordial Dyad, the two poles, Purusha and Prakriti for the Hindu tradition, does not mean to negate the One, the Supreme Being, the Principle that, apparently, has halved itself to produce the whole Cosmos (in the same way a child plays two characters engaged in a dialog), without losing its unitary characteristic. It is a serious mistake to forget that the primordial Dyad derives as a determination (which means a limitation) from the absolute, immutable and eternal One.

There are situations though when the cosmogonic doctrine, eroded and impoverished, insisted on the primeval Duality, as in the case of Manicheism (or in Eastern Europe, where Bogomilism exerted an influence); yet even then it is enough to rearrange the elements into their right places to reestablish the truth, in the same

---

[1] This *principial* pair is Purusha-Prakriti in the Hindu tradition, or Heaven-Earth in the Far-Eastern tradition.

way as, in other cases, when falling down from the Dyad to the feminine pole as exclusive, we can reconstitute the original reality. In various traditions, the production of manifestation is indissoluble related to the archetypal couple (Apsu – Tiamat, Qian – Kun, An – Ki, Anshar – Kishar, Fu Xi – Niu Wa, Purusha – Prakriti, Shu – Tephnut, Geb – Nut); the ancient Iranians had, as a primordial pair, the twin brothers Ahura Mazda – Angra Mainyu, born from the primeval and eternal god Zurvan Akarana: the light was Ahura Mazda, and the darkness Angra Mainyu. This duality was especially highlighted in Manicheism which, forgetting the mutual Principle, insisted on the couple good-bad, even though in the universal manifestation any other pair could represent the *principial* duality; the choice of this particular couple good-bad cannot be explained but by a sentimental and individualistic tendency.

Of course, if we take into account that good and bad symbolize superior realities and not only moral notions, their choice can be accepted, especially since in different traditions good and bad (sufferance also) are often utilized to symbolize the distinction between the immortal and invisible world and the mortal and visible one, with individual man more easily grasping the metaphysical realities through the intermediary of the sensitive elements. Yet there is the danger of forgetting the symbolic meaning, the same way decayed ancient civilizations came to worship the symbolic supports (mineral, vegetal or animal) for themselves as such and not as tokens of God.

Forgetting the one-without-a-second Principle and employing the dyad good-bad led to the false Christian problem with respect to the origin of evil; however, the moral point of view has no power beyond the individual domain and thus cannot solve metaphysical questions. For this reason, Good and Evil must be considered emblematically as poles of manifestation. The Gnostic sects, Bogomils, Paulicians and Cathars greatly appreciated the duality good-bad. The Bogomil cosmogony, for example, considered two brothers, Michael and Satanael, the former participating in a spiritual way in Creation, and the latter corporeally; the invisible and immortal world corresponded to good and light, while the visible and mortal world to bad and darkness.

The human mind is a dangerous tool that, like water, can give life or can flood, that is, can help or produce confusion and error. The mental moulds, naturally, accept as true the doctrine of duality and frivolously neglect that all the pairs are, in fact, contained in the One-without-a-second. Today, many individuals speak lightly about *yin-yang* as a token of duality, neglecting without a trace of responsibility the fact that the white half has a black point and the black half a white point, signs of their affiliation to Unity.[1]

That is, in the Islamic tradition's view, exactly Noah's mistake, who neither knew how to reconcile the One and the multiple, nor to blacken the white and whiten the black; Muhammad, in comparison to Noah, did not admonish the people in the day time (white) and separately in the night time (black), but he called his people nightly during the day and daily during the night (Muhyiddin Ibn 'Arabî, **Kitâb Fusûs al-Hikam**).

For the one who knows that all the dualities derive from the immutable and eternal One, even the errors of the diverse dualistic doctrines can be repaired and the truth reinstated; in other words, despite the dualist characteristic of some Gnostic doctrines it is possible to rediscover, beyond the error, the reality; in this way, the Gnostic mistakes are highlighted even more.[2]

---

[1] We use the word "affiliation" in its original sense (Latin *filius*).

[2] On the other hand, the Gnostic text **The Gospel of Philip** affirmed: "Light and darkness, life and death, right and left, are brothers of one another. They are inseparable. Because of this neither are the good good, nor the evil evil, nor is life life, nor death death [there is no pure *yang* or pure *yin*, but always *yang* and *yin*, in various proportions]" (**The Nag Hammadi Library**, Harper San Francisco, 1990, p. 142); however, **The Gospel of Philip** is, among the Gnostic writings, a text that deserves our attention. In addition, let us mention another text, Gnostic apparently, **The Thunder: Perfect Mind**, in which the woman-thunder said: "For I am the first and the last. I am the honored one and the scorned one. I am the whore and the holy one. I am the wife and the virgin. I am the mother and the daughter... I am knowledge and ignorance. I am shame and boldness. I am strength and I am fear. I am war and peace" (**Nag Hammadi**, p. 297).

In the Balkans, there is a cosmogonic myth, considered to be of Bogomil origin, in which God and Satan represent the duality.[1] We should immediately quote René Guénon to reestablish the truth: "Many, deceived by appearances, imagine the existence in the world of two opposite principles, who fight for supremacy, an erroneous concept, which in a theological language comes to say that Satan is at the same level with God, a concept assigned, rightly or wrongly, to the Manicheans" (Guénon, **Le règne**, p. 357).[2] This pair, God and Satan, is called in some of the variants Brother and Non-Brother, that is, Brother and Anti-Brother, corresponding in a way to the Good and Supreme God and the Evil God of the Gnostics.

In the Christian tradition, the pair, Christ and Anti-Christ, is not a balanced pair; the Anti-Christ has no access to the spiritual and super-individual domain, it has no access to the *Greater Mysteries*, and the same inequity exists between good and evil, or initiation and counter-initiation.[3] In the same way, the Brother and the Non-Brother are not equal. The appellation "Non-Brother" suggests various comments: it could mean that God and Satan represent the fundamental pair of contrarieties, yet, in fact, Satan is nothing compared to God, it is a "non-god"; it could also imply that they actually are some sort of "brothers," having a common origin.[4]

---

[1] For this myth and its variants in South-Eastern Europe and Asia, see Mircea Eliade, **Zalmoxis the Vanishing God**, Univ. of Chicago Press, 1972, pp. 77 ff.

[2] And Guénon added: "There are today many individuals who are, in this sense, «manicheans» without knowing."

[3] As Guénon said, "beneficent" and "maleficent" are not symmetrical. The latter is something unstable and ephemeral; the former has a permanent and definitive characteristic. It means that at the end the good will prevail and the evil will vanish, since only due to the sectarian and dualistic views do we have the illusion of two opposite and equal forces. Moreover, when we surpass the duality, the "beneficent" will also disappear (Guénon, **Le règne**, pp. 372-3).

[4] It is important to heed Guénon's sayings: "The «counter-initiation» we must say, cannot be assimilated to a purely human invention, which would be no different from the «pseudo-initiation.» In fact, it is more than that, and to be so effectively, it must, in a specific mode, and with regard to its origin, derive from the unique source to which is attached every initiation, and, generally speaking, everything that manifests in our world has a «non-human» element" (Guénon, **Le règne**, p. 351).

From a worldly perspective the Brother and the Non-Brother are the two faces of the same and unique Principle. The former, like Purusha, produces the universal manifestation actualizing it through his divine presence; the latter, like Prakriti, produces substantially (or "materially") the Cosmos. Of course, we should not take these comparisons too far; but we can try to bring some sense into this matter. Following the traditional perspective, we might say that the World was produced by a *principial* Dyad: the "essential" pole, the supreme and unique cause, activates the "substantial" pole that produces the universal manifestation, which, even if it generates the elements of Existence, remains a plastic and passive principle. To understand the generation of the world the human mind needs to conceive a primordial pair, a primeval duality, which has as a symbolic support the corporeal union between a man and a woman; the Supreme Being (with whom Purusha is essentially identical) must therefore split in two (or it doubles itself), in the same way Eve had to be born by "splitting" Adam.[1]

Sometimes the Brother and the Non-Brother are twins, which alludes to the two halves of the World Egg, and to the twin pair immortal-mortal. In some versions, God (the Brother) is alone at the beginning (Ishwara, the pure Being of the Hindu tradition), and he throws his sceptre (or staff, or axe) into the Waters,[2] activating them; as a consequence, a huge tree grows from the Ocean (*Axis Mundi*, Ygdrasill of the Scandinavian tradition) and at its roots sits the Devil (Satan, the Non-Brother, the dragon[3]). The tree as *Axis Mundi* necessarily requires two ends, two poles and so, Satan (the inferior pole) is a determination of the One, of God (Ishwara), who doubles Himself. The Devil dives into the Waters, *following God's commandment*,

---

[1] In Hebrew, *isha* (woman) derives from *ish* (man). We may add that even worse than the error of an irreducible duality is the "matriarchal" syndrome, which sees Prakriti as the only principle, since all the elements of the Three Worlds were produced by her; it is like saying that, because only the woman gives birth, she is the only generative parent (of course, we have here the natural process in mind).

[2] The supreme Principle, one-without-the-second, produces the worlds "by simply way of sport," as pastime (**Brahma Samhitâ** XVII).

[3] In the Scandinavian tradition, a dragon gnaws forever at the root of the ash tree, Ygdrasill.

and brings from the abyss sand or dust (the plastic substance containing the dormant possibilities of manifestation, hibernating in the mud) to create the World; yet the World does not coagulate (the sand cannot stick together) and it is necessary for God's Name to be uttered, the name symbolizing the essence without which the universal manifestation cannot be really produced. From this handful of sand or dust (actually mud[1]) the Brother (as Demiurge) fabricates a cake around the tree (again He plays like a child), and on this central cake both will rest. Yet, while the Brother falls asleep (which means He is spiritually wide awake), the Non-Brother works frenetically, trying to throw his Brother into the Waters; in fact, what we see here is, from one point of view, the activity of God's energy (*shakti*). The Non-Brother acts now as the Principle's *shakti* (while the Principle is immutable and non-working) and as a result the cake starts to widen, becoming larger and larger, developing in all the directions the Non-Brother was pushing the Brother. The scene symbolizes the production of the universal manifestation from the World Egg (the cake) and again, it is not Purusha who visibly generates the Cosmos, but Prakriti. First, a smooth, plane and indefinite expanse is created; then, to make the world finite, following the Non-Brother's advice, the Brother will wrinkle the expanse, producing mountains and valleys, lakes and swamps, fields and hills.

In a version, God, after He created the smooth, plane and indefinite expanse, sent the bee to ask the hedgehog for advice on how to limit the earth. And the hedgehog came up with the idea of wrinkling the expanse, producing mountains and valleys, and accomplishing Creation. We notice that in all the versions of the cosmogonic legend there is an endeavour to reconcile the *principial* Infinite with the worldly finite; for the Gnostic sects, obsessed with the cosmogony, to which they connected the salvation of man, this Infinite-finite relation had a special importance.

The pair, bee-hedgehog, is very curious. No doubt, the bee is the messenger of God (Brother), while the hedgehog appears as a

---

[1] The symbolism of the mud would require a separate elaboration.

substitute for Satan (Non-Brother), and in some legends the hedgehog is precisely the devil; on the other hand, the hedgehog is very wise, very skillful with regard to worldly things, the Greeks considering it the most knowledgeable creature. In other words, the hedgehog is both the emblem of the inferior pole and that of the Being in manifestation. Of course, a question emerges immediately: why the hedgehog? To answer, we should represent the dyad Brother – Non-Brother, geometrically, as the center and the circumference of a circle, that is, as One (the center) and multiplicity (the indefinite number of points of the circumference), or Being and Existence. Coming back to the pair, bee-hedgehog, it is easy to note that both the bee and the hedgehog have the spine as common element; the difference is that the bee has *one*, while the hedgehog has a *multiplicity* of spines. And from here, the solution of the riddle: evidently, the bee is One and the hedgehog the multiplicity.

The bee, with its unique spine – central axis, capable of flying (representing the super-individual states), the alchemist that transforms the nectar of multiple flowers into the one-and-only honey (the food of immortality), is the symbol of the celestial Principle. Clement of Alexandria alluded to the spiritual symbolism of the bee. "He, the true, the Sicilian bee, gathering the spoil of the flowers of the prophetic and apostolic meadow, engendered in the souls of his hearers a deathless element of knowledge" (I, 1)[1]; "Or go to the bee, and learn how laborious she is; for she, feeding on the whole meadow, produces one honey-comb" (I, 6).[2] We should mention the biblical episode about the spiritual essence of the bee, related to Samson: "[Samson looked] at the carcass of the lion, and there was a swarm of bees in the lion's body, and honey. He took up some honey in his hand and ate it" (**Judges** 14:9).[3] Yet, it is

---

[1] vol. I, p. 355.
[2] vol. I, p. 371.
[3] We explained the meaning in **The Everlasting Sacred Kernel**: "The lion is a well-known emblem of the Sun; the zodiacal *Leo* is the house of the sun. At the highest level, the lion symbolizes the supreme Principle. It is also the spiritual father. On a lower level, the lion is an emblem of justice and of the warrior-king. Killing the lion, Samson obtains temporal power. The golden honey is an eminent symbol of divine

interesting that Vergil narrated a comparable episode regarding the Arcadian bee-master, Aristaeus, the son of Apollo (we note that Apollo is an emblem of the spiritual sun). Aristaeus was worshiped (especially in the ancient Arcadia) as a god and was considered the one who taught the human race the use of the vineyard (like Noah) and of the bees; both the wine and the honey have initiatory properties. Vergil narrated that Aristaeus, in order to be purified of his crime (he caused the death of Eurydice, Orpheus' wife), followed the advice of Proteus to sacrifice four bulls; after nine days (the number of nights Odin, the god of wisdom, remained hanging from the ash tree, Ygdrasill), "Here, to be sure, a miracle sudden and strange to tell of they behold: from the oxen's bellies all over their rotten flesh creatures are humming, swarming through the wreckage of their ribs. Huge and trailing clouds of bees..." (IV, 534-558).[1]

René Guénon wrote in a letter (year 1935) about this episode: "some time ago, I was made aware of Aristée's story about the bees in Vergil's «Georgics»; there is here, for sure, something that would deserve close examination"; and later: "Apropos of the bees, I noticed a similitude between Aristée's bull and the «primordial Bull» of the Persian tradition, from whose body emerged all the creatures.[2] There is also a bizarre similarity between the Latin name of the bee, *apis*, and the Egyptian name of the sacred bull."[3]

On the other hand, the hedgehog, which rolls into a tight, spiny ball for protection, represents the Cosmos, the World; yet, if the

---

wisdom. It is the solar nurture, the spiritual immortal food. Honey represents the transformation of multiplicity, of mundane existences into celestial Unity, the leap from ignorance to knowledge. The way the bees change and unify the different nectars of the multicolored flowers into one kind of honey illustrates the spiritual transformation. Honey is found inside the lion as the sacred kernel is found inside profane skin. Spiritual wisdom is in the cavity of the heart; temporal power is the concealment, which safeguards wisdom. Eating this honey, Samson obtains sacerdotal power" (pp. 29-30).

[1] Virgil, **The Eclogues The Georgics**, Oxford Univ. Press, 1983, p. 127.

[2] In this case, the swarm of bees represents the multiplicity born from Unity. This symbolic image is another attempt to make the human mind understand the mystery of the production of multiplicity from One.

[3] Guénon added, in his correspondence, that the bee could be a symbol of royalty, since the Chaldean word *sâr* means both "prince" and "bee."

hedgehog is identified with the Non-Brother itself (in the various legends they are interchangeable), the bee is not God, but the "messenger" of God (gr. *aggelos*, Hebr. *maleak*); she is "God's angel," the emblem of the spiritual and heavenly influences,[1] while the hedgehog, despite his worldly wisdom, is subordinated to God as the Non-Brother is subordinated to the Brother. That is why the hedgehog and the Non-Brother participate in the earthly cosmogony, in the creation of this world, "down, below," and, even more specifically, in the creation of the uneven surfaces, of the irregularities of the earth, the real Demiurge, the unique Demiurge, being in fact the Brother who, even if he apparently pairs with the Non-Brother, is superior to this one, and uncreated, in the same way Purusha, even though he pairs with Prakriti, is superior to her, being actually identical to Ishwara.[2]

Here is unveiled now the bottom of the dualistic error: for the Gnostics, as well as for others, the coexistence of One and multiple produced the affirmation of a duality that lost its true meaning. In fact, there is no pair of bee-hedgehog type, like One and multiple; what the legend actually describes is the reality of the multiple contained and generated from One.[3] Only for our limited mind is it

---

[1] This image alludes to the symbolism of the swarm of bees coming out from the Bull's body. The bees are the "rays" that awaken the possibilities of Prakriti.

[2] Mircea Eliade's position in this respect is at least curious. He erroneously considered the Brother a *deus otiosus*, a mentally and physically (?) weary god, who needs the Non-Brother's help. Eliade ignored the traditional data, which for sure he was familiar with; for example, in the Far-Eastern tradition, *wu-wei*, the divine "non-action" is an essential concept. Eliade wrote: "in point of fact, God had scarcely worked at all; it is the Devil who dived three times... this unexpectedly negative note, present in the figure of God, becomes even more marked in the second part of the myth, when God admits his inability to solve a small postcosmogonic problem and has to ask advice from the Devil or the hedgehog. ... God, who had seemed to be omniscient, displays a strangely diminished intelligence; ... and not only the Devil knows the solution to his problem but also the hedgehog" (**Zalmoxis** 86-87): a total profane opinion.

[3] René Guénon and Ananda K. Coomaraswamy used geometrical symbolism to illustrate this truth: they considered the circumference of a circle as having an indefinite number of points (the multiplicity), and moving along the rays towards the center, the circumference becomes smaller and smaller and the points more and more crowded, until in the end they fuse into the center as a unique point.

necessary to conceive a pair generating the world, having the One as superior pole and the multiplicity as the inferior pole.[1] For these reasons the Non-Brother is the one that produces earthly irregularities, indicating changeability, while the Brother generates the indefinite even expanse, symbolizing the *principial* immutability and the primordial state announced by the prophet Isaiah and Saint Luke.[2]

There is, with regard to the multiplicity, a problem, somehow subtle, which we have already mentioned in connection to the Tower of Babel symbolism: that is, the difference between multiplication and scattering. From a traditional perspective, the multiplicity derived from One is perfectly normal; the anomaly appears when this multiplicity attempts to become independent, detached from the One, and this represents separation, sectarianism, and scattering. Satan or the Non-Brother reigns not upon the multiplicity contained and manifested by One, but upon the scattering and dispersion; therefore the Tower of Babel episode has a satanic aspect related to the revolt of those who built it, and actually any revolt, angelic or human, against the normal hierarchy contains this aspect.[3] Of course, in reality, there is nothing independent from the One and separation and scattering represent an erroneous point of view, a heretical perspective, in the same way

---

[1] As Guénon said, the Anti-Christ is the most "illusioned" one, because of the dualist error (Guénon, **Le règne**, p. 370).

[2] "A voice of one calling in the desert: «Prepare the way for the Lord; make straight in the wilderness a highway for our God, make straight the paths of our God. Every valley shall be raised up, every mountain and hill made low; the rough ground shall become level, the rugged places a plain. And the glory of the Lord will be revealed, and all mankind together will see it. For the mouth of the Lord has spoken»" (**Isaiah** 40:3-5); "Every valley shall be filled in, every mountain and hill made low. The crooked roads shall become straight, the rough ways smooth" (**Luke** 3:5).

[3] In **Zohar**, as we have already mentioned, there is a connection between Nimrod and Babel. "Cush was the father of Nimrod, who grew to be a mighty warrior on the earth. He was a mighty hunter before the Lord; that is why it is said, «Like Nimrod, a mighty hunter before the Lord.» The first centers of his kingdom were Babel..." (**Genesis** 10:8-12). Related to this, René Guénon affirmed that the origin of the counter-initiation was such a revolt that occurred long ago, in the past (in a previous secondary cycle).

the profane does not exist as a domain, rather what exists is a profane point of view.

In the Romanian "tradition," Satan, taking advantage of the fact that Noah was away from home, came to his wife and asked her a lot of questions about her husband; yet only after the Devil gave her a jar of boiled wine and she became drunk, did the wife betray Noah's secret and confessed that he was building a boat in the woods.[1] Satan ran to the forest, where he found a pile of timber ready for the construction of the Ark, and the Devil scattered the whole pile in such a way that each piece of wood was completely separated from the others. When Noah found out the devilish thing, he made a plank of maple wood and started to knock it with a gavel or a small mallet gathering back the scattered wood.[2] The symbolism is transparent: Satan is responsible for the scattering and Noah, through a sacred gesture, "reunites what was scattered,"[3] restoring the Unity, or better yet, restoring the multiplicity in Unity.[4]

Regarding the Demiurge, René Guénon published, in 1909, in *La Gnose*, under the alias Palingénius, an article named precisely **Le**

---

[1] The biblical episode about Samson contains the same theme of the traitorous wife (with respect to an essential secret); regarding the jar of wine, we note that in the **Bible** Noah is the one who is drunk.

[2] This plank is a sacred object in the Christian Orthodox Church, and is called in Greek *semantro*, "seal," and in English "a special monastery bell" (since like a bell, it emits a sound having as its purpose the gathering of the community).

[3] It is well-known that this formula is an important Masonic initiatory expression. Also, we should add the Islamic saying: "Those who break the covenant of Allah after ratifying it, and sever that which Allah ordered to be joined, and (who) make mischief in the earth: Those are they who are the losers" (**Qur'ân** 2:27).

[4] Such a gesture, with an initiatory meaning, can be found in different traditions, a well-known episode being the gathering of Osiris' scattered body. As we will see in a next chapter, Noah is the prophet of the transcendent Unity, but not of an immanent multiplicity (as Ibn 'Arabî stated). Regarding Noah's wife, in **Qur'ân** (66:10), she is an example of an unbeliever (her name was Wâila, which should be compared to Wâhela, Lot's wife, who was in confederacy with the men of Sodom). The Gnostics developed the theme of Noah's wife; she appears under the name of Norea, the daughter of Adam and Eve. Norea set fire to the Ark, because God (Ialdabaoth for the Sethians, an inferior and arrogant God, that is, the Non-Brother) did not want to let her survive the flood and because Noah's God is considered the evil God. In other Gnostic texts, this God, who sent the flood, is opposed by Sophia, the Wisdom that saved Noah in the Ark.

Démiurge (Guénon, **Mélanges**, pp. 9 ff). Since the article is not signed with his real name, we quote it with caution, and only because it has a connection with our subject. The author states from the beginning that "the origin of evil" is a grave dilemma of the Christian world: *Si Deus est, unde Malum? Si non est, unde Bonum?*, a dilemma which reminds us of Omar Khayyám's quatrain: "When the Maker formed nature/ Why imperfect was the venture/ If it is good, why departure/ And if bad, why form capture?" Palingénius underlined that the mentioned dilemma cannot be solved considering Creation as the direct work of God, but only by accepting a dyad, a primeval pair that is responsible for the creation of the world. The Principle is unique, infinite and perfect; it is the prime Cause that produces all things; yet being perfect how could it produce imperfection? The solution is found in delineating One as a primordial dyad. From a *principal* point of view, evil or imperfection does not exist, because all the imperfections, partial disorders, and relative disarray are synthetically comprised in the total perfection and order; on the other hand, from a worldly perspective, when all things are viewed as distinct, analytically and fragmentarily, the evil is forced to exist because the world cannot be without duality, and the common man, as an worldly element, cannot understand the world but through duality, through distinction; for the same reason, to permit the human mind somehow to comprehend, total Perfection was divided in Non-Being (non-manifestation) and Being (universal manifestation), even though, in fact, the non-manifestation contains *in principio* the manifestation and there is no real distinction between those two.

Evil emerged only as a consequence of division, of tendency toward multiplicity (or better yet, toward scattering), by separating the things from their common Principle, their Perfection. The biblical fall is nothing else than the first distinction between good and evil, that is, the entrance into multiplicity, into Satan's domain, the domain of the Gnostics' Demiurge, since for these the Demiurge was the creator of the multiplicity, of the world of duality, the world of good and bad. This Demiurge is the Adversary, attempting to stop man from surpassing the domain of individuality, and,

Palingénius said, this demiurge is actually within man, representing the tendency toward distinction, toward separation, toward limitation. The Demiurge, as a sectarian power, is *princeps hujus mundi* as a reflection of Adam Kadmon, having no reality and existence by itself, being a shadow, a tenebrous and inverted reflection of the Supreme Being. Yet this Demiurge does not represent only evil, but the couple good-evil, as an emblem of multiplicity and only if we consider the pair unity-duality associated to good-evil, it appears as an expression of evil. As a creator, the Demiurge first produced division, but the Demiurge exists only so long as the division exists; then, as formative god, the Demiurge produced individual existence, organizing "matter" and creating multiple forms; however, all this creation was imperfect since it was related to the Demiurge (in a Gnostic sense) and not to the supreme Principle. For the Gnostics, man can go beyond the domain of separation ruled by the Demiurge, through Gnosis, that is, through an integral Knowledge (a synthetically, not an analytical one).

A deep precipice separates Gnosis from Gnosticism, similar to the one between Tradition and traditionalism. True Gnosis is the transcendental and absolute Knowledge, while Gnosticism is syncretism (Guénon, **Franc-Maçonnerie**, II, pp. 167-8). Gnosis is the traditional Knowledge that constitutes the common foundation of all initiations and their goal.[1] Clement of Alexandria promoted Gnosis for the Christian tradition; he defined the Gnostic as "perfect man" (IV, 21), the only one capable of comprehending and of explaining the secret things of the Spirit (VI, 15), the one who obtains Gnosis through virtuous behaviour and an intellectual attachment, and who has to ascend beyond the sphere of creation and sin (IV, 25), the one who perfectly imitates God (II, 19), the one called wise by Solomon (VI, 14); "the Gnostic is a perfect man, up to the measure of full stature" (VII, 11); "the Gnostic is consequently divine, and already holy, God-bearing and God-

---

[1] Guénon, **Franc-Maçonnerie**, II, pp. 257, 260, the article **La Gnose et la Franc-Maçonnerie**, signed Palingénius, year 1910.

borne... mixing, then, the serpent with the dove" (VII, 13)[1]; Gnosis, Clement of Alexandria also suggested, is for the few and not for the many (I, 1). [2]

Yet Gnosis is not a particularity of the Christian tradition. It is well-known that in the Hindu tradition, *jnâna-marga*, the way of knowledge, perfectly taught by Shankarâchârya, has as its goal absolute and supreme Gnosis,[3] and to this Gnosis René Guénon referred. Guénon wrote:

> The importance [of knowledge] is not a characteristic of «Gnosticism» only, but a general characteristic of any initiatory teaching, of any form; the knowledge is always the supreme goal, and all the rest represents only various means to reach it. We have to be careful not to confound «Gnosis,» which means «knowledge,» with «Gnosticism,» even if the latter derived its name from the former; however, the name «Gnosticism» is vague and it seems that, in fact, was applied without distinction to very different things. (Guénon, **Ésot. Chrét.**, p. 65)

---

[1] This "mixing" represents the "Feathered Serpent," symbol of the Principle.
[2] See also Jean Tourniac, **Principes et Problèmes Spirituels du Rite Écossais Réctifié**, Dervy, 1969, pp. 174-175, where a compendium (concerning Gnosis and Gnosticism in Clement of Alexandria's work) can be found. Michel Vâlsan underlined that, in conformity with Origen, "the true light" is the spiritual influence of Gnosis (Vâlsan, **Initiation**, p. 167).
[3] The words *gnosis* and *jnâna* derive from the same root.

CHAPTER XII

GNOSTICISM AND OCCULTISM

IN ANOTHER ARTICLE, SIGNED Palingénius, Guénon wrote:

Gnosis, in its highest and widest sense, is knowledge; true Gnosticism cannot be therefore a school or a particular system, but must be first of all the quest for the integral Truth. ... Gnosis must thus expel all those doctrines [based on experiment] and find support only in the orthodox Tradition contained in the scriptures of all nations, Tradition that, in fact, is everywhere the same, despite the diversity of forms taken in order to match each race and each epoch. Yet, here also we have to be careful to differentiate between the genuine Tradition and all those erroneous interpretations and fantasist commentaries offered in our days by a multitude of schools which are more or less occultist. (**Mélanges**, pp. 176, 178)

This text was published in the period 1909-1911, when René Guénon was a member of the *Gnostic Church of France*,[1] an episode of Guénon's life to which some gave too much importance.

---

[1] We note that the *Gnostic Church*, even if it counted members like Matgioi (Albert de Pouvourville) and Abdul-Haqq (Léon Champrenaud), had close affinities with the occultists and theosophists. Regarding Albert de Pouvourville and Léon Champrenaud, called Simon and Théophane in the *Gnostic Church*, they published a book, **Les enseignements secrets de la Gnose** (republished by Archè, 1999) in which Gnosis is defined as "a traditional doctrine with constitutive cosmogonic and metaphysical elements" (p. 7) that takes the man from the present state and guides him toward the light that is God Himself; the man appears to be now in the

The fact of the matter is that Guénon, in this obscure period, completed a symbolic dive into tenebrous regions, with his pseudonyms as silent witnesses.[1] Let us give Guénon's opinion about the neo-Gnostics (and implicitly about the *Gnostic Church*) whom he had the opportunity to know directly:

these «neo-Gnostics» did not receive anything through any sort of transmission, and there is just an attempt to «reconstruct» [the Gnosticism] following some documents, however very fragmentary, which are at everybody's reach; and you can believe the confession of one who had the occasion to notice these things from nearby and therefore knows what it is truly all about. (Guénon, **Ésot. Chrét.**, p. 65)[2]

Evangelic "outside darkness," which separates him from his origin and end, that is, God; and the "outside darkness" is, from a cosmogonic point of view, the informal chaos, the rough stone, and from a metaphysical perspective, ignorance (p. 8).

[1] About this period see Gilis, **Introd. Guénon**, 1985, pp. 45-49, and also our *Introduction* in **Agarttha, the Invisible Center**. Jean Borella, in an article of 1982, **Gnose et gnosticisme chez René Guénon** (**René Guénon**, Les Dossiers H, L'Age d'Homme, 1997) developed in detail the history of Gnosticism and touched the problem of Guénon's affiliation to the *Gnostic Church*. Let us mention briefly that Borella had asked how come that Guénon joined this *Church*, when he clearly made a distinction between Gnosis and Gnosticism; the author answered that Guénon on purpose penetrated the neo-Gnostic ambiance, knowing its fantasies, but later, Borella concluded (due to some terms used by Guénon in his articles signed with alias) that Guénon had "evolved" in this period, breaking up with a certain environment. Here it is what René Guénon said in 1931: "A quarter of a century since we were involved with initiatory matters, we never changed our perspective… we changed so little, that it can be found under pseudonym articles having a content which was integrally reproduced in some of our recent books" (Guénon, **Comptes rendus**, pp. 119-121). We wonder why Borella and others like him think that they know better than Guénon what really happened? Or why they believe Jean Reyor and other "biographers" rather than Guénon himself? In fact, it is a flaw of our modern world, in accordance with the individualism: it is better preferred to have an interpretation that fits the interpreter's mentality, instead of getting information (and also comprehension, without it the information being useless) directly from the source; various orientalists and occultists work in the same way, not telling the historians researching the lost civilizations (they don't have a direct source and just extrapolate our modern mentality).

[2] In some of his reviews, René Guénon wrote: "We did not have but a mediocre interest for Gnosticism, first because it is difficult today to truly know what this was in reality, and then, because its Greek form is unattractive for us. … The word «Gnosis» means «Knowledge» and has nothing to do with «Gnosticism» and we never considered it otherwise" (Guénon, **Comptes rendus**, pp. 119-121).

True Gnosis is of super-human origin and the Gnostic receives the initiation that leads to it through an uninterrupted transmission, which in the case of the Christian has its source in Christ. Clement of Alexandria named first of all James, Peter, John and Paul perfect Gnostics, and then the other Apostles. "For prophecy is full of Gnosis, inasmuch as it was given by the Lord, and again explained by the Lord to the Apostles. ... And is not by Gnosis it may become entitled to immortality?" (VI, 8). The severance of the transmission chain lowered Gnosis into Gnosticism, and the authentic esoteric data, which can be still recognized in the Gnostic texts, have been mixed with an exoteric perspective and altered by individualism. The birth of so many Gnostic sects does not represent but the strong effects of individualism and the loss of the initiatory transmission. Guénon wrote: "The Ismaelians, the Druses, the Nozairi, etc. are nothing else but «sects» (*firâq*), where there always reigns some confusion between esoteric and exoteric; in their initiation, there is an «obscure» aspect because of their deviation from the genuine tradition" (**Quelques pages oubliées**, p. 216); we can tell the same thing about the Gnostic sects. We noticed that sectarianism, beside individualism, constitutes the sign of the antitradition and we observe such characteristics in Gnosticism too.[1] Porphyry, in his **Life of Plotinus**, mentioned that in the time of Plotinus there "lived many Christians and, beside them, heretics [sectarians] derived from the old philosophy [ancient Greek]. ... They mislead many, being themselves misled. ... For this reason Plotinus criticized them, and even more, he wrote an entire book, which we called *Against the Gnostics*."[2]

It does not mean that the Gnostics of the early Christian years did not possess authentic initiatory data; yet besides those who, like Clement of Alexandria, stayed attached to the orthodox tradition,

---

[1] For a look at some significant Gnostic sects see, among many other titles, H. Leisegang, **La Gnose**, Payot, 1971.
[2] See also Plotinus, **The Six Enneads**, Encyclopaedia Britanica, 1952, II, 9; Plotinus rejected, one after another, the Gnostic errors and accused them of getting secret inspiration from Greek philosophy and especially from Plato's teachings, but they dishonored them, interpreting erroneously these teachings (II, 9, 6).

many intervened directly modifying the doctrine and the rites, revolting against the Christian exoteric order, and, taking Saint Paul for example, considered themselves directly inspired by God. This is the great danger of false prophets, who have existed from the Gnostics' times to nowadays, reflecting the great revolt of the Tower of Babel episode: the error of thinking that you as an individual can be similar to the gods; the intervention of some powerful individual elements constitutes an antitraditional work, which we witness today, more than ever.[1] The historians and other modern scholars who have written about Gnosticism put forward the question of why the Gnostics were considered "heretics," doubting the Fathers of the Church's criticism; they have forgotten a fundamental fact: these Fathers lived when the Gnostics lived, and they knew exactly what it was all about, in the same way as in our time the insides of different social and political phenomena are known. It is more than probable that among those declared heretics there were genuine initiates, yet in these sorts of situations the half measure is not acceptable. It is similar to the situation of a common man who can drink alcohol without restriction, while for an alcoholic drinking is forbidden. For this reason Guénon was so tough about everything heterodoxic, including Buddhism; the healing of a sick organism requires tough and rigorous measures.[2]

However, it is important to demolish the illusions that could persist with regard to Gnosticism, and we must warn that, regardless of the initiatory data transmitted by the Gnostics in the first centuries of Christianity, it is not possible today to talk about a "Gnostic initiation"; all that was valid in Gnosticism died long ago, for lack of regular and orthodox transmission.

The early years of the Christian tradition were agitated, and the descent from esoteric to exoteric did not happen smoothly and without commotions. There was no unanimity on the individual

---

[1] The modern people are attracted to neo-Gnosticism (in the same way they like the Runes and the Celtism) because it is intricate, rebel and heterodox, promoting the individualism.

[2] As Coomaraswamy said: the great illusion is to try to make compromises, in the way Christianity does today (Coomaraswamy, **Letters**, p. 308).

level and we cannot consider that all the individuals, as a homogenous block, decided to become public. It is reasonable to accept that a part of the sects and so-called heresies appeared due to the protest of individuals in possession of some initiatory data, individuals who were shocked by the direction Christianity took; yet, in the majority of cases, these sects, in their turn, shifted toward exotericism, combining the authentic initiatory data (mysteries) with individual innovations, which doomed them as heresies.

To understand what we are trying to say, let us take a well-known example, the snake's symbolism. Some Gnostic sects appreciated the snake image in a special way. The serpent, as any other symbol, accepts many interpretations, yet synthetically it offers two aspects, completely opposite to each other, a beneficent and a maleficent one.[1] From an exoteric point of view, in the Christian tradition, the serpent became a satanic element, even though the opposite face was not unknown.[2] From an esoteric perspective, the snake contains symbolism related to the initiatory voyage and to other spiritual aspects, which could appear for exotericism as heretical ideas. When the Gnostic texts were discovered at Nag Hammadi, many were surprised to see the serpent regarded not as the devil that tempted the primordial human pair, but as the symbol of divine wisdom. This is the reason why some teachings cannot be unveiled to the general public, but they have to be guarded by the esoteric domain; and also for this reason it would be absurd to think that an eso-exoteric Christian tradition is possible. An arbitrarily exteriorization of the esoteric data leads only to confusion and heresy. For common believers, an evil serpent (beast, devil) which is at the same time good (and divine) is unacceptable and will only mislead them. With regard to the Gnostic sects that worshipped the serpent, they purely and simply lost the maleficent aspect of the snake, as the helix wound on the *Axis Mundi*.

---

[1] Hermes' two snakes symbolize these two aspects.
[2] In Christianity, the bishop's staff ends with a serpent's head, the beneficent one; the Gospel mentions the serpent's wisdom (**Matthew** 10:16). On the other hand, the serpent caused Adam's fall.

The Gnostic texts discovered at Nag Hammadi originated in the early years of Christianity, in those obscure times when the exoteric tradition was taking shape. In that epoch, many Gospels, Acts and Apocalypses circulated, telling about Jesus' and the Apostles' miracles, gestures and teachings from different points of view, threatening the newly emerged Christian tradition with a deadly sectarianism, a sectarianism so dear to the modern world. Many of the discovered Gnostic texts used Christian terminology, with references to the Judaic tradition, and declared that they present the secret teachings of Jesus, hidden from the many, that is, from the exoteric Church, and accessible only to the few (the initiates). Some texts affirmed that Christ did not come to redeem the world, but as a spiritual master or guide, that is, an initiatory master.

In **The Gospel of Thomas**, Jesus declared: "He who will drink from my mouth will become like me. I myself shall become he, and the things that are hidden will be revealed to him" (50:108) (**Nag Hammadi**, p. 137), and: "When you make the two one, and when you make the inside like the outside and the outside like the inside, and the above like the below, and when you make the male and the female one and the same, then you will enter the Heavenly Kingdom" (37:22) (**Nag Hammadi**, p. 129),[1] words with an initiatory meaning. In the same way, in **The Dialogue of the Saviour**, Jesus asked: "Who is it who seeks and who is it who reveals," and answered that it is one and the same (126) (**Nag Hammadi**, p. 247). Also, **The Gospel of Philip** suggested that resurrection might be obtained while alive, before death (**Nag Hammadi**, p. 149); such an idea has an initiatory and *oriental* background, being similar to what in the Hindu tradition is called *jîvan-mukti*, "the liberation while alive."[2]

---

[1] See also Elaine Pagels, **The Gnostic Gospels**, Vintage Books, 1989, pp. xx, 129.
[2] Obviously, many teachings remained unwritten. Tertullian compared the Valentinian initiation to the Eleusinian Mysteries, underlining that the neophytes followed years of difficult trials, and they had to be mute (like the Pythagoreans) (Pagels 140). In her book, Pagels confounded initiation with an individual psychical experience, and the esotericism with Freud and Jung's psychoanalysis. We may quote a conclusion though: "[The Nag Hammadi texts] suggest that Christianity might have

The Gnostics have generalized Saint Paul's "occurrence," stressing that many, even though they saw and physically heard Jesus, did not understand Him, that the Apostles confused spiritual vision with corporeal resurrection, and so, it is possible for Christ to appear anytime to one or another in spirit, even if, like Saint Paul, He was not known physically (in some cases just for the reason that those individuals were born later). In **The Gospel of Mary [Magdalene]**, Mary Magdalene saw Jesus in an ecstatic vision and not corporeally resurrected (**Nag Hammadi**, p. 525), and in the **Apocalypse of Peter**, Peter had a similar vision in which Christ insisted that He is spirit and not body (Pagels 11-12, **Nag Hammadi**, p. 373). Such a teaching is dangerous, then and now. It permits to anyone to intervene individually, and therefore Gnosticism is so soaked with individualism. This teaching disregarded the regular, orthodox and uninterrupted transmission.[1] We should remember that Saint Paul went to Jerusalem and was accepted by Peter and James, "the brother of Jesus," who validated his mission and his vision on the road to Damascus. Of course, for

---

developed in very different directions – or that Christianity as we know it might not have survived at all. Had Christianity remained multiform, it might well have disappeared from history, along with dozens of rival religious cults of antiquity. I believe that we owe the survival of Christian tradition to the organizational and theological structure that the emerging church developed" (Pagels 142).

[1] It is most surprising that Antoine Faivre, following Abellio, criticized Guénon for heeding and stressing too much the uninterrupted characteristic of the initiatory transmission. On the contrary, without this characteristic there are only revolt and individualism, which are the ingredients of counter-initiation. The notion "orthodox and uninterrupted transmission" means maybe little to the modern mentality, yet it is fundamental and indispensable; the one who teaches the others transmits something he has received, and if he received nothing, he obviously transmits nothing. Sure, the Gnostics claimed that they received the teachings through visions, yet the influence of their individualism is pretty obvious even now, when we read their texts. Such a situation exists in the modern world, full of false prophets; for this reason Guénon was implacable and without mercy with respect to all the occultist, theosophist and spiritualist inventions. Any doctrine which today claims that it derived from a "vision" or from an exotic and secret source is suspect. One of the signs that allows us without error to identify such fakes is the sectarianism they produce. We may note that Saint Paul was an exception, which enforces the rule, that is, the necessity of a regular transmission.

modern man, it is very difficult to understand why Saint Paul was considered orthodox but not the Gnostics who claimed to have similar visions; yet this only because they do not have the capacity to penetrate the secret things.[1] In various traditions there is an initiatory trial in which the neophyte must choose the genuine divine maiden between two twins; who among the modern people might pass such a trial?[2]

One of the reasons why the Church inflexibly stressed the human aspect of Jesus Christ and His bodily resurrection was due to the

---

[1] In modern times, there was a permanent tendency to promote the possibility of a "spontaneous" initiation, without the need of a regular and uninterrupted transmission through an initiatory organization, revealing the thirst of the profane people for comfort and illusory reassurance. Even those who claimed they met to discuss and understand better Guénon and Tradition, blamed Guénon that he tried to limit and restrict the initiatory possibilities for modern man (see for example, "Actes du colloque international de Cerisy-La-Salle" already quoted). Let us stress: even if there are some exceptional cases of "irregular" or "spontaneous" initiations, these are of no interest for the majority of individuals in quest of a spiritual way. It is the ego that tries to deceive them, claiming such an initiation as accessible and affordable. We do not want to increase the separation between Guénon's perspective and those of Schuon and Evola, but we must mention here Evola's complaints with regard to Guénon's tough attitude when it comes to initiation. Evola even said that what René Guénon affirmed with respect to initiation "is not very consolatory" (Julius Evola, **La Doctrine de l'Éveil**, Archè, 1976, p. 288), or the truth has nothing to do with consolation (as Guénon stated very clearly). Evola, due to his position and nature, was a Westerner and could not accept the truth about the Occident and its lack of initiatory ways. For this reason he had to reject Guénon's teachings and consider a sort of "auto-initiation" (which would connect the neophyte directly to the Most High, without the need of a regular initiation or a initiatory organization). Evola's attitude is a very common one. It can be found in any modern classroom; when the students do not know how to solve a problem, they try to alter the problem and adapt it to their limited knowledge. Since Evola, bound by an Occidental nature, could not solve his initiatory problem, he tried to change and adapt the initiatory laws to his necessities. We see something similar in the case of Schuon, who, attempting to become a spiritual master not only for Muslims, but also for Christians, had to promote the idea of a Christian eso-exoterism with initiatory capabilities. In both these cases – it is easy to note – a prize was at stake. On the other hand, René Guénon, so strict about the initiation and its rules, was completely disinterested.

[2] Irenaeus warned that the Gnostics, even if they have a similar language, spread blasphemies. And common man, because of such a similar language, cannot discriminate the Gnostics from the Church, in the same way he or she cannot discriminate the emerald from common glass (Pagels 32).

danger of individualism and of mental phantasmagorias.¹ All the spiritual masters warned how difficult and deceiving the initiatory

---

[1] In the **Acts of John** (Pagels 73), John said that Jesus never left any footprints, nor did He ever blink His eyes, which proves His spiritual not human nature. On the other hand, there is in Rome a church called *Domine Quo Vadis*, where are kept the footprints of Jesus, left by Him when He was walking on the Via Appia, meeting Peter. Peter was trying to run from Rome, to escape martyrdom. The **Acts of Peter** (**Apocryphal NT** 333) described that Peter, seeing Jesus, asked, "Domine, quo vadis?," and Christ answered: "I go into Rome to be crucified again." And only then did Peter return to the city and suffer martyrdom. We can see the difference between Peter and Jesus, as between human and divine. The apocryphal **Acts of Peter** was used both by Ananda K. Coomaraswamy and Michel Vâlsan. Coomaraswamy used it in his article **The Inverted Tree** (Ananda K. Coomaraswamy, **Traditional Art and Symbolism**, ed. de Roger Lipsey, Princeton Univ. Press, 1977, p. 395), an article considered by Guénon when he wrote his **L'Arbre du Monde**. The fall of man is one with the head downwards, as an inverted tree. And he needs a "rectification." In the **Acts of Peter**, Peter asked to be crucified upside down, to stress the decadence of humankind, in comparison to Jesus' upright position on the cross. In another version, **Pseudo-Marcellus**, Peter said: "My Lord Jesus Christ who came down to earth from heaven, was crucified on the earth with the cross standing upright, and now he deigns to call me, to come from earth to heaven. For this reason, my cross must be placed upside down, so that my steps may point towards heaven. I am not worthy to be crucified like my Lord." Michel Vâlsan considered the **Acts of Peter** of great interest from a symbolic point of view. He said that the horizontal branch of the cross represents the human nature of Jesus and the vertical branch the divine nature (Michel Vâlsan, **Références islamiques du "Symbolisme de la Croix,"** Ét. Trad., no. 428, 1971, pp. 275 ff.). More than that, Peter crucified upside down symbolizes human nature and Christ crucified upright, the divine nature. Peter is the rock and foundation of the Church, the vicar of Christ, but on earth, for humankind and from humankind. Christ, on the other hand, even if He is human, His humanity is an "upright" one, not an "upside down" one. One of the meanings of *Kenosis* is that Jesus Christ, being on the cross, is, at the same time, present in the Three Worlds: on earth as man, suffering the crucifixion, in the *Inferno*, as divine Son, liberating humanity from the chains of its sins, and in heaven beside the Father and the Holy Spirit. And the first chapter of the **Gospel of John** is helpful regarding *Kenosis*. With respect to *Kenosis*, we would like to quote Saint Paul with the part from where *kenosis* derives, just to compare it to Meister Eckhart's words. "Who, being in very nature God, did not consider equality with God something to be grasped, but made himself nothing [emptied, *ekenosen*, himself], taking the very nature of a servant, being made in human likeness. He humbled himself and became obedient to death – even death on a cross! Therefore God exalted him to the highest place" (**Philippians** 2:6-9). Meister Eckhart said: "You have to descend in order to ascend. Not because there is a difference between descent and ascension. The supreme ascension consists in the profound abyss of humility. The deeper is the abyss, the higher is the ascension. The

journey can be without guidance and how easily the inferior psychical forces can be confused with divine visions; they stressed how vulnerable the mind and the psychic are and how easily, when opened apparently to receive divine grace, they can be invaded by adverse forces.

The Gnostics considered that some of Jesus' disciples hid a part of the esoteric teachings transmitted to the few, but they are just echoing specific paragraphs of the **New Testament**: "The knowledge of the secrets of the kingdom of heaven has been given to you, but not to them" (**Matthew** 13:11). And again we might give the example of Saint Paul, who, caught up to the third heaven, learned ineffable mysteries and secrets:

I know a man in Christ who, fourteen years ago, was caught up to the third heaven. Whether it was in the body or out of the body I do not know – God knows. And I know that this man – whether in the body or apart from the body I do not know, but God knows – was caught up to paradise. He heard inexpressible things, things that man is not permitted to tell. (**2 Corinthians** 12:2-4)

Though, Saint Paul uttered them: "No, we speak of God's secret wisdom, a wisdom that has been hidden and that God destined for our glory before time began" (**1 Corinthians** 2:7), which suggests an opening towards the exoteric, in the same way the entire Paulician activity to christianize the nations indicated. Valentinus, the famous Gnostic, claimed that he received Saint Paul's secret teachings through his disciple, Theudas, which is interesting, because we can observe how, willy-nilly, there is an endeavour to build an uninterrupted regular transmission to justify the doctrine's validity.[1] It is worthy to review Saint Paul's words:

---

high and the profound are one and the same." We may say that the distance between God and God is the distance from the most profound to the most high.

[1] Many Gnostics, even if they claimed to possess secret data, hastened to expose them in their Gospels and texts, which does not exclude the persistency of some hidden esoteric elements. Not only Saint Paul, but also the other Apostles, including Mary Magdalene, were considered teachers by the Gnostics, to justify their theories and give them weight; and it is easy to understand why there was division even

But I am afraid that just as Eve was deceived by the serpent's cunning, your minds may somehow be led astray from your sincere and pure devotion to Christ. For if someone comes to you and preaches a Jesus other than the Jesus we preached, or if you receive a different spirit from the one you received, or a different gospel from the one you accepted, you put up with it easily enough. ... For such men are false apostles, deceitful workmen, masquerading as apostles of Christ. And no wonder, for Satan himself masquerades as an angel of light. (**2 Corinthians** 11:3-4, 13-14)

Even though these words allude to some exponents of the Jerusalem Church, they could be as well applied to those Gnostics who claimed to be similar to Saint Paul; yet, as Irenaeus complained, those "daily invented something new" (Pagels 19), their individualism having nothing in common with the Paulician teachings. Irenaeus accused that the Gnostics "boast of being inventors and discoverers," basing their writings on their own imagination, and attributing their psychical (mental and emotional) experiences to the divine Word. The Gnostics, added Irenaeus, believed they are invested with the supreme power and thus rejected the authority of the Church[1]; and Irenaeus gave as example Marcus' group, Marcus being one of Valentinus' disciples who founded a Gnostic group in Lyon (where Irenaeus was bishop in A.D. 177). The members of this group thought they are initiates, liberated from the power of the Demiurge, and therefore beyond the authority of the bishop, that is, Irenaeus, who was for them the exponent of the Demiurge. Through initiation, it was claimed, each member received the gift of communicating directly with the Holy Spirit. At their meetings, they

---

among them. One of the first Gnostics, Basilide of Alexandria, claimed that he invented nothing, and he just exposed the esoteric teaching of Christ, following Matthew and Peter's transmitted data; yet Basilide introduced many individualistic elements, personal inventions, which he presented at one time as derived from Noah's sons; he invented complicated names for prophets to impress his auditorium and he imposed on his disciples, like Pythagoras, that they be mute for five years (Leisegang 141-143); it is almost useless to warn that, like Basilide, we could list many false masters of the modern times who, using various notions stole from genuine traditions, mixed with their personal fantasies, mislead naive people.

[1] We note that René Guénon stressed that we have to obey the exoteric law. Pagels compared these Gnostics with the Protestant movement (Pagels 46-47).

participated in drawing lots, and whoever received a certain lot was designated to take the role of priest or bishop, or prophet (Pagels 41), which means the rejection of hierarchy and suggests a type of "equalitarianism" found also in some genuine initiatory organizations of Christian esotericism. Sure, Irenaeus concluded that the Gnostics and the Valentinians were Satan's representatives and warned that even some priests from his congregation were secretly Gnostic initiates; for Irenaeus, there could not exist two teachings, an exoteric and a secret one, but only the one derived from the Apostolic succession, and for this reason the secret Gnostic meetings could not have any other goal but evil (Pagels 45).

It is obvious how easy it was to be in error. The cases of the Templars and of the Masons are well-known in our history, how they were denigrated, how fabricated stories were spread about their satanic practices, etc. Esotericism and genuine Christian initiatory organizations, even if integrated into the Christian tradition, due to their nature always generated the public and the Church's suspicion. On the other hand, exactly this secretiveness allowed some people to imitate and mock the authentic organizations, where under similar appellations they created profane groups and sects, of individual (or even satanic) origins. In the case of primitive Christianity, various groups functioned at the border between falsehood and truth, and we can only repeat what René Guénon said that it was an obscure epoch impossible to fully decipher today. What we know for sure is that there was a mission to establish an exoteric tradition, which had to overcome many difficulties and in this process of exteriorization the esoteric teachings were sacrificed, altered, abused and hidden.

However, our persistence with regard to Gnosticism is not accidental. Many of its characteristics can be found today in the religious, pseudo-spiritualist, neo-occultist and neo-theosophist sects and currents. The theosophists, for example, considered themselves the successors of the antique Gnosticism, preaching a "secret teaching" and calling, *avant la lettre*, the Alexandrian Gnostics "theosophists." Heterodoxic Gnosticism, based on individualism and syncretism, though it wanted to be a "secret wisdom" and the keeper of a secret "gnosis," strove to become public, writing and spreading its doctrines; likewise, modern Occultism issues manuals "for dummies"; in the same way any technical equipment or method is accompanied today by a manual of instructions, "the user's guide," (carefully wrote not to challenge the brain), so modern Occultism publishes all kinds of manuals and dictionaries helping everybody to practice and become a good occultist, gnosticist or *New-Age*-ist. With regard to the "secret," the only secret thing of the theosophists and occultists is the source of their teachings and doctrines; and only because there is no regular, orthodox and uninterrupted transmission of non-human origin, as in the case of genuine esotericism, the real source of the Occultism, an individual one, is kept secret.[1]

René Guénon wrote:

We have reached the situation when we cannot utter the word «esotericism» without somebody thinking immediately about occultism or other similar things, where there is no genuine esotericism at all; it is unbelievable how the most unjustified claims are easily admitted by the very people who would be the most interested in rejecting them. ... There is also another confusion, the one of thinking that it is possible to translate «esotericism» with «gnosticism»; here we are talking about authentic old concepts, yet their interpretation is also false and inexact. It is difficult today to know precisely what the old doctrines really were, those reunited under the generic name «gnosticism,» among which there are many distinctions; yet, as a whole, it seems that we find here more or less distorted oriental ideas, probably misunderstood by the Greeks, and dressed in imaginary forms that are incompatible with pure intellectuality; we can find, of course, interesting things, less mixed with heteroclite elements, less dubious and with a more valid significance. (**Orient et Occident**, pp. 197-198)

In the same way Gnosticism used diverse genuine traditional data, belonging to Christianity, Judaism, Greek Mysteries, and the Oriental doctrines, combining them in a complicated syncretism, so modern Occultism embraces everything it can get from the esoteric and pseudo-esoteric heritage that survived through the centuries, altering

---

[1] In 1997, **The Only Tradition** was published, a work dedicated to Mircea Eliade in which the author combined Theosophism with Guénon and Coomaraswamy. Alvin Moore Jr. unveiled the author's mischievous intent to identify Tradition with Theosophism and considered the work not only a nothing but sinister.

and counterfeiting it, inventing illusory initiations and developing fake doctrines marked by individualism. To give one example, in 1988, a book was published called **Les maîtres de l'occultisme** (translated into English in 1991 as **The Occult**), in which under the occultist umbrella are mentioned pell-mell, without shame, esotericism, gnosticism, Masonry, Rosicrucianism, spiritualism, theosophism etc.; moreover, René Guénon was labeled as the "Karl Marx of esotericism" and the "Karl Marx of occultism."[1]

Guénon clearly defined Occultism as being identical to pseudo-esotericism (Guénon, **Franc-Maçonnerie**, I, p. 213). "Occultism is something very recent. ... This term was, it seems, used for the first time by Eliphas Lévi, and we think that he probably was its inventor."[2] "The occult sciences," René Guénon wrote also, "existed before the invention of the term; they contained Magic, Alchemy, Astrology." Indeed, at the beginning of the 16th century, Cornelius Agrippa founded the term "occult," making it famous with his work **De Occulta Philosophia Libri Tres**. Agrippa used the notion "occult," noticing how all the antique mysteries required secretiveness and how they were forbidden to be exposed to the general public, and he quoted Plato, Pythagoras, Porphyry and Apuleius (Agrippa, **Occult**, p. 443).[3]

---

[1] Since the book was published in 1988, it missed by one year seeing what became of Karl Marx. For those who personally know what Communism really was, even mentioning Karl Marx is an insult.

[2] René Guénon, **L'Erreur Spirite**, Éd. Traditionnelles, 1984, p. 61. It is interesting that Eliphas Lévi, despite his mixed occultism, wrote about the Gnostics: "The name of Gnostic was not always rejected by the Church. Those fathers whose doctrine was allied to the traditions of St. John frequently made use of this title to designate the perfect Christian. Apart from the great Synesius, who was an accomplished Kabalist but of questionable orthodoxy, St. Irenaeus and St. Clement of Alexandria applied it in this sense. The false Gnostics were all in revolt against the hierarchic order, seeking to level the sacred science by its general diffusion, to substitute visions for understanding, personal fanaticism for hierarchic religion. ... The Council of Nicaea saved the world. ... Gnosticism, Arianism, Manicheanism came out of the Kabalah misconstrued" (Eliphas Lévi, **The History of Magic**, Samuel Weisser, 1999, pp. 171, 174).

[3] In the time of the Renaissance, and when Rose-Cross were still active, there was in the Occident a more or less esoteric effervescence, or better yet, a hermetic one. Yet to say, as a recent work does, that the "traditionalistic philosophy" derived from

Today, what we see of Occultism and Gnosticism presents no mystery: there are only individual fantasies, which can be interesting from the profane point of view, for the profane scholar or researcher, even for the common people on the hunt for sensational; yet nothing of this modern pseudo-esotericism allows a real initiation or a genuine gnosis. More than that, Gnosticism and Occultism became nutriment for various antitraditional authors, even some agents of counter-initiation, who produced delirious works and only a flood *à la* Noah could stop them.

There is a last Gnostic element though, which we must now elucidate. One of the most famous Gnostic texts is **Pistis Sophia** and it is known that Sophia played an important role in the various Gnostic sects and texts. Yet Sophia was also an important notion for the early Christian tradition, in relation with the Near-West.

Marsilio Ficino, the "renaissance perennialist," is completely out of order, not only because the expression "traditionalistic philosophy" is a miserable invention, but also especially for rewarding that epoch with a merit it did not have.

CHAPTER XIII

THE NEAR-WEST

RENÉ GUÉNON SYMBOLICALLY divided the world into "Orient" and "Occident," not so much from a geographical point of view, as from a traditional perspective, calling the profane and modern world the "Occident," and the still living traditional societies, the "Orient." The "Orient," said Guénon, contains three major regions: the Far-East, with China and Indochina (where the Daoism flourished), the Middle-East represented by India (the Hindu tradition), and the Near-East considered by him identical to the Islamic tradition. In this classification, North America becomes the Far-West. That is nothing new actually. Guénon followed the terminology in use during his times, the Far-West, for example, being a well-known American emblem, and so the Far-East being for China. Only the Middle-East, which he identified as India, is now, due to an excessive obsession for shortness, the common designation for the region containing all the countries from Egypt to Iran, a region that includes what was in the past called the Near-East; and the Near-East has shifted to the west, almost becoming for the Western world a label for Eastern Europe.

In fact, Eastern Europe is more likely the Near-West, and we can complete Guénon's classification by adding the Middle-West as representing Catholic and Protestant Europe, and the Near-West as designating the Orthodox Christian countries. Considering the whole picture, it is interesting to note the similarity between the

Near-West and Near-East, the two regions occupying a central position, which empowered them with a special function.

The Near-East and the Near-West have been at one point in the past, the bridge or, using an Islamic term, the isthmus (*barzakh*),[1] which, more than separating the Occident and Orient, has operated as a mediator, facilitating not only the traders' voyages and the exchange of various merchandise, but especially making possible the communication of ideas, information and knowledge. Despite the opinion, erroneously established, that the West is a direct inheritor of Greek and Roman civilizations, this isthmus has been, in fact, the fundamental agent, which transmitted to Europe the Greco-Roman learning, the ancient sciences and philosophy, influencing in an essential manner the constitution of the medieval traditional society, without diminishing, of course, the contribution of the West-European populations. In one of his articles, written at the end of his life, René Guénon said:

> Most of the Europeans haven't properly evaluated the importance of the contribution they have received from the Islamic civilization.... It is important to note that the European universities don't show this influence in their teachings in history .... It is very weird to see the Europeans considering themselves the direct inheritors of the Hellenistic civilization, when the facts invalidate this claim. The historical reality has established without doubt that Greek science and philosophy have been transmitted to the Europeans through Muslims. (**Aper. sur l'ésot. isl.**, pp. 76-7)

Indeed, browsing the history textbooks and reviewing the main facts, it is easy to see the fundamental role played by the Near-East in the birth and development of the Occidental civilization, culminating with the Middle Ages when the Christian traditional society became mature and powerful. The Near-West played the same role, even stronger in some respects.

In his article, René Guénon stressed the influence of Islam; but, before its emergence, the Christian religion started its growth

---

[1] About the meaning of *barzakh* see Titus Burckhardt, **Mirror of the Intellect**, State Univ. of New York Press, 1987, pp. 193 ff.

precisely in that part of the world. The first bishoprics are founded there, in the Near-East and Near-West, excepting Rome, which had a privileged position as capital of the Roman Empire. After the first council of Constantinople, in A.D. 381, the same isthmus sheltered the four great patriarchies: Antioch, Alexandria, Jerusalem and Constantinople. This is a normal development, hence in those centers early Christian communities prospered. Despite Rome's claims to supremacy, based on the Evangelical statement, "You are Peter and on this rock I will build my Church" (**Matthew** 16:19), the Gospels also affirm that Christ's first disciple was Peter's brother, Andrew, the Apostle who preached in the Near-West, covering Thrace and Scythia. "One of these two who became followers of Jesus after hearing what John had said was Andrew, the brother of Simon Peter. He first found his brother Simon and said to him, «We have found the Messiah» – which means the Christ (the Anointed)" (**John** 1:40-1). Andrew's testimony is essential and appears as a revelation; he is the first, after John the Baptist, to declare explicitly that Jesus is not "a messiah," or another prophet, but the Messiah.

Yet this special region is not only the preaching area of Jesus' first disciple; it is also the source of the main Christian vocabulary. Here, for the first time, appeared the appellative "Christian": "It was at Antioch that the disciples were first called «Christians»" (**Acts** 11:26). The word "church" (like the German *Kirche*) derived from the Greek *Kyriakon*, "the House of God," and the French *église* (and Italian *chiesa*) came from another Greek word, *ekklesia*, which means "assembly."[1] Without diminishing the authentic importance of Rome as a primeval bishopric in the history of Christianity, it has to be stressed, though, that an extraordinary effervescence developed in the Near-West and Near-East during the first Christian synods, under the reign of the Byzantine Empire (the Western Roman Empire being historically in agony). This spiritual tumult was maintained, in spite of deviations and erroneous sects, by esoteric Christian currents, some of which were banished as heresies, others

---

[1] In the same way, Andrew's name is Greek (*andros*, "man"). Peter's name, even if apparently a Latin word, meaning "the rock," originates from the Greek *petra*.

going into hiding, yet all of them leaving visible and invisible traces. The Armenian Church, the Coptic Church, and the Ethiopian one, are good examples of some visible traces. The influence played by the Monophysites and Nestorians is less visible on an esoteric level. Both heresies, preserving elements of the primitive Christianity, have successfully flourished in the Near-West and Near-East. The Nestorians and the Armenian and Coptic Monophysitism became mediators between the Orient and the Occident, having a subtle influence, still not clearly deciphered, upon the Western Crusaders. During the Crusades, in the city of Nicosia, for example, there coexisted an Armenian cathedral, a Maronite church, a Coptic church and a Nestorian one; in Famagusta, Coptic monasteries and Nestorian churches prospered together. Monophysite Armenia was a transmitter of the Chivalric rites and Masonic arts, which came, despite the opposition of the Byzantine official religion, to enrich the content of the Crusades; at the beginning of Armenian Christianity, the 4th century Armenian apostle, Saint Gregory the Illuminator, wandered the country with a square in his hand, praising the "Grand Architect of Heaven and Earth," and being the patron of Armenian masons. At the same time, the Nestorians (or those who activated under this name) spread from the Near-East and Near-West to the Middle and Far-East, covering Egypt, Syria, North Africa, Mesopotamia, Persia, Mongolia, India, and China, functioning as counselors and secret advisers, in exoteric and esoteric domains; in these positions, they brought a subtle contribution to the birth of Islam, and later they were among the Christian physicians, astronomers and philosophers that lived at the Islamic royal courts, as in the time of Harun al-Rashid.[1]

This succinct journey into early Christian history highlights a significant aspect: if the West-European world was not the direct inheritor of the Hellenistic civilization, neither was Islam. The Arabs, Moors or Saracens, received the various information and knowledge through the diverse Christian currents developed inside the

---

[1] For a detailed analysis on Nestorians and Monophysitism, from an esoteric perspective, see Jean Tourniac, **Lumière d'Orient**, Dervy-Livres, 1979.

Byzantine Empire, and we could say that the only successor, *de jure* and *de facto*, of the Greco-Roman civilization, has to be considered the Christian Byzantine Empire, including without reservation the heresies, too.

Early Christianity in the Near-East and Near-West assimilated the Greek sciences, with Alexandria being a very good example.[1] Saint Paul stressed from the start that "the Jews demand miracles and the Greeks look for wisdom" (**1 Corinthians** 1:22), the Greeks' *philo – sophia*, "the love for wisdom," being the most appreciated, as Clement of Alexandria and other Fathers of the Church confirmed, since Clement considered Greek philosophy a preparatory science for Christian theology.

The Byzantine Empire was incontestably the direct continuator of the Greco-Roman civilization; here, in the Near-West, the union of Hellenism and Latinism took place, and only here is it truly acceptable to use the hyphen in the expression "Greco-Roman."[2] Byzantium, as Eastern Roman Empire, was the sole valid inheritor of Rome, and during the reign of the famous emperor Justinian, the official documents were still written in Latin; only later was Latin completely replaced by Greek, the first *basileus* of Greek language being Maurice, at the end of the 6th century. The Byzantines were the "Romans," and the Saracens and Turks always called them "Rumi." The Byzantine Empire became, after the collapse of the Western Roman Empire, the only genuine "Romania," where for a long time the Greek language was known as "the Romaic language" and the emperor bore the title *basileus ton Romaion*, "the emperor of the Romans."[3]

It is essential to understand, though, that the Byzantine Empire was not an ordinary successor of the Greco-Roman culture and

---

[1] Alexandria was also a powerful Gnostic center.

[2] Byzantium was Roman in its customs, Hellenic in its culture, and Oriental in its methods of government. See Louis Bréhier, **Vie et mort de Byzance**, Albin Michel, 1969, p. 27. We may add that it was as well "Oriental" in its spirituality, where "Oriental" does not refer necessarily to the geographical location.

[3] See the *Introductions* in Thomas F. Mathews, **Byzantium**, Prentice Hall, 1998 and in Charles Delvoye, **L'art byzantin**, Arthaud, 1967.

structures; Byzantium was primarily a Christian Empire, the first Christian temporary power ever established, with Orthodoxy being the cement that unified the various populations (which now would be considered different nations), fastening them to one – the traditional society of the Orthodox Christians, governed by the emperor who was the vicar of God on Earth. Hence, the appellation "Rumi" became for Muslims the equivalent for "Christians."

If the Orthodox religion was the force that consolidated and united the Empire, it also caused, with its increasing intransigency and rigidity, the flight of valuable spiritual and intellectual elements. This is the tragedy of the traditional societies. The foundation of a regular traditional kingdom or city implies a sacrifice, that is, a sacred "cutting." The kingdom's border or the city's wall represents the sacred "cutting"; what is inside the wall (or border) designates "order" (in Greek *cosmos*) and the sacred; what is outside is "chaos," the profane and the "darkness." For a specific traditional society, its capital-city symbolizes the Center of the World, an image of the Supreme Center, the Pole. At the beginning of present humankind there was one and only one spiritual Center; together with the evolvement of our cycle, from the "Golden Age" to the "Iron Age," the primordial and only Tradition has multiplied into secondary traditions, all valid, and the unique Center has generated secondary spiritual centers. A paradoxical situation appeared: the different traditional centers started to fight against each other in the name of the absolute Truth, each one considering itself the possessor of the real Tradition and the only sacred heart of the World, while the others were the "chaos" and the profane.[1] In the same way, the Orthodox Byzantine Church, in order to consolidate its structure, started to persecute all the other Christian factions, labeling them as "heresies" and forcing them to find shelter in the neighborhood. The Near-East (Islam) became the first beneficiary from this action,

---

[1] We must stress though that this fight was only external, since internally there was always a peaceful and spiritual connection among them; the well-known example is the entente that existed between Christian and Islamic esotericism.

the fugitives spreading the Greco-Roman sciences among the Muslims.

The first academic school was founded at Constantinople in the year 330, under the high patronage of the emperor Constantine the Great; in 425, under the emperor Theodosius II, it became the University of Constantinople.[1] Other "pagan" universities, converted to Christianity, continued to function at Antioch, Alexandria, Beirut, Gaza, and Athens, teaching, among other subjects, Arithmetic, Geometry, Astronomy, Music, Natural Sciences, and Medicine. Yet the emperor Justinian closed the University of Athens for its Neoplatonic tendencies, and after that, the *magisters* were recruited from among the Orthodox Christians exclusively; as a result, valuable teachers migrated to Gundeshapur, in Persia, which became a famous Islamic learning center. The same thing happened some decades earlier, when the emperor Zeno closed the School of Edessa, in 489, the Nestorians who were teaching there being forced to relocate to the Orient.[2]

During the birth of Islam, the Orthodox Christian Church was already shaken by diverse "heresies." The new Islamic religion was seen as no more than a new Christian "heresy," which came to enhance the dangerous influence of others upon the stability and unity of the Byzantine Christian Church. As a defensive reaction, Byzantium had to banish the pagan sciences taught at the universities, and Byzantine education became completely controlled by the Church. This was the historical moment when Greco-Roman learning started to migrate from the Near-West to the Near-East, i.e., from Orthodox Christianity to Islam. Moreover, the expansion of Islamic power caused the universities at Alexandria, Beirut and Antioch to fall under Muslim domination.[3]

---

[1] Philip Sherrard, **Byzantium**, Time-Life Books, 1966, p. 136.
[2] See René Taton (editor), **Histoire générale des sciences**, Presses Universitaires de France, 1966, tome I, part III, chap. II (the Arabic Science).
[3] We must not, though, simplify too much the Byzantine religious history. The times of the synods were very troubled and hazy times. Of course, to stabilize Orthodox religion, the emperor and the heads of the Church had to fight against the pagans (Bréhier 28), and condemned Christian deviations, like Gnosticism, or the doctrines

Curiously enough, for a long time, despite the divergences between the Byzantines and Muslims, the Near-East and Near-West were very close; in comparison, a fissure separated the Middle-West and Near-West, a fissure that became a precipice full of intolerance and adversity. For this reason, Islam would be the main beneficiary of the Greco-Roman heritage. During the Umayyad dynasty and then, the Abbasid dynasty, Byzantine artists and scholars, together with the Persian ones, had an important role in organizing the Islamic empire. The official documents of the Saracens were written in Greek; the Arabic coins were similar to the Byzantine ones; the Byzantine architects and masons built mosques; soldiers, deserting the Byzantine army, became generals of the Muslims; Byzantine women became mothers of caliphs. The famous Saint John of Damascus was a high dignitary at the Umayyad court, and Nestorians and Monophysites enjoyed complete religious freedom in the Islamic territories, a freedom they could not have in Byzantium.

Byzantine learning joined the Persian and Hindu contributions, everything being melted and remolded into a new shape, specifically Islamic; Islam, assimilating this rich heritage, would elaborate its own Muslim sciences, and in this form knowledge was transmitted, particularly during the Crusades, to the Middle-West. The Arabic scientific *corpus* was significantly indebted, besides the importance of Persian and Hindu influences, to Byzantine scholarship; in his **Tabaqât al-Umam**, Sa'îd al-Andalusî said that India was "the source of wisdom, law and political art," the master in the science of numbers, geometry, astronomy and medicine, yet after that, he named the ancient Greeks as "the men of the highest rank, the most

---

of Nestorius, the patriarch of Constantinople, and of Arius. The Arian heresy had spread among the Goths and other Teutonic tribes, so when emperor Justin, in 524, banished the Arians, the Empire lost Germanic support (Bréhier 31). For that reason, intransigency was alternated with tolerance, and strong attempts were made to convert the Monophysites to the official Orthodox dogma, and for many years the Monophysitism heresy was allowed at Constantinople, even if censured in Syria and Egypt, in hope of a chimerical conciliation (Bréhier 33, 53).

respected scholars" (Taton, *ibid.*).[1] The first translations from Greek to Arabic took place during the Umayyad dynasty, at the end of the 7th century, when – Ibn al-Adim said – the caliph Khalid called from Egypt some Greek philosophers who could speak Arabic perfectly, and asked them to translate, from Greek and Coptic, some books of Alchemy.[2] An important role in spreading the Near-Western learning, through translations, was played by the two famous intellectual centers, Nisibis and Gundeshapur. In the Assyrian city of Nisibis, a Byzantine Christian school was founded at the beginning of the 4th century, and Saint Ephraem Syrus was in charge of it; when the Persians conquered Nisibis, the school moved to Edessa, and later, when the emperor Zeno closed it, moved back to Nisibis. The school became a great Nestorian university, and contributed to the translation into Syriac of Greek treatises. Gundeshapur, the academic Neoplatonic center, also initiated numerous translations from Aristotle, Galen, Hippocrates, Euclid and others. The learning and the teachers would migrate in time to the Arabian Peninsula and to Baghdad. The Arabs themselves would hunt for the Greek manuscripts from the Byzantine Empire, and sometimes they would ask for books for war compensation (Clot, *Ibid.*).

The Arabic learning *corpus*, in this way consolidated, radiated together with the Islamic expansion to the Middle-West, first to Spain, Sicily and the south of Italy, and then to Charlemagne's Empire, being translated into Latin. Even today we are able to see vivid evidence of the Islamic influence just considering the terminology we use in our Western sciences.[3] Of course, the

---

[1] It should be understood that we refer here to the Greek exoteric learning in the first place.
[2] André Clot, **Haroun al-Rachid et le temps des Mille et Une Nuits**, Fayard, 1986, chap. IX.
[3] See, for example, the following sciences: Alchemy and Chemistry (even the word "alchemy" has an Arabic origin; besides, we mention: alcohol – *al-koh'l*, alembic – *al-anbiq*, alkali – *al-qali*); Astronomy and Navigation (azimuth – *as-sumût*, nadir, zenith, Algol – *al-ghûl*, Aldebaran – *al-dabarân*, admiral – *amir*); Mathematics (algebra, algorithm); and so on. The Arabic influence in Mathematics was very strong. In the time of Charlemagne, the Middle-West assimilated the abacus, the astrolabe and the Arabic figures or "ciphers" (in French, *chiffre*), of Hindu origin, where the word

Byzantine civilization also had a direct influence upon Western Europe. Nicholas of Cusa was an eminent example of this influence. In the spring of 1437, the Pope sent Nicholas to Constantinople as an official envoy; thus, he had a chance not only to learn directly about the Byzantine culture, but also to discover Orthodox spirituality, while visiting sacred Mount Athos and reviewing the works of Dionysius the Areopagite. Cusanus confessed that, when he was on the ship returning from Constantinople, he received divine grace and light.

The Palatine Chapel, *Capella Palatina*, built in the center of Charlemagne's capital-city, Aix-la-Chapelle, is another exquisite example. The Chapel's architecture imitated the Byzantine church of San Vitale of Ravenna, which, in its turn, copied the basilica of Hagia Sophia of Constantinople. When Constantinople became the new center of the Roman Empire, it was called "the New Rome" (Sherrard 31) or "the second Rome" (Mathews 19). Constantinople was, like Rome, a sacred center, the city being founded on seven hills (Sherrard 33), obeying the laws of sacred geography and symbolizing the seven *dwipas* of the Hindu tradition (Guénon, **Roi**, pp. 57-8). Aix-la-Chapelle (or Aachen) was also called by Charlemagne's contemporaries, "the second Rome" or even "the New Jerusalem," which means an implicit admittance of the Near-Western influence, especially when Alcuin called Aachen "the New Athens," considering Charlemagne's educational program.[1]

There is a fundamental difference, though, between Rome and Constantinople: "the New Rome" is a Christian capital, the first Christian official center, having the church built at the heart of the city, while in Rome the Christian temples were located on the

---

"cipher" derives from Arabic *al-sifr* = void, zero. The great Arab mathematician Ibn Musa al-Khwarizmi, teacher at the "House of Wisdom" in Baghdad, a university that followed the model of Alexandria, introduced the decimal system and elaborated the first book of Algebra (Arabic *al-djabar*); the word "algorithm" comes as an alteration of the name al-Khwarizmi. For the Arabic contribution to Mathematics see Carl B. Boyer, **A History of Mathematics**, John Wiley & Sons, 1991, pp. 225 ff.

[1] Richard E. Sullivan, **Aix-la-Chapelle in the Age of Charlemagne**, Univ. of Oklahoma Press, 1963, pp. 31-2, 150.

outskirts (Mathews 20, Sherrard 34). In this respect, Constantinople was not an imitation of Rome, while Aix-la-Chapelle was a reflection of Constantinople.

In fact, a superb illustration of the fundamental meaning of Tradition is unveiling before us. The essential difference between a profane and a sacred society is that the profane one has cut its ties with the Principle; on the contrary, in a traditional society, every gesture, every activity was a sacred one, imitating what the gods did *in illo tempore*, at the beginning of the world. A traditional man knew that mankind, at the moment of birth, was blessed with a holy lore, the Tradition descended from Heaven, which continued to live in all the day-to-day activities. For the profane man, this descent is just a legend. Etymologically, the word "tradition" describes this uninterrupted transmission of the divine lore and principles from the beginning of our human cycle; any break in this chain of transmission causes the fatal fall from sacred to profane. For that reason, Rome has considered itself the direct continuator of Troy, and Troy – it is well-known – was the symbol of the spiritual center, a projection of the supreme Center. Aeneas carried to Italy the Palladium – the sacred statue of Pallas Athena, which had descended from Heaven as a divine token of Troy; this story symbolizes the transmission of the sacred lore from Troy to Rome, the Palladium, like the Holy Grail, being a symbol of the Tradition itself. In the same way, Constantinople became the continuator of Rome, Constantine the Great bringing the Palladium from Rome to the new capital (Sherrard 33), a gesture that reveals the unbroken transmission of the sacred Tradition, even if Rome is a "pagan" society and Constantinople represents a Christian one.[1] On the other hand, Aix-la-Chapelle lacked this continuity, and its epithet of "second Rome," like Charlemagne's title of "Roman emperor," was just an imitation.

Constantine the Great was the patron of many churches, the most important ones being Hagia Sophia, in the center of the city,

---

[1] Note the same continuity in the case of the sacred temples. The Christian churches are built upon the ruins of the pagan temples.

and the Church of the Holy Apostles (Sherrard 34)[1]; in 532, the emperor Justinian rebuilt the famous *basilica*, Hagia Sophia, as it is known today. The name of the *basilica* deserves attention.[2] The Near-West proved to be not only the inheritor of the Greco-Roman civilization, not only the dwelling of the first Christian empire, but also a "kingdom of wisdom." The marriage between the Orthodox religion and Sophia, illustrated exoterically by the name of the most important church, suggests the existence of an esoteric kernel and of an intellectual tradition. And we are not talking about the outside appearance of the Byzantine monasticism.[3]

Orthodox monastic life is an important coordinate of the Near-West. Sacred Mount Athos, with its inaccessible monasteries is famous. The Orthodox monks secluded in caves or in the desert are well-known. Monasteries built like fortresses are legendary and could represent a fine illustration of the Orthodox spiritual path.[4] Orthodoxy, after the chimerical attempt to attract the Monophysites and others, never promoted an aggressive proselytism. On the contrary, the Orthodox monks, like the Hindu seers or other

---

[1] The basilica of St. Mark in Venice is a replica of the Holy Apostles church. The famous icon of the Blessed Virgin Nikopeia, placed on St. Mark's altar of the north transept, carried by the Venetians into battles at the head of the army, is, in fact, a Byzantine icon abducted from Constantinople during the Fourth Crusade.

[2] The churches in Thessaloniki, Edessa, Ohrid, Nicaea, and the Kiev's cathedral are also called Hagia Sophia (Mathews 9, 164, and Meyendorff 259). Moreover, the capital-city of Bulgaria is Sophia, Bulgaria belonging to the posterity of Byzantium.

[3] We should say that Orthodox Christianity kept an "Oriental" kernel, while official monasticism was more of an "Occidental" type, which could, though, be a cover for esotericism.

[4] Monasticism flourished in the Byzantine Empire; in the 6th century, there were eighty-five monasteries in Constantinople alone; books about the lives of great monks became best sellers in Byzantium (Sherrard 27). At the same time, the Near-West, and especially Constantinople, was a huge reliquary (Sherrard 34). Many valorous Christian relics formed a holy web, the infrastructure for the activity of the divine blessing, proving that Constantinople was a "New Jerusalem," an image of Heaven (Sherrard 96), the relics being the support for Heaven's spiritual influences. Constantinople, as a genuine spiritual center and image of the Heavenly Jerusalem, was girdled with formidable walls, the sacred "cutting," which protected and separated the holy city from the exterior darkness and chaos. In a 5th century ivory plaque (Sherrard 15), the "New Rome" was represented as an empress wearing a crown symbolizing the walls of Constantinople.

genuine initiates, tried to hide and escape the curiosity of the external world, answering questions very reluctantly, and often playing the role of the ignorant, the same way the Tibetans did when asked about the Lord of the World.[1]

The Orthodox seers built a strong wall around their inner spirituality, similar to the ramparts of the monasteries: it is the sacred "cutting," separating the light from darkness, the wisdom from ignorance. The supreme Sophia reigned inside this wall of silence, the churches' name being just an external reflection. If the monks, and not the official clergy, were the main athletes of the spiritual domain (Sherrard 99), the monastic life was also just a robe for something much more profound: a divine and everlasting wisdom.

It is interesting to compare the name of the Near-Western and Middle-Western churches. In Western Europe, the cathedrals are usually called "The Church of Our Lady," or in French, *Notre Dame*. Orthodoxy praised the Virgin equally, calling her "the Mother of God," the Orthodox icons with the Mother of God being famous. There are also churches bearing the name "Mother of God," yet the most important church was called Hagia Sophia. Obviously, "Holy Wisdom" is the equivalent of *Notre Dame*.[2] In the Middle Ages, in Western Europe, the Virgin was a symbol for esoteric spirituality, she was *Madonna Intelligenza*. Much earlier, in the Near-West, the divine Sophia became part of the Christian tradition, expression of an esoteric core. Yet only secondarily "Holy Wisdom" was in the Near-West an equivalent for the Mother of God; in the first place, it represented Jesus himself, as *Logos* (Meyendorff 259 ff.). "Wisdom has built herself a house, she has erected her seven pillars" (**Proverbs** 9:1); in the same way, Constantinople on its seven hills was the "city of wisdom" and the Orthodox Church was the house

---

[1] Marco Pallis' criticism regarding Guénon's "Le Roi du Monde" and its lack of historical reality are a result and an example of this tactic of dissimulation. See **René Guénon**, Le Dossiers H, L'Age d'Homme, 1997, pp. 145 ff.

[2] René Guénon wrote about St. Bernard: "He liked to name the Holy Virgin *Notre-Dame*, under his influence, this name was generally used after that. St. Bernard was a genuine «knight of Mary» and he considered St. Mary his «dame,» in a Chivalric sense" (**Saint Bernard**, p. 20).

of God's Wisdom. The Holy Sophia came down as Jesus, the first earthly "house of wisdom" being the Mother of God, the Virgin, the holy womb of the *Logos*. An old Syriac manuscript presented an icon of the Mother of God carrying Jesus inside an oval form (the World Egg), the Virgin having king Solomon at her right and Holy Wisdom at her left (Meyendorff 263). Solomon himself is an emblem of Wisdom, being considered the wisest king and the builder of the Temple. And his name is related to Peace.

When Constantine the Great laid the foundations of Hagia Sophia, he also built another church, which became the first cathedral of the "New Rome," and it was called Hagia Eirene, "Holy Peace" (Mathews 21). Sophia, wisdom, is strongly related to Peace. In different traditions, Sophia and Peace are the ingredients of the Heart, when spiritual realization or Liberation (Hindu *moksha*) is completed. In Hindu tradition, the greatest spiritual master, Shankarâchârya, wears a name related to "quietness" and "peace" (Sanskrit *santi*).[1] In Chinese tradition, the legendary *Huang-ti*, the Yellow Emperor, is also called "Peace." In the Judaic and Christian traditions, Melchisedek is "the king of Salem," i.e., the "king of Peace"; also Solomon means "the peacemaker."[2]

René Guénon, explaining the Tradition, called "non-manifestation" which the Hindu tradition referred to as *Turîya*, "the Fourth," the supreme state of *Âtmâ* (**Mândûkya Up.** I, 7). For our rational mind it is almost impossible to describe the non-manifestation, the domain of *Brahma nirguna* and of Meister Eckhart's Godhead. There are, though, some characteristics that can suggest this supreme state, such as: silence, void, non-action (the Chinese *wu-wei*) and complete quietness. Sophia and Peace belong to

---

[1] His name means "the peacemaker." See Paul Martin-Dubost, **Çankara**, Seuil, 1973, p. 10.
[2] In fact, in any tradition, the most important role of a ruler was to establish and maintain peace. We may add that, for example, in the mythology of the Norsemen, Frey, the god of peace, came down on earth again and again, impersonating kings of Sweden and Denmark. His son, Frodi, ruled Denmark in the time of Jesus, and he was called "Peace." See H. A. Guerber, **Myths of the Norsemen**, Dover Publ., 1992, p. 128.

this state too, and the fact that the first important churches of the Near-West were named Hagia Sophia and Hagia Eirene makes us wonder. As we saw in a previous chapter, Orthodoxy covered a sacred kernel, which was known in the outside world as Hesychasm, a name derived from Greek *hesychia*, "quietness, peace."

"The Prayer of the Heart," as we have already said, plays a major role in Hesychasm, indicating the siege of the Holy Sophia and of the divine Eye.[1] Even if *apophatic* theology, similar to the Hindu doctrine of *neti, neti*, "not this, not this," is more appropriate as a way of spiritual knowledge, and high above the "affirmative theology," the light of negative theology is ultimately also a discursive reasoning in which the mind develops its thinking, negating all the attributes assigned improperly to God. The only adequate way for directly seeing the Divine Light is above and beyond the mind and individuality, is the Intellectual vision obtained by quieting (*hesychia*) the mind and the soul, and realizing the Super-luminous Night within the Heart. This Super-intelligible Light, perceived during the enduring Prayer of the Heart, and seen in an unseen way and known in an unknown way, unveils not God but Super-God (*hyper-theos*), identical to Meister Eckhart's Godhead. It is the Light of transfiguration: Jesus' "face shone like the sun and his clothes became as white as the light" (**Matthew** 17:2); it is, with respect to the teaching of the **Psalms**, the vision of God, "clothed in majesty and glory, wrapped in a robe of light" (**Psalms** 104:2); it is the absolute Light, without alteration or shadow of a change (**James** 1:17).

This sacred kernel, which is still hiding in the Near-West, was so essential and fundamental for Orthodox Christianity, that in the 6th

---

[1] There is another reason why king Solomon was so appreciated, besides his connection with Sophia and Peace, and the building of the Temple. "The Lord gave Solomon immense wisdom and understanding, and a heart as vast as the sand of the seashore. The wisdom of Solomon surpassed the wisdom of all the sons of the East and all the wisdom of Egypt" (**1 Kings** 5:29). "The Lord said, «I give you a heart wise and shrewd as none before you has had and none will have after you»" (**1 Kings** 3:12). Solomon is wise and peaceful because he has a divine and infinite heart in which Sophia and Hesychia found shelter.

century, when Hagia Sophia became the heart of Constantinople, Byzantine iconography insisted on presenting a symbolical scene called "Healing of the Blind." Jesus applies a finger to one eye of a blind man (Mathews 100-4), a gesture that illustrates the opening of the inner Eye. Moreover, a legend said that the first founder of Constantinople was Byzas who asked the Delphic Oracle where to establish a new city, and the Oracle told him: "Opposite the blind" (Sherrard 31). The Delphic Oracle was right again: Constantinople, the spiritual center of the Near-West, unifying the Holy Sophia, the Peace and the Prayer of the Heart, became precisely the "opposite of the blind." And even if today modern civilization has taken over, the Near-West hides somewhere, in its depths, the ever-young Sophia. This Sophia, like the true Gnosis, even if inaccessible for Westerners (that is, for the modern people, including those from the Near-West) represents the "Oriental" marrow of Hesychasm.

CHAPTER XIV

NOAH AND THE NEAR-EAST

WE UNDERLINED AT THE beginning of this study that one of the characteristics of the Great Disarray is the division or the sectarianism, which flourished during Saint Paul's time and continued to prosper, more or less visible, under the same or different garments, until nowadays. We saw in the previous chapters, from a traditional perspective, some aspects of this division and their consequences. The question is: what are the remedies, or, even better, are there still efficient remedies today to heal the scattering and the division?

The question is so fundamental that the only answer we are allowed to give is a parabolic one; in fact, we already know an example represented by the foundation of the Christian tradition, where such a dogmatism and solidification was needed for the Church to stabilize its unity, that it had to expel and eliminate all the dissident Christian currents.

The organization of Christianity as an orthodox tradition is a sacrifice with more than one face. Having a messianic function, Christianity could not remain at the esoteric or prophetic level. It was not enough to prophesize the end of times and ask the nations to repent, as, for example, Isaiah and Jeremiah did; there was the need to save the whole Occident (the Roman Empire). For this reason, Christ came down and became man, suffered the crucifixion and rose after three days. In the same way, Christianity "came down" and became an exoteric tradition. In concert with these facts, Saint

Paul strove to unite the nations, who worshiped the idols and the pagan gods, and make them vassals of the transcendent Unity – the one-and-only God, the Most High.

If Christianity was the force that saved and regenerated the Occident, it also caused, with its increasing intransigency and rigidity, the flight of valuable spiritual and intellectual elements, as we saw in the chapter about the Near-West. Moreover, we must not forget that the Christian tradition not only passed from esotericism to exotericism, but also from a monotheist (Judaic) ambience to a polytheist one (the Roman Empire). In other words, as Saint Paul's letters showed, the problem was to annihilate the "pagan" gods and rituals, which brings us to an essential matter, that of the relation between One and multiplicity. Christianity tried to solve it, on the one hand, by discreetly integrating gods and rituals into the transcendental unity of the Christian religion, promoting the numerous angels and the cult of the saints, and on the other hand, by introducing the Divine Names, as Saint Dionysius the Areopagite registered them.

Christian tradition built an Ark (the Church)[1] which was prepared to save the many, not only the few, and for this reason it descended into the exoteric domain. To make the Ark float without danger a one-and-only captain was needed, a one-and-only law, the same rules for everybody; any revolt or sectarianism would have endangered navigation and forced, as reaction, the expulsion of the sectarians from the ship; on the other hand, due to its messianic characteristic, nobody was refused on it, and there was not only wrath against the decayed world but also salvation.

We note also the difference with regard to Noah's mission. For the Christians, Noah is indissolubly related to the flood and appears, being "a righteous man, blameless among the people of his time," God's favorite, a chosen one who "walked with God"; "But Noah found favour in the eyes of the Lord" (**Genesis** 6:8-9), and not His Wrath. The Orthodox Church considers that Noah invented the

---

[1] The boat is one of the Church's symbols.

semantro.[1] God – it is said – did not order Noah to build only the Ark but also the sacred plank, that replaced the bells and, knocking it, everyday Noah gathered the masons to work, and admonished and warned the population about the flood. The Orthodox monasteries even today use the *semantro*, as do the churches, especially for Easter, yet almost nobody thinks of Noah's times.

Saint Paul's letters, permanently read in the church, are similar to the sacred plank, *semantro*, and to the bells, since Saint Paul, like Noah, admonished the decayed people, announcing the Second Coming, *Parousia*, in the same way as Noah announced the flood. And yet there is a difference between the Noachite mission and the Christian one, a distinction stressed by the Judaic Kabbalah with respect to the difference between Noah and Moses.

Saint Paul, like Noah, announced the imminent coming of the Judgment and it is possible that some of the first Christians even waited for the Second Coming to occur during their life. Yet, as we explained at the beginning of this work, the only concession that was made to us was that we ignore the time when the end will come. Therefore, Saint Paul wrote:

Now, brothers, about times and dates we do not need to write to you, for you know very well that the day of the Lord will come like a thief in the night. While people are saying, «Peace and safety,» destruction will come on them suddenly, as labour pains on a pregnant woman, and they will not escape. But you, brothers, are not in darkness so that this day should surprise you like a thief. You are all sons of the light and sons of the day. We do not belong to the night or to the darkness. (**1 Thessalonians** 5:1-5)[2]

Hence, the Day of Judgment will come when everybody will least expect it.

---

[1] In Arabic, this sacred plank, this "special monastery bell" is called *nâkûs*, and in Greek, *semantro*, "seal."

[2] "Every nation has its term; so whenever their deadline comes, they will not postpone it for an hour, nor will they advance it" (**Qur'ân** 7:34). "They may ask you about the Hour: «When will it arrive?» Say: «Knowledge about it rests only with my Lord; He Alone will disclose its time. Things will seem heavy in Heaven and Earth; it will simply come upon you all of a sudden!»" (**Qur'ân** 7:187).

But because of your stubbornness and your unrepentant heart, you are storing up wrath against yourself for the day of God's wrath, when his righteous judgment will be revealed. God «will give to each person according to what he has done.» To those who by persistence in doing good seek glory, honour and immortality, he will give eternal life. But for those who are self-seeking and who reject the truth and follow evil, there will be wrath and anger. There will be trouble and distress for every human being who does evil: first for the Jew, then for the Gentile; but glory, honour and peace for everyone who does good: first for the Jew, then for the Gentile. (**Romans** 2:5-10)

The Day of Wrath announced by Saint Paul corresponds to the Day of Flood predicted by Noah. Yet this Wrath is not inexorable since "God did not appoint us to suffer wrath but to receive salvation through our Lord Jesus Christ" (**1 Thessalonians** 5:9) and in this declaration is hiding the difference in comparison to Noah.

In the Judaic Kabbalah,[1] Noah is considered a "righteous man" (and "blameless"), *Zaddik*, a quality suggested also by the fact the he "walked with God." The "righteous man" refers initially to a spiritual station, but this qualification appears in the exoteric domain too, like in the case of Joseph, or of James, "the brother of Jesus," who is called James the Just or James "the Righteous One" (the *Zaddik*); this term can be found as well in the Qumran's documents and the "Gnostic" gospels.[2] *Zaddik* is "the world's pillar (fundament)" and we remember that Saint Paul considered Peter, John and James, "the brother of Jesus," as the three pillars of the Church.[3]

---

[1] **Zohar**, I, 59 b (vol. I, p. 193).

[2] In **The Gospel of Thomas**, the disciple asked Jesus: "We know you will leave us. Who is going to be our leader then?" And Jesus answered: "No matter where you reside, you are to go to James the Just, for whose sake heaven and earth came into being" (**The Secret Teachings of Jesus**, Vintage Books, 1986, p. 21). The idea of "spotless" in the sense of spiritual righteousness exists also in the official Gospels: "For I tell you that unless your righteousness surpasses that of the Pharisees and the teachers of the law, you will certainly not enter the kingdom of heaven" (**Matthew** 5:20).

[3] The "pillar" has a rich symbolic meaning, related to the *Axis Mundi* and the spiritual center. The "pillars of Hercules" are well-known (**Sacred Kernel**, p. 37), as well as the two pillars on Enoch. In this latter case, it is said that the pillars were made of different materials to resist, the one water, the other fire; one was placed in Syria, the

The Judaic Kabbalah stressed more than once the harmony between heaven and earth, which in Christianity is said as "on earth as it is in heaven" (**Matthew** 6:10). For example, *Knesseth-Israel* from below corresponds to *Malkuth*, "Kingdom," and to Shekinah as divine presence in the world; but there is also a *Knesseth-Israel* from above, celestial, and every (sacred) activity the Community of Israel does on earth imitates the divine archetypes: "When we are told that the whole land of Israel came and folded itself under Abram, this refers to another holy supernal land which God has and which is also called «the land of Israel.» ... and it is called «the land of the living» (**Zohar** III, 84 a).[1] The Community of Israel only superficially means the Jewish people, in the same way as Islam bears a universal spiritual significance, beyond the particular Arabic point of view. This Community represents especially "the traditional society" as "explication" of a spiritual center, and is therefore a sort of earthly paradise, image of the Heavenly Paradise. In a perfect case, the Kabbalistic disciple hides in this *Knesseth-Israel*, which he essentially represents, and follows Shekinah's way to unite with the Community of Israel from above, with God, being also the intermediary through whom the whole community will rise to the Most High, and the community being the intermediary through which the whole world will do the same. *Sephira Malkuth* designates *Knesseth-Israel*, yet, as we said, not as Jewish people in a common sense, but as an "organism" (in the same way the *sephirothic* Tree is an "organism"), as world, as kingdom, as spiritual center and also as king, that is, as illuminated man, who, in some specific epochs, can fall from sacred to profane. In the middle of this *Malkuth* (a "kingdom" that can be in man's heart) resides the divine presence, Shekinah, the perfect mediator

---

other one in Ethiopia, with Syria and Ethiopia being symbolical names with respect to the spiritual center. The "pillars of Enoch" symbolize two spiritual and initiatory centers to which were given the treasure of primordial knowledge to be kept along the centuries (see René Guénon's notes in **Quelques pages oubliées**, Études Traditionnelles, no. 427, 1971, p. 211).

[1] Vol. 5, p. 97. We saw that Guénon considered the name "Israel" as representing the assembly of the initiates.

nearby the king (**Zohar** II, 51 a),[1] very similar to the Babylonian goddess Ishtar.

Generation of the universal manifestation necessarily means the beginning of cosmic divorce, and the Judaic Kabbalah calls this "Shekinah's exile," the divine presence leaving the Holy One, blessed be He (*Kaddosh-Baruch-Hu*), and going away, farther and farther; the theme of the exile obsesses the Judaic tradition. We could say that the whole modern world is in exile, in diaspora, from this point of view, the Jews' exile being somehow the visible model of worldly diaspora. In fact, a double exile takes place: on the one hand, Shekinah's exile with respect to the Holy One, blessed be He, and on the other hand, Israel's exile with regard to Shekinah, who becomes the hidden sun, where this exile represents "the misery" (*daleth*) when the candle of Ishtar's worshiper becomes extinct; the man falls then into ignorance and profanity, since the exile refers not only to the Community of Israel but also to each individual. The straightening means evidently the beginning of a new cycle, after all the scattered ones in diaspora are reunited, after "my scattered family will come back together" (as a Babylonian hymn to Ishtar tells), when Shekinah will unite with *Kaddosh-Baruch-Hu*. The union is first of all, of course, an initiatory one, of spiritual essence, symbolizing the union of the Self with Brahma (in the Hindu tradition), the Supreme Identity when *jîvâtmâ* breaks the worldly chains and reveals his splendour as *Âtmâ*, identical to Brahma.

We witness an attempt to reconcile two points of view, one transcendental, the other one immanent. In all the genuine traditions, the Principle is at the same time the Most High (transcendent) and the Heart or the Center (immanent). A traditional society of "righteous men" respects and imitates the things from the High, and at the same time it is in harmony with the spiritual kernel (center) from where it receives its reality and the kernel is *Zaddik*, "the pillar of the world."

In Noah's times, there were no more "righteous men" in the exoteric domain, and Shekinah was in exile. In other words, the

---

[1] Vol. 3, p. 156.

harmonious communication between heaven and earth broke, and the esoteric domain became dry; the spiritual influence withdrew from the world, due to the lack of "righteous men." To regenerate and straighten the world "ten righteous men" were needed, yet at the time of the flood only Noah (and his sons) was found blameless, and only with him did God make a Covenant having as an earthly token the ark, and as a celestial token the rainbow (**Zohar**, I, 67 b).[1] It is interesting that Noah's embarking on the Ark (of this Covenant) is considered a union similar to the union in the highest, being therefore a symbol of a supernal archetype; as the river derived from the supernal waters watered the paradisiacal Garden, fertilizing it, and then the river parted into four to produce the world (**Genesis 2:10**), in the same way the union of Noah with the Ark will produce future generations that will multiply upon the earth (**Zohar**, I, 59 b).[2]

As Guénon explained (**Symboles**, pp. 173, 175), the ark from below is analogous to the rainbow from above modeling a complete cycle. The rainbow represents the superior Waters, the ark the inferior Waters and they come together, united in order to regenerate the world and produce a new cosmic cycle. The Judaic Kabbalah says that the greatest sin of the flood generation was that Noah's contemporaries did not let the union between the superior and inferior Waters occur, that is, due to the corruption, crimes and injustice reigning among the people, heaven and earth became completely separated. That is why they were punished with water. The waters of the flood were burning like fire, emerging boiling from the abyss: they corresponded to the inferior Waters[3]; at the

---

[1] Vol. I, pp. 223, 241. The Ark of this Covenant is equivalent to the Garden of Eden, that is, with the spiritual center; on the other hand, the Ark is the World Egg that contains the seeds of the future cycle. The union of Noah with the Ark suggests the union with the Principle from an immanent point of view, as a response to the Covenant with the transcendental God (Noah has already walked with this God).
[2] Vol. I, p. 193.
[3] We note that in Greek mythology Minos was killed in a barrel with boiling water; the connection between Minos and the cosmic cycles is known. Regarding the combination fire-water, besides the alchemical symbolism, we should observe that it illustrates *coincidentia oppositorum*, which will be present at the end of times, when the

same time, heaven opened and humankind was flooded with the waters from above: they corresponded to the superior Waters.¹ In this mode the two types of waters came together to punish mankind in proportion to its sin (**Zohar**, I, 62 a, 68 b).² The end of the world means the reassembling of the World Egg as it has been at the beginning, it means the reunification of the superior and inferior Waters as they have been before Genesis.

We reach now a capital problem. From a cosmologic point of view and from the doctrine of cosmic cycles perspective, the flood is something normal and logical. When a world has exhausted its possibilities, it has to die and a new one will be born. From an initiatory point of view, salvation (regeneration) of the world is logical and so Noah appears as an ambiguous character.³

---

end and the beginning are one; we already noted that "the pillars of Enoch" represent the water and the fire.

[1] We mentioned in the *Introduction* that the Greek flood is described as a combination of the waters from above (controlled by Zeus) and from below (controlled by Poseidon).

[2] Vol. I, pp. 202, 228. "Noah's folk denied it long before them; they rejected Our servant and said: «He is crazy!» and he was rebuffed. ... So We opened Heaven's gates for water to pour down. We drilled the earth full of springs and the waters met at a command which had been decreed" (**Qur'ân** 54:9-12).

[3] For example, Judaic esotericism considers that Noah brought sin into the world: "Noah himself drew death into the world, through his own sin, of which is written, «And he drank of the wine and was drunken, and he was uncovered within his tent»" (**Zohar**, I, 63 b, vol. I, p. 207); on the other hand, we saw what Guénon said about Noah and the initiatory symbolism of the wine. For Saint John Chrysostom, Noah's drunkenness is a debauchery, yet if it is an initiatory "drunkenness" then Noah's uncovering is equivalent to a revelation and that is why Ham was punished (in the same way as in **Chymische Hochzeit Christiani Rosencreutz**, those who saw Venus naked were punished). With regard to this Biblical episode, we should note that here is suggested the difference between the exoteric and the esoteric. "Ham, the father of Canaan, saw his father's nakedness and told his two brothers outside. But Shem and Japheth took a garment and laid it across their shoulders; then they walked in backward and covered their father's nakedness. Their faces were turned the other way so that they would not see their father's nakedness. When Noah awoke from his wine and found out what his youngest son had done to him, he said, «Cursed be Canaan! The lowest of slaves will he be to his brothers.» He also said, «Blessed be the Lord, the God of Shem! May Canaan be the slave of Shem. May God extend the territory of Japheth; may Japheth live in the tents of Shem, and may Canaan be his slave.»" (**Genesis** 9: 22-27). Philo explained the episode: "In the first place, because

Noah and The Near-East

A perfect spiritual realization supposes not only an ascendant initiatory way, but also a descendant one, the two phases being comparable (as Guénon affirmed) to the two halves of a circle[1]; the descendant half is related to the *avatâra*'s function (*avatarana* means in Sanskrit "to descend"), a function, which, compared to Christ, Noah did not have. In the Islamic tradition there is a difference between *walî* and *nabî*: the former is an initiate for himself, the latter for the others (Guénon, **Initiation**, pp. 256-262); *walî*, said Guénon, lacks something, and such a "lack" we find in Noah's case: it is about Mercy.[2] Only when a straightening is no longer possible, the kernel of Tradition and the spiritual seeds gather in the Ark to get ready for a new cycle and the old world is completely destroyed. Yet the initiates have the obligation of striving for a regeneration and revivification of the world in which they operate and that is what

---

he [Ham] did not report the involuntary evil of his father to one brother only, but to both of them; and no doubt if he had any more he would have told it to them all, as he did in fact to every one he could; and he did so with ridicule in his very words, making a jest of what ought not to have been treated with laughter and derision" (QG II, 71, **The Works of Philo**, Hendrickson Publishers, 1997, p. 837). Philo also suggested that the three brothers, Shem, Japheth and Ham, correspond to good, indifferent and bad, which we may interpret in various ways. First, it is possible to compare this triad to the three *gunas* of the Hindu tradition and to Lao Zi's sayings: "When the best pupil hears about Dao he practises it assiduously; when the average pupil hears about Dao, he seems now to keep it and now to lose it. When the worst pupil hears about Dao, he laughs out loud. If he did not laugh, Dao would be unworthy of being Dao" (**Dao De Jing** XLI). Ham, who did laugh, is the worst pupil and relates to *tamas* (the *guna* directed downwards); Shem corresponds to *sattwa* (the *guna* directed upwards). On the other hand, we may say that Ham represents exotericism, while his brothers illustrate esotericism; or, in more details, Ham should be related to the "outside darkness," Japheth to exotericism and Shem to esotericism. From a Christian point of view, Shem would indicate the Jews and Japheth the Greeks (or the Gentiles). Eventually, we note that Flavius Josephus and some other traditions considered that Ham was perpetuating the teachings of the Giants and of the fallen angels, after the flood (in the **Bible**, Nimrod is Ham's grandson), which shows Ham as the ancestor of the present counter-initiation.

[1] Even if we obtain the same diagram as the one composed by the ark and the rainbow, here the two semicircles are "vertical" not "horizontal"; there is though a close connection between the two diagrams.

[2] Allâh's greatest name, synthesizer, is *Er-Rahmân*, "the Merciful"; in the same way "the Prayer of the Heart" in Hesychasm is nothing else than divine Mercy.

happened in the cases of Christianity and Islam. If Noah had operated as a *nabî* maybe the flood would have been avoided. The change of the cycles comes only when all other means are exhausted; therefore the initiates' intervention is compulsory.

When the individuals are "righteous," Shekinah, the divine presence, is among them; but when the world is decayed and full of sins, the people throw Shekinah into exile: this was the flood generation, Noah's people (**Zohar**, I, 61 a).[1] When there is one "righteous man" in this world, Shekinah joins him and does not leave him; and Noah was allowed to embark on the Ark only because he was "righteous," since nobody else but the righteous (*Zaddik*) can unite with the Ark (**Zohar**, I, 66 b).[2] When the righteous men multiply the earth is fruitful.[3] When the sinners multiply the waters dry (the earth becomes a desert and the heart solidifies). God, even if He destroyed the sinners in the time of Noah, He wanted to spare the world, yet couldn't find a redeemer to save the world from His Wrath.[4] The world's salvation required the existence of "ten righteous men," and besides Noah nobody was "righteous."[5] With regard to Noah, all his efforts were required to save himself and repopulate the world (**Zohar**, I, 67 a, b)[6]; that is all Noah was capable of, and if from a cosmologic point of view his role is beneficent, from an initiatory point of view he appears with a "lack."[7]

That is the difference between Noah and Moses. The latter, even if he admonished the population, gave the Law and saved them.

---

[1] Vol. I, p. 198.
[2] Vol. I, p. 219.
[3] See also **Qur'ân** 7:57-58.
[4] Since, in fact, Mercy not Wrath is the essential characteristic of God.
[5] In the Sodom episode, Abraham asked God: «May the Lord not be angry, but let me speak just once more. What if only ten [righteous men] can be found there?» God answered, «For the sake of ten, I will not destroy it» (**Genesis** 18:32).
[6] Vol. I, pp. 222-223. "When the sinners were destroyed in the time of Noah, God was anxious for the preservation of the world, but could see no one who might save it from His wrath; for the whole efforts of Noah were required to save himself and to repeople the world."
[7] Noah "was righteous only by comparison with his contemporaries" (**Zohar** I, 67 a).

Compared to Moses, Noah did not intervene to save his contemporaries; he let them perish. Moses, on the other hand, offered his life in change for salvation of his people; Noah saved himself and left the world in God's hands. Moses planted Shekinah in the middle of Israel, risking his life for it. Even if Noah was a "righteous man," he was not holy enough to make God consider him qualified to save the world. Noah should have had mercy for others, since when the sinners multiply, the "righteous man" suffers first for their sins. On the other hand, Noah "walked with God," and he was saved in the Ark, having the mission of repopulating the world; moreover, he daily admonished and warned the people and asked them to repent because the flood was coming, and the Wrath of God was awakened, and it is written that the one who admonishes the sinner "saves himself and is not involved in the punishment which befalls them" (**Zohar**, I, 67 b-68 a).[1]

In the Islamic tradition, the hierarchy of spiritual realization has, at the top, three stations: one occupied by *rasûl* and the other two we already mentioned (*nabî* and *walî*). *Rasûl*, who occupies the highest station (*maqâm*), is "the messenger of God" and manifests the greatest divine attribute, that of being Merciful (*Er-Rahmân*), in all the worlds (*rahmantan lil-âlamin*) (Guénon, **Initiation**, p. 261), this function having a universal characteristic. *Rasûl* is God's favorite, chosen to "reveal" the Tradition into the world again when a change of cycles occurs, in order to save the world (or a part of it) from decadence, profane and ignorance, and to establish a new spiritual center and a new traditional society equipped with a sacred Law (Sanskrit *Dharma*). "The messengers of God" are very rare during a human cycle and manifest themselves only when a major crisis develops. The station occupied by *rasûl* contains implicitly the qualities of *nabî* and *walî*. *Nabî* is a divine "messenger" as well, yet the area of his function is limited to a particular people. *Nabî* means literally "prophet" and, in comparison to *rasûl*, does not bring a new law, does not found a new society, but admonishes the people to come back to the existing Law and to the still operating society, in

---

[1] Vol. I, pp. 223-225.

the same way the biblical prophets scolded the Jews to return to Moses' Law and follow it in all the details. *Nabî* is at the same time a *walî*, that is, a "saint." *Walî* is the one "close to God," the one who "walks with God," and therefore his station is considered by some higher than that of *nabî*; yet, in fact, the latter is a *walî* who has also a "mission" with regard to a group of people.

We observe that Noah appears as a *walî*, since he "walked with God" and saved himself; but Noah seems to be also a prophet, a *nabî*, whose mission was the endeavour to straighten a specific people, daily warning about the flood. For the Islamic tradition though, Noah is even more than that: he is a *rasûl*, the first "messenger of God" on earth from a long series of "messengers" (which includes Abraham, Moses, Jesus and Muhammad). Muhammad is considered the last "messenger" for present humanity's cycle, and Jesus is the one who will come to earth for the end of times.

Noah, as the first "messenger of God," plays an important role in the Islamic tradition.[1] He is often mentioned in the **Qur'ân**. In sûrah *Al Arâf*, the "messengers of God" are listed starting with Noah. It is an important sûrah that depicts a vast picture with regard to human infidelity and decadence, beginning with Adam's sin; the worshipers of (satanic) idols are condemned and also the lack of faith in the one-and-only God. The sûrah opens with "Follow the revelation given unto you from your Lord, and follow not, as friends or protectors, other than Him" (7:3), in the way Adam and Eve did. A part of humankind ("the righteous men") accepted the signs and the way of God, yet others rejected the messengers and the signs,

---

[1] When the holy Kaaba was built, it is said in the Islamic tradition, the corner (angle) of the black stone was empty and Abraham sent Ishmael to find the stone; in a way, this stone is the thrown keystone that must be found (like the Holy Grail) through an initiatory process. Ishmael embarked on the quest, yet, meanwhile, Tirmidhi said in **Asâr al-hajj**, the mountain Abu Qubays (nearby Kaaba), moved from Khorassan to Mecca and offered to the "intimate friend" (*al-Khalîl*, Abraham), with God's permission, the black stone; this black stone, when the flood took place, Noah gave it to Abu Qubays (Charles-André Gilis, **La doctrine initiatique du pèlerinage**, Les Éditions de l'Oeuvre, 1982, p. 86).

and they took beside God the evil ones as protectors, falling into error (7:30); these, even if God created them, do not know to be grateful and were full of arrogance (7:10, 36). *Al Arâf* is the veil that separates the righteous ones who will go to heaven from the evil ones who will go to hell (7:46); the heights (*al arâf*) suggest the wall that divides heaven from hell.

We sent Noah to his people. He said: «O my people! worship Allâh. You have no other god but Him. I fear for you the punishment of a dreadful day!» The leaders of his people said: «Ah! we see thee evidently wandering (in mind).» He said: «O my people! No wandering is there in my (mind): on the contrary I am an apostle from the Lord and Cherisher of the worlds! I but fulfill towards you the duties of my Lord's mission: Sincere is my advice to you, and I know from Allâh something that you know not.» But they rejected him, and We delivered him, and those with him, in the Ark: but We overwhelmed in the flood those who rejected Our signs. They were indeed a blind people! (7:59-64)

The sûrah goes on naming other "messengers of God" (starting with Hûd), and showing how the disbelievers rejected them. Moses occupies an essential place; even though he also wasn't followed, not all the people building the golden calf as an idol were decayed, and Moses chose seventy men with whom he saved the rest from punishment and installed the Law (7:103-160). Another sûrah, called *Hûd*, talking again about the "messengers," presents Noah and his message, the infidelity of his people, the building of the ark and Noah's salvation; the sûrahs *Poets* and *The Moon* stress how Noah was accused of being an impostor, and in the sûrah *The Spider* again Noah is presented as the "messenger of God." Eventually, there is a short sûrah, called precisely *Noah*, in which Noah complains to God: "My Lord! Lo! I have called unto my people night and day. But all my calling does but add to their repugnance. And lo! whenever I call unto them that Thou may pardon them they thrust their fingers in their ears and cover themselves with their garments and persist (in their refusal) and magnify themselves in pride" (**Qur'ân** 71:5-7). And Noah added: "My Lord! Leave not one of the disbelievers in the land. If Thou should leave them, they will mislead Thy slaves. ... My

Lord! Forgive me and my parents and anyone who enters my house believing, and believing men and believing women, and increase not the wrong-doers in anything save ruin" (71:26-28).

This attention paid to Noah in the **Qur'ân** is due not only to the fundamental importance of the theme, but also to the fact that the Noachite mission was a "preview" of the Muhammadian one. For this reason Islamic esotericism supplied profound commentaries on the subject, like the ones written by the greatest spiritual master, Muhyiddin Ibn 'Arabî in his **Kitâb Fusûs al-Hikam**.[1] The third chapter of this work is dedicated to Noah (Nûh) and from the beginning we are warned: "It is well known that the sacred Laws, when uttering about God the Most High, use a language that has for the common believer an apparent meaning; while, for the elite, it comprises the totality of meanings" (p. 115). Then, Ibn 'Arabî stressed that Allâh is both "without" and "within," therefore we should consider both His transcendence and immanence, suggesting that we must surpass the superficial significance of the Qur'ânic text about Noah and penetrate the initiatory meaning. And from this initiatory point of view Noah presents a "lack," not the same one as underlined by the Judaic Kabbalah, but equally important. The ambiguity of the Noachite symbolism only underlines the complexity of the crisis in the vicinity of the change of cycles, as well as that of the esoteric and initiatory perspective in comparison to the exoteric one. And everything we describe here about Noah could be transposed to today.

Ibn 'Arabî wrote:

Through transcendence, you condition Him and through immanence you limit Him. If you do both, you are on the right track. You are an Imâm and a Master of Knowledge. Who affirms «pairness» [duality] is an associator [making the mistake to associate something to God][2]; who talks about «impairness» [singularity, excluding multiplicity] a unionist [making the mistake to neglect the mystery of One and multiple]. ... Allâh the Most

---

[1] We use Gilis' French translation and commentaries (Ibn 'Arabî, **Le Livre des Chatons des Sagesses**, Éd. Al-Bouraq, 1997).
[2] It is what Noah contested at his people.

High said: «Nothing is in His likeness,» proclaiming so His transcendence, «and He is the One who listens and sees,» proclaiming His immanence. The Most High said: «Nothing is His simile,» proclaiming His immanence and the existence of a double, «and He is the One who listens and sees,» proclaiming so His transcendence and His incomparability. (p. 118-119)

Meister Eckhart uttered the same metaphysical paradox: "You have to descend in order to ascend. Not because there is a difference between descent and ascension. The supreme ascension resides in the profound abyss of humility. The deeper is the abyss, the higher is the ascension. The high and the profound are one and the same." And Nicholas of Cusa in his famous **De docta ignorantia** declared:

God is within everything, because He is an infinite center; without everything, because He is an infinite circle; penetrating everything, because He is of an infinite diameter, the principle of everything being the center, the end of everything being the circumference, the middle of everything being the diameter, efficient cause being the center, formal cause being the diameter, the terminal cause being the circle, the center producing the being, the diameter ruling, and the circle keeping.

The great master Ibn 'Arabî continued:

If Noah had gathered for his people the two modalities of appeal [immanent and transcendent], the folk would have listened to him. But he called them loudly, and then whispering and secretly; and then he told them: «Beg the Lord for forgiveness: He is indeed the eternal forgiver.» Noah said as well: «I called the population day and night and my appeal had no other effect than to increase the aversion.»[1]

Ibn 'Arabî showed the difference between the Noachite mission (*risâla nûhiyya*) and the Muhammadian one (*risâla muhammadiyya*): the people did not respond to Noah's appeal because there was a discrimination (*furqân*) between transcendence and immanence; yet the true reality is at the same time discrimination (*furqân*) [between One and multiple] and synthesis (*qur'ân*), this synthesis including

---

[1] The quotations are from the **Qur'ân**, sûrah *Nûh*.

discrimination, but the reverse not being possible; for this reason *qur'ân* is Muhammad's privilege, since *risâla muhammadiyya* unites the two aspects. And Muhammad, compared to Noah, did not call the people day and night, but he called them "nightly" in the daytime, and "daily" in the nighttime.

In comparison with *risâla muhammadiyya*, which has a universal and integrative characteristic, addressing all the people, Gilis observed, *risâla nûhiyya* is restricted to a specific nation, having a goal of installing limited traditional unity; therefore Noah asked the population to leave the idols and the multiple divinities, to come and obey the transcendent Unity, which means to abandon the previous traditional forms.[1] *Risâla muhammadiyya* on the other hand, integrated the previous traditions, like the Judaic and Christian ones, and included the deities of the Arab tribes; for this reason Noah, Hûd and Jesus are among the "messengers of God" before Muhammad's arrival. The Islamic tradition realized the synthesis of immanent and transcendent, because it contains a metaphysical doctrine and accepts beside the exoteric domain an esoteric one, to the latter belonging the writings generating perplexity of Ibn 'Arabî. The limitation to an exoteric domain imposes only the aspect of a transcendental Unity, like in Christianity. From a metaphysical perspective, the perfect reality occurs when we consider not only the non-manifestation but also the manifestation, not only the ascendant spiritual realization but also the descendent one, not only One but also the multiple. For this reason in Hesychasm there are the uncreated energies that correspond to the divine attributes and which, from a metaphysical point of view, are exactly the "idols" of Noah's folk. Therefore Ibn 'Arabî considered that Noah's mission

---

[1] The Judaic and Christian traditions also stressed this particular aspect of Noah's function. Noah's seven laws or commandments are well known, the first one referring to prohibition of idolatry and praise of one transcendental God. We may note that there were erroneous opinions which identified the Noachites with Masons and considered the seven commandments as the "Constitutions" of Masonry. In fact, the tradition that Noah received the seven laws when God made His Covenant after the flood was introduced to Masonry in 1736, by Anderson, who wanted to promote the moral aspect.

was limited, because he did not know how to solve the mystery of "One and multiple," since "the Most High is at the same time the origin of unity and multiplicity."

If the exoteric tradition is the same (the circumference, the fruit's skin), referring to the transcendental One, the initiatory ways (*turuq*), belonging to the esoteric domain, are multiple (the circle's radius), they are all aiming at the One (the center, the kernel, the immanent One), and in this mode the One and the multiple are reconciled (see Guénon, **L'ésot. islam.**, pp. 14-15). From a metaphysical point of view, the "idols" of Noah's people can be considered these initiatory ways (*turuq*), each "idol" being nothing else but a face of Allâh. On the other hand, to push the ambiguity of Noah's symbolism to the limit, the danger is the appearance of error and sectarianism, as Gilis stressed (vol. I, pp. 142-145); *risâla nûhiyya* offered the needed stability for a traditional society, a stability reached through Noah's appeal to an exoteric unity for all and to submission to the transcendental One, the multiplicity of "idols," that is, of ways and laws, of particular prophets, leading to confusion, heresy and sectarianism, especially at the end of the cycle. That is what forced the Christian tradition to "descend" into the exoteric domain and to reject all the other "Christian" currents; that is also the motivation for *risâla muhammadiyya* to establish an exoteric Law and integrate the previous traditional forms to prevent any contradiction and dispute among the regular and authentic traditions, which exacerbate at the end of times.

Today, not too many understand the universal function and the metaphysical essence that are hidden in *risâla muhammadiyya*; the spiritual and symbolic meanings are often forgotten, and the Islamic exotericism itself expressed more than once incomprehension with regard to Ibn 'Arabî's teachings; in the same way, Judaic and Christian exotericism seem to have lost the *absconditorum clavis*, the key of the secret things.

CHAPTER XV

SAINT PAUL AND HISTORICISM

ONE OF THE GREAT DANGERS that threatened the esoteric domain and, even more, the exoteric domain, especially during the "Iron Age," was "historicism," if we are allowed to use such a barbarism. Like "individualism," "historicism" derived its power from the fact that, by definition, human beings live in the world, as individuals – makers of history, and at the very moment when the "sense of eternity" was lost, that is, individuals lost the divine vision, all their judgments with respect to the "secret things" were reduced to the erroneous and narrow individualistic and historical perspective.[1] Today such a perspective chokes almost all the attempts to rise toward the super-mental truth. The first that suffered was the exoteric domain, due to its accessibility to the general public, and it is known how the Christian Church tried to adapt to the "progress of history," making compromises and absurd concessions in its attempt to reconcile the sacred plane with that of the profane sciences, proving a serious lack of comprehension of its own domain. Even less should history intervene in the esoteric domain; if the exoteric field has the role of reconciling the two powers, spiritual and temporal, the esoteric domain must not be

---

[1] The great danger of "historicism," as well as of "individualism," consists, of course, in the fact that man is an individual and historical being; for this reason, to use a common example, it is easier to give up smoking than to follow a diet: you can live without smoking but not without food.

affected by the historical point of view. For this reason, any opening of an initiatory organization toward "historicism" means a breach opened for the antitraditional and counter-initiatory forces.

In a traditional society, profane history (and, consequently, the chronology of historical facts) has a peripheral place.[1] Even if it is difficult for modern man, obsessed with exact data and being hypnotized by time and duration, to accept a non-historical and non-temporal perspective, this existed in the traditional civilizations, which had a mentality closer to eternity than to temporality.[2] Also, it is not about an annihilation of history and we cannot accept Mircea Eliade's expression "the fear of history"; but we have to permit each element of the universal manifestation to take its hierarchically suitable place.[3]

---

[1] Therefore, it is wrong to consider, as the scientists often do, the various buildings and objects discovered by the archeologists and belonging to lost civilizations, as being just calendars.

[2] See Guénon, **Introduction**, pp. 35 ff. Generally, in a traditional society the chronology is symbolic, referring to the cosmic cycles, and the sacred texts were beyond time, having a non-human origin; however, the teachings were transmitted usually in an oral mode and their written registration was made in a relatively recent epoch: hence the absurdity of trying to find a date for the scriptures. In a recent work about Saint Paul, we saw an intense endeavour to establish a chronology as precise as possible with regard to his life; it is hard to believe that knowing the exact date when the letters were written can help us to understand their message.

[3] See Mircea Eliade, **Le mythe de l'éternel retour**, Gallimard, 1979, pp. 163 ff. From a metaphysical perspective, the Principle is both non-manifestation and manifestation, silence and sound, One and multiple; for this reason in a traditional society there is no "fear of history," in the same way an "eternal return" is absurd ("history repeats itself"); the traditional seer knew very well that the perfect circle is both center and circumference, that is, both immutable principle and changeable world, and a traditional doctrine does not have the goal of saving people from "the fear of history" or the "world's terror," but of reintegrating the world into the eternal principle, "to gather the scattering ones." In a traditional society, man did not live with fear of history, that is, with fear of day-to-day life; on the contrary, the traditional or righteous man celebrated life as a manifestation of the Principle and found in it symbolic supports to help him rise beyond it; on the other hand, the traditional man knew that the "circle" of individual history is only a spire of the universal helix, and did not pay attention, more than necessary, to history and chronology (in comparison to some Gnostics who considered the spire a closed circle). Another Romanian thinker, André Scrima, underlining the difference between the Western and the Eastern Church with regard to history, suggested that the Catholic and Protestant

Mircea A. Tamas

And it is not about inventing an individual method to avoid "the fear of history," artificially imagining a theory of cycles where the historical events and characters gain a non-historical and archetypal value; on the contrary, history (like geography, astronomy, etc.) illustrates, in conformity with the law of correspondence, the supernal truth. As Guénon said, it seems that Christianity lost the symbolic characteristic of the cross, seeing it only as the sign of a historical event[1]; yet, in fact, the two points of view do not exclude each other, and the latter is, somehow, a consequence of the former (Guénon, **Croix**, p. 12). Forced by the heresies,[2] the Christian Church had to insist upon the human nature of Jesus and so, upon His historical and corporeal aspects, forgetting sometimes that Christ is an *avatâra*, and His birth at the winter solstice, at midnight, is the normal descent (Sanskrit *avatarana*) of an *avatâra* through the gate of gods (*dêva-yana*, *Ianua Coeli*).[3] This insistence helped the modern authors to promote a very human Jesus and also a very human Saint Paul.[4]

Churches have contributed, more or less unwittingly, to the opinion which makes the Occident *fons et origo historiae*, since modern history is a Western creation, which spread world-wide. Scrima considered also that Western colonialism is responsible for what is happening today in the Near-East, Israel and the Arabic countries, by forbidding this part of the world to have access to history. In fact, the Occident took advantage of the fact that the Near-West (the Orthodoxy) and the Near-East (Islam) considered history from a traditional point of view, which has nothing to do with some kind of "fear of history" or even with a "refusal of history" (André Scrima, **Duhul sfânt şi unitatea Bisericii**, Ed. Anastasia, 2004, pp. 76-79, in Romanian).
[1] Since the historical cross was the "weapon" that killed Jesus, it is absurd to think that the Christians would praise it, if it had not had a profound symbolic meaning. Therefore, rejecting the cross and then, kissing it, has an initiatory significance, also related to the two Peters, the one before and the one after Pentecost.
[2] We have in view here especially the Docetism (gr. *dokein*, "to seem"), which considered that Jesus only seemed to have a body, that He was not really incarnate. Docetism developed in Gnosticism and Manicheism, then in Bogomilism, taking various forms. Michel Vâlsan had the opinion that, generally, those who talked about Docetism did not really understand it, and from an initiatory point of view there were in Docetism very interesting elements (Michel Vâlsan, **Références islamiques du "Symbolisme de la Croix"**, Études Traditionelles, no. 428, 1971, p. 278).
[3] See Guénon, **Symboles**, pp. 240-241.
[4] The Council of Chalcedon proclaimed: "one and the same Son, our Lord Jesus Christ, perfectly divine and perfectly human, truly God and truly man" (see Paul

Actually, the only type of "terror" that could be taken into consideration is related not to history itself, but to the loss of any correspondence between this one and the superior principles, and so, it does not concern the authentic traditional societies; it can be detected in some incomplete civilizations, like the one of the Aztecs (less spiritual than that of the Toltecs), where an intense obsession with regard to the end of the cycle made them stress the importance of the calendar and of the sacrifices. We also find some traces in the Western medieval society (which did not have a pure intellectual doctrine), the Millennium "fear" being a well-known phenomenon. On the other hand, no "terror" can be found in the profane societies, at least officially, having avoided any allusion to the end of times and to the Wrath of the Gods. It is also the attitude of Noah's contemporaries.

In the **Apocalypse of Paul**, the angel led Saint Paul to Paradise where, among others, he met Noah who said:

Blessed are you, Paul, and blessed am I that have seen you the beloved of the Lord. ... I am Noah that was in the days of the flood: but I say unto you, Paul, that I spent a hundred years making the ark, not putting off the coat which I wore, and I shaved not the hair of mine head. Furthermore I kept continence, not coming near mine own wife. And I besought men at that time, saying: Repent, for a flood of waters comes upon you. But they mocked me and derided my words; and again they said unto me: This is the time of them that would play and sin as much as they will: for God looks not on these things, neither knows what is done of us men, and moreover there is no flood of waters coming upon the world. And they ceased not from their sins until God blotted out all flesh that had the breath of life in it. But know you that God loves one righteous man more than all the world of the wicked. Therefore blessed are you, O Paul, and blessed is the people that has believed by your means. (**Apocryphal NT** 553)[1]

Evdokimov, **L'Orthodoxie**, Desclée de Brouwer, 1979, p. 141). The Fathers of the Church said: "Christ, truly God and truly man... became what we are, to make us become what He is" (Evdokimov 140). In time, the correspondence between the two natures became more and more incomprehensible.

[1] Saint Augustine condemned, like the majority of the Christian authorities, the **Apocalypse of Paul**, as being a fake. It is said that the manuscript was discovered, following a divine sign, in Paul's house, in Tarsus, Cilicia, in a box made of marble,

The apocryphal text is in concert with what we have already presented about Noah; yet we note, on the one hand, Saint Paul's redeeming mission, and on the other hand, the comparison between Noah's contemporaries, full of "historicism," and the "righteous men" who followed Saint Paul's teachings.

We may call "historicism" both the adversity and the lack of understanding which confronted Saint Paul in his apostolic pilgrimage, and an aspect of the same "historicism" can be found in the modern commentaries regarding Saint Paul's function. We remind the authors of these commentaries what Meister Eckhart said: "Nobody can understand or explain Saint Paul's writings if they don't possess the Spirit of Saint Paul's writings and sayings."

As we said at the beginning of this study, Saint Paul was a special and mysterious character, his function in the early years of Christianity generating various reactions; even today these contradictory reactions are still alive, many of them being influenced by the "historicist" point of view; they do not possess the Spirit of Saint Paul's writings, and are of little value. Some critics spoke about the Hellenism brought by Saint Paul, which altered primitive Christianity, and considered that Orphism influenced the passage from the Judaic Christianity to the Hellenistic one, from the historical deed of Jesus to the mystical one, where Saint Paul's teachings were only a translation of the Orphic doctrine. Others, more recently, saw in Saint Paul just a frustrated Jew who became anti-Semitic (*sic*).[1] Thousands of pages were written about this subject, which in many of them was reduced to profane history and to modern mentality; the authors highlighted Saint Paul's unstable and irascible nature, his dispute with the Jerusalem Church, the difference he made between the historical Jesus and the divine

---

buried under the floor, yet this is also, it seems, just an invention. Anyway, in **The Divine Comedy** (**Inferno** II, 28), Dante alluded to Saint Paul's visit to Hell and Paradise, registered in the **Apocalypse of Paul**.

[1] The word "anti-Semitic" is another example of modern abuse with respect to language. In any dictionary, "semite" is defined as "a member of any people speaking a Semitic language as their native tongue. Jews and Arabs are Semites" (**Gage Canadian Dictionary**, Gage Publishing, 1983, p. 1020).

Christ, the fact that he did not know Jesus directly and in person, etc. It is amazing how stubborn the modern authors can be in their search for answers to problems of a divine and sacred order using "historicist" methods, as well as their fear of admitting the sacred perspective, considered by them and their readers as "unscientific." Even more astonishing is the fact that the exponents of "historicism" waste their time on characters belonging to the sacred history: it is impossible to understand why, if they refuse the traditional and super-human point of view, they choose subjects belonging precisely to the traditional and divine domain.

First of all, let us remember what Saint Paul himself declared: "I will not venture to speak of anything except what Christ has accomplished through me in leading the Gentiles to obey God by what I have said and done, by the power of signs and miracles, through the power of the Spirit. So from Jerusalem all the way around to Illyricum, I have fully proclaimed the gospel of Christ" (**Romans** 15:18-19). Such affirmations are constantly repeated in his letters. Saint Paul from the beginning presents himself as: "Paul, a servant of Christ Jesus, called to be an apostle and set apart for the gospel of God. ... Through him and for his name's sake, we received grace and apostleship to call people from among all the Gentiles to the obedience that comes from faith" (**Romans** 1:1, 5, **1 Corinthians** 1:1); "Paul, an apostle, sent not from men nor by man, but by Jesus Christ and God the Father, who raised him from the dead" (**Galatians** 1:1). And Saint Paul specified the regular and indispensable transmission: "For what I received I passed on to you as of first importance: that Christ died for our sins according to the Scriptures, that he was buried, that he was raised on the third day according to the Scriptures, and that he appeared to Peter, and then to the Twelve" (**1 Corinthians** 15:3-5); and his teachings are in concert with the sacred texts and the apostolic doctrine, accepting also the priority of Peter. Are there any reasons to doubt his affirmations? Even some exponents of "historicism" admitted that the doubt is a completely unproductive method (despite what the antitraditionalist Descartes said), and if there are no strong proofs, we have no reasons to doubt, for the sake of doubting, the existing affirmations.[1]

On the other hand, **The New Testament** insists on presenting the apostles' doubts, from Thomas to Peter, including their doubts regarding the resurrection, when the disciples were still in a "historicist" phase[2]; it is a lesson for the future generations, illustrating what it means to be without the Spirit and Gnosis; for this reason, the Fathers of the Church strongly stressed that the Christian tradition has, as essential fundament, Faith, opposing doubts and discursive reasoning.[3]

Saint Paul continued: "I want you to know, brothers, that the gospel I preached is not something that man made up. I did not receive it from any man, nor was I taught it; rather, I received it by revelation [*apocalypseos*] from Jesus Christ" (**Galatians** 1:11-12); "Although I am less than the least of all God's people, this grace was given me: to preach to the Gentiles the unsearchable riches of Christ, and to make plain to everyone the administration of this mystery, which for ages past was kept hidden in God, who created

---

[1] However, if we doubt Saint Paul's sayings, why should we believe the profane authors, who promote this doubt? If we deny Saint Paul, considering him, in comparison to James, "the brother of Jesus," the one who altered primitive Christianity, as some modern authors do, why should we accept James? Why should the texts with regard to James be more credible than Saint Paul's letters? And can we be sure which James we are talking about? This type of "historicism" is purely and simply absurd.

[2] The Templars' initiation alludes to this phase.

[3] Faith is the exoteric aspect of true Gnosis. "And without faith it is impossible to please God, because anyone who comes to him must believe that he exists and that he rewards those who earnestly seek him. By faith Noah, when warned about things not yet seen, in holy fear built an ark to save his family. By his faith he condemned the world and became heir of the righteousness that comes by faith" (**Hebrews** 11:6-7). "Nessuno comunque perfetto per virtù morali e intellettuali, e secondo abito e secondo operazione, si può salvare senza fede" (Dante, **Monarhia**, II, 7): "No one can be saved without faith, no matter how perfectly endowed he might be in the moral and intellectual virtues" (Dante, **Monarchia**, Cambridge Univ. Press, p. 77). In Dante's text there is though a secret meaning, Faith being rather the *Fede Santa*, having a central role for *Fedeli d'Amore*, we note that the initials F. S. can be interpreted as *Fides Sapientia*, the exact translation of the Gnostic *Pistis Sophia* (Guénon, **Ésot. Chrét.**, p. 67).

all things" (**Ephesians** 3:8-9). Saint Paul is openly confessing the intent "to descend" the esoteric teachings into the exoteric domain.[1] "We have not received the spirit of the world but the Spirit which is from God, that we may understand what God has freely given us. This is what we speak, not in words taught us by human wisdom [Gnosticism] but in words taught by the Spirit [Gnosis], expressing spiritual truths in spiritual words. ... But we have the mind of Christ" (**1 Corinthians** 2:12-13, 16). "I have been crucified with Christ and I no longer live, but Christ lives in me. The life I live in the body, I live by faith in the Son of God, who loved me and gave himself for me" (**Galatians** 2:20).

These affirmations are essential. In accordance with them, Saint Paul cannot be measured with the earthly square, but with the heavenly compass; in accordance with them, the individuality of Saint Paul has no importance, the only important things being his illumination and his mission given to him by the divine power; in accordance with them, any attempt to write Saint Paul's biography is doomed to failure, and cannot touch the truth when written from a historical or worldly position; in accordance with them, what we should understand are the profound teachings, the Gnosis transmitted by the Apostle, and not Saul's individual characteristics or the date when the letters were written. For this reason Saint Paul went up to Jerusalem, and met only with Peter and James.

But when God, who set me apart from birth and called me by his grace, was pleased to reveal his Son in me so that I might preach him among the Gentiles, I did not consult any man, nor did I go up to Jerusalem to see those who were apostles before I was, but I went immediately into Arabia and later returned to Damascus. Then after three years, I went up to Jerusalem to get acquainted with Peter and stayed with him fifteen days. I saw none of the other apostles, only James, the Lord's brother. (**Galatians** 1:15-19)

---

[1] We note that here it is not about a differentiation such as Saint Paul – Gentiles – exoteric domain, and Jerusalem Church – Jews – esoteric domain.

This is another important confession. Let us first quote a sacred text: "The angel of the Lord appeared to her and said, «You are sterile and childless, but you are going to conceive and have a son. ... No razor may be used on his head, because the boy is to be a Nazirite, set apart to God from birth»" (**Judges** 13:3-5). The son is Samson, who was what the Judaic tradition called *nazirite*, i.e., "vowed to God"; no razor shall touch a *nazirite*'s head (**Numbers** 6). Samson's mother was barren and the birth of the child was announced by an angel; we remark the similarity with the Christian tradition where Elizabeth was also barren and the angel announced to her the miraculous birth of John the Baptist[1]; moreover, Saint Mary was, not barren, but a virgin, and an angel told her about the birth of an *avatâra*.[2] Saint Paul is also a *nazirite*, as he himself declared, not in the sense of an *avatâra*, like Christ or even Samson to some extent, but obviously with a divine mission. For this reason, he did not ask other people, and his visit to Jerusalem was only for the sake of the exoteric law, to maintain the chain of transmission and to receive in a regular way the mandate from Peter and James.[3] For sure, what Saint Paul wrote in his letters he also communicated to Peter and James, "the brother of Jesus," and they believed him (otherwise they would have expelled Paul).

---

[1] "But the angel said to him: «Do not be afraid, Zechariah; your prayer has been heard. Your wife Elizabeth will bear you a son, and you are to give him the name John. ... He is never to take wine or other fermented drink, and he will be filled with the Holy Spirit even from birth" (**Luke** 1:13-15).

[2] From a symbolic point of view we may consider Jesus of Nazareth as *nazirite*.

[3] Some people were intrigued by this short and exclusivist visit to Jerusalem, considering that normally Paul should have stayed as much as possible in order to find out all the historical details regarding Jesus. In those times, the spreading of information occurred faster and easier than modern scholars imagine, and Paul, who was against the Christians at the beginning, was surely informed of what and whom he persecuted. We are not talking here about a common man, so those who imagine a Paul eager for gossiping and worldly talk, are totally mistaken. Very curious is Saul's first gesture after the illumination: he disappeared in Arabia. Some considered that in Arabia Saint Paul started his mission, which is doubtful, since Peter and James' approval was missing. These three years have rather a pure spiritual meaning.

Saint Paul and Historicism

> Fourteen years later I went up again to Jerusalem, this time with Barnabas. I took Titus along also. I went in response to a revelation and set before them the gospel that I preach among the Gentiles. But I did this privately to those who seemed to be leaders, for fear that I was running or had run my race in vain. ...they saw that I had been entrusted with the task of preaching the gospel to the Gentiles, just as Peter had been to the Jews. For God, who was at work in the ministry of Peter as an apostle to the Jews, was also at work in my ministry as an apostle to the Gentiles. James, Peter and John, those reputed to be pillars, gave me and Barnabas the right hand of fellowship when they recognized the grace given to me. (**Galatians** 2:1-9)

We observe again Saint Paul's concern to keep unbroken the chain of transmission and have the approval of the Christian "pillars"; otherwise, his work would have been an individual one.[1]

Nonetheless, as the letters prove (which otherwise maybe would have not been written), Saint Paul was contested, not only by the Jews who considered him a traitor with respect to the Law,[2] but also by some Judaic Christians of the Jerusalem Church. Doubtless, if these enemies had won, Christianity would have remained for a while a small sect, among many other Judaic sects, probably disappearing after the destruction of the Temple; the Roman Empire would have fallen into chaos and only a flood and another Noah could have come. It is possible that Saint Paul's adversaries were a faction of the Jerusalem Church, thinking that sectarianism was in fashion in those days, a faction more interested in a special type of "historicism." The fact that they took the pains to follow Saint Paul's

---

[1] In the **Acts of the Apostles** it is said that in Asia Minor "some went out from us [the Jerusalem Church] without our authorization and disturbed you, troubling your minds by what they said. So we all agreed to choose some men and send them to you with our dear friends Barnabas and Paul" (**Acts** 15:24-25). And further it is stated that Saint Paul was obeying the regular transmission: "As they traveled from town to town, they delivered the decisions reached by the apostles and elders in Jerusalem for the people to obey" (**Acts** 16:4).

[2] There is nothing abnormal here (taking into consideration that Christ was crucified for the same apparent reasons). We should not forget that any particular tradition believes that it is the Center of the World, rejecting the other forms (of course, exoterically).

tracks, only to undo what the Apostle did, and only to confuse the new Christians, suggests a spiritual blindness.[1]

Regarding the Second Coming of Christ, Saint Paul wrote to the Thessalonians: "and to wait for his Son from heaven, whom he raised from the dead, Jesus, who rescues us from the coming wrath" (**1 Thessalonians** 1:10). This affirmation, like others, has created another problem for Saint Paul. His declaration, taken in a worldly, historicist sense, made the new Christians believe that Paradise was at hand, that they did not have to work anymore or to suffer or to abstain from various pleasures, since Jesus' coming was imminent, and becoming Christians they were already redeemed. As we said, nobody knows when the last hour will be, and what Saint Paul, like Noah, was preaching did not refer to a specific date.[2] "Now, brothers, about times and dates we do not need to write to you, for you know very well that the day of the Lord will come like a thief in the night" (**1 Thessalonians** 5:1-2); "we ask you, brothers, not to become easily unsettled or alarmed by some prophecy, report or letter supposed to have come from us, saying that the day of the Lord has already come" (**2 Thessalonians** 2:2).[3]

Saint Paul was in a delicate position. His letters are full of high spirituality and sacred symbolism and we can ask ourselves how much the people, just christianized, understood from his, sometimes very intellectual, words. We should not be surprised if some of the new Christians accepted his sayings only at a historicist level, having no vocation for divine things. "Don't let anyone deceive you in any way, for that day will not come until the rebellion occurs and the man of lawlessness is revealed, the man doomed to destruction. He will oppose and will exalt himself over everything that is called God or is worshiped, so that he sets himself up in God's temple, proclaiming himself to be God" (**2 Thessalonians** 2:3-4); such a prophecy, more actual than ever, could not be understood by a mind

---

[1] On the contrary, Saint Paul did not go to places where others went before him.
[2] Noah, some traditional data said, tried for 950 years to straighten his folk; so, it did not mean that the flood came immediately after he started to admonish the people.
[3] It is possible that this opinion about the imminent coming of Christ explains, at least partially, the attitude of the Jerusalem Church.

anchored in the common history, and we may assume that then, like today, there was a number, more or less significant, of new Christians who accepted the new doctrine for very individualistic reasons.

For the historians, one of the difficulties with respect to the birth of Christianity was the apparent opposition between Paul and James, "the brother of the Lord," which was translated as an opposition between Judaism and Hellenism.[1] As we stressed, following Guénon, the origin of Christianity was enveloped in obscurity and it was not about external fighting and quarrelling, not about historical events, but about the "descent" of the tradition from the esoteric domain to the exoteric one. If we do not forget this truth, we can read with more profit the documents of primitive Christianity.

Saint Paul did not deny Judaism, and neither did Jesus, since He said, "Do not think that I have come to abolish the Law or the Prophets; I have not come to abolish them but to fulfill them" (**Matthew** 5:17)[2]; in the same way, the Islamic tradition came to accomplish the universal Law, incorporating the Judaic and Christian

---

[1] Some analyzed in details the four Gospels trying to discover how the transition from Judaism to Hellenism occurred; they asked, of course, the question: "why exactly four Gospels?" For the one who studied all the so-called apocryphal and un-canonical Gospels, Acts and Apocalypses, delineated from the profane and historicist point of view, the question has no sense. Everything that should have been told is there, in the **New Testament**.

[2] In the episode regarding the Canaanite woman, Jesus affirmed: "I was sent only to the lost sheep of Israel," and added: "It is not right to take the children's bread and toss it to their dogs" (**Matthew** 15:24, 26), alluding to "Do not give dogs what is sacred; do not throw your pearls to pigs. If you do, they may trample them under their feet, and then turn and tear you to pieces (**Matthew** 7:6). Yet the Canaanite woman replied: "Yes, Lord," she said, "but even the dogs eat the crumbs that fall from their masters' table." "Then Jesus answered, «Woman, you have great faith! Your request is granted.» And her daughter was healed from that very hour." We note also the Christian expression, "Only in his hometown and in his own house is a prophet without honor" (**Matthew** 13:57). And: "These twelve Jesus sent out with the following instructions: «Do not go among the Gentiles or enter any town of the Samaritans. Go rather to the lost sheep of Israel»" (**Matthew** 10:5-6); yet, after resurrection, Jesus urged the Apostles: "Therefore go and make disciples of all nations, baptizing them in the name of the Father and of the Son and of the Holy Spirit" (**Matthew** 28:19).

traditions' prophets, including Jesus. The apparent dispute is a misunderstanding. Both the Christian and Islamic traditions were destined, in conformity to the divine plan, to make sacred the nations which otherwise would have fallen into secular profanity; they had the mission to renovate the world establishing external spiritual centers for self-determining traditions, even though related. On the other hand, the Judaic tradition, by definition, could not accept the change. Any secondary orthodox tradition, especially in the exoteric domain, thinks about itself as the only keeper of the truth and the sole heir of the primordial Tradition; one of its basic rules is the immutability and the unaltered conservation of the initial traditional data.[1]

Initially, Buddha did not want to change the "Brahmanic" tradition, even though Buddhism appeared as a revolt of the royal caste, mainly because of the epigones; he came to renovate and regenerate the old tradition, and the Brahmans declared Buddhism a heterodox doctrine and made it disappear from India. Similarly, Judaism could not be but outraged by the idea of a renovation,

---

[1] Boccaccio's story told in his **The Decameron**, with regard to the dispute between Saladin and the Jew Melchizedek is well-known. Saladin asked Melchizedek (who alludes to the Lord of the World) to decide which one of the three religions (Judaic, Islamic and Christian) is the true one. Melchizedek answered with a parable: "there once was a rich man and among the precious gems in his treasure he owned a ring – the most beautiful and priceless of rings [the primordial Tradition]. He wanted the ring to stand out from the rest and remain in the family as a permanent bequest; so he issued instructions that whichever of his children was found possessed of the ring as part of his inheritance, he was the one to be considered his heir. This ring passed from hand to hand from one heir to the next [the uninterrupted transmission] and eventually came into the possession of a man who had three sons. He loved them equally and could not for the life of him decide which of them to leave it to. He had a good goldsmith secretly make another two rings identical with the first. At his death each son was secretly given his own ring. When their father was dead, they each claimed the title of son and heir [the claim of each secondary tradition to be the only true one]. Now the rings, as they discovered, were identical to such a degree, there was no way of telling which one was the original, and the question of which of the three was the true heir to their father remained unresolved. It still is" (Oxford Univ. Press, 1993, p. 41, tr. Guido Waldman). We may note that Boccaccio belonged to the initiatory organization *Fedeli d'Amore*, and his story suggests that from an esoteric perspective this problem was resolved, or even better, never existed.

completion or surpassing of Moses' Law, a Law that brought salvation to the Jewish people, in comparison to Noah who brought them the flood.[1]

The Jews accepted James with his Jerusalem Church, which functioned between 40 and 60 A.D., since Judaism considered it a "sect" as were many others of those times (some of them with an apocalyptic characteristic, others with a militant and political one)[2]; some sources even presented James as a member of the Judaic sacerdotalism of the Temple. Eusebius also said that James, "the brother of the Lord," "was holy from his mother's womb," "he drank no wine or strong drink, nor did he eat meat. No razor came near his head," that is, he was a *nazirite*, like Samson and Saint Paul. Even though, it seems that James made some compromises with the "historicist" aspect of the Old Law, and could be connected to the fact that he did not leave Jerusalem, contrary to the other Apostles; in comparison to James, Saint Paul is situated in an order beyond the "historic" plane.[3]

If some modern authors, belonging to historicism, exaggerated James' role and tried with wrath to eliminate Saint Paul who trespassed the Judaic Law, others, including some traditionalists, could not accept the idea of Christianity derived from Judaic

---

[1] Even if the Judaic tradition considers that, after the flood, Noah received from God the seven commandments, a precursor of Moses' Law.

[2] Eusebius in his **History** showed that James was nicknamed the Just and was the first bishop of the Jerusalem Church; of course, his nickname suggests a connection with Qumran and the Essenes' sect; the Jerusalem Church and the Qumran community had some common traits, both disappearing almost at the same time, after the destruction of the Temple. Eusebius said also that James was generally named "the brother of Jesus" and he received the Jerusalem bishopric directly from Jesus; however, Saint Paul named him the pillar of the Church. Clement of Alexandria considered James an Apostle (even though James did not leave Jerusalem) and a participant in Gnosis: "and really pertaining to the true Gnosis, such as were James, Peter, John, Paul" (VI, 8) (vol. II, p. 343).

[3] Saint Paul was accused, by those who chased him in Asia Minor to undo what he did ("certain men came from James," **Galatians** 2:12), of being a false apostle, an impostor, a satanic instrument, etc. The common modern man may ask the question, how did the Fathers of the Church know to choose between the wheat and the darnel, to worship Paul and reject the Gnostics? This question has no answer only from a "historicist" perspective.

esotericism[1]; in fact, to those the concept, expressed by Guénon, of a descent of Christian tradition from esotericism to exotericism, which implies that the Christian way was initially "simplement un ésotérisme" (*sic*), looked insulting. The expression "just an esotericism" uttered by a traditionalist is representative with respect to the position of those who intervene in questions of an initiatory order that are beyond their expertise. It is indeed impossible for an exponent of historicism, traditionalist or not, to understand that not the spiritual is contained by the corporeal, but the corporeal by the spiritual, and the greater is not contained by the lesser, but the lesser by the greater. Regarding the esoteric domain, even if, *principially*, it is compatible with any exoteric domain, from an initiatory point of view there must be an attachment to a traditional exotericism

---

[1] See, besides Vâlsan's sayings, Charles-André Gilis, **Introduction à l'enseignement et au mystère de René Guénon**, Les Éd. de l'Oeuvre, 1985. Gilis, in a chapter of his book, *Les origines de la religion chrétienne* ("The Origins of the Christian Religion") considers three consecutive stages: 1. Jesus' messianic and terrestrial mission inside Judaism; 2. Christian Judaism after Jesus' death; 3. Roman Christianity (the "church" founded by Saint Peter). For the first two stages Gilis preferred to use "Christian revelation" instead of "Christianity," since Jesus' terrestrial mission was situated within the Judaic tradition. Gilis, following Vâlsan, considered Christian revelation as a new initiatory path within Judaism; Jesus attempted to "transform" the Judaic tradition to fit his universal mission. The second stage, Gilis continued, was an intermediary one, and it was voluntarily obscured by the third phase (Roman Christianity); therefore, in Saint Paul and Saint Luke's writings, Saint Mary and her spiritual function were almost ignored. The passage from the second to the third stage was operated not by Christ, but by the Holy Spirit, who inspired the disciples to establish an independent religion, an exoteric tradition, different and outside Judaism; and Gilis insisted in stressing more than once that Christianity, as an autonomous traditional form, separated from Judaism, was founded by the Holy Spirit, not by Christ; also, its descent into the exoteric domain occurred at the same time as its separation from the Judaic tradition. Pentecost was the moment when the third stage started. Yet we have to add that, even if Gilis mentions – briefly – Saint Paul's influence in the foundation of the Roman Christianity, he does not specify that in this particular case not the Holy Spirit, but Christ brought illumination to Saul. As we stressed a few pages earlier, Saint Paul himself confessed: "Paul, an apostle, sent not from men nor by man, but by Jesus Christ and God the Father, who raised him from the dead" (**Galatians** 1:1); "I want you to know, brothers, that the gospel I preached is not something that man made up. I did not receive it from any man, nor was I taught it; rather, I received it by revelation [*apocalypseos*] from Jesus Christ" (**Galatians** 1:11-12).

(Guénon, **Initiation**, p. 73); and there is no doubt that Christianity was born from the womb of the Judaic tradition.[1] Some people supposed that Christianity originated from "the Christian universal center, beyond all distinctions." We see again a very unlucky expression, used frequently by the exponents of historicism, who imagined, one after another, a Gallic universal center, a Dacian universal center, a North-German one, etc. The author who talked so easily about a "Christian universal center" was full of confusion; even if he had a "historicist" mentality, he tried to introduce traditional notions, but for him Christianity appeared to be a *Deus ex machina*. Hoping to contest René Guénon, he affirmed that, in fact, the incarnated Word founded Christianity and not an initiatory anonymous organization or some invisible superior character, since the Essenes for example could not save the decayed world.

First of all, a universal Center does not have an epithet, or a name, since otherwise it would not be universal.[2] Second, the manifestation of Tradition into the world follows very precise rules and laws, which do not contravene the possible and are very real, even positive. As in our world a square circle is impossible, in the same way the operation of the divine presence does not occur as a *Deus ex machina*, but in an established community, which, in the case of Christianity, was an esoteric one. Eventually, the validation of Christianity obeyed the same sacred rules: that is the meaning of the three Magi (Guénon, **Roi**, p. 36),[3] as well as Melchizedek's

---

[1] We should remember the episode of the Canaanite woman. Some tried to explain that in a Judaic ambiance it would have been impossible to deify Christ, and only a Greco-Roman ambiance allowed this; here is another error of a historicist interpretation that reverses the normal order. Some said that if Christianity had been a Judaic esotericism, it would have been impossible for it to save the decayed Western world, which proves again that for many the term "esotericism" means nothing.

[2] About the symbolism of the center see Guénon, **Roi**, and our **Agarttha, the Invisible Center**, Rose-Cross Books, 2003.

[3] Guénon wrote: "The homage offered to Christ when he was born, in the three worlds that are their domains, by the authentic exponents of the primordial tradition [the Magi], is at the same time, we stress, the proof of the perfect orthodoxy of Christianity with respect to this one [the primordial Tradition]." This homage underlines as well the Christian mission to become an autonomous tradition.

significance, who represents the Lord of the World.¹ René Guénon stressed that "the Judeo-Christian tradition distinguishes two priesthoods, one «in the order of Aaron,» the other «in the order of Melchizedek»; and the latter is superior, in the same way Melchizedek is greater than Abraham (from whom was derived the tribe of Levi, and consequently the family of Aaron)." And Guénon added in a note that we could say, as a result, that the New Law (Covenant) is superior to the Old Law (Guénon, **Roi**, p. 51).²

We will come back with regard to this important subject. For now we should note that Melchizedek represents the Lord of the World in the Judeo-Christian tradition (Guénon, **Roi**, p. 48):

> Then Melchizedek king of Salem brought out bread and wine. He was priest of God Most High, and he blessed [*berakoth*] Abram, saying, «Blessed be Abram by God Most High [*El Elion*], Creator of heaven and earth. And blessed be God Most High, who delivered your enemies into your hand.» Then Abram gave him a tenth of everything. (**Genesis** 14:18-20)³

Saint Paul wrote:

---

¹ René Guénon wrote in a letter to Vasile Lovinescu (May 1935): "On ne peut pas dire qu'une tradition soit «primordiale» par là même qu'elle est fondée par un Avatâra, car il ne peut y avoir, par définition même, qu'une tradition primordiale pour un Manvantara. D'ailleurs, une telle tradition (qu'il s'agisse du Christianisme aussi bien que de toute autre) est nécessairement constituée dans un milieu déterminé, dont les conditions influent sur la forme qu'elle revêt, et qui este toujours en relation avec les formes traditionnelles préexistants ; la «descente» directe de l'Esprit (c'est là le sens propre du mot Avatâra) n'y change rien. Il y a là quelque chose qu'on pourrait en somme comparer à la naissance d'un être individuel, qui est déterminé assurément par l'influence du «Soi», mais aussi par les conditions du milieu où elle se produit (ce qui peut être représenté géométriquement par l'intersection d'une verticale et d'une horizontale)."

² Saint Paul said about Christ: "For it is declared: «You are a priest forever, in the order of Melchizedek.» ... Because of this oath, Jesus has become the guarantee of a better covenant" (**Hebrews** 7:17-22). "A better covenant" refers to the fact that, though born in the Judaic ambiance, Christianity had the mission to save the Western world, which needed a new Law.

³ In the Gnostic text **Pistis Sophia**, Melchizedek is, like Manu of the Hindu tradition, "The Great Receiver of the eternal Light" (Guénon, **Roi**, p. 52).

Saint Paul and Historicism

This Melchizedek was king of Salem and priest of God Most High. He met Abraham returning from the defeat of the kings and blessed him, and Abraham gave him a tenth of everything. First, his name means «king of righteousness»; then also, «king of Salem» means «king of peace.» Without father or mother, without genealogy, without beginning of days or end of life, like the Son of God he remains a priest forever. (**Hebrews** 7:1-3)

Melki-Zedeq is presented as the divine Orphan, as the Stranger, who surpassed the individual order, being of a non-human nature; he is superior to Abraham, since Saint Paul affirmed:

Just think how great he was: Even the patriarch Abraham gave him a tenth of the plunder! Now the law requires the descendants of Levi who become priests to collect a tenth from the people, that is, their brothers, even though their brothers are descended from Abraham. This man, however, did not trace his descent from Levi, yet he collected a tenth from Abraham and blessed him who had the promises. And without doubt the lesser person is blessed by the greater. (**Hebrews** 7:4-7)

And Abraham accepted this superiority, paying the "tenth"; the Judeo-Christian tradition distinguished, as we mentioned, two priesthoods, one "in the order of Aaron," the other "in the order of Melchizedek," the latter being, as Saint Paul said, superior; and Saint Paul added: "In the one case, the tenth is collected by men who die; but in the other case, by him who is declared to be living." And "Because of this oath, Jesus has become the guarantee of a better covenant" (**Hebrews** 7:22), since He is "priest forever, in the order of Melchizedek," being born not from the sacerdotal tribe of Levi, but from the royal tribe of Judah (Guénon, **Roi**, pp. 49 ff.).[1]

---

[1] The residence of Melchizedek, Guénon wrote, could be Agarttha. Of course, it is not about a "Christian universal center," but about the supreme Center; also the Lord of the World's transmission is of an initiatory order and not an exoteric one, hence its superiority.

CHAPTER XVI

GREAT TRIAD AND HOLY TRINITY

SAINT PAUL DESCRIBED MELCHIZEDEK as "Without father or mother, without genealogy, without beginning of days or end of life," which referred, of course, not to his social and historic status, but to his sacred function as Lord of the World. Melchizedek is an orphan and a stranger in a divine sense; he is not from this world and does not obey time and history. Saint Paul added that he was "like the Son of God"; Christ, invested by the three Magi, was also Lord of the World.

To understand the profound significance of these things, we should note some "historicist" authors' affirmation that in the Gospel we find hate for Jesus' family and hence for James, "the brother of Jesus"; this affirmation is not only absurd, but also a divider.[1] It is related to ignorance and an individualist perspective, which, however, was also present in Jesus' time. "If anyone comes to Me and does not hate his father and mother, his wife and children, his brothers and sisters, yes, even his own life, he cannot be My

---

[1] Historicism can only extend the characteristics of the modern mentality upon all societies and civilizations, alive or dead, traditional or profane. This fundamental error of trying to explain sacred gestures and writings using modern judgment makes historicism consider the Gospels as some common texts, similar to newspapers and magazines, which hide insinuations and hints, gossip and envy, calumny and sensational facts.

disciple (**Luke** 14:26; **Matthew** 10:37).[1] "Now Jesus' mother and brothers came to see him, but they were not able to get near him because of the crowd. Someone told him, «Your mother and brothers are standing outside, wanting to see you.» He replied, «My mother and brothers are those who hear God's word and put it into practice.»" (**Luke** 8:19-21). No doubt, the Evangelic text refers not to a worldly hate, but to a spiritual way, following the model of Melchizedek; nowadays, the great spiritual master Ramana Maharshi stated the same idea.

There were many discussions with regard to Jesus' "family." Some assumed that James was his step-brother, having a different mother, even a different father, or that he was a "cousin"[2]; there was also the confusion between James, "the brother of Jesus" (James the Lesser) and James, John's brother (James the Greater). However, the Christian texts abounded with such confusions regarding the names, like in the case of Mary, being almost impossible for the "historicist" scholars to identify the many Marys of the Gospels. In the same way, there were many characters named Judah, Simon, Herod, Matthew, etc. Saint Peter was called either Simon, or Cephas, and sometimes it is hard to say who that Cephas was.

The problem is that the **New Testament** is a sacred text, which cannot be treated like a profane book, of history for example.[3] Its logic is closer to that of the fairy tales, myths and other symbolic narratives.[4] As a sacred text, it accepts multiple levels of meanings, the historic one being very exterior. Necessarily, as any other sacred

---

[1] We note that it is not about rejecting only the family, but also one's own life, a historical and worldly life, that is, the ego and the individual aspect. We would not have insisted upon this obvious meaning, if we had not seen prominent scholars completely lost in historicism.

[2] In the apocryphal texts, Joseph appears as an old man, with grown up children, being forced to accept Mary into his house.

[3] And the truth of a sacred text is not a subject of doubt or investigation. Ananda K. Coomaraswamy wrote: "Anything for example, that is true for Plato, the Gospels, Islam, Hinduism and Taoism, I am prepared to regard as true, and rather for me to understand than to question" (Coom., **Letters**, p. 15).

[4] We understand the fairy tale and the myth not as "stories for children" but as initiatory and traditional vestiges. See **Sacred Kernel**.

writing, it describes a sacred history, a sacred geography, sacred gestures that can be easily found in other authentic traditions. In the Hindu tradition, Aditi is Daksha's daughter, and Daksha is Aditi's son; Sûrya, the sun, is both Aditi's husband and son. Dante stated: "Oh nobilissimo ed eccellentissimo cuore che ne la sposa de lo Imperadore del cielo s'intende, e non solamente sposa, ma suora e figlia dilettissima!"[1] And the examples could go on and on. The confusion of names and kinship, found in the **New Testament**, represents rather a protective veil against historicism and means a willing participation in the obscuration of the early years of Christianity. What we really read as history is a sacred story, an absolute myth that corresponds to all the levels of the universal manifestation, and therefore, it has its projection in the human history. We are not talking here about a simple man, called Jesus, whose historic facts were, afterwards, mythicized and deified; but about a "descent" (*avatarana*) of the divine into the world, and hence, the historical and worldly events are reflections of the divine order, obeying the immutable law of correspondence for the various degrees of Reality.

Therefore, the massacre of the children ordered by Herod, who was afraid that Jesus would take his throne, is not only a historical event, but also an archetypal one, since it is found in various traditions, including the fairy tales,[2] and is related to the doctrine of the cosmic cycles, as well as to the initiatory process, the old king being the dragon. Jesus' escape to Egypt is also a symbolic, not only

---

[1] Dante Aligheri, **Convivio**, Biblioteca Universale Rizzoli, 1999, p. 196, III, 12, 14; "O most noble and most excellent heart which is intent upon the spouse of the Emperor of the heavens – and not the spouse only, but sister and daughter best beloved!" (Dante, **The Banquet**, Anma Libri, 1989, p. 110); and also: "Vergine madre, figlia del tuo Figlio" ("Virgin mother, daughter of your Son") (**Paradiso**, XXXIII, 1).

[2] For example, in the Greek mythology, Acrisius was afraid that his new-born grandson, Perseus, would kill and replace him; similarly, Laios was scared that his son, Oedipus, would kill him and take his reign. For the same reason, the Pharaoh ordered, when Moses was born, that all the new-born children to be killed.

historical event.¹ The same universal and symbolic or mythical meaning transmit both the birth of John the Baptist and of Jesus, separated by an interval of exactly six months: the former was born at the summer solstice, the latter at the winter solstice (since He was an *avatâra*); John the Baptist is the worldly reflection of Jesus, the two of them being similar to the twins from the fairy tales, representing the two halves of the World Egg. However, John the Evangelist, who was "the most beloved" of the disciples, replaced Christ, to enhance the similitude and to allow two Saint Johns, each one related to a solar gate.² There is no coincidence that Jesus was born in Bethlehem, a name that means "House of Bread," spiritual bread.³ There is as well a mythical dimension in the fact that at Jesus' birth [the beginning], an ox and a donkey guarded the new-born in the manger, the former at his right, the latter at his left, in the same way as at His crucifixion [the end], "Two robbers were crucified with him, one [the good one] on his right and one [the bad one] on his

---

¹ "The voyage to Egypt" is primary a symbolic expression, often signifying an initiatory degree that any neophyte has to achieve, including the exponents of priesthood and royalty. Plutarch (**De Iside et Osiride**, Univ. of Wales Press, 1970, p. 131) affirmed that the seers of Greece, Solon and Thales, Plato, Eudoxus and Pythagoras visited Egypt to learn its mysteries and teachings. Diodorus Siculus (**Bibliotheca Historica**, I, 23, 2, IV, 25, 3) wrote about Orpheus' journey to Egypt, where he "perfected his knowledge and became among the Greeks the most learned in mysteries and theology." "The Egyptian priests," Diodorus added, "narrated that Orpheus, Musaios, Melampus, Daedalus, Homer, Lycurg of Sparta and Solon of Athena went to Egypt" (I, 96, 2). Also Strabo wrote that Zalmoxis traveled to Egypt. Eventually, we should remember that Abraham, Moses and Joseph took the same voyage.

² John was the only Apostle who witnessed the crucifixion and to him Jesus entrusted his mother. "When Jesus saw his mother there, and the disciple whom he loved standing nearby, he said to his mother, «Dear woman, here is your son,» and to the disciple, «Here is your mother.»" (**John** 19:26-27); thus Jesus indicated that John was his substitute.

³ Beith-Lehem was called previously Beith-El, "House of God," and is a representation of the Center of the World (Guénon, **Roi**, p. 77). "Jesus said to them, «I tell you the truth, it is not Moses who has given you the bread from heaven, but it is my Father who gives you the true bread from heaven. For the bread of God is he who comes down from heaven and gives life to the world.»" (**John** 6:32-33).

left" (**Matthew** 27:38).[1] Saint Mary is a virgin because she corresponds to Shakti from the Hindu tradition and she is mother of *avatâra*, which charges her with a universal meaning (even if the Christian theology has a particular perspective with regard to the Blessed Virgin). Not by chance Jesus said: "Let the little children come to me, and do not hinder them, for the kingdom of God belongs to such as these. I tell you the truth, anyone who will not receive the kingdom of God like a little child will never enter it" (**Luke** 18:16, **Matthew** 19:14).[2] And it is no coincidence that Jesus chose twelve disciples; in the same way Aditi has twelve sons, the Greeks and Germans have twelve gods, the Zodiac has twelve signs, and there were twelve tribes of Israel.[3] For the same universal and symbolic reason, there are four Evangelists, since there are four cardinal points; and their emblems (man or virgin, lion, bull, eagle) are found in the Judaic and Chaldean traditions. Eventually, Jesus died on the cross because he is the Universal Man, integrating the six spatial directions, that is, the whole universe.[4]

---

[1] We may note that the ox and the donkey are not mentioned in the Gospels. There is though a hint in the **Bible**: "The ox knows his master, the donkey his owner's manger" (**Isaiah** 1:3). In the **Acts of Pilate** the two malefactors are called Dysmas and Gestas (**Apocryphal NT**, p. 103). René Guénon indicated the symbolism hidden here, and we can see that even apparently insignificant details have more than historical meaning.

[2] In the Hindu tradition, the seer, *sannyâsi*, has three attributes: *bâlya, pânditya* and *mauna*. The last two refer to Gnosis and solitude. The first one, *bâlya*, "child-like," means that the *sannyâsi* realizes a status comparable in purity, undifferentiated simplicity, and unconsciousness, to the status of a child (*bala*). See **Sacred Kernel**.

[3] Guénon wrote: "We can see in the number of twelve Apostles, a sign, among many others, of the perfect conformity between Christianity and the primordial Tradition (**Roi**, p. 39).

[4] The Christian theologians considered (and still do) the myth a simple fable and a human invention, rather than a sacred and "non-human" mystery; therefore, they rejected the "mythical" nature of the Gospels and we were also criticized for our perspective here. The Church, fighting various "heresies," had to stress continuously the human nature of Jesus and the "historicity" of his life. Yet our point of view is above the theological perception and the differences between particular traditions. Mircea Eliade, in an article called **Survivals and Camouflages of Myths**, affirmed: "The earliest Christian theologians took the word [myth] in the sense that had become current some centuries earlier in the Greco-Roman world, i.e., «fable, fiction, lie.» They therefore refused to see a «mythical» figure in Jesus and a «myth» in the

Therefore, what could stir mainly interest for Jesus' "family" does not refer to common history, but to the sacred. In the Far-Eastern tradition, the Holy Family is called the Great Triad, composed of Heaven (Father), Man (Emperor, Son, Mediator) and Earth (Mother). The Great Triad is the *principial* Family: "What constitutes **Yi Jing**, what makes it perfect and colossal, is the fact that it contains Dao of Heaven, Dao of Man, and Dao of Earth. It reunites the three efficient causes and each one is double, that is six in total." This triad, found in various other traditions, cannot be an equivalent of the Christian Holy Trinity. René Guénon explained that, if in the Great Triad the first and the last terms are somehow symmetrical and complementary, in the Holy Trinity, the second term derives from the first one and the third (corresponding to the second term of the Great Triad) is not the son of the other two. In fact, Guénon wrote:

«the operations of the Holy Spirit» with regard to Christ's birth correspond to the Heavenly Father's activity of presence (in the Hindu tradition Purusha)[1]; the Virgin, on the other hand, is a perfect image of Prakriti, designated by the Hindu tradition as Earth; with regard to Christ himself, he obviously is identical to the Universal Man.[2] Hence, if we want to find a concordance, we should say, using Christian theology's terms, that Triad does not concern the generation of the Word *ad intra*, which is included in the concept of the Trinity, but the generation *ad extra*, that is, in conformity with the Hindu tradition, the birth of Avatâra in the manifested world.[3]

Messianic drama. From the second century on, Christian theologians had to defend the historicity of Jesus against the Docetists and the Gnostics as well as against the pagan philosophers" (**Symbolism, the Sacred, the Arts**, Crossroad, 1990, p. 32).

[1] The Holy Spirit corresponds to the stork that brings the new-born. The stork, like the swan, heron, etc., is the "feathered serpent," unifying Heaven and Earth, and alluding to *avatâra* as Universal Man and Mediator. In the Christian tradition it is said: "Therefore be as shrewd as snakes and as innocent as doves" (**Matthew** 10:16), and Clement of Alexandria wrote about the Gnostic that he unifies the serpent and the dove (VII, 13); the dove is an emblem of the Holy Spirit.

[2] René Guénon wrote in the footnote: "We stress again, related to this, that we do not want to deny the «historical» aspect of some events as such, but, on the contrary, we consider the historical facts as symbols of a superior reality, and only for this reason they are interesting for us."

[3] René Guénon, **La Grande Triade**, Gallimard, 1980, pp. 20-22.

The Blessed Virgin, as mother of *avatâra*, Guénon stated,[1] corresponds rather to Shakti of the Hindu tradition, Prakriti being her "terrestrial" projection; Shakti, like Shekinah of the Judaic Kabbalah, is the divine Maiden. *Mâyâ-Shakti* is the superior aspect of the Virgin, woman and mother within the Principle, and "she is first of all, the Principle's Shakti, the same and one with the Principle, its «maternal» aspect" (Guénon, **Hind.**, p. 102); *Mâyâ-Prakriti* is the inferior aspect, woman and mother within the world, "and she is also, with regard to her birth in the manifested world, Prakriti."

If we try though to find a triad similar to the Far-Eastern one, that is, a Holy Family, we have to heed the triplet Joseph, Mary and Jesus. Saint Mary represents in this case passive Perfection, *Kun* in the Far-Eastern tradition, the feminine principle as Shakti, the divine Maiden, symbol of Gnosis and Sophia, of (divine) Love and Mercy, mother of *avatâra*. Christ is obviously the Universal Man, the Son of Heaven, and the Emperor. And we still have Joseph… Joseph should correspond to the celestial Father, yet he is the earthly mortal father, he is what the initiatory scenario calls "the inferior (or unworthy) husband," token of the ego, of the psycho-corporeal individuality, which must be transformed, destroyed and recovered during the initiatory process, the real, immortal husband, token of the Self, of the Spirit, being the Holy Spirit, the lightning of the Far-Eastern tradition, who produces the miracle of the virgin becoming mother.[2] Consequently, we find another triad, "the family triangle" (Holy Spirit, Mary, Joseph), which, in fact, can be reduced to a couple, the duality Holy Spirit – Saint Mary, in the very moment when the "unworthy husband" is annihilated.[3]

---

[1] See, for example, **Mâyâ** (**Études sur l'hindouisme**, Éd. Trad., 1979, p. 101).

[2] Of course the Holy Spirit is not the celestial Father, but his Activity, therefore the equivalent of the lightning. We should stress that our hermeneutical endeavour does not want to insult Joseph's status (as defined inside the Christian religion), but to bring it to a "mythical" level.

[3] In **Yi Jing**, hexagram no. 41, *Suên*, it is said: "When three people journey together, their number decreases by one and then each man finds a companion. Indeed, in the universe everything exists as couples; one and two, by their contrast they are the origin of the birth of all beings; three is therefore too much and must decrease."

Great Triad and Holy Trinity

The theme of a "family triangle" is typically initiatory. In the tradition of the ancient Greeks, for example, Hercules, one of the greatest initiatory heroes, has as parents a triad composed by Zeus and Alcmene, plus the "inferior husband," Amphitryon; the "triangle" is obvious since Zeus took Amphitryon's appearance.[1] Zeus took Amphitryon's place, the Holy Spirit took Joseph's place, in this mode *avatâra*, the Son of Heaven can be incorporated into the world. In the **Gospel of Matthew** is written: "While the Pharisees were gathered together, Jesus asked them, «What do you think about the Christ? Whose son is he?» «The son of David,» they replied. He said to them, «How is it then that David, speaking by the Spirit, calls him 'Lord'? If then David calls him 'Lord,' how can he be his son?»" (22:41-46). In one of David's psalms (110) it is said indeed: "The Lord says to my Lord: «Sit at my right hand until I make your enemies a footstool for your feet. ... You are a priest forever, in the order of Melchizedek.»" Christ Himself warned that His Father is not the earthly David, but God and the Holy Spirit.

The fact that David was named instead of Joseph is not random, since David himself is an illustration of a minor *avatâra*. Moreover, David was part of a "family triangle," and he took the place of Bathsheba's husband, Uriah, becoming the father of the wisest king, Solomon.

The existence of the "family triangle" in Christianity does not compensate for the lack of a Great Triad. For this reason the Gnostics strongly promoted one. There is the possibility that some esoteric data saved by the Gnostics contained such a Triad, yet it is even more probable that they were influenced by other traditions. Guénon wrote:

---

[1] The superior and the inferior "husbands" appear as twins: the immortal-mortal pair. Another famous example is the pair Ulysses – Penelope. Penelope is not only the patron of spiritual realization, but also she is the cosmological activity of God. It is said that Penelope was weaving a shroud for Laertes (**Odyssey** II, 95). Each night she was undoing the work she did during the day. Weaving the web symbolizes the production of the World, the *Fiat Lux*, while dissolving the web during the night means the absorption of the Cosmos back into the Principle. Penelope is the divine Maiden and the suitors represent our lowest passions and appetites, the "inferior husband."

It is true that some Christian sects, more or less orthodox, claimed to make the Holy Spirit feminine, and so, they wanted to qualify him as Mother; yet is very probable that they were influenced by a false assimilation of the Trinity with a triad, which shows that such errors are not exclusively modern. Moreover, the feminine characteristic attributed to the Holy Spirit is in disaccord with his role, essentially masculine and «paternal,» in the birth of Christ. (Guénon, **Triade**, pp. 20-21)[1]

The Holy Trinity is a "masculine" triad. Of course, there is an extraordinary veneration for the Blessed Virgin, but she is excluded from the sign of the cross and from the fundamental Christian trinity. The persistence of underlining the "masculine" aspect does not refer, evidently, to what historicism would call misogyny and inequality between man and woman. It is a question of sacred symbolism. The Christian tradition had the mission of regenerating the world, or better said, a part of it. In all the orthodox traditions, the superior pole is masculine and the inferior one feminine, since the earth supports and the heaven covers.[2] One of the characteristics of the end of times is amnesia regarding the masculine pole and the feminization of the existence. Such a "feminization" takes place today in the modern world and, even if apparently we might think that the women, in their struggle to be equal with men, have become too masculine, in fact, exactly the opposite is true, because "feminization" must be understood first of all in relation with *yin* of the Far-Eastern tradition. When Christianity became an exoteric tradition, one of its first operations was to reinstate the reign of *yang*, that is, of the masculine pole; taking into consideration the

---

[1] Coomaraswamy compared the Holy Trinity with the Three Lights of the Hindu tradition: a Father in heaven [Âditya], a Son of Fire on earth (from where he rises to heaven) [Agni, the eternal *avatâra*] and the common Breath [Vâyu]; even more precisely the Three Lights are identical with the three Christs of Gnosticism (Ananda K. Coomaraswamy, **Autorité Spirituelle et Pouvoir Temporel, dans la perspective indienne du gouvernement**, Archè, 1985, p. 69).

[2] It is interesting that this symbolism can be found in Masonry; yet many masons, who execute the related gesture, have no clue about its real meaning and universality.

unfavorable moment of the present cycle, this reinstating had to be well underlined.[1]

Nonetheless, to complete spiritually the Western Christian society, it was necessary to make allowance for its more royal than sacerdotal characteristic. And here intervened the role of the Virgin, as a saintly supplement of the Holy Trinity. The super-veneration of the Blessed Virgin corresponded to the *bhakti* aspect, very important for the Western world; this aspect had to be taken into consideration and guided toward a sacred target. In fact, Christian esotericism gave Saint Mary the supreme dimension, establishing a close relation between Love and Knowledge, that is, between *bhakti-mârga* and *jnâna-marga*.[2]

In the Hindu tradition, in the Judaic Kabbalah, in Greek mythology and in fairy tales, the initiatory stories present a supreme endeavour, the finding of the divine Maiden. The Virgin (even if, historically, she doesn't appear as such) has various names: Helen of Troy, Beatrice, Pistis Sophia, Madonna Intelligenza, Sîtâ, Ariadne, etc., symbolizing absolute Knowledge, divine Light and heavenly Love.

Dante's love for Beatrice, for example, is an initiatory way; this way (*dao*, in Chinese tradition, *marga*, in Hindu tradition), developed under the sign of *rajas*, corresponds to the royal caste, *Kshatriya*, for whom the Virgin had a most high significance, as proved by different initiatory organizations of the Western Middle Ages, like *Fedeli d'Amore* and the Templars. When Beatrice resumes her throne

---

[1] In the Gnostic text, **The Gospel of Thomas**, at the end, Peter requested: "Let Mary leave us, for women are not worthy of [eternal] life." And Jesus replied: "I myself shall lead her in order to make her male, so that she too may become a living spirit resembling you males. For every woman who will make herself male will enter the kingdom of heaven" (**Nag Hammadi** 138). Yet here it is not about misogyny and not even about the superiority of man in the world. The change of the female into male refers to the "reversing of the poles," applied microcosmical; it means that the woman who accomplished a spiritual realization reaches the superior pole, which is symbolically masculine.

[2] This supreme Love is identical with the divine Mercy. Schuon noted that in Islam Saint Mary is considered a symbol of Mercy (*Rahmah*) (**Forme**, p. 114).

in the third tier of the Mystic Rose,[1] a bright triad is unveiled to us: Virgin Mary at the top, Eve in the second tier, and in the third tier, beside Beatrice, Rachel (symbolizing contemplation); St. Bernard de Clairvaux, servant of the Blessed Mary and the patron of the Templars, is Dante's supreme guide who facilitates the vision of the Virgin.

Luigi Valli, in an important work about Dante,[2] focused on *Donna Sapienza*, the Sophia.[3] He stressed that Dante identified Beatrice with active Intelligence or Wisdom (p. 82).[4] Such symbolism, he wrote, can be found, much earlier, among the Gnostics, who had introduced in their doctrine the feminine characters Ennoia and Sophia, but also in the **Bible**, where Rachel had the same significance (pp. 86, 91). However, René Guénon, praising Valli's study and his extraordinary documentation, underlined the author's lack of an "initiatory mentality" and his rather "historicist" point of view; "it is not enough «to make history,» and, besides, did the people of the Middle Ages make «history for the sake of history»?" (**Ésot. Chrét.**, pp. 55-56). Chivalry, to adjust to the human mentality, Guénon wrote, had a preponderant feminine principle, the *Madonna*. This feminine aspect of Divinity can be found in India, where it is called Shakti, an equivalent, in some respects, of the Hebrew Shekinah. The function of the feminine principle, Guénon said, appears also in Catholic exotericism, due to the importance of the Virgin. The Mystic Rose from St. Mary's litanies is of initiatory origins and is motivated by the connection to Wisdom (Sophia) and to Shekinah (**Ésot. Chrét.**, p. 63).[5]

---

[1] See Dante, **The Divine Comedy, Paradiso**, XXX-XXXII.
[2] Luigi Valli, **Il linguaggio segreto di Dante e dei "Fedeli d'Amore,"** Roma, "Optima," 1928.
[3] Valli's work has as *motto* Compagni's verses: "L'amorosa Madonna Intelligenza,/ Che fa nell'alma la sua residenza,/ Che co la sua bieltà m'ha 'nnamorato" (p. 79).
[4] Guénon wrote: "«The active Intellect,» represented by *Madonna*, is «the celestial Ray,» which constitutes the link between God and man and which leads the human being to God: it is the Hindu *Buddhi*" (Guénon, **Ésot. Chrét**, p. 63).
[5] As an old Syriac manuscript shows, the Blessed Virgin as Shakti is carrying Christ inside her oval form, which, from one point of view, suggests that she is the "outer"

For the Christian Church, the Saintly Virgin is, first of all, *Theotokos*. The "paternity" of the Heavenly Father, corresponds to the "maternity" of the Mother of God, *Theotokos*, in the human domain (Evdokimov 149). That is why Guénon considered the symbolism of the Black Virgin as referring in the first place to Prakriti. He wrote: "We have to understand that the Christian tradition, not considering separately the «maternal» aspect of the Principle, has to adopt, at least explicitly, in respect to the conception about Theotokos, only the second point of view we just indicated" (Guénon, **Hind.**, p. 103). The two points of view are: the Virgin is considered as Shakti (*Natura naturans*, the Black Virgin as Supernal Darkness), and the Virgin is considered as Prakriti (*Natura naturata*, the Black Virgin as *materia prima*). The Orthodox Church, even if it considered the Virgin as *Theotokos*, that is, as Prakriti, praised even more the Virgin as Saint Sophia, that is, as Shakti, as the Black Virgin of the Super-luminous Darkness. Guénon and Coomaraswamy stressed that Shakti, the divine "art" of the Principle, is identical to Wisdom, Sophia, in which case she is the celestial mother of the *avatâra* (Guénon, **Hind.**, p. 102). And only as Saint Sophia, is the Virgin equivalent to Jesus, in the same way Shekinah is to the Messiah.[1]

Sophia and Christ is the "inner" Sophia. Almost all of the famous statues of the Black Virgin present the Mother of God with her Son in her lap. It is interesting that, usually, the authors who studied the symbolism of the Black Virgin, in connection with the sacred meaning of the colour black, disregarded completely the fact that the child Jesus is also black. We developed this aspect in our work **Din negura de vremi**, Mirton & Rose-Cross Books, 2003 (in Romanian, the chapter **The Black Child**). We may note though St. Bernard's words: "What He [Christ] appears is corporeal and death. One is seen and the other is believed. Bodily sense declares that He is black. Faith proves that He is fair and beautiful. He is black only to the eyes of the foolish. For to the minds of the faithful He is altogether beautiful. He is black but beautiful – black in the opinion of Herod, beautiful in the confession of the thief and in the faith of the centurion" (Saint Bernard, **On the Love of God**, Mission Press, 1943, p. 114); St. Bernard expressed here the exoteric and common meaning of the colour black.

[1] Yet the common Christian exoteric viewpoint considers the Blessed Virgin as an aspect of Prakriti within the world. St. Bernard stated: "Beyond all doubt the Mother of the Lord was holy before she was born. ... I, for my part, believe that she received a more ample blessing which not only sanctified her in the womb, but also preserved

Luigi Valli assumed that the medieval initiatory organization *Fedeli d'Amore* (which venerated *Madonna Intelligenza*) derived from the ancient Gnosticism, and he compared Beatrice to Pistis Sophia; moreover, Valli suggested that Rose-Cross was as well of Gnostic origin, and Gnostic ideas can be found in Dante's work (pp. 421-2).[1]

Sophia played an important role in the Gnostic sects; the most famous Gnostic text, **Pistis Sophia**, states that *Pistis Sophia*, that is, "The Faith in Wisdom," had her home in the 13th Æ*on*, between Light and the World, yet a deceitful light tempted her down, into the obscure world, where she became a prisoner. Jesus' mission was to descend and save her, bringing Sophia back home to the 13th Æ*on*.

No doubt, the Gnostics highlighted, sometimes to the maximum, the function of the feminine principle. Without understanding the Church's perspective of promoting the Holy Trinity better than a Great Triad, the Gnostics expressed their disaccord and sectarianism by strongly endorsing the feminine aspect. Again, they are at the

---

her thereafter free from sin throughout her life [St. Bernard was also saying: "And who would venture to say that a child filled with the Holy Spirit still remained a child of wrath...?"]. ... I say that she conceived of the Holy Spirit, not that she herself was conceived of the Holy Spirit; that she gave birth as a virgin, not that she was born of a virgin. ... It remains that she was sanctified after her conception, when she was already in the womb" (St. Bernard of Clairvaux, **Seen through his Selected Letters**, Henry Regnery Company, 1953, pp. 203-206). Therefore, the well-known (black) statues representing St. Anne, St. Mary and Jesus as a triad should be interpreted with caution. On the other hand, some legends suggested that, after St. Joachim died, St. Anne married Cleophas, by whom she became the mother of Mary Jacobé; after the death of Cleophas she is said to have married Salomas, to whom she bore Mary Salomé. In other words, St. Anne – following these legends – is the Mother of The Three Marys (see the next chapter) and from a mythical point of view accepts a vaster symbolism. And we should mention here the old belief (the 4th century) that St. Anne was also a virgin and conceived without the participation of a man, an error condemned by the Church (and by St. Bernard).

[1] Guénon, correcting Valli, wrote: "the real Rose-Cross were not at all of «Gnostic origin»" (**Ésot. Chrét.**, p. 57). We note that in the article **La Gnose et la Franc-Maçonnerie**, of 1910, signed Palingénius, it is said: "modern Masonry as we know it today is the result of a partial fusion of Rose-Cross (which conserved the Gnostic doctrine of the Medieval times) with the old guilds of masons and builders" (**Franc-Maçonnerie**, II, p. 260), yet the author was thinking to the authentic Gnosis, since he added: "we insist that the Masonic initiation, like any other initiation, aims to obtain the integral Knowledge, which is the Gnosis, in the true sense of the word."

edge between truth and falsehood, because Saint Mary, as we saw, is a fundamental element in the Christian exotericism and esotericism.

Marcos, one of Valentinus' disciples, claimed that the "naked" truth descended upon him in the shape of a woman: "I would like to show you the Truth, herself; I brought her down, so you can see her without a veil and you can comprehend her beauty" (Pagels 20). The symbolism of the Truth as a nude woman is not something heretical and belongs to the esoteric domain, being known in various traditions; that is the hidden meaning of Acteon's punishment, after he surprised Diana naked, and the blinding of Teiresias, who saw Pallas-Athena naked, bathing in the Hippocrene fountain. Unfortunately, Marcos exposed and used this symbolism for his individual goals.[1]

---

[1] Saint Paul confessed: I "was caught up to the third heaven" (**2 Corinthians** 12:2-4); "the third heaven" is the heaven of Venus, the goddess related to Cyprus Island, and it is believed that Saint Paul, *Lo Vas d'elezione* (**Acts** 9:15), founded the first church in Cyprus. *Fedeli d'Amore* had seven degrees, corresponding to the initiatory ladder, "the third heaven" meaning the third degree of the hierarchy, the degree where salvation (*saluto*) was obtained, a ritual celebrated on the day of "All Saints" (Guénon, **Ésot. Chrét.**, p. 59). Guénon noted also, as Luigi Valli did, when he suggested the link between Dante and the Templars (p. 425), that the Templars' headquarters was Cyprus (at Limassol), a direct connection existing between Cyprus, Venus, "the third heaven" and the symbolism of copper (Guénon, **Ésot. Chrét.**, p. 68). In his initiatory journey, on the fifth day, Christian Rosenkreutz reaches a subterranean vault, illuminated by a huge precious stone; a triangular tomb, crowned by a *copper* vessel, hid the beautiful goddess Venus, and Rosenkreutz, opening a *copper* trap-door, could contemplate Venus naked (Jean-Valentin Andréae, **Les Noces Chymiques de Christian Rosencreutz**, Éd. Traditionnelles, 1994). The nude Venus is equivalent to the unveiled Isis, representing "sacred love"; she is Shakti, the divine Maiden, and the mother of the *avatâra*. The nude Venus is the "naked Truth," and that is the hidden meaning of Titian's famous painting "Sacred and Profane Love" (Schuon was, it seems, inspired by this symbolism). We may note that, like Acteon and Teiresias, Christian Rosenkreutz would have been punished, because he saw Venus naked, but he escaped punishment fulfilling the initiation (only profane people cannot see the Truth). On the other hand, the Greek Mysteries, and also the Western initiations, imposed nudity on the neophyte; Plotinus wrote (I, 6, 7): "to those that approach the Holy Celebrations of the Mysteries, there are appointed purifications and the laying aside of the garments worn before, and the entry in nakedness" (Plotinus, **The Six Enneads**, Encyclopaedia Britannica, 1952, p. 24).

Simon Magus, who proclaimed himself the supreme power of God, declared a prostitute, Helen, the Wisdom descended from Heaven, Ennoia, Mother of All; he suggested a pair Father-Mother (Brahma-Shakti), their union bringing universal salvation (Leisegang 49). In the Valentinian doctrine, the pairs multiply exuberantly: Bythos and Sophia generate Christ. Christ and the Holy Spirit (who is feminine, sister and wife) engender Jesus (Leisegang 27). In **The Gospel of Thomas**, Jesus has, besides his terrestrial parents (Joseph and Mary), divine parents: The Father of the Truth and the Holy Spirit (feminine)[1]; in **The Gospel of Philip**, the Holy Spirit is the Mother of All.[2]

Mary Magdalene had a special position in the Gnostic doctrines. The same way Simon Magus had the prostitute Helen as a partner, Jesus was associated with Mary Magdalene. **The Gospel of Philip** says: "And the companion of the [Savior] is Mary Magdalene. Jesus loved her more than [all] the disciples [and used to] kiss her often on her [mouth]" (63. 32, **Nag Hammadi** 148). In another Gnostic text, **The Gospel of Mary**, Mary Magdalene is the first one to have the vision of the risen Christ, and to her Jesus talks first. Yet also in the **New Testament**, it is written that

Mary Magdalene and the other Mary went to look at the tomb. There was a violent earthquake, for an angel of the Lord came down from heaven and, going to the tomb, rolled back the stone and sat on it. His appearance was like lightning, and his clothes were white as snow... The angel said to the women, «Do not be afraid, for I know that you are looking for Jesus, who was crucified. He is not here; he has risen, just as he said. Come and see the place where he lay. Then go quickly and tell his disciples: "He has risen from the dead and is going ahead of you into Galilee. There you will see him." Now I have told you.» So the women hurried away from the tomb, afraid yet filled with joy, and ran to tell his disciples. (**Matthew** 28:1-10)[3]

---

[1] See **The Secret Teachings of Jesus**, Vintage Books, 1986.
[2] **The Gospel of Philip** states: "Some said, «Mary conceived by the Holy Spirit.» They are in error. They do not know what they are saying. When did a woman ever conceive by a woman?" (**Nag Hammadi** 143). **The Gospel According to the Hebrews** affirms: "My mother the Holy Spirit" (**Apocryphal NT** 2). Obviously, the Gnostics' perspective was a Great Triad and not a Holy Trinity.
[3] We find the same story in **Luke** (24:1-10).

"When Jesus rose early on the first day of the week, he appeared first to Mary Magdalene, out of whom he had driven seven demons. She went and told those who had been with him and who were mourning and weeping. When they heard that Jesus was alive and that she had seen him, they did not believe it" (**Mark** 16:9-11). And St. John remarks the same thing: the risen Jesus appeared to Mary Magdalene first (**John** 20:1-18).

If in the **New Testament** we don't find any disputes, besides the one referring to the Apostles' mistrust, the Gnostics suggest a rivalry between Mary Magdalene and Peter; the latter had the following reaction to Mary's words: "Did he really speak with a woman without our knowledge and not openly? Are we to turn about and all listen to her? Did he prefer her to us?" (**The Gospel of Mary**, 17:18, **Nag Hammadi** 526).

We should not be surprised by this rivalry, because the Gnostics opposed, very often, the official Church, and we understand from Saint Paul's letters that Christianity, just born, had as its main enemy, not Roman and Judaic persecutions, but sectarianism, rivalry and disagreements within itself. This sectarianism was, of course, generated by humanistic and individualistic views, and from this perspective we will never understand why Jesus appeared to Mary Magdalene first. However, the statement that Mary Magdalene was the prostitute who washed Jesus' feet and dried them with her hair (**Luke** 7:44) has no other base but the fact that this event was followed in **The Gospel of Luke** by the first mention of Mary Magdalene, together with the twelve disciples, "After this, Jesus traveled about from one town and village to another, proclaiming the good news of the kingdom of God. The Twelve were with him, and also some women who had been cured of evil spirits and diseases: Mary (called Magdalene) from whom seven demons had come out" (**Luke** 8:1-3).

CAPITOLUL XVII

THE THREE MARYS

WHO IS, IN FACT, MARY MAGDALENE? is the logical question that immediately surfaces in our minds. The Gospels contain statements such as: "Near the cross of Jesus stood his mother, his mother's sister, Mary the wife of Clopas [Cleophas], and Mary Magdalene" (**John** 19:25); "Among them were Mary Magdalene, Mary the mother of James and Joses, and the mother of Zebedee's sons" (**Matthew** 27:56); "After the Sabbath, at dawn on the first day of the week, Mary Magdalene and the other Mary went to look at the tomb" (**Matthew** 28:1); "Some women were watching from a distance. Among them were Mary Magdalene, Mary the mother of James the younger and of Joses, and Salome" (**Mark** 15:40). Consequently, the question should be reformulated thus: "Who, in fact, is Mary?" since many Marys surrounded and accompanied Jesus.

It is interesting that, as there are two James, James the Greater (Zebedee's son) and James the Lesser (Jesus' "brother"), the same way the Christian Church celebrates two Marys: Saint Mary the Greater and Saint Mary the Lesser. The difference is, compared to James, that here there are not two different Marys, but one and only, the Blessed Virgin, Saint Mary the Greater marking *the Assumption* of the Saint Virgin (August 15th) and Saint Mary the Lesser marking her *Nativity* (September 8th). Such a partition of the Virgin into two Marys, as well as the multitude of Marys in the Gospels, have nothing to do with a "historicist" point of view (which cannot

The Three Marys

function without concrete data and for which the multiplication of Mary creates an irremediable confusion), but belongs to the sacred science of the traditional symbols. In respect to this science, the multitude of Marys represents just aspects or attributes of the unique feminine principle, which, in its turn, is not different from the Supreme Principle.

The partition of the feminine principle into two aspects can be found in various traditions. In the Hindu tradition, the Principle's divine spouse is not only Shakti (in heaven), but also Prakriti (on earth). In the Judaic Kabbalah, the Bride or *Matrona* is, both, the higher Shekinah and the lower Shekinah. The Moon, writes Guénon, is, at the same time, *Janua Coeli* and *Janua Inferni*, Diana and Hecate, corresponding to the solstitial doors.[1] In the same way, Mary the Greater corresponds to heaven, where the Saint Virgin rises (*the Assumption*), and Mary the Lesser to earth, and so Christian tradition transmits, even if in a veiled manner, the same meanings as any other orthodox tradition; more than that, this symbolism illustrates the Evangelic adage "on earth as it is in heaven" (**Matthew 6:10**).[2]

---

[1] Guénon, **Dante**, p. 22. In **Vâjasanêyi Samhitâ**, the Night (*râtrî*) and the Day (*ahas*) are the wives of Indra, the Sun, and they are also the mothers of Buddha, Mahâ-vîra, or Krishna (in Buddha's case, for example, the queen Mâyâdevî is his immortal mother, and his aunt, the second wife of king Shuddhodana, is the mortal mother). Also in the Hindu tradition, Sanjnâ, Twashtri's daughter and the Sun's wife, being incapable of resisting the solar fire, hired Chhâyâ in her place (in Sanskrit, *chhâyâ* means "shadow," "optical illusion" and "copy"). In Greek mythology, Ixion, in love with Hera, was deceived like the Sun was, and he gets, instead of the supreme goddess, her "shadow," a cloud, Nephele. In the Judaic tradition, Moses has two mothers (in fact three: a corporeal one, an intermediary one who nurses him, and, eventually, the divine virgin, the Pharaoh's daughter); Abraham has two wives, Sarah and Hagar; also in the Judaic tradition, the twelve sons of Jacob have two double mothers (the sisters-wives Lea – the active way, and Rachel – the contemplative way, and their two maids).

[2] Meister Eckhart said: "The Virgin Mary, before becoming Mother of God in her humanity, was Mother of God in her divinity, and the birth in heaven is illustrated by the birth of God as human being" (quoted in Jean Hani, **La Vierge Noire et le mystère marial**, Guy Trédaniel, 1995, p. 112). Meister Eckhart said also about Christ, "that his birth from a spiritual Mary was much more joyful than that from a corporeal Mary" (quoted in Coomaraswamy, **Autorité Spirituelle**, p. 57). The

In the **Bible**, the partition into "heaven" and "earth" ("the world above" and "the world below") is stated from the beginning: "And God said, «Let there be an expanse between the waters (*hammayim*) to separate water from water (*mayim lamayim*).» So God made the expanse and separated the water under the expanse from the water above it. And it was so. God called the expanse «sky»" (**Genesis 1: 6-8**).[1] The symbolism of waters as Universal Possibility was well explained by René Guénon and is common to different traditions. The Babylonian cosmogony, recorded in the **Enuma Elish**, starts with: "When in the height heaven was not named,/ And the earth beneath did not yet bear a name,/ And the primeval Apsu, who begat them,/ And chaos, Tiamat, the mother of them both/ Their waters were mingled together..."; yet another translation goes like this:

When there was no heaven, no earth, no height, no depth, no name, when Apsu was alone, the sweet water, the first begetter; and Tiamat the bitter water, and that return to the womb, her Mummu, when there were no gods. When sweet and bitter mingled together, no reed was plaited no rushes muddied the water, the gods were nameless, natureless, futureless, then from Apsu and Tiamat in the waters gods were created...

The freshwaters or sweet waters stand for Apsu, the abyss, a masculine principle; the saltwaters of the seas or the bitter waters represent Tiamat, the feminine principle. In the Judaic Kabbalah,

---

Gospel of Philip affirmed that "Adam came into being from two virgins, from the spirit and from the virgin earth" (**Nag Hammadi** 152); on the other hand, it underlines the importance of One: "Christ, therefore, was born from a virgin to rectify the fall which occurred in the beginning" (this Gnostic text, contrary to others, insists on the one-and-only origin of the duality).

[1] The **Bible** starts with "In the beginning God created the heavens and the earth," yet the translation is not a faithful one; for example, "God" is in fact "Gods" (Hebrew *elôhîm*) and "heavens" (plural) refer to "waters" (*sâmayim*); we have to distinguish between "waters" (*mayim*) and "sea" (*yam*) or "seas" (*yam-mîm*). See William R. Harper, **Introductory Hebrew Method and Manual**, American Publication Society of Hebrew, Chicago, 1886.

The Three Marys

Malkuth (the lower Shekinah)[1] is "the reservoir where the waters coming from the supernal river [the higher, celestial river] mingle together,"[2] and we can assume that the celestial river originates from a supernal reservoir (the higher Shekinah).[3] The bitter and sweet waters of the Babylonian cosmogony could be compared to the two aspects of *Malkuth*, but also to the episode of **Exodus** (15:23-25): "When they came to Marah, they could not drink its water because it was bitter [*marah*].[4] That is why the place is called Marah... Then Moses cried out to the Lord, and the Lord showed him a piece of wood. He threw it into the water, and the water became sweet." Some authors regard the name Mary (Miryam or Mariam) derived from *mar-yam*, "bitter sea"; even if etymologically it seems less than probable, from a symbolic perspective it makes a lot of sense, considering what we just said. We discover two Marys: a bitter one (the Virgin without the *avatâra*, barren)[5] and a sweet one (the Virgin as mother of *avatâra*).[6] In fact, the sweet Mary (the freshwaters)

---

[1] Another equivalent of *Malkuth* is *Sabbath*, which refers to the idea of "peace"; the Arabic term *Sakînah* signifies the Great Peace, corresponding perfectly to *Pax Profunda* of Rose-Cross (Guénon, **Roi**, pp. 24, 54).

[2] Paul Vulliaud, **La Kabbale juive**, Émile Nourry Éd., 1923, I, p. 509; see also Guénon, **Roi**, p. 55.

[3] The moon has two aspects (Diana and Hecate), the same as Shekinah, the "divine presence," has: "There is a Shekinah called «handmaid,» and there is a Shekinah called «the daughter of the king»" (**Zohar** II, 94 b, vol. III, p. 283); "Nor is to be thought that the body which harbours the daughter of the king shall be sold into the power of earthly crowns of defilement... Which is the body of the King's daughter? Metatron; and this same body is identical with the handmaid of the Shekinah." The handmaid is the lower Shekinah; the King's daughter is the higher Shekinah.

[4] It is curious that in Latin, a similar word, *amarus*, also means "bitter."

[5] She is equivalent to Sarah, Hannah – Samson's mother (1 **Samuel** 1:6), and Elizabeth, John the Baptist's mother (**Luke** 1:7); Mary "the bitter" is also comparable to the "sad" Ariadne. We should recall also the following fragment from **Numbers**: "Then the priest shall put the woman under oath and say to her, «If no other man has slept with you and you have not gone astray and become impure while married to your husband, may this bitter water that brings a curse not harm you»" (5:19).

[6] This one is equivalent to the "joyful" Ariadne. On the other hand, it would be interesting to refer to Ananda Coomaraswamy's studies regarding the emptied and barren dragon (after the sacrifice) and the full one (before the sacrifice); also we may observe the correspondence with the new and the full moon.

represents Shakti and the bitter Mary (the saltwaters) is an equivalent of Prakriti.

Conversely, there is also a three-way partition, like, for example, in the case of the three Wise Men. The Magi are the regents of the Three Worlds, which in the Hindu tradition are symbolized as Earth (corresponding, in microcosms, to *Corpus*), Atmosphere (the intermediary realm, *Anima*) and Heaven (*Spiritus*),[1] and in Dante's work as: *Inferno, Purgatorio* and *Paradiso*. A three-way partition can be found in the Judaic Kabbalah: "These are the three supreme Names, which «no eye hath seen, apart from thee, God» (**Isa.** LXIV, 8)" (**Zohar**, II, 97 b)[2]; "The *beth* has two parallel lines and a third joining them. What do these signify? One for heaven, one for earth, and one for the Holy One, blessed be He, who unites and receives them... These represent three supernal and closely connected holy lights" (**Zohar**, III, 36 a).[3] These three invisible lights suggest a striking similarity with the three (invisible) roots of the "Inverted Tree." Yet, even in the domain of the *sephiroth* we can distinguish this configuration "light upon light." The first three *sephiroth* (*Kether, Hokhmah* and *Binah*) compose *Arikh Anpin* ("the longer face," similar to Mary the Greater) and correspond to the three heavenly lights (*tri rocani*), mentioned by Shri Aurobindo in his works.[4] The other seven *sephiroth* compose *Ze'eir Anpin* ("the shorter face," similar to Mary the Lesser).[5] The letters *Aleph, Yod* and *Nun* symbolize the three supernal lights and they constitute the word *Ain*; in

---

[1] Here the earth and the heaven represent Worlds and not the two Poles, masculine (Heaven, Purusha) and feminine (Earth, Prakriti).
[2] Vol. III, p. 294.
[3] Vol. IV, pp. 394-5. This doesn't exclude the two-way partition: "If one lamp is placed above another and the lower one is lit, the smoke as it ascends kindles the upper one also" (**Zohar**, III, 35 b).
[4] Some traditions suggest that, complementary to the three *gunas* (masculine) of Prakriti, there are three lights (feminine) of Purusha. The two triads should be compared to **Yi Jing**'s trigrams *Qian* and *Kun*. Also, in the early Christian Church two trinities were considered, one superior and invisible, the other inferior and visible; see **Les Mystères des lettres grecques**, by Apa Seba (assumed to be a hermit of the 5th century), in **Science Sacrée**, no. 5-6, 2004, p. 111.
[5] See Gershom Scholem, **Kabbalah**, Meridian Book, 1978, p. 141.

consequence, *Arikh Anpin* means the Non-Being (*Ain*), the invisible face, God as Being not yet manifested (before the creation of the "six days"); *Ze'eir Anpin* signifies the visible, revealed face, the six days of the Creation and the *Sabbath*.

Light upon light upon light. It represents the altar of the fire, in three degrees, belonging to the Vedic sacrifice, *agnihotra*, where there is built an altar of five bricks, in three degrees. The sacrifice, as **Maitrâyanîya Up**. unveils, symbolizes a more profound one, an inner sacrifice, the sacrificer erecting the altar within himself, when he decides to leave this world and become a *sannyasin*. Through *agnihotra* is kindled the flame in Ishtar's heart (as a Babylonian hymn says); *jîvâtmâ* becomes fire that consumes *jîva* revealing *âtmâ*, the upper light, in its splendour.

The laying of the altar of the fire by the ancients was a brahman-sacrifice. Therefore the sacrificer, while laying these fires, must think upon them as the âtman. ... The fire [Self] which, abiding in the heart-lotus, eats food is the same as the fire which, abiding in the sky, the solar fire [Brahma], eats all creatures for its food. For this lotus is âkâsha. The four regions and the four intermediate regions constitute its leaves. ... Brahma has two forms, an embodied form and a disembodied one. The embodied form is the untrue form; the disembodied form is the True, it is Brahman, it is Light.[1] The Light is the Sun. The Sun is OM. That became the Self. This Self separated himself into three. OM has three mâtrâs. Through these three mâtrâs all this is woven on Brahman, warp and woof. The world was at first unuttered. Prajâpati, who is the Truth, having performed tapas, uttered one after the other Bhûr! Bhuvar! Swar! These three mâtrâs are the essence of Prajâpati's body. Swar is the head, bhuvar the navel, and bhûr the feet, the sun the eye of this body... The Eye is Prajâpati-Truth.[2]

---

[1] We note the partition into two; here is presented a metaphysical perspective, the supreme Principle as non-manifestation and manifestation. It is possible though to apply this symbolism to Christ as divine (disembodied) and human (embodied).

[2] See **La Maitrâyanîya Upanishad**, Fayard, 1973 (tr. Jean Varenne) and **The Maitrâyanîya Upanishad**, Mouton & Co., 1962 (tr. J. A. B. van Buitenen). Prajâpati is equivalent to the Hebrew *Adam Kadmon* (the synthesis of the *sephiroth*) and to the Islamic Universal Man (*al-insân al-kâmil*).

The three Lights could be, consequently, related to the Three Worlds. In Greek mythology, Theseus had three luminous wives (sometimes considered sisters): Ariadne ("the pure one"), Phaedra ("the radiant, beaming one") and Aigle ("the shining, luminous one").[1] Various groups of three maidens are often present in Greek myths. On a cameo we see the three Charites perched between a bull's horns (above the bull are also seven stars),[2] the triplet of maidens being an "explication" (in Nicholas of Cusa's view of the word) of the one-and-only Virgin; the bull is not any bull, but "the noble Bull" symbolizing Dionysus.[3] The Greeks deemed also that the three Horae represented the three phases of the moon (the moon waxing, full and waning) and probably the same three-way partition of the moon was recognized in Crete, where Minos (Pasiphaë's husband) sacrificed to the three Charites (Harrison, **Themis**, pp. 189, 192, 389)[4]; it is acceptable to think that Ariadne, Phaedra and Aigle are, in the same way, aspects of the one-and-only lunar Virgin. Yet in the Greek tradition, besides the three Horae, Charites and Moirae, the symbolism directly connected to the moon is the one of the triple Hecate, the queen of the Three Worlds: Selene (Heaven), Artemis (Earth) and Persephone or Hecate (Hell); Hecate was described as having three heads or faces, which were associated to the phases of the moon.

Expressing the Three Lights as the three phases of the moon has the important advantage of suggesting that, in fact, the triplet is One, and only from an exterior point of view appears multiple. On the other hand, the Three Lights could be related to the sun, moon and

---

[1] Ariadne's mother, Pasiphaë, was the Sun's daughter and also "shining." Theseus' mother, Aethra, the virgin loved by Poseidon, was, similarly, "the luminous one." Ariadne, on the other hand, has two aspects: the "bitter" one and the "sweet," joyful one (when she received Dionysus' love), the two forms corresponding to the solstitial doors of the lunar god Janus.
[2] Jane Ellen Harrison, **Themis**, Merlin Press, 1989, pp. 205-6.
[3] Dionysus is sometimes represented as a bull, having an important function in the *Mysteries*; the bull's horns bear lunar symbolism.
[4] Apollodorus, **The Library of Greek Mythology**, Coronado Press, 1975, p. 86, III, 210. Orpheus also has considered the triple maidens as the phases of the moon.

stars as described in the fairy tales,[1] but even then we are told that these three lights are equivalent to the three fairies (or swans) manifesting themselves at the summer solstice.[2]

We read in **The Book of Revelation**: "A great and wondrous sign appeared in heaven: a woman clothed with the sun, with the moon under her feet and a crown of twelve stars on her head. She was pregnant and cried out in pain as she was about to give birth" (12:1-2). The Christian tradition applied this apocalyptical image, partially, to the Virgin Mary, who was pictured standing or sitting (on a throne) on a lunar crescent, identified with the moon.[3] Sometimes, in these illustrations, a cross replaced the Virgin and a "historicist" explanation supposed that it represented a token of the Christians' victory against the Turks. In fact, the meaning belongs to the domain of sacred symbolism.[4] It is important also to understand that, even

---

[1] The same Lights are present in the Masonic Lodge.

[2] In the Hindu tradition, the Three Universal Lights are: Agni, Vâyu and Aditya, each one governing a World. "The three primordial lights fertilize the worlds" (**Rig Vêda** VII, 33, 7); "The powerful bull with three faces is the husband, who fertilizes the eternal dawns" (**Rig Vêda** III, 56, 3); see Coom., **Autorité**, p. 67. Regarding the solstitial (solar) doors, it is interesting that the janitor is a lunar god, Janus. The symbolism of the triple Hecate appears stressed in Shakespeare's **A Midsummer Night's Dream**, and we may note that the events of the play take place at summer solstice (see **Sacred Kernel**).

[3] Obviously, in all these cases we have mentioned, the maiden represents the light of *Gnosis*, of the invisible and uncreated energies, of the divine presence, and it would be a fundamental error to identify her with the physical moon; in the same way the moon and the sun symbolize higher realities, the virgin corresponds to these realities. We can see a statue of the Blessed Mary standing on the lunar crescent above the door of Saint John church, in Parma, Italy.

[4] A pillar having the cross on top of the lunar crescent can be seen in the Austrian city of Klagenfurt; the same symbol appears on top of the tower of an old wooden Orthodox church in Transylvania. In Alchemy, we find the Blessed Virgin sitting in the lunar crescent and nourishing the Child (Michael Maier, **Symbola aureae mensae**, Frankfurt, 1617), Christ being the "philosophical stone" (see Gareth Roberts, **The Mirror of Alchemy**, Univ. of Toronto Press, 1994, p. 80). We may note that the lunar crescent crowns the head of the Egyptian god Thoth. Sometimes, the lunar crescent holds the Pentagram, as it appears in the Islamic tradition (**Le Voile D'Isis, Tradition Islamique**, no. 176-177, 1934, p. 327). There is the suggestion that one Gnostic sect merged Jesus with Orpheus: an engraved ring stone shows a character crucified on a cross and above that a lunar crescent and seven stars (probable the Pleiades); an adjacent inscription mentions *Orpheus Bachicos* (André

though Saint Mary is associated with the moon, implicitly she, as in **The Book of Revelation**, is also related to the sun and the stars.[1]

The lunar crescent is the symbolic equivalent of the cup (or vessel) (Guénon, **Symboles**, p. 45); the cup signifies also Christ's heart (solar), and the sacred meaning of the Holy Grail is well-known (Guénon, **Symboles**, p. 39). Coomaraswamy wrote: "Usually, the Grail Cup is identified to the Moon (Soma); in fact, the moon (soma) is nourishment for the Sun, who receives and assimilates it, this food corresponding to the one found in Buddha's begging vessel, this vessel being, like the sun, the Grail Cup."[2] There is, as we see, a continuous *hierogamos* between the sun and the moon and we shouldn't be surprised that the Virgin, symbolizing the supreme Sophia, appears as a lunar Maiden.[3] Coomaraswamy also wrote:

> King Soma is a victim: down here, Agni is the eater, Soma the food; above there, the Sun is the eater and the Moon his food[4]; when the eater and the food (*adya, purodâsha*, the sacrifice cake) are united, we talk about the eater and not about the food. ... It is a wedding consummated in the night before the rising of the new moon... There are inseparable connections between initiation, wedding, death and digestive assimilation; ... there are many terms used in the texts, related to the unification of the multiple in One,

---

Boulanger, **Orphee, rapports de l'orphisme et du christianisme**, F. Rieder et cie, 1925).

[1] Let us observe that Joseph compared his family to the sun, moon and stars (**Genesis** 37:9). The famous painting of Saint Mary of Guadalupe shows the Virgin standing on the lunar crescent radiating solar light and dressed in a cloak full of stars. The legend says that, in 1531, Saint Mary appeared to Juan Diego, a 55 year-old Mexican (Aztec), and she gave him the mysterious painting. It is remarkable that almost at the same time, in 1519, Saint Mary standing on the lunar crescent appeared to Jean de Baume la Cotignac, in Provence, France. Cotignac became an important place of pilgrimage, as did Guadalupe (the church is close to Mexico City).

[2] Ananda K. Coomaraswamy, **La Doctrine du Sacrifice**, Dervy-Livres, 1978, p. 127.

[3] In the Hindu tradition, Damayanti, miraculously born, with the help of a *brahmana*, represents the divine Maiden. She is described as a luminous being, a pearl, a lightning, and especially as the moon; she is compared to the full moon that drives away the darkness, to the lunar crescent, to the moon among the clouds, to the chaste Rohinî, the lunar god's favorite wife.

[4] See **The Śatapatha Brâhmana**, Motilal Banarsidass Publishers, Delhi, 1995, part IV, p. 398 and part V, p. 16 (X, 6, 2, 1-3, XI, 1, 6, 19).

which imply at the same time death and wedding, such, for example: *api-i*, *êko bhû*, *sambhû*, *samgam*, *samdhâ*, cf. *teleo*, to get married, to die, to perfect [Greek *teleo* corresponds to Latin *initiari*, being utilized in *Mysteries* to define the spiritual initiation]. (Coom., **Sacrifice**, pp. 195-6)

The same way a vessel can be a cup or a boat, the lunar crescent is the symbolic equivalent not only of the cup but also of the boat. In Mesopotamia, the lunar god, Nanna, was depicted traveling in a boat having the shape of the lunar crescent, and the ends of the boat were compared to the horns of a young bull.[1] The bull's horns allude to a lunar symbolism and we saw that Dionysus was compared to a bull. However, there are images of Dionysus in a boat, and some legends tell about the god coming from the waters; it is said that, at the festival of his epiphany, Dionysus comes back from the waters in a black boat.[2] The Romans considered that Saturn, the regent of the Golden Age, came from the seas, and was received with a lot of respect by Janus, the lunar god; that is why a ship was engraved on Roman coins (Macrobius, **Saturnalia**, I, 7, 21-22). The symbolism of the boat coming into the harbour with a precious load (a redeemer god, an initiator, or a miraculous child, for example) is similar to the meaning of Noah's Ark that carried the sacred kernel of the new world.

The Christian tradition took over the saint tokens of Janus. First, his keys (Janus being the "janitor" of the solar doors) became Saint Peter's (and the Pope's) golden and silver keys; the golden key belongs to the *Greater Mysteries*, the silver one to the *Lesser Mysteries*, corresponding to the Sun and the Moon.[3] Secondly, Janus' boat became one of Saint Peter's emblems and that of the Church itself

---

[1] **Encyclopédie des Symboles**, Le Livre de Poche, 2000, p. 176. On the other hand, the ancient Egyptians used the well-known symbol of the solar boat, highlighting a three-way partition similar to that of the phases of the moon: child in the morning (Herpi), adult at noon (Re) and old at sunset (Atum).

[2] Otto, **Dionysus**, Indiana Univ. Press, 1965, pp. 162-3.

[3] René Guénon, **Autorité Spirituelle et Pouvoir Temporel**, Véga, 1976, pp. 102-103. Normally, the golden key belongs to the Papacy to open the way toward the Heavenly Paradise, and the silver key is given to the emperor who guides toward the Earthly Paradise.

(Guénon, **Autorité**, p. 106). More than that, the Blessed Mary was considered to be a living Ark that contained the Logos.[1] As Guénon stressed, the symbol of navigation, used also by Dante, represents a spiritual journey, in the Christian tradition, Saint Peter's boat leading to the Heavenly Paradise. Guénon wrote: "The harbour towards which humankind should aim is «the sacred island» that stands immovable in the middle of the agitated waters, and which is «the Salvation Mountain,» «the Peace Sanctuary»" (Guénon, **Autorité**, p. 108).[2] The symbolism of navigation towards the Island-Center can be found also in the Rosicrucian texts; Christian Rosenkreutz, on his fifth day of initiation, after he saw the naked Venus, is invited to a journey on the sea, to assist the rebirth of the royal victims, and the ships will navigate as a pentagon to a square island. Yet, the sea-journey (to which Dante alluded in **Monarchy**) could symbolize, as we have already suggested, a "descent" (*avatarana*) of a divine messenger or of an *avatâra*, in order to establish a new tradition or a new secondary center, the annual rites celebrating this event renewing the world every time. The Christian tradition contains such a sacred significance, related to the foundation of Christianity in Western Europe.

A legend tells that, after Christ's crucifixion, some of his disciples, who were direct witnesses of His glory and power, were forced to leave the Holy Land. They were embarked, against their will, on a boat (without paddles or sails) and abandoned to the sea. Such a symbolic gesture is not new. It can be found in different traditions, usually related to the birth of an *avatâra*. Moses, Perseus, Sargon,

---

[1] In **A Midsummer Night's Dream**, Shakespeare presented, in a very subtle mode, a "lovely boy" of "an Indian king," meant to be the regent of the new Cosmos, of the new cycle. He is the spiritual seed and the golden germ of the new world, that is why his mother, the Virgin, is compared by Shakespeare to a ship, an Ark, the "World Egg" floating on the primordial Waters (II.I.123-134); see **Sacred Kernel**, p. 98.

[2] Guénon noted: "If there are in the Gospels words and deeds that allow us directly to assign the keys and the boat to Saint Peter, that is because the Papacy, from its origins, was predestined to be «Roman,» due to the situation of Rome as capital of the Occident" (Guénon, **Autorité**, p. 106). We may add that Saint Paul's letter addressed to the Romans indicates the same thing.

The Three Marys

Dionysus,[1] heros of the fairy tales, etc. are forced into an ark and thrown into the waters to perish. In the Christian case, the abandoned ones were: Mary Jacobé, Mary Salomé, Mary Magdalene, Lazarus and Martha, Maximinus and Sidonius (the blind from Jericho). The boat floated with them, reaching the shore at the mouth of the Rhône River, to a place which today is called Saintes-Maries-de-la-Mer (Provence, France). From there, Mary Magdalene and the others spread the Word of the Lord in Gaul, leaving behind only the two Marys, Salomé and Jacobé. Here, over an ancient temple, was built a church dedicated to the Virgin Mary, called at the beginning *Sancta-Maria-de-Ratis*, that is, "Saint Mary of the Boat," and then *Sancta-Maria-de Mari*, "Saint Mary of the Sea" (Sainte-Marie-de-la-Mer).[2]

From a historical point of view, it is not known exactly who the two Marys were; we have already seen the confusion regarding the name Mary. Mary Jacobé is considered to be either Cleophas' wife and the Virgin's sister (**John** 19:25), or the mother of James (Jacob) and Joses (**Matthew** 15:40), or just the mother of James (Jacob) (**Luke** 24:10), which explains her nickname Jacobé. Salomé is supposed to be the wife of Zebedee and the mother of John and Jacob (**Matthew** 20:20).

Yet the story of the two Marys has an additional important episode. The legend says that, when they were forced to embark, a black maiden, Sarah, begged to be taken in the boat and, using Salomé's cloak as a boardwalk, she stepped, like Christ, on the

---

[1] A legend of Laconia says that Cadmus, enraged by his daughter's love affair, had her (Semele) and the boy (Dionysus) thrown into the sea (Otto 162).
[2] A. Chapelle, **Les Saintes-Maries De-la-Mer, l'église et le pèlerinage**, Bélisane, 1997, pp. 15 ff. We may note that the Grail's legends contain an episode full of substance regarding the symbolism of the vessel. There is a miraculous ship, reached by three knights of the Holy Grail: Galahad, Bors and Perceval; we note the Chivalric triad. The miraculous ship is not any vessel, but it symbolizes the spiritual center, guarding the Tradition transmitted over the ages (**The Quest of the Holy Grail**, Penguin Books, 1969, p. 214). We add that Apuleius stated that Isis appeared from the sea, and the rites celebrating the goddess contained an episode about launching a sacred ship (Lucius Apuleius, **The Golden Ass**, Penguin Books, 1985).

waters, reaching the boat; one version considers that Sarah was the handmaid of the two Marys, Jacobé and Salomé.[1]

This social position of "handmaid" is, of course, a symbolic one. The colour black refers to the symbolism of the Black Virgin and the "servitude" refers to humility in respect to God. "Sitting down, Jesus called the Twelve and said, «If anyone wants to be first, he must be the very last, and the servant of all.»" (**Mark** 9:35). In the same way, Sarah is a "handmaid" only from a spiritual point of view, her name meaning in fact "princess"; she is an aspect of the Black Virgin.

The cult of the Black Virgin is well-known. It is said that the "official" start of this cult occurred in the 11th century (Hani 23). Generally, the immediate explanation of the Black Virgin is the one that considers her as *Terra Mater*, *Magna Mater*, or *terra nigra* of the Alchemists; this interpretation is not wrong, of course, but it could be deceiving, because it is close to all those fantasies that regard the "chthonian gods" and "gods of vegetations." René Guénon also wrote that the Christian Virgin "is a perfect image of Prakriti, designated by the Far-Eastern tradition as «Earth»; we can see this especially in the symbolical images of «the black virgins,» the colour black symbolizing here *materia prima* and its indistinct character" (Guénon, **Triade**, p. 21).

Guénon's statement requires a clarification, indispensable for the economy of the present work. René Guénon later wrote more thoroughly about an important subject, after Coomaraswamy published some articles regarding the symbolism of "the two nights." The article **Les deux nuits** was published in 1939 (Guénon, **Initiation**, p. 239) and, compared to what he wrote in 1937-1938, brought deeper teachings; here Guénon unveiled the symbolic correspondence between the three initiatory deaths (and the three rebirths) and the "three nights," related to the three levels: corporeal, psychical, and spiritual. Considering that "the night" was the phase of darkness needed to pass from one initiatory degree to another, or

---

[1] Another version states that Sarah was the handmaid of the *three* Marys, Salomé, Jacobé and Magdalene (see Jean-Paul Clébert, **The Gypsies**, Penguin Books, 1967, p. 179).

from a degree of the universal manifestation to another, Guénon underlined the essential significance of the two extreme "nights": one, understood as infernal darkness, as chaos, the other one, understood as supernal darkness (the super-luminous darkness of the non-manifestation), this second meaning being usually ignored. The night of chaos referred to the "material" indifference, as an inverted reflex of the *principial* indifference of the non-manifestation, of the supernal night. This night with its chaotic indifference, applied to the whole universal manifestation, is precisely that of Prakriti, the maternal pole identical to *materia prima* of the ancient cosmological doctrines of the Occident, signifying the state of pure potentiality, the reflected inverted image of the *principial* state of the non-manifested possibilities.[1] Guénon went even further in his articles published at the end of his life, in 1947-8, when he unveiled, without any restraints, the metaphysical symbolism of the colour black and the difference between Shakti and Prakriti.[2] Of course, he wrote that the Black Virgin of the Christian tradition is Prakriti ("the Earth" of the Far-Eastern tradition), but only in the context of the Great Triad, the Holy Spirit being the divine Activity of Purusha ("the Heaven") and Christ the Universal Man, the Mediator between Heaven and Earth (Guénon, **Triade**, p. 21); also, this equivalence is particularly Christian (especially related to Christian exotericism, which cannot see the supernal significance of the colour black and of the Black Virgin, as a universal symbol) (Guénon, **Hind.**, p. 103).

To permit the human mind to grasp somehow what is impossible to understand in a rational, discursive way, the Principle (even if unchangeable and immutable, without duality and immovable) is considered to act through his "energy" (*shakti*), which is feminine compared to him. Shakti is the divine Maiden, the lunar Virgin, Sophia, Helen of Troy, *Madonna Intelligenza*, Dante's Beatrice, as

---

[1] Guénon presented the fundamental specification that the production of manifestation has to be seen in an ascending sense (from the maternal chaos towards cosmos and light, the *prakritian* cosmogony), as well as in a descending sense (from the super-luminous, paternal darkness, the *purushan* cosmogony).
[2] See **Le blanc et le noir** and **Les «têtes noires»** (**Symboles**, pp. 134, 306), and also **Mâyâ** (**Hind.**, p. 101).

target of the spiritual realization. Shakti is the "dark cloud" of the Judaic tradition, the Black Virgin as celestial Queen who, due to the Principle's "non-active activity" (*wei wu-wei* of the Far-Eastern tradition), generates the spiritual influences. These influences descend upon Prakriti, representing the divine Activity of Purusha, and in consequence, Prakriti emerges from her indifference and produces the universal manifestation. Prakriti is Shakti's projection and the Black Virgin is, at the same time, Shakti and Prakriti.[1]

"Dark am I, yet lovely, O daughters of Jerusalem, dark like the tents of Kedar, like the tent curtains of Solomon. Do not stare at me because I am dark, because I am darkened by the sun" (**Song** 1:5-6); this Biblical text represents the Christian motivation for the cult of the Black Virgin; Sarah of Saintes-Maries-de-la-Mer is such a Black Virgin.

Yet more than that, Sarah, or better yet, the Saint Sarah, is the protector of the Gypsies. Every year the Gypsies from all around the world gather at Saintes-Maries-de-la-Mer, in the vault of the church, where the black statue of Saint Sarah is, and celebrate her. As Guénon showed, the elected queen of the Gypsies bears the name Sarah (Guénon, **Franc-Maçonnerie**, II, pp. 31-32). A legend tells that Sarah, called also *Kâli* ("the dark one"), was a Gypsy woman, the leader of a tribe living on the shores of the Rhône River. In those times, a ritual was celebrated every year, in which the Gypsies carried the statue of goddess Ishtar into the sea-waters; one day, Sarah had a vision that revealed to her the coming of the three Marys. And when they arrived, Sarah helped them and the saints baptized her (Clébert 179). In memory of this event, in May, every year, the Gypsies gather at Saintes-Maries-de-la-Mer and carry the black statue of Saint Sarah

---

[1] "Shakti is the maternal «power,» «the divine Activity.» Therefore, she is inherent to Brahma or to the supreme Principle; she is incomparably higher than Prakriti; Prakriti is, in fact, only a reflection of Shakti in the «cosmologic» order. We remark the inverted analogy: the supreme Activity is reflected in the pure passivity and the «almightiness» of the Principle is reflected in the potentiality of *materia prima*. Shakti, as the divine «art» abode in the Principle, is identical to the «Wisdom,» Sophia, and, in this case, she is the mother of Avatâra. Using the Western terminology, Shakti is *Natura naturans*, and Prakriti – *Natura naturata*, even though both are named *Natura*" (Guénon, **Hind.**, p. 102).

into the sea. Actually, they join the Christian festival that celebrates the two Marys, Salomé and Jacobé, whose statues are also carried to the sea.[1]

One who enters the church at Saintes-Maries-de-la-Mer is impressed by the sacred simplicity of the temple. Yet what amazes one most is that, upon entering, one's eyes perceive not one altar, as it usually is, but three. There are three altars, arranged vertically, symbolically marking the Three Worlds. The middle altar, that at the floor level, has the statue of the Blessed Virgin in close proximity. Up close to the ceiling, there is a niche with a chest containing the relics of the Saints Marys suggesting the high altar. Eventually, in the subterranean vault there is a very old altar, having the black statue of Sarah nearby. Here we rediscover the "lights" of the Three Worlds. Sarah's subterranean vault and the colour black could make us believe that we are dealing with Prakriti's or Hecate's domain. In fact, to understand completely the symbolic meaning, we have to consider also the significance of the underground spiritual center and of the super-luminous darkness. Actually, we may say that Sarah is "the black face" of the Virgin Mary and, therefore, subtly identical with her.[2] However, the church was consecrated to the Blessed Virgin, and so, even if apparently there is no correspondence, we are allowed to think that the three altars, that is, the Three Worlds, are in direct association with the Three Marys: Sarah – the Virgin Mary, Mary Salomé and Mary Jacobé.[3] Yet we can go even further: from a

---

[1] Regarding May: the name of this month derives from Maia, Hermes' mother, to whom it was consecrated; in the Christian tradition, May became "the month of Mary," due to an assimilation, which was not only phonetic, between Mary and Maia (René Guénon, **Formes traditionnelles et cycles cosmiques**, Gallimard, 1980, p. 135). Maia was one of the seven Pleiades, the seven stars we saw above the bull.

[2] In the Islamic tradition, in the **Qur'ân**, *sûrah* called "Mary" represents Saint Mary "fasting," not in regard to food but to speaking, that is, showing Mary mute and indicating with her finger the new-born Jesus. On the other hand, an anecdote, found at the beginning of one of Ibn 'Arabî's works, tells about a black handmaid, who was dumb, and who, at the question, "where is Allâh?," indicated the sky with her finger (Charles-André Gilis, **Marie en Islam**, Éd. Trad., 1980, pp. 16-17). The similitude between the two women is, somehow, as that between Saint Mary and Sarah.

[3] In 1357, Jean de Venette even wrote a poem called *The Three Marys*, and at Mignières, a church of 11th century was consecrated to the Three Marys (Chapelle 54-

symbolic point of view there is only one and the same Virgin, the Three Marys being, as in the case of Hecate, her three faces.[1]

The Romanian traditional data bring a confirmation, apparently unexpected, to our conclusion. A Christmas carol says: "And it was built a White Great Monastery/ With nine altars/ And nine golden thrones./ In the greater altar/ Is Saint Mary the Greater,/ In the lesser altar/ Is Saint Mary the Lesser./ In the middle altar/ the Mother of God sat."[2] We should note, first, that the White Monastery, as we showed in another work, is an equivalent of Agarttha, the Center of the World[3]; any church, like the one of Saintes-Maries-de-la-Mer, is a projection of the Monastery in the world. Then, we observe that the White Monastery has three altars: a greater, a lesser and a central one, similar to the church of the Saints Marys from the south of France. Eventually, we remark that the three altars belong to the Three Marys: Saint Mary the Greater, Saint Mary the Lesser and the Mother of God; yet all the three names refer to one and the same Mary, the Blessed Virgin, the mother of Christ.

---

55). As we mentioned earlier, some legends considered St. Anne the mother of these three Marys.

[1] Coomaraswamy clearly showed that the Three Lights of the Hindu tradition are, in fact, the one-and-only Light, the solar Spirit that appears as Agni, Vâyu and Âditya in relation to the Three Worlds. "The three regents of the Worlds" are not different principles, but the same principle with different functions. The Three Lights are the three-headed Light, "the Sun with three heads" (Coom., **Autorité**, pp. 67-69).

[2] Geticus, **La Dacie hyperboréenne**, Etudes Traditionnelles, 1936-1937.

[3] See **Agarttha, the Invisible Center**, Rose-Cross Books, 2003.

CHAPTER XVIII

PILGRIMAGE AND TOURISM

BEFORE CHRISTMAS, IN THE YEAR 1448, "the good king" René, Comte of Provence, ordered an excavation of the area where the Marys and Sarah were buried. Thus, the saintly women's relics were discovered, and Sarah's crypt as it appears today is a vestige of that time.

As a result of the event, the worship of the St. Marys became official, and the relics were laid, in the presence of the King René, Queen Isabelle, bishops and nobles of Provence, in a wooden painted ark and placed in the high altar. From then on, Saintes-Maries-de-la-Mer became a shrine and its population turned into the guardians of the relics, and even today the term "guardian" remained in use, though rather associated with guarding horses and bulls.[1]

The church of the St. Marys was already a station for the famous pilgrimage to the tomb of Saint Jacob of Compostella, yet when the relics were discovered it became an important shrine, generating an autonomous pilgrimage.[2] Today this pilgrimage is still alive and it

---

[1] René Guénon wrote an article called **Les Gardiens de la Terre sainte (Symboles)** in which he explained the symbolism of the "guardian," which refers firstly to the Center of the World and only then to a particular center as the Holy Land, the Templars being its guardians.

[2] Already in 1338, the Saint Marys Confraternities were mentioned. There were famous pilgrims registered who came to the Church of the St. Marys, begged for divine help and got it. They spread the cult of the Three (two) Marys in France after that.

occurs two times a year: on May 25, the day of Mary Jacobé, and on October 22, the day of Mary Salomé. More important and better known is the May fête when, beside the Christian pilgrims, the Gypsies gather to celebrate Saint Sarah. On the afternoon of May 24, the ark with the relics is brought down, and also the Gypsies take the statue of Saint Sarah to the sea; the next day the St. Marys are taken, in their boat, onto the waters.

Just as the notion "guardian" hides a sacred meaning, so the pilgrimage is more that an exoteric rite, hiding a sacred kernel. The pilgrimage to Saintes-Maries-de-la-Mer was part of the *Via Tolosana*, which started in Arles, passed Saintes-Maries-de-la-Mer, reached Toulouse, and from there, through Auch, Montesquiou, and Morlaàs crossed the border to Spain and eventually reached Compostella. In each place, city or village, through which the pilgrims passed, there was a church, a chapel, or a shrine. Each place represented a spiritual station and for this reason, the pilgrimage, in its highest signification, symbolized an initiatory journey.[1]

Of course, the common pilgrims, like the ones who went to Jerusalem or, on their knees, followed the labyrinth traced on the tiled floor of the cathedral, were not conscious of the initiatory meaning, yet they knew that, accomplishing the pilgrimage, at least once in a lifetime, they could reach "sainthood," that is, they could share the blessings of the visited places. It was also obvious that, for those with a callous heart, and for those who completed the pilgrimage just superficially, for the eyes of the others, or waiting for

---

[1] Besides *Via Tolosana*, we should mention *Via Podiensis*, *Via Turonensis* and *Via Lemovicensis*. The first pilgrim to Compostella was considered to be the king of Asturia, Alfonso II the Chaste, in 9th century, A.D. It is said that, having been killed by Herod in Judea, Saint Jacob was carried by a miraculous ship to Galicia, where his coffin was towed by bulls; Galicia was the only region which partially resisted the Arabic invasion and from here Requonquista and its legends started. The cult of Saint Jacob, a local one at the beginning of the year 800, became general when the first archbishop of Compostella, Diego Gelmirez, helped by the monks of Cluny, organized the pilgrimage to Saint Jacob's tomb. The various itineraries of the pilgrimage to Compostella were marked by initiatory stations covered externally by cathedrals, inns, hospitals, shrines, fairs, itineraries guarded by a Chivalric Order and organized by a "guide" of the pilgrims.

a reward, the result was proportional. On the other hand, for the initiates, that is, for those who were conscious of the sacred journey's meaning, the pilgrimage represented an initiatory operative rite, which allowed them at each church, temple, or shrine to receive the divine influence and support for their personal spiritual efforts.

Dante stated:

For «pilgrim» may be understood in two ways, one general and one particular, in as much as anyone journeying from his own country is a pilgrim. In the particular sense, pilgrim means someone who journeys to the sanctuary of St. Jacob [James] and back. It should be understood that those who travel in the service of the Almighty are of three kinds. Those who travel overseas are called palmers, as they often bring back palms [from Jerusalem]; those who go to Saint Jacob's shrine in Galicia are called pilgrims, because the burial place of Saint Jacob was further away from his country than that of any other apostle; and romeos are those who go to Rome.[1]

It is interesting that, previous to this definition of the pilgrim, Dante wrote:

Some pilgrims were passing along a road, which runs almost through the center of the city where that most gracious lady was born, lived and died. These pilgrims, it seemed to me, were very pensive as they went their way; and so, thinking about them, I said to myself: «These people seem to be journeying from far away, and I do not think that they have ever even heard about my lady; they know nothing about her, indeed their thoughts are on quite other things than those that are around them here; perhaps they are thinking of their friends at home.» (**Vita Nuova**, XL, p. 96)

Dante's "gracious lady" was not so much Beatrice, but *Madonna Intelligenza*, the target of the initiatory pilgrimage. The fact that the pilgrims passed along the sacred road without knowing or thinking of her, referred to "the many" who followed the ritual of this holy journey without getting profoundly involved, engaging in just a

---

[1] Dante, **La Vita Nuova**, Penguin Books, 1969, XL, p. 97.

superficial participation.¹ In the fairy tales and other initiatory writings, if the neophyte looks back and remembers his family (the world), he is lost and fails initiation. Dante suggested that many pilgrims thought not of the *Madonna*, but of home and friends, therefore dooming themselves to fail.

Sure, even in the times of the Crusades the medieval society was not an "ideal" one, but it allowed a development of spirituality and, more importantly, it presented the needed support for the initiatory process, illustrated by the multiple pilgrimages, the Crusades, the Troubadours' literature, the building of the cathedrals, etc.²

The Latin word *peregrinus*, from which is derived *pilgrim*, Guénon wrote (**Franc-Maçonnerie**, I, pp. 52 ff.), signifies at the same time "traveler" and "stranger," both having initiatory meanings and being used in *Compagnonage*. The pilgrim, like the *companion*, was a "stranger" embarked on a spiritual journey. Masonry (even the modern one) used the name "journey" for the symbolic initiatory trials; however, in various traditions, the initiatory degrees were often described as parts of a journey (on land or sea) and the journey sometimes became a warlike one (the Crusades, the Trojan war); in religious terms, even terrestrial life is a journey, a pilgrimage aiming at the Earthly Paradise.

The initiates are "noble voyagers," hiding in the crowd of common travelers. The initiates' pilgrimage, Guénon showed, has to be related to the "royal art" and the "royal caste" (*kshatriya*), and to Hermeticism, with Saint John corresponding to metaphysics and

---

[1] Any rite in which the individual does not participate with his entire being is a wasted one. Moreover, an initiatory realization implies a theoretical training and an indispensable theoretical knowledge (see René Guénon's letter of 1918, L'Age D'Or, **René Guénon**, Pardès, 1987, p. 99). In the case of the exoteric rites, the training is more "moral" and sometimes not even so.

[2] Those who think that only modern civilization, the great supporter of the hyper-developed "tourism," made traveling possible, forget the intense voyages that took place in the ancient and medieval times; yet then, the causes were not usually profane, but constituted a part of a sacred life and a spiritual training. The pilgrimage is a good example; thousands of people were continuously on the move: priests, monks, knights, merchants, troubadours, masons, thieves, beggars, jongleurs, etc. carried initiatory data.

pure intellectuality, and Saint Jacob to the "traditional sciences"; everything that was transmitted using the pilgrimage belonged to this "intermediary" domain. It is interesting that the pilgrims' insignias were the staff and the shell, corresponding to Purusha and Prakriti of the Hindu tradition represented by *vajra* (lightning, scepter) and *shankha* (shell, in the Tibetan tradition the shell being replaced by the ritual bell, *dilbu*).[1] The pilgrim is a traveler through the Cosmos; he is the Mediator, the Man who reunites Heaven and Earth due to this spiritual voyage. All the pilgrims who went to Compostella, following "Saint Jacob's way," carried the shell, illustrating, among other meanings, the pilgrim's status of vassalage with respect to God.[2]

Ibn 'Arabî wrote: "During the pilgrimage, the servant is dominated by the station of servitude, *Maqâm al'-ubûdiyya*, obeying all the restrictions through which the wisdom escapes the rational. It is, somehow, a work of pure adoration, which cannot be accomplished but with the qualifications of a vassal." And: "Allâh calls the pilgrims only to test them and to make them see the one faithful to the status of vassalage. Therefore the most part of the pilgrimage's rules are related to worshiping, without a rational cause or meaning."[3]

Muhyiddin Ibn 'Arabî's words indicate the importance of pilgrimage in Islam; at least theoretically, every Muslim should complete the pilgrimage's rites, which makes it an exoteric ritual, even though it is a reflection of an initiatory process, representing a voyage to the Center of the World, a voyage that each one, proportional to his capability, assimilated and was transformed by accordingly. In the same way, during the pilgrimage of the medieval voyagers to Compostella or to Jerusalem, besides the exoteric crowd, there were the "chosen" ones for whom the journey was a "materialization" of an inner, spiritual voyage. The Islamic

---

[1] A lama has the *vajra* in his right hand and the *dilbu* in his left hand. The bell, like the shell, hides the primordial sound. The Tarot contains the pair staff – cup.
[2] Vassalage in medieval times had a much deeper significance than the one the historians suggest, who considered it a humiliating state of servitude.
[3] About the Islamic pilgrimage see Charles-André Gilis, **La doctrine initiatique du pèlerinage**, Les Éd. De l'Oeuvre, 1982.

pilgrimage, the *hajj*, has two parts: *umra* or "the lesser pilgrimage," which could be completed anytime and contains: the initial consecration (*ihrâm*), the rite of circumambulation around Kaaba (*tawâf*), followed by a prayer at Abraham's station (*Maqâm Ibrâhîm*) and *sa'y* (the race between the two rocks Safâ and Marwa); the greater pilgrimage, the *hajj*, occurs just once in a year, and is composed of *wuqûf* ("the halt" of the pilgrims at the foot of the merciful mountain, Jabal ar-Rahma, on the plateau Arafa), *ifâda* ("the overflowing," when the pilgrims descend to Minâ and then to Mecca). Having arrived to Mecca, the pilgrims carry out the *tawâf* around Kaaba, and then they spend the night at Minâ (*layalat al-qarr*, "the stabilization night"). Yet, Ibn 'Arabî stressed, even if it is the greater pilgrimage, *hajj* is limited by the fixed date when it has to take place, while *umra* does not depend on the time, which suggests that only the target is beyond any kind of limitations, the ways being forced to obey more or less important determinations. The pilgrimage to Mecca means to leave the "outside darkness," to penetrate the Cosmos surrounded by the Great Wall, covered by the circular mountain, and for this reason Ibn 'Arabî dedicated a large part of the chapter concerning the pilgrimage to the "state of holiness" through which the pilgrims reach the harmonious concordance with the primeval state symbolized by the sacred area (*haram*) that surrounds Mecca.[1]

Any authentic pilgrimage achieves such a "state of holiness." Each stage, marked by a holy place, allows the pilgrim to leave the profane standpoint and step inside the sacred domain. And we don't have in view only the initiatory aspect. The exponents of the exoteric domain have also the possibility of enjoying this "state of holiness"; it is an important fact, which should be better understood by those who want at any price to consider the Christian religion an eso-exotericism, fearing that Christianity is at a lower level than other traditions or religions. Only those, who Dante described in such a

---

[1] *Haram* is Adam's heritage, since Allâh ordered the angels to guard Adam's Tent; the angels composed a circular barrier, with their backs to the "outside darkness," to stop the demons and the *djinns* from entering the sacred land.

gentle manner as we saw above, will remain in the "outside darkness." Only those, who, instead of having the heart full of love for God, visit the sacred places full of wrath and anger, those who are more interested in others' business, thinking of themselves as little gods, only those will have no part of the "state of holiness." For them, the pilgrimage is, in fact, a sort of tourism. And tourism is the "pilgrimage" of the modern world.

Tourism is a recent invention, being motivated, generally, by curiosity and the need for entertainment, that is, by profane reasons. There are, of course, travelers drawn by, apparently, more serious motives, such as scientific, social, cultural, etc. grounds; these belong to the modern "historicism." Far be it from us to suggest that the seer or the spiritual master was against traveling. Saint Paul (as well as the other Apostles) is a good example of a "traveler"; also, the spiritual masters' writings often contain allusions to landscapes and places they visited. In the same way, today, there are people who, under the guise of tourists, hide a higher goal.

Yet, modern tourism is something totally different. It is a tornado of continuous unsettledness, of unlimited curiosity and greediness, the greediness with regard to the desire to visit as many "tourist objectives" as possible and in the fastest way; it is the anxious need to memorize, using the available high-tech, all the visited places, for the sake of the ego, to gallop along the various vestiges (the older the better), to rush from one temple to another, from one museum to another, to hunt masterpieces, famous objects and names. Modern tourists do not usually enter a church to pray; they go inside hypnotized by their nicely printed guides that tell them where and what to search for and admire, giving them a lot of useless details, and you can see on their faces the satisfaction when they have succeeded in identifying the objective their guide indicated. Modern tourists do not see the church as "the house of God" and they do not "feel" the divine presence. They look at the ornamentation, paintings, architecture, which do not transmit to them anything sacred and which are, for them, just dead things. If they discover an article made by a well-known artist, the tourists will accept the spending of a few more minutes of their busy schedule, and then they will run toward another "three star" objective. Modern tourists are, from all points of view, "wandering" and "wayward" individuals. One of their favorite objectives is the museum. We do not want to be cynical, yet what would be the reaction with regard to those vandalizing graves and cemeteries? Of course, every normal person would be outraged and infuriated, and would expect the perpetrators to be punished. On the other hand, what would be the reaction hearing the news that a group of scientists discovered an Egyptian mummy, or opened a prehistoric grave, or penetrated a very old sanctuary? No outrage here. The news would be accepted as normal. But this news is not normal. What the modern and so-called civilized society does is desecration on a large scale. The dubious enthusiasm of the archeologists to dig out and exhume corpses and associated objects is an outrage that the "scientific" cover cannot excuse. The fact that these objects end in a museum as "public" goods does not change the significance of the gesture. Even if the archeologists dig up not graves, but vestiges of houses, sanctuaries, etc., they look like poor beggars rummaging through garbage cans; moreover, irresponsibly, they put everybody at risk, by also digging out associated infectious germs.[1] Their "hungriness" is labeled "scientific," even though, too often, it is just simply and purely indecent curiosity. The idea of exposing to the public all the "discoveries" is suspect. To unveil to all what was supposed to remain hidden is a desecration. Just the same, the tourist visiting old castles and famous mansions is mostly attracted to one room: the royal bedroom, because it suggests an intimate space very tempting for human curiosity.

Talking about old castles, we may note modern man's attraction to antiquities and, in general, for all that is old. Besides the absurd passion for useless objects belonging to some momentary

---

[1] And we don't have in mind here so much the physical germs, but the subtle ones. René Guénon wrote about "the moderns' relentlessness to excavate vestiges of the past ages and lost civilizations, which they are incapable to really understand" and the danger related to this dubious activity due to "the nature of the subtle influences which remained attached to these vestiges and which, unnoticed, were freed by the excavations" (Guénon, **Le règne**, p. 238).

"celebrities," the attraction to antique objects replaces, in the modern world, the worshiping of holy relics from the traditional societies. It is, indeed, a mockery of the relics' cult. If the holy relics and the sacred places were supports for a spiritual influence, the collectable objects of modern man have no real value, and their old age does not mean much. Let us take, for example, a Roman vessel. This one will appear to the modern individual as priceless and its commercial value is considerable. Yet the vessel is not at all more special than it was in the time when the Roman or Greek potter made it; on the contrary, it is less valuable because it has lost its utility. For this reason, a vessel made today by a real potter who uses the traditional art of pottery is at least as precious as the ancient vessel. Therefore an artist (in the sense given by Ananda K. Coomaraswamy) who has vocation and makes a votive painting, following the sacred rules and suffering the necessary purifications, produces a masterpiece not different from the old ones.

Nonetheless, the tourist's schedule continues with admiring a building because a "celebrity" lived there. It is difficult to understand why that particular building deserves more attention than another one. The tourist can be heard saying, with great satisfaction, "I saw Jane Austen's house!," like suggesting that this event changed his or her life. We find here again a mockery, with the visit to a famous house replacing the pilgrimage to sanctuaries and shrines.

If a building deserves to be studied, it should be for completely different reasons.

CHAPTER XIX

MASONRY AND THE CONSPIRACY THEORY

THE CHRISTIAN TEMPLE, like any other traditional buildings, is an image of the Cosmos; moreover, it symbolizes the Center of the World and the House of God. Its building process follows a divine archetype, representing first of all the Heavenly Jerusalem, which confers universality both on the Masonic operations and the temple itself. In the **Old Testament**, there are enough examples underlining the divine influence involved in the building of a temple: Bezalel (like Oholiab), who built the Tabernacle and the holy Ark, was filled by God "with the Spirit of God, with skill, ability and knowledge in all kinds of crafts, to make artistic designs for work in gold, silver and bronze, to cut and set stones, to work in wood and to engage in all kinds of artistic craftsmanship" (**Exodus** 35:31-33); God inspired Solomon and Ezekiel's Temples, and Noah's Ark was built following the measures given by God. We note the same "artistic" technique, which we find in the Hindu tradition: the artist (we are using the word in the sense Coomaraswamy defined it), throughout contemplation, visualizes first the heavenly model in its integrality, using an authentic spiritual process; then, the artist translates this model to the physical world. The Christian temple continued the Judaic tradition, and Eusebius compared Saint Paulin, the bishop of Tyre and the founder of the church built in that city based on divine inspiration, to Bezalel. Saint Paulin, like Bezalel, built in his spirit an exact image of Christ, of the Word, of Wisdom, and of the Light, raising afterwards a magnificent temple, dedicated to the Most High, following the model of the perfect temple – a visible emblem of the invisible temple.

As in the case of the Hindu temple, the construction of the Christian one started with the "orientation" ritual, the shadow of a central post (around which was traced a circle) marking the East-West axis (morning and evening); then, using two other circles, the square was drawn. The Christian temple, it is well-known, has the altar oriented to the East, Christ being *Oriens*, the rising Sun. As the Hindu temple encompasses Purusha, as the *stûpa* is Buddha's body, so the Christian temple is Christ's body; in a way, His archetypal sacrifice allows the raising of the Church. "Jesus answered them, «Destroy this temple, and I will raise it again in three days.» The Jews replied, «It has taken forty-six years to build this temple, and you are going to raise it in three days?» But the temple he had spoken of was his body" (**John** 2:19-21). On the other hand, the temple is *ecclesia*, that is, the believers' assembly (the Buddhist *Sangha*), the gathering of the "chosen" ones. When Christ becomes the keystone of the edifice, the "chosen" ones will be transformed into the precious stones of the Heavenly Jerusalem. The Christian temple is at the same time the cosmic Mountain, *Axis Mundi* and the Center. It is the Cosmos, the World; it is the House of God and Christ's body; it is, eventually, the believers' assembly (who are the stones of the edifice), and also the body of each believer. As the Principle "fills" the Universe, which is his House and his Body, so the "divine presence" lives in the temple, and Christ lived in His human body; similarly, the spiritual influence, the grace, comes down into the body-temple of the neophyte aiming at salvation.

Yet not only does the temple as such offer symbolic meanings, but also its components. In the Hindu tradition, *gopuram*, the gates, surpass the temple with respect to their splendor. In the Christian tradition, the portal of the church is, in a way, its most complete double (from a symbolic perspective). The gate's shape makes it an image of the Cosmos and, at the same time, is Christ's insignia: "Therefore Jesus said again, «I tell you the truth, I am the gate for the sheep. ... I am the gate; whoever enters through me will be saved»" (**John** 10:7-9).¹ To cross the portal of the temple means to pass from the profane to the sacred domain, from one state to another; therefore in different traditions the gate has an important symbolic function, and for this reason they are flanked by *dwarapâlas*, the guardians that allow only the qualified ones to pass. On the other hand, the whole temple is a Gate: concerning the spiritual center Luz, Beith-El, Jacob affirmed: "How awesome is this place! This is none other than the house of God; this is the gate of heaven" (**Genesis** 28:17).²

The famous building that represented the House of God in Judaism, having a significant role in the Christian tradition as well, was Solomon's Temple.

The biblical narrative regarding Solomon's Temple hides a rich meaning, beyond the particular traditional form to which it belongs. First of all, we note the process of Jews' "stabilization" or "coagulation" when their spiritual center, the Jerusalem Temple, was raised. The masonic work (in its operative sense) was not typical for nomads, therefore Solomon had to call foreign builders to erect the Temple; in the same way, the construction of Kaaba was conducted by foreign craftsmen. Solomon's Temple, made of wood and stone, was covered with precious stones and gold, being symbolically equivalent to Heavenly Jerusalem; its shape was parallelepiped-like, and the Holy of Holies was cubic. The two pillars made of bronze could be compared to the Hindu subtle channels, *ida* and *pingala*, or to Hermes' two serpents, or to Hercules' columns. The three floors of rooms around the Temple could represent the cosmic "frame," but also the labyrinth; or, from a different point of view, they are a token of the Three Worlds, and the spiral stairs suggest the degrees of universal Existence. The Temple was built on Mount Moriah, an

---

[1] For the symbolism of the gate and of the temple see Titus Burckhardt, **Principes et methodes de l'art sacré**, Dervy-Livres, 1976, and Jean Hani, **Le Symbolisme du Temple Chrétien**, Guy Trédaniel, 1978.

[2] The name of Babylon signifies the same thing: "the gate of heaven."

equivalent of the Hindu Meru, *Axis Mundi*[1]; no tool made of iron desecrated the edifice, with bronze being preferred as a reminder of a better age. The architect was the great master Hiram, or Adoniram, or Hiram-Abif, the Widow's son ("King Solomon sent to Tyre and brought Hiram, whose mother was a widow from the tribe of Naphtali," **1 Kings** 7:13-14). We have here all the symbolic elements of a myth or of an initiatory fairy tale, and it is easy to understand why Free-Masonry adopted them as a foundation-stone or a corner-stone.

The Masonic rituals have as their core the well-known myth of Hiram. Three companions envied the great master Hiram and wanted to know from him the master's "secret." They hid into the Temple, at three of the cardinal points (south, north and east). Hiram entered the Temple through the western gate (the temple had an eastern orientation, like the Christian churches); then, he tried to exit through the southern gate, but the worker hiding there attacked him. Hiram ran to the northern gate and again, the second companion confronted him. Eventually, the great master looked for escape at the eastern gate, yet the third worker was waiting and he killed his master. After seven days, king Solomon started an investigation, and Hiram's vanished corpse was found and brought to the Temple.

Through this myth, Free-Masonry established itself as a direct heir of the "Solomonic" tradition. There are some obvious reasons why, when the Masonic initiatory organization was constituted, it adopted from so many other myths precisely the one regarding the construction of Solomon's temple. On the one hand, the Masons were part of the Christian traditional society, and Christianity owed a lot to Judaism and had a special esteem for Solomon (related to Sophia); on the other hand, the initiatory data carried by the Western Masonic guilds were of Oriental origin. Yet it does not mean that the

---

[1] Mount Moriah was the support for seven consecutive edifices: the Altar of Abraham; the Threshing-floor of Ornan; the Altar of David; the Temple of Solomon; the Temple of Zerubbabel; the Temple of Herod; the Mosque of Omar. The last one, the Orthodox Christian tradition from Mount Athos connects to the end of times.

problem of the origins could be considered in a simplistic way. In India, *kammâlar*, the masons' guild was the heir of Vishwakarma, the Great Architect of the Universe; the Egyptians had also such types of corporations. Plutarch said that Numa, the Roman king, was the one who instituted the crafts and their guilds, the so-called *collegia fabrorum*. When the Roman Empire fell, that did not mean the complete disappearance of the Roman craftsmen, even though violent changes took place before the consolidation of Christian society. Sometimes the vestiges of the *collegia fabrorum* hid in the monasteries, not only because they had there the liberty to operate without interference, but especially because their art was connected to the priesthood to which it truly belonged. However, the survival of the Byzantine Empire meant the survival of the old Roman guilds that continued to function in the Near-West, and there is no doubt that the Byzantine influence had marked the Western Masonic art, already in the times of Charlemagne; but mostly during the Crusades, at the same time as the birth of the Chivalric Orders, Masonry found its fulfillment.

There is a strict difference between speculative Masonry and the operative one, the former deriving from the latter. The operative Masons' art was an efficient support for an authentic spiritual realization. Speculative Masonry, due to the worldly conditions, represented a decline, even if any initiatory path requires a theoretical preparation. Operative Masonry was mainly an initiatory organization of the Christian Middle Ages that transmitted uninterrupted spiritual and initiatory data derived from various orthodox sources. Operative Masonry offered to those who were qualified the support of the Masonic craft to complete the *Lesser Mysteries* and to achieve an effective spiritual realization. Masonry, besides Alchemy, Chivalry, and Hermeticism in general, constituted the Christian esoteric domain, the sacred kernel of the medieval Christian society. The Masonic guilds possessed not only a secret with respect to their craft (as the profane scholars believe), but first of all an initiatory secret, veiled by the masonic profession. Within operative Masonry, an initiatory and traditional education took place, the knowledge being transmitted orally and through symbols. The medieval builders and architects possessed an inexpressible operative secret, of an initiatory nature, yet even though "operative," this Masonry was also, we may say, "speculative," since it mastered the art of numbers and that of geometry, transmitted by the Pythagoreans; with the help of these arts, the Masons "planned" the effective spiritual realization.

Operative Masonry had three degrees: apprentice, fellowcraft and master mason. In the Middle Ages, after the apprentice worked for some years, if he proved to be qualified he was admitted into the Lodge to become a fellowcraft or companion. In other words, the apprentice was still in the "outside darkness," in the labyrinth, his entrance into the Lodge representing the birth within the Cosmos (the "illuminated cave"). As a fellowcraft, the mason became in control of the masonic art, taking possession of the cosmologic art and it was his duty to ramble through the Cosmos, effectively regenerating and mastering it. The fellowcraft was, therefore, a "pilgrim," a "stranger," wandering into the world, from one construction site to another, covering an inner initiatory path.

It is known that the construction sites and the cathedrals were milestones of the medieval pilgrimage and we stress that we are confronted with an amazing secret, typical for the Middle Ages society. The pilgrim's itinerary, a corporeal reflection of the initiatory path, encompassed a cluster of spiritual elements to which contributed the Chivalric Orders and the "noble voyagers," anonymous characters disguised as pilgrims, monks, companions, gypsies, and troubadours, who spread *les chansons de geste*. In such an environment, the fellowcrafts practiced their profession, rebuilding the Cosmos and praising the Great Architect of the Universe. On his return from this pilgrimage, the fellowcraft would become a master.

The waning of operative Masonry and the waxing of the speculative one occurred at the beginning of the 14th century, at the same time as the brutal obliteration or the Templars. Also then, in 1313, a papal bull dismantled, at Lyon, the "pontiff brothers" guild, and in 1326, the Council of Avignon interdicted all confraternities outside the Church. The "one hundred years war" ratified the change of cycles and, after its end, we may say that operative Masonry, even if it maintained a long agonizing survival, especially through the *Compagnonage*, lost its reason to be. The operative secret, though, did not disappear so easily, but was transmitted further and, as surprising as this would seem, some masonic symbols were saved by the art of typography, which was just instituted as a guild.

It seems that in the 16th century, "amateurs" started to be currently "accepted" into operative Masonic Lodges, yet without doubt, clerics, physicians and members of Chivalry had been members much earlier. Whatever might have been the cause of the "accepted masons'" admittance, we note that the Masonic craft was "chosen" to support further the initiatory vocation. While the initiatory possibilities of the other crafts died, Free-Masonry was reorganized, inheriting the symbols and the spiritual data of operative Masonry, adding to these the initiatory vestiges of Chivalry and pilgrimage. The Protestants had an important role in the foundation of modern Masonry.[1] This should be related to the Rosicrucian movement, which tried to inspire, without success, a "reformation" of the decaying Christian society. It seems that after the genuine Rose-Cross retreated to Asia (shortly before speculative Masonry was founded), what remained in Europe were some traces of Rosicrucianism that survived mostly related to Protestantism, replacing the lost initiatory and spiritual kernel with "morality" and "humanitarian" views. Of course, we must not think that speculative Masonry was just a sort of Protestant movement.

In the 18th century, both in England and France the Grand Lodges were created and the Scottish Rite was introduced. At the same time, baron Hundt, in Germany, founded the Strict Observance. This Masonic turmoil, started in the 18th century, intermingled with other "esoteric" waves, more or less profound and legitimate, and here we can find the origins of the modern pseudo-initiation, since at this time there was a proliferation of various pseudo-initiatory and pseudo-spiritual societies, which will play an

---

[1] The Scot James Anderson was a Presbyterian pastor. Jean-Theophile Désaguliers was a Huguenot.

important role in the development of the Great Disarray at the end of *Kali-yuga*.[1]

Today, for the modern world, Masonry has nothing to do with operative Masonry and initiation. It is seen, in the best of the cases, as an association promoting charitable works and moral principles. And even modern Masons consider these characteristics as fundamentally defining their organization. For the common people, without prejudices, Masonry is a male society, very mysterious, with secret rites, a kind of exclusive club. And for many, whose minds were infected by gossip and superstitions, Masonry is a huge net of conspirators and manipulators, aiming at world domination.

Before discussing the conspiracy theory, we must sadly remark on how the spiritual symbolism of the Lord of the World has decayed today to an upside-down position, being considered the lowest materialistic insignia. When Pilate "summoned Jesus and asked him, «Are you the king of the Jews?,»" Christ answered: "My kingdom is not of this world" (**John** 18:33, 36). Yet, for the modern mentality, as well as for Jesus' persecutors, it is impossible to understand a non-historical empire, a non-materialistic and non-worldly one. Therefore, today, the idea regarding the domination of the world, of the ephemeral and changeable world, is used as the supreme goal in various scenarios. In Sci-Fi literature, the aliens have one ambition: to become the masters of the terrestrial world; in the occultist and pseudo-esoteric texts, all the secret societies have an objective of governing the world. The great secret of the initiatory organizations, past or present, is, in the modern perspective, either a document, or a material treasure, or a proof regarding the right to govern the world.

---

[1] The 18th century was wrongly called "the age of enlightenment." Illuminism was erroneously considered a cultural movement, with a philosophical tint and socially committed, that tried to open the gates toward knowledge, freedom, democracy, and people's "enlightenment," and against the feudal system and theology. In fact, the problem is much more complicated; the real age of enlightenment was the Middle Ages (called "the dark age" by historicism), because only the spiritual domain can be related to light. Illuminism is a mockery, a desecration of genuine spirituality and pure intellectuality.

With respect to the conspiracy theory, we might underline that it is one of the most efficient methods of using and manipulating historicism. It is something often encountered in daily individual life, a notorious tactic. If somebody breaks a china plate, rainy weather is responsible, or the kid who asks too many questions, or the bad score of the favorite team, something external, and never one's own inability. It becomes serious when such an attitude extends from an individual to an entire nation. If a nation has problems, history and geography are responsible. And inside history it is easy to find scapegoats, true of false. One way is to blame predecessors. Usually a new government will declare from the beginning: "the past government transmitted to us a heavy heritage," shifting the responsibility to others. A second way is to blame the neighbours (and here geography intervenes): always the neighbouring countries are potential enemies and they could be excellent scapegoats. The third way is the conspiracy theory: very efficient today, since one does not lie more than necessary; it mingles the truth and falsehood. Everything occurring in the world is a result of a fantastic conspiracy. For the weak and sentimental individuals, the conspiracy theory is the key for all the problems and evil things. Unfortunately, this is like saying that the dearest dream of a fish is to swim.

In other words, of course important individuals and organizations plan and create various scenarios years in advance. Even something trivial, like a trip, has to be planned in some way, if you want it to succeed. In the profane world, it would be surprising if it was different. Yet, this becomes very distressing when the conspiracy theory confuses the profane domain with the sacred one, the temporal world with the spiritual one; to accuse, for example, Jesus of conspiracy, suggesting that He tried to take the worldly throne of Israel goes beyond any admissible limits.

If somebody really wants such an impossible combination (profane-sacred), the only valid thing would be to apply the theory of the cosmic cycles; yet such an application needs qualified and competent persons, who might be able, by particularization, to explain the "destiny" of people and civilizations, unveiling a "conspiracy" on a cosmic scale applied to various races, ages and nations of terrestrial humanity.[1] Moreover, if we indeed consider the conspiracy theory and the adjacent one (regarding the domination of the world), we should thoroughly study the real situation of *Kali-yuga* and what the Wrath of the Gods means. We should understand what *princeps hujus mundi* signifies and what the apocalyptic doctrine of the "adversary" represents, since, in fact, only the influence of some "adverse" forces in the historicist plane made it possible today for authentic initiatory and traditional organizations to be desecrated and accused of conspiracy and maleficent rites.

Today, there are innumerable conspiracy theories based not on traditional data or on the doctrine of the cosmic cycles. These theories take advantage mainly of the people's appetite for gossip and coffee shop secrets. As various individuals, when they meet, lack essential subjects to discuss and share all sorts of worldly "secrets," connected usually to the words and deeds of some specific characters ("celebrities" if possible), so the conspiracy theories deal with "secrets" on a historicist level, unveiling to the public all kind of historicist gossip and fabricated stories. And Free-Masonry, due to its nature, was used as a favourite element by the authors of these theories.[2]

---

[1] Such an attempt was made by Gaston Georgel (**Les Quatre Âges de l'Humanité**, Archè, 1976). Yet Giovanni Ponte wrote to us, years ago: "Is it really possible to study [the ancient civilizations] in a traditional way? Is there not a danger, which has to be taken into account, regarding the individualistic interpretations, as it happened to Gaston Georgel?"

[2] As an example, we mention two well-known theories: the first one pretends the existence of the so-called *Illuminati*, who were at the same time Masons, having as their objective the domination of the world; the second one refers to the *Protocols of the Elders of Sion*, related to the *Illuminati*. The name *Illuminati* derives from the Bavarian "illuminati" of Weishaupt, an antitraditional sect that has nothing to do with genuine Masonry. Regarding the *Protocols of the Elders of Sion*, that is an old story, which has been revived again and again in the hope that maybe somebody would believe it. René Guénon, with regard to the *Protocols*, said: "a serious and indeed hidden organization, whatever its nature would be, does not leave behind written documents" (René Guénon, **Le Théosophisme, histoire d'une pseudo-religion**, Éd. Traditionnelles, 1982, réédition augmentée de textes ultérieurs, p. 414). The "sources" for the *Protocols*, Guénon stated, are: a pamphlet by Maurice Joly against Napoleon the third, published at Brussels in 1865; the novel **Biarritz** by Hermann Goedsche and the novel **Le Baron Jéhova** by Sidney Vigneaux, published at Paris,

For the common people, the existence of a secret organization always produced distrust and animosity, since, by definition, the public is based on all that is public and everything that is hidden and unknown irritates. As mentioned before, the pleasure a tourist experiences when stepping inside the bedroom of a "celebrity" is also due to the opportunity to penetrate a "secret" and "intimate" place. Today, when nothing is considered "intimate" anymore, an organization like Masonry is difficult to accept. The mass-media's slogan, "the public has the right to know," is very well known. It is abused and used to hunt all sorts of gossip and intimacies and so-called "secrets," when, in fact, the information people need and have a right to know should be of a totally different nature.[1] At the same time, the public is always focused on "uncommon" individuals (called today "celebrities"), exactly because they look different from the common people (who constitute the "public"). Therefore, a conspiracy theory, which implicates a secret famous organization, will have, obviously, much more success than an unknown one. Free-Masonry, with its links to Rosicrucians and Templars, represented an ideal target for the exponents of the conspiracy theory.

The obliteration of the Order of the Temple is a good example of the profane mentality's reaction with regard to a secret organization. Generally speaking, in a society that has lost its traditional characteristic the idea of a "state inside the state," that is, the

---

in 1886 (there are some resemblances with Alexandre Dumas' novel **Joseph Balsamo**); the *Protocols* "borrowed" almost verbatim from these documents. The *Protocols*, Guénon concluded, are a fake, but it does not mean that there was not a "plan" designed by the antitraditional and counter-initiatory forces, which are linked with what we were saying about *Kali-yuga* and the cosmic cycles. The influence of "literature" in spreading this sort of antitraditional theories is remarkable, an influence that continues to act today. Regarding the *Protocols*, we may note a droll detail: in the French newspaper *Lyon Figaro*, of November 18, 2002, Claudio Mutti was accused of being the author of the *Protocols*, which would have made him over one hundred years old (René Guénon showed that the probable date of the fake document is 1901).

[1] Of course, people should be informed with regard to the social, political and economical order, and they should know the "secrets" regarding illegal activities. But there is a tendency to bury the really important issues in a huge amount of gossip and intimacies.

existence of an autonomous group, having its own rules different from the official ones (yet not against the official laws governing that country), is inconceivable. Like Free-Masonry later, the Order of the Temple became unbearable and was destroyed. If Masonry survived (even if there were epochs when it was totally prohibited), that was due to the passage from "operative" to "speculative" and, especially in modern times, due to its opening to the world, where in its ranks were accepted many individuals who, in normal times, would not have a chance of becoming Masons without possessing the necessary qualifications. As speculative Masonry, the organization comprised among its members preeminent characters belonging to the government, either princes and kings or presidents, who assured its survival. Yet, it did not mean, as the Templars were accused of all types of absurd crimes, that Masonry did not suffer the same accusations.[1] The antitraditional forces, perfidiously, took advantage of the fundamental law of traditional symbolism, which stipulates that not only does a symbol, by definition, accept an indefinite number of meanings, but also it always has two faces, one beneficent, and the other maleficent, since our world is based on duality. In different epochs, the beneficent meaning was lost, and only the maleficent one remained; in this mode, Saturn, the king of the "Golden Age," became an ogre, and was even identified with Satan (his symbolic weapon, the scythe, became the tool of Death); similarly, the wolf lost its luminous and spiritual aspects, remaining in the people's memory as the "bad wolf"; the same thing happened to the colour black. Correspondingly, the Templars' rites and emblems were interpreted in a maleficent sense (or they were simply invented). And likewise, the Masonic pentagram was confused (malevolent or not) with a satanic insignia; yet the five-point star is a symbol of the Microcosms and only by degeneration did it begin to be used in some satanic ceremonies.[2]

---

[1] The "Morgan case" is well-known in North America.
[2] The pentagram was not only a Masonic emblem, but also a Rosicrucian one, symbolizing the initiate, that is, "the perfect man." The mockery that presents the satanist with a pentagram on his chest is part of a larger action, a counter-initiatory one, aiming at the desecration of the traditional symbols. We may note that the

It is very important to make a distinction between an initiatory organization, as the Templars and Masonry, and a society, group, association or sect, even if secretive. The initiatory organizations[1] belong to the esoteric domain, while the religious sects, for example, refer to exotericism, the word "sect" signifying (from an etymological point of view) "scission," that is, scattering; to deny the esoteric for the sake of exoteric, Guénon stressed, means to deny precisely the link and the effective communication with the spiritual center of the world. It is true that sometimes religious sects were generated by an imprudent propagation of esoteric elements, more or less comprehended; yet, this does not mean that esotericism should be confused with religious heresies or sects, where the deviations were always due to "unqualified" individuals, incapable of an authentic knowledge. An example might be the Gnostics or the Cathars. To claim that an initiatory organization derives from a religious sect is equivalent to saying that the outside produced the inside, the circumference generated the center, the inferior caused the superior, and the body made the spirit. Evidently, the truth is precisely the opposite, since the body cannot "encompass" the spirit, but the spirit comprises the body (the lesser cannot contain the greater). For this reason, today, all these illusions regarding initiation, by artificially reviving the Gnostic doctrines, etc. only increase the Great Disarray.[2]

Coming back to the initiatory organizations, it must be stressed that (even secret) societies and associations are the expression of an individual initiative. Their rules and regulations, their organizational style, the oath and meetings, represent a typical individual

---

"adverse" forces, not at all negligible, know only to imitate, their role being to steal the traditional elements and desecrate them in an infernal mode. For the common people, such an action generates an irremediable confusion, and that is what these forces want. There are other examples we could mention. Guénon stated that the apocalyptic number 666, "the number of the Beast," is also a solar number, as well the lion is, at the same time, Christ and Antichrist's emblem. The confusion between the luminous aspect of the symbol and its dark side constitutes "satanism" (Guénon, **Roi**, p. 30).

[1] About this see Guénon, **Aperç. sur l'Init.**, pp. 72 ff.
[2] Gnosticism is a temptation for the modern mentality, being heretical.

"bureaucracy," while an authentic and superior initiatory organization is usually invisible, without any outside traces, and the case of the Rose-Cross is the best known; or, if they manifest their presence, they would need only initiatory rites and traditional symbols. Only on special occasions may the initiatory organizations take an external form similar to that of a society, as occurred with Masonry; yet even then it would be wrong to consider them secret societies, since many of the esoteric organizations possessed an initiatory secret that is incommunicable because of its very nature and not due to some external interdictions. However, profane societies copied, more or less, traditional organizations, aping their content, and therefore we have to be very careful when we want to characterize a visible organization.[1]

An initiatory organization does not usually leave written evidence, and that is one of the reasons why the historians will never fulfill their profane curiosity. For this reason, anytime the individual founders (without traditional attachments) of a group are exactly known, we can be sure that it is not an initiatory organization. An initiatory organization, Guénon stressed, is indeed "ineffable"; it is not submitted to contingencies and no worldly power can dismantle it (as in the case of a profane society), since the quality of its members is permanent and cannot be withdrawn, remaining real and operant, as long as one single "member" stays alive (in the case of the Templars, the "initiatory secret" was transferred to Masonry).

Diverting the initiatory organization's energies toward social, sentimental and moral objectives diminishes its effectiveness; yet, especially when it becomes implicated into the political domain, the decay is irremediable. On the other hand, there were circumstances

---

[1] As an example, Guénon wrote, we should mention the "Bavarian Illuminati," who represented an antitraditional society, that is, a profane one, and which was organized as an imitation of Masonry; on the other hand, Carbonarism, even though similar to *Illuminati* (because of its revolutionary activity), was originally an initiatory organization based on craft, which severely degenerated, with its members losing the meaning of their rites and symbols. It is obvious that we have to be cautious when we want to specify the nature of an organization, especially since the name (like "Illuminati") can easily deceive us (Guénon, **Aperç. sur l'Init.**, p. 83).

when an initiatory organization inspired one or more external, but genuine traditional organizations, due to their attachment to the initiatory organization that "generated" them, the latter guiding them in an "invisible" way, through a subtle activity of presence and "non-action" (the Far-Eastern *wu-wei*).

Speculative Masonry, by its opening to the many, to which we should add the unfavorable moment of the evolving human cycle, weakened and allowed, because of this very weakness, a lot of so-called Masonic organizations, in fact counterfeit groups based on individual initiatives, to be born.[1] If true Masonry is based on a regular and uninterrupted transmission, all the pseudo-Masonic societies and associations have a fantasist origin. Therefore, when some amateurish authors write that Masonry was an important factor in starting the French Revolution, for example, and they introduce the conspiracy theory, it is willingly forgotten that, in those times, in Germany, France, Russia, and Scandinavia, kings and princes were members of Free-Masonry, which made Queen Marie Antoinette exclaim: "Everybody is a Mason! So, where is the danger?"[2] Yet the danger was not Masonry itself, but exactly the fact that "everybody is a Mason"; since, this "dilution" of Masonry was a true misfortune, which permitted the manifestation of deviated individuals (among whom, of course, were Masons belonging to the regular lodges) and of dubious and profane societies dressed in Masonic clothes.[3]

One of the problems related to Free-Masonry that haunted the imagination of the modern world was the secrecy. From a historicist point of view, of course, it is impossible to understand that the "initiatory secret" is a mystery first of all because it is inexpressible,

---

[1] As Guénon said, "Regarding the Masonry, we must say that the infiltration of the modern ideas, to the initiatory mentality's detriment, made Masonry not one of the agents of the «conspiracy,» but one of its first victims" (Guénon, **Franc-Maçonnerie**, I, p. 110).
[2] On the other hand, the opinion that the revolutions are spontaneous is as well erroneous.
[3] The Masonic terms "assembly" and "convention," gestures and rituals, mode of organizing, were adopted by revolutionaries and are used today by political parties.

containing super-human truth that cannot be limited by words. Then, the point of view of an initiatory organization is not a worldly one, and as Saint Paul cannot be judged by human standards, so it is absurd to try to explain initiation by profane means. What characterizes all this amateurish "literature" that focused upon the Masonic secret is the endeavour to invent something sensational and corporeal, which could represent the "secret." Yet, unfortunately for historicism, as much as we boast about the human imagination, its possibilities are limited to few scenarios.

Let us try to trace logically these scenarios. An option would be to consider Jesus an alien, and that the Templars and the Masons knew this secret. Yet there is nothing new here, since some decades ago a campaign was launched to convince the public that all the gods are aliens coming from other planets. Another option would be to consider the "secret" a precious document[1]; yet in this case the "secret" is still unveiled. We can imagine that the document hides an even bigger secret: that, for example, the true God is the one worshiped by the Templars and not by the Catholic Church; this idea is a very old one, and we have seen that the Gnostics used it. We might suppose that the Templars and the Masons were some sort of satanists, but we cannot see how this "secret" is a secret, when such accusations accompanied Christianity all along, and Jeanne d'Arc and the Templars were publicly punished for this very reason. Another option would be to consider that the Templars hid a "secret" used to blackmail the Catholic Church.[2] Yet what is the reason for the blackmail? For power? For money? Impossible, because then we alter the basic truth about the Templars.[3] And if the Templars had a secret which could be used to blackmail the papacy, this should have been related to a false religion or a false God; but the Templars were strong defenders of the Catholic religion.

---

[1] We could consider the "secret" some kind of treasure, but Dumas already exploited it in his **Count of Monte-Cristo**.
[2] We must comment that the obsession of some authors with the Templars and Catholicism is more than weird.
[3] However, such a hypothesis is too modern. Only the modern man thinks that everything is money and power.

As we may note, there are not too many scenarios. Various authors have tried all these options and all their works, at the end, deflated since they could not unveil a secret sufficiently sensational to stand for a real "secret." All the works had one element in common: they referred to Jesus and, more or less subtly, were against the Catholic Church. In fact, to write a best-seller regarding this subject it is enough to have at hand a list of keywords, such as: Gnosticism, Masonry, Templars, Grail, Knights of the Round Table, Rosicrucianism, Jesus, Jerusalem Church,[1] Essenes, *Protocols of the Elders of Sion*, conspiracy theory, etc., and to connect them as cleverly as possible. Of course, it does not mean that the best-seller also has to tell the truth.[2]

---

[1] In a recent book it is considered that James and the Jerusalem Church transmitted to the Templars the Masonic "secret"; the absurdity and ignorance that characterize each page of this work are amazing. We note that some Gnostics had a special attraction for James, "the brother of Jesus," yet, almost certainly, they used him as a pretext to expose their doctrine; in **The First Apocalypse of James**, Christ states: "James, my brother. For not without reason have I called you my brother, although you are not my brother materially" (**Nag Hammadi** 262).

[2] One of the sure signs that could point out such a phantasmagoria (which often has a malevolent purpose) is its critical view regarding the medieval Christian traditional society (considering that this represents "the dark age"), and also its favorable views regarding the Renaissance and the "age of enlightenment."

CHAPTER XX

ROSICRUCIANISM AND TYPOGRAPHY

IF MASONRY ALLOWED ALL KINDS of aberrations related to the conspiracy theory, Rosicrucianism did not have the same success. The reasons are quite obvious, the first being the impossibility of "historizing" Rose-Cross. Even though Rosicrucianism can be traced to Masonry, even though many organizations called "Rosicrucian" emerged, they never constituted an initiatory organization such as Masonry, many of them being "Rosicrucian" only by name. Nobody could ever identify a genuine Rose-Cross.

René Guénon warned that there is a great difference between Rose-Cross and Rosicrucianism (Guénon, **Aperçus sur l'init.**, pp. 241 ff.). The true Rose-Cross never constituted a visible organization, all the groups that were born, starting with the 17th century and which could be qualified as Rosicrucian, did not have among their members a Rose-Cross, since the Rose-Cross functioned invisibly, similar to the messengers of Agarttha. The name Rose-Cross designates an initiatory degree, a spiritual state, and was not an association, an organization, or an identifiable group. The symbol of Rose-Cross (the rose in the center of the cross) expresses the perfection of the human state, describing the reintegration of the being in the center of this state, and the full expansion of human possibilities starting from this center.[1] Nevertheless, the name "Rose-Cross" was used, we should take note, for some particular spatial and temporal conditions, that is, for Christian society starting with the 16th century; in other circumstances there would have been a different name. Everything, Guénon stated, is indicated by the "legend" of Christian Rosenkreutz, who must not be considered a historical character, but rather a "collective entity."[2] The general significance of the "legend" is that the initiates of Christian esotericism, after the brutal disappearance of the Order of the Temple, seemed to have saved themselves and reorganized, in accordance with Islamic esotericism, but in a very secretive, invisible manner, having no visible institutions as support. The *Superiores Incogniti* who inspired this reorganization were, it seems, the Rose-Cross, the genuine Rose-Cross, so different from the later Rosicrucians. The "legend" of Christian Rosenkreutz seems to illustrate this reorganization. The Rosicrucians, on the other hand, were selected individuals, operating within the frame work of visible organizations, yet no one had acquired the spiritual degree of a Rose-

---

[1] The initiatory state of Rose-Cross refers to the Earthly Paradise and to the *Lesser Mysteries*, and only analogously we can transpose it to the *Greater Mysteries* and to Heavenly Paradise; Hermeticism also is about cosmology and not metaphysics. In the Middle Ages, one of the important emblems of the Blessed Virgin was the rose, which was called exactly *Rosa Mariae*. The Rose of Jericho has been called Saint Mary's Rose and a legend is told that "when Joseph and Mary were taking their flight into Egypt one of these roses sprang up to mark every spot where they rested." In medieval Germany, *Marien Roselen* was the name given to the Virgin (Arthur Edward Waite, **The Brotherhood of The Rosy Cross**, University Books, New York, pp. 88-9). The Blessed Virgin had an essential influence upon the Order of the Teutonic Knights, as it had upon Dante, Shakespeare and Christian Rosenkreutz. We may note that the headquarters' name of the Teutonic Order, established in Romania and then in Poland, was Marienburg, "the city of Mary"; also, the complete title of the Order was "the Teutonic Order of Holy Mary" (Jean Tourniac, **De la Chevalerie au secret du Temple**, Editions du Prisme, 1975, p. 16). And maybe it is not a coincidence that Rosicrucianism surfaced in Germany and that Christian Rosenkreutz was "German."
[2] Yates suggested that **The Alchemic Wedding of Christian Rosenkreutz** alluded to the wedding of princess Elizabeth (the daughter of James I, king of England) to Frederic V, the Palatin elector, in the year 1613 (when the Rosicrucian manifestos emerged). However, the election of Frederic as king of Bohemia started the "thirty years war" (Frances Yates, **La lumière des Rose-Croix**, Retz, 1978, pp. 13, 15, 41, 90).

Cross. It is said that, after the end of the "thirty years war" and the Peace of Westphalia, in 1648, the last genuine Rose-Cross retired to the Orient, wherever this "Orient" might be.[1]

Yet Rosenkreutz's "legend" also suggests that Germany was chosen as fertile land for the endeavour regarding the revival of the Western Christian society.[2] Luther, the visible exponent of the Reform, had as his seal a cross with a rose, that is, a "rose-cross,"[3] and it seems that Rose-Cross attempted, invisibly, to straighten out the Christian religion and society, but failed; on the contrary, this attempt amplified the decadence, illustrating, in a way, the very limits of the inspirers.

In these convoluted times, Valentin Andreae lived in Tübingen, Germany. He was a Protestant cleric whose grandfather supported Luther. Andreae's coat of arms contained a Saint Andrew's cross encompassed by four roses; also, the fact that he fought for a Christian Republic and a "True Christian Union," promoting an absolute fraternity, brotherly love, a pure Christian life, simplicity, and meditation, made many consider him the author of the three Rosicrucian works printed in Germany at the beginning of the 17th century. These are, in fact, the collective works of an anonymous group, which possibly the Andreae family joined, but what we should note is the ambience and the circumstances associated with the publishing of these Rosicrucian documents; the spiritual reform of the genuine Rose-Cross was distorted and reflected in the world as a, more or less, exoteric reform, tainted with Hermetic and Alchemical elements.

Let us observe also the guild of typographers' role in spreading Reform ideas, and the relation between the Rosicrucians and the typography as an initiatory craft seems more than a coincidence. Joseph de Maister underlined the disadvantage of writings compared

---

[1] Sédir, **Histoire et Doctrines des Rose-Croix**, Bibliothèque des Amitiés Spirituelles, 1932, p. 40. Guénon confirmed Sédir's sayings.
[2] Michael Maier affirmed though that Germany, where the headquarters of Rose-Cross was situated, is not the geographical country, but a symbolic land (Sédir, **Hist.**, p. 64).
[3] Waite, **Rosy**, p. 101, Sédir, **Hist.**, p. 64.

to oral transmission, the mistake of the Protestants being precisely to prefer Scripture to Tradition. For a Catholic from the 15th century, typography was an invention of the Antichrist, since it was spreading heresy. On the other hand, in Masonry, even if the oral transmission was fundamental, the writing was, like in other traditions, a support for initiation. Moreover, some Rosicrucian printed books were charged by their authors with special influences aiming at some particular disciples embarked upon an initiatory journey.

The printing of the Rosicrucians texts, at the beginning of the 17th century, has to be viewed almost as a modern act of "popularization." **Fama** (in 1614) and **Confessio** (in 1615) were published in Germany, at Cassel. **The Chemical Wedding of Christian Rosenkreutz in the year 1459** was published in 1616, at Strasbourg; however, the beginning of the 17th century was not the moment when the Rose-Cross was born (as the printed documents would suggest), but when its activity was ending. Germany was the country of the famous typographers Gutenberg and Johan Fust, while Strasbourg (where Gutenberg worked) was not only an important Masonic center, but also one of the typographers. In 1623, the people could read, on the walls of Paris, the following poster: "We, the Deputies of the Higher College of the Rose-Cross Brotherhood do make our stay, visibly and invisibly, in this city, by the grace of the Most High, to Whom turn the hearts of the Just. We demonstrate and instruct, without books and distinctions, the ability to speak all manners of tongues of the countries where we choose to be, in order to draw our fellow creatures from error of death." Or: "He who takes it upon himself to see us merely out of curiosity will never make contact with us. But if his inclination seriously impels him to register in our fellowship, we, who are judges of intentions, will cause him to see the truth of our promises; to the extent that we shall not make known the place of our meeting in this city, since the thoughts attached to the real desire of the seeker will lead us to him and him to us." The three documents printed in Germany, unveiling the symbolic legend of Christian Rosenkreutz, were related to the Parisian manifestos, aiming at the same goals (Wisdom, the way to the "infinite treasure," "a universal reform").

The Chemical Wedding of Christian Rosenkreutz is, though, more than an allegorical Alchemical treatise. **Fama** ends with a violent criticism regarding the so-called Alchemists, "the ungodly and accursed gold-makers," who "abuse the credit which is given to them" and "hold the transmutation of metals to be the highest point and *fastigium* in philosophy." These villains even suggest "that God would be most pleased with those who could make great store of gold – they hope with unpremeditated prayers to attain an all-knowing God and searcher of all hearts." And against them **Fama** stated: "but we by these presents publicly testify, that the true philosophers are far of another mind, esteeming little the making of gold, which is but a paragon, for besides that they have a thousand better things." Fama warned also against the printed books: "Also we do testify that under the name of Chymia many books and pictures are set forth in *Contumeliam gloriae Dei*, as we will name them in their due season, and will give to the pure-hearted a catalogue, or register of them. And we pray all learned men to take heed of these kinds of books; for the Enemy never rests but sows his weeds, till a stronger one does root them out." **Confessio** as well said: "In conclusion of our Confession we must earnestly admonish you, that you cast away, if not all yet most of the worthless books of pseudo chemists, to whom it is a jest to apply the Most Holy Trinity to vain things, or to deceive men with monstrous symbols and enigmas, or to profit by the curiosity of the credulous." And also: "You that are wise eschew such books, and have recourse to us, who seek not your money, but offer unto you most willingly our great treasures" (Yates, **Rose-Croix**, pp. 274, 283). It is an open confession that Christian Rosenkreutz's legend is a sacred tale about spiritual realization, using symbols regarding initiation and not the Alchemical processes and techniques as such.

It is interesting that in **The Chemical Wedding of Christian Rosenkreutz**, at one moment, the printed books, which want to deceive the readers, are judged, and a "Catalogue of Heretics or *Index Expurgatorius*" is established, which gave a hint of the dangers of typography. In **Fama**, the Rosicrucians asked the European scholars to be cautious with the books they read; yet these same scholars were encouraged to communicate in writing the result of their meditations. Despite this stimulus to the "popularization" of wisdom and the criticism regarding some books, the Rosicrucians deemed typography as a sacred science, "the science of letters." It is said in **Confessio**:

> These characters and letters, as God [The Great Typographer] has here and there incorporated them in the Sacred Scriptures, so has He imprinted them most manifestly on the wonderful work of creation, on the heavens, on the earth, and on all beasts, so that as the mathematician predicts eclipses, so we prognosticate the obscurations of the church, and how long they shall last. From these letters we have borrowed our magic writing, and thence made for ourselves a new language, in which the nature of things is expressed, so that it is no wonder that we are not so eloquent in other tongues, least of all in this Latin, which we know to be by no means in agreement with that of Adam and Enoch, but to have been contaminated by the confusion of Babel.[1]

We might note the relation with the Islamic doctrine of the "science of letters" (*ilmuh hurûf*), where the Rosicrucian *Liber Mundi* is (like in the Islamic doctrine) the Cosmos, and letters represent the eternal essences and divine ideas, which the supreme Pen has written simultaneously.[2] To learn the Book of the World, to be able to read it and even to write in it, the Rosicrucians needed a sacred tongue, since the European tongues were profane and inadequate to

---

[1] In Apa Seba's manuscript about the Greek letters, quoted previously in Chapter XV, the hermit considered the Greek letters of the alphabet as the elements of the universal manifestation (**Les Mystères des lettres grecques**, p. 22); and, "initially, there were the language and the letters of the Syrians ["Syrian speech" (*loghah sûryâniyah*)], that is the profound language of the Chaldeans. These letters were known in the days of Enoch. Regarding this language of the Syrians, the twenty-two letters of it were used by all the grammarians until the Tower of Babel episode and the confusion of the tongues. These Syrian letters were not invented by men, but traced by the hand and finger of God, who engraved the letters on a table of stone" (p. 140).

[2] The legend said that Christian Rosenkreutz, when he was sixteen years old (very "young," like any hero of the fairy tales), arrived at Damcar, in *Arabia Felix* ("Happy Arabia"), where the seers had already been waiting for him for many years; there Christian learned the Arabic language, became versed in the cosmic "miracles," and translated *Liber Mundi* into Latin, taking the book with him. The legend suggests an Islamic influence upon the Middle-West, as we have already mentioned.

transmit the metaphysical truth: therefore the Rosicrucian nostalgia for "Adam's tongue"; that is as well the meaning of the Parisian manifestos' hint with regard to "the ability to speak all manners of tongues." At the same time, the capacity to predict future events is based on the "science of letters," in close relation with Astrology; as Ibn Khaldun explained, the Muslim seers could predict (using the numerical values assigned to the letters) various events and even operate changes, influencing human and world destinies, since the letters corresponded to Macrocosms and Microcosms. The Rosicrucians, similarly reading in the Book of the World, saw the end of times getting closer, and tried to reform Western society. On the other hand, the "science of letters" constituted an excellent initiatory base for the typographer, since the art of typography appeared to be a direct application of the "science of letters." To print the **Bible**, that is, the **Book** (*bible* meaning "book"), signified a sacred imitation of the divine archetypal process of *Genesis*. From an initiatory point of view, *Liber Mundi* was the "divine Message" (*Er-Risâlatul-ilâhiyah*), the archetype of all the sacred books (Guénon, **Symboles**, p. 71).[1]

---

[1] Masonry was also related to the "science of letters," since the neophyte was embarked on a quest for the Lost Word (and the initiatory degrees had a connection with reading and writing). In the Islamic tradition, "red sulphur" was the initiatory degree of the one who could write in the *Liber Mundi*. In fact, Universal Man is also the Book, and Ibn 'Arabî said that the Prophet was constituted of letters. Universal Existence is an immense book, *Kitâb tadwînî*, in which Allâh wrote with the Pen-Intellect. In the Judaic Kabbalah, the twenty-two letters of the alphabet were the cosmogonic elements of the universal manifestation. In the Hindu tradition, the Three Worlds and the four conditions of *Âtmâ* were marked by letters: "Âtmâ, considered from the point of view of the syllable, is OM. Considered from the standpoint of the letters (constituting OM), the quarters (of the Self) are the letters (of OM), and the letters are the quarters. The letters are A, U and M. The waking state (the corporeal domain), the first element, is A. The state of dream (the subtle domain) is the second letter U. The sleep state (the informal world) is the third element, M. The fourth state is Turîya, without element, the partless OM, beyond conventional dealings, the limit of the negation of the phenomenal world, the non-dual. Om is thus the Self to be sure" (**Mândûkya Up**.). In the Christian tradition, Christ is A and Ω, He is the Logos composed of letters, and, "In the beginning was the Word, and the Word was with God, and the Word was God." In Gnosticism, the letters of the Greek alphabet are the parts of Alêtheia: A and Ω represent the head, B and Ψ the

Yet, as the Reform lost control, so did the art of typography; instead of remaining an initiatory art, it shifted soon to the profane domain.¹ Under the protection of the "printed word syndrome," the art of typography became desecrated; without any discrimination, all sorts of books were published, that significantly contributed to building a profane mentality.² Nowadays, Rosicrucian warning with respect to the books we read and the need of selection (between the genuine books and the ones aiming to deceive the reader) is more actual than ever.

There is though a positive aspect. Printed works can be, in the present unfavorable circumstances, a real support in assimilating a theoretical knowledge belonging to the traditional domain. They do not replace an authentic spiritual master, are not a substitute for an initiatory attachment, but they are able (of course the genuine traditional books) to offer support for meditation and help for a theoretical accomplishment, which is indispensable in any normal spiritual realization. Yet, we have to understand, even if indispensable, the theoretical training is just an introduction to the effective spiritual realization. Guénon wrote: "In any doctrine that is metaphysically complete, like the Oriental doctrines, the theory is always accompanied or followed by an effective realization, for which it is only the necessary base; no realization can be initiated without a theoretical preparation" (**Introduction**, p. 146). This theoretical preparation has nothing to do neither with the modern methods used in schools, nor with those of the scholars, the academic and erudite methods aiming the "cultivation of the spirit" belonging to the profane domain.

---

neck, Γ and X the shoulders and the hands, Δ and Φ the chest, and so on, until we reach M and N, which represent the feet.

¹ There is though an important difference between the art of typography and the art of calligraphy. The former, involving "mechanical" techniques, was from the beginning open to profane influences.

² "The printed word syndrome" refers to the fact that the modern individual prefers to believe the printed word rather than the oral word. Even today there are people who say, "It is true because it was printed in the newspaper."

Any exclusively «bookish» learning has nothing to do with the initiatory instruction, even if considered in its theoretical stage. [...] What is exclusively a bookish study belongs to the most outer education; and if we insist, that is because there are confusions when the study refers to books with an initiatory content. The one who reads such books like a «cultivated» person, or the one who studies them in an erudite manner and uses profane methods, will not be closer to genuine knowledge, since he brings dispositions that don't allow him to penetrate its real sense, nor to assimilate it at some degree. [...] Completely different is the case of those who, considering these books as «supports» for their inner effort (these types of books having precisely this function), are able to see beyond the printed words and find in them corroboration and an occasion for developing their own possibilities; and here we allude to the symbolic characteristic of the language. (Guénon, **Aperç. sur l'Init.**, pp. 218-9)

As we see, initiatory knowledge and traditional instruction have nothing in common with erudition.[1] Therefore, Ramana Maharshi, when he was asked if he read a specific book, answered:

I have not read anything. All my learning is limited to what I learned before my fourteenth year. Since then, I have had no inclination to read or learn. People wonder how I speak of **Bhagavad Gîtâ**, etc. It is due to hearsay. I have not read **Gîtâ** nor waded through commentaries for its meaning. When I hear a *sloka*, I think its meaning is clear and I say it. That is all and nothing more. Similarly with my other quotations. They come out naturally. I realize that the Truth is beyond speech and intellect. Why then should I project the mind to read, understand and repeat stanzas, etc.? Their purpose

---

[1] Regarding the spiritual domain, erudition (which is an assembly of quantitative data and bibliographical references) has no power. There is no common denominator between erudition and genuine esotericism. The true spiritual masters are not scientists or just erudite individuals; in the same way, Tradition and profane culture are not at the same level. Let us not be misunderstood: we have nothing against erudition and culture, sometimes they are even helpful, and we know too well that they are part of our modern world. But we do not see why each element should not be placed at its normal degree of the hierarchy. Also it is hard to understand why the erudite scholars feel the need to poke their noses into the esoteric domain, which they do not comprehend; or why the philosophers think they have a right and even an obligation to analyze genuine metaphysics. Of course, what happens is the exacerbation of "individualism," that is, of the antitraditional spirit in the modern world, when everybody thinks they have the right to touch on any subject, in the same way as everybody thinks they can perform any function.

is to know the Truth. The purpose having been gained, there is no further use engaging in studies.[1]

There are some, aware of the importance of René Guénon's work, who have suggested that its study allows one to obtain a spiritual influence and even an effective initiation; that his work, in the present difficult circumstances, would exempt us from participating in the exoteric rites and in the exoteric domain in general, and would offer a new spiritual way. Is it possible? Yet Guénon himself asked this question and answered without equivocation:

Cannot the books with an initiatory content, for qualified individuals and pupils with the necessary vocation, serve as carriers in the transmission of a spiritual influence? Is it not enough for an initiation, in such cases, to read these books and exclude the direct contact with a traditional «chain»? [...] That would be contrary to the fact that an oral transmission is, everywhere and always, deemed as a necessary condition in genuine traditional education; therefore, putting traditional learning in writing cannot replace the oral transmission, and that is so because, to be indeed valid, it implies the existence of a «vital» element, which the books cannot carry. Some might protest that, considering various stories with respect to the Rosicrucian tradition, a number of books have been charged with influences by the very authors, which is indeed possible, as well as it is for any other object. Yet, even if admitting this fact, it could not be more than some specific copies prepared in a special way for this purpose; moreover, each of these copies should be destined exclusively to a disciple to whom it would have been handed directly; and it would not replace the initiation that the disciple had already acquired, but offer an efficient help, when during his personal efforts the disciple would use the book as support for meditation. (Guénon, **Initiation**, pp. 58-59)

Consequently, Guénon's works are for the modern man, we might say, indispensable for a theoretical preparation aiming at a spiritual realization and should be used, with great efficiency, as support for meditation. Yet these works do not confer an initiation and do not replace other requisite elements to accomplish an effective

---

[1] **Talks with Ramana Maharshi**, InnerDirections, 2000, pp. 315-316.

realization. One of Guénon's books, printed in thousands of copies, does not become special only because it ended up in our hands. It cannot be considered help as a physical object, but only due to its content and what it may transmit.[1]

The problem was so important that René Guénon insisted upon it on more than one occasion. As the printed books more and more flourished and spread, so flourished errors. Not only have all sorts of books, with noxious and false content, spread into the world, but a "bookish fixation" (now challenged by the Internet) has developed, which included the idea of being "self-taught" and rejected the importance of oral transmission.[2] Guénon wrote:

[For the neophyte embarked upon a spiritual realization], a book's content is nothing else than a support for meditation, in a ritual sense we might say, similar to other symbols of different orders. If the one who meditates upon an initiatory writing establishes, indeed in this way, a connection with an influence coming from the author, which is really possible if the specific writing belongs to a traditional form and, especially, to a particular «chain» (to which the neophyte himself belongs), this, far from replacing an initiatory attachment, is, on the contrary, only a consequence of this attachment (which the neophyte already possesses). Therefore, from all the standpoints, we absolutely cannot envisage a bookish initiation, but only, in

---

[1] We must though insist that René Guénon's work is not a work "of exposure" or "of popularization," to match the public's curiosity for "esoteric secrets." René Guénon's work is not a manual to prepare someone with a view to initiation, or a manual informing about esotericism. It is not just an introduction to other traditional writings. Guénon's work represents a metaphysical teaching, complete and autonomous, and the one who succeeds in comprehending and really assimilating it, even though he does not obtain an initiation or an effective realization, acquires a perfect theoretical knowledge.

[2] Martin Lings wrote: "On the one hand, like an old man who has become irrepressibly granulous in his senility, the human race produces a ceaseless flow of books, and we may be certain that incomparably more is written than what reaches the stage of print. ... They share with the mass media the blame of distracting man from the essential, but they are far less dangerous than the writings of those literary, philosophic and scientific «heroes» of the hour which serve to indoctrinate their readers with error in various forms and in general to imprison them within the limitations of the modern outlook" (**The Eleventh Hour**, Quinta Essentia, 1987, p. 78).

some conditions, an initiatory use of the books, which is something totally different. (Guénon, **Initiation**, pp. 62-63)

Yet in the modern world, even the initiatory use of the books is very rare. The majority of people do not have the necessary spirit of discrimination to choose the beneficent book from the maleficent one. They often look for easy reading, or purely and simply they give up reading books. And those who have the chance to have in their hands an initiatory work do not have the vocation or the initiatory attachment to properly use the book. Already in Guénon's days there were few really interested in traditional studies[1] and we can note the same thing throughout the ages.[2]

In fact, the modern individual lacks the proper language to understand an initiatory book, since, a new confusion about the language has occurred in our days, and for the one without a traditional guide, a sacred text looks like it is written in an unknown tongue. And when the Rosicrucians declared: "We demonstrate and instruct, without books and distinctions, the ability to speak all manners of tongues of the countries where we choose to be, in

---

[1] The lack of interest is often the consequence of the lack of qualification, yet the interest for traditional studies does not mean acquiring automatically an initiatory qualification. The case of Guénon's collaborator, Marcel Clavelle (Jean Reyor) is a good example.

[2] There is though a mysterious law saying that always the ones who really look for such books will find them and the author should worry only to produce a work which conforms to the truth, without caring if the work will have readers or not. Saint Philotheus, Saint Gregory Palamas' biographer, registered how Palamas started to write. After a period of serious ascetic and divine meditations, Saint Palamas retreated to a Hesychastic hermitage on Mount Athos. One day, after two hours of prayers and divine meditation in complete silence, he fell into a kind of sleep and entered a state of divine contemplation. He saw himself holding a vessel full of milk, which, suddenly, started to overflow. The milk then changed into a marvelous wine that flew onto his clothing and hands, spreading an extraordinary perfume. Then a man "full of light" showed up, who told Palamas that he had to share with others this divine liquid, and not let it be wasted, since it is the God's grace. Saint Palamas, very reluctant, argued that there are not such people to relentlessly quest these sorts of teachings. Yet the divine apparition answered that Palamas had to do his duty and leave it in Jesus Christ's care to find such people.

order to draw our fellow creatures from the error of death," they did not refer to the profane language but to the initiatory one.

CHAPTER XXI

LANGUAGE DISARRAY

AT THE BEGINNING OF THE PRESENT human cycle the primordial Tradition was identical to the Word, as the first affirmation of Silence; this Word synthesized the metaphysical knowledge without a discursive elaboration. When the cycle evolved and declined, when humanity through its centripetal movement left the Center and started to fall farther and farther, the Word changed into words and, what for the primeval human beings looked obvious and natural and could be grasped by intellectual intuition, had to be explained, ramified, and explicated, dressed in clothing matching the cycle's moment. There are many symbols (the symbol constituting the most adequate language for transmitting metaphysical truth) that changed and decayed at the same time with the increase of human ignorance, in conformity with the law of the cosmic cycles.

Silence – Word – words: it is the language's journey, symbolizing the "evolving" of the universal manifestation. In the Hindu tradition, the Word generated the Three Worlds, by uttering the three ritual exclamations: "Bhûr, Bhuvar, Swar – these three, indeed, are the Vyâhrtis [the ritual exclamations]. Besides them, Mahâcamasya knew a fourth one – Maha by name. It is Brahma; it is the Self, Âtmâ [the non-manifestation, The Fourth, Turîya]. The others are the limbs. Bhûr, indeed, is this world [the Earth, the corporeal manifestation], Bhuvar is the intermediate space [the Atmosphere, the subtle manifestation, still formal], Swar is the other world [the Heaven, the informal and super-individual manifestation]" (**Taittiriya Up.**, I, 5,

2). The Word is the overall principle, and for this reason **Taittirîya Upanishad** also said: "Maha [the Greater Word] is the Sun [as Principle sustaining the universal manifestation]. Bhûr is the Fire [the anterior, inferior states], Bhuvar is the wind [the unifying element], Swar is the sun [the posterior element, the superior states],[1] Maha is the Moon [as midnight Sun]."

Muhyiddin Ibn 'Arabî wrote: "All the existences are «the Words of Allâh» that never end; since all are nothing else than the word «Let it be» (*kun*), which is the Word of Allâh." The Christian tradition explicitly stated: "In the beginning was the Word" (**John** 1:1), which corresponds to the Hindu primordial sound, *Parashabda*. The Word is the expression of the Thought, of the divine Intellect, of Silence; it is "the Word without words," as Zhuang Zi said. As Ibn 'Arabî said, "Allâh uttered the sound not after a preliminary silence, nor after a silence of reflection [that is, not in a temporal succession], but through an eternal Word (*qadîm*), without beginning and end, like His other attributes. With this Word He talked to Moses and He called it Torah; with this Word He talked to David and called it Psalms, to Jesus and He called it Gospel, to Muhammad and He called it «Descent» (*al-Tanzîl*) and «Discrimination» (*al-Furqân*) [names of **Qur'ân**]."

The difference between the Word and the words is huge, especially when the latter are desecrated, as occurs in the modern world. In any traditional society the words, as projections of the Word, constituted the ritual sounds capable of operating upon the world in accordance with their semantic quality, "the talking and the walking," that is, the word and the deed, representing a harmonious couple; therefore when God uttered *Fiat Lux*, there was light.[2] At

---

[1] Fire, Wind and Sun are the lights of the Three Worlds.
[2] In a traditional society, Coomaraswamy stated, what an individual, who "has the authority to utter," utters is "said and done" (Coomaraswamy, **Autorité**, pp. 25-26). The king (the temporal power) does not "do" with his hands, but with *fiat*, with his edicts; he is the "Word" that actualizes the intentions (Thought) of the spiritual authority, making them become effective. This is the wedding, in a traditional society, between Thought (Intellect) and Word, expressed by the priesthood (masculine) and royalty (feminine). Any of the king's words which are not inspired by a sacerdotal thought (being therefore

the same time, as can be read in **Sepher Yetsirah**, the word is associated with the name, and the production of the universal manifestation, that is, of the beings that constitute it, means "to name" these beings. The name plays an important role in various traditions, being, however, in a specific order of reality, a substitute of the supernal pole. "The Lost Word" is an equivalent of "God's Name" and to utter this name signifies an operation upon reality, signifies using the "power of the keys," to lock and unlock. In this respect, there is an interesting episode from Saint Sylvester's life, in which the magician Zamvri, belonging to the Judaic tradition, uttered the name of God in a wild bull's ear, killing it instantaneously, and Saint Sylvester resurrected it by uttering the name of Christ.[1]

Silence – Word – words. The Silence symbolizes the metaphysical Void, it is the hidden Dragon representing the Non-Being, the metaphysical Zero, the supreme Principle, called in the Hindu tradition *Brahma nirguna*; the Word is the Plenitude, the Pleroma, the One, it is the visible Dragon, the Being, *Brahma saguna*, the first determination of the Non-Being, the Principle of the universal manifestation. The Word without words belongs to the non-manifestation: it is the "not uttered utterance"; the duality of the words belongs to the manifestation. The words represent the multiplicity, the universal manifestation generated and sustained by the visible Dragon's sacrifice which, through its sacrifice, allows it to be cut into pieces and multiplied, like Purusha, like Osiris, like the Word that is cut into words, like Christ who shared His body and blood at the Last Supper.[2] The morsels of bread offered to the Apostles are Christ's words, which afterwards multiplied, in the same

---

an independent operation) is a heresy, a revolt, a heterodoxy, something satanic, since "the Word is uttered inspired by the Spirit" (**Aitareya Brâhmana**, II, 5, Coomaraswamy, **Autorité**, p. 40).

[1] In the Gnostic writing **The Gospel of Philip**, it is said: "One single name is not uttered in the world, the name which the father gave to the son; it is the name above all things: the name of the father. For the son would not become the father unless he wore the name of the father" (**Nag Hammadi** 142).

[2] The words generated by the sacrifice of the Word become nutriment for the beings. The real meaning of "cannibalism" illustrates this very symbolism.

way as the Evangelic bread multiplied due to Jesus' miracle; yet these words, this bread, have a double reality: an apparent, illusory one, representing the manifestation, the world, and a hidden, permanent one, illustrated by the Christian tradition through Jesus' sayings: "Man does not live on bread alone, but on every word that comes from the mouth of God" (**Matthew** 4:4); "Heaven and earth will pass away, but my words will never pass away" (**Matthew** 24:35). Christ is the Word, and the bread (erroneously translated as "the daily bread") symbolizes the Word, therefore Jesus was born in *Beith-Lehem*, "the House of Bread."[1]

The words inside the universal manifestation take different hierarchic degrees, the "greater words" (the ritual, sacred, stable words), situated at the top, compose the sacred languages; at the bottom are the profane words, which change, multiply, alter their meaning, appearing as conventional elements, without a principle. We can see a major distinction between the sacred and profane language, oral or written.[2]

In conformity with the Islamic tradition, the primordial, or "Adam's," tongue is the "Syrian speech" (*loghah sûryâniyah*), yet the name alludes not to the actual country Syria, but to "the Sun's land," *sûryâ* in Sanskrit being the name of the sun (Guénon, **Symboles**, p. 69); "the Sun's land" is one of the names of the primordial Center. In **Qur'ân**, Solomon exclaimed: "O you people! We have been taught the speech of birds" (27:16). "The speech of birds" (*ullimna mantiqat-tayri*) is the angelic tongue, that is, the speech of the super-

---

[1] In **The Gospel of Philip** it is said: "Man used to feed like the animals but when Christ came, the perfect man, he brought bread from heaven in order that man might be nourished with the food of man" (**Nag Hammadi** 143). Herodotus narated the story about the Phrygians, who were considered of greater antiquity than the Egyptians because the first word a child uttered was *becos*, which was the Phrygian name for bread.

[2] There are tongues like Chinese, Sanskrit, Hebrew, and Arabic, which are closer to the primordial tongue than the Western ones; the Chinese ideograms, like the Egyptian hieroglyphs, compose an exclusively sacred language, close to the primordial one, and the Hebrew and Arabic languages contain characteristics favorable to initiatory instruction (we have in mind firstly the numerical values of the letters).

individual states, and the only way it can be explained to the human mind is to consider it as a "music of the spheres," a versified, rhythmical song, in harmony with the celestial vibrations. Its projection into the world is exactly the "Syrian speech," which – reflection of the heavenly music – is a rhythmical language and an Islamic tradition transmitted that Adam, while still living in the Earthly Paradise, used rhymes when he spoke; however, Guénon affirmed, the "science of the rhythm" is the fundament for any type of communication with the supernal states.[1] "Here is the reason why the sacred Books were written in a rhythmical language, which makes them something totally different than some profane «poems.» However, at the beginning, poetry was not this vane «literature» as it became by decaying, due to the decline of the human cycle" (Guénon, **Symboles**, p. 77).[2]

The rhythmical language is closely connected to the oral transmission of the tradition. In a traditional society, "a man can only

---

[1] Djalâl ad-Dîn Rûmi said: "In the music's rhythm a mystery is hiding: if I had unveiled it, I would confuse the world." "Saul's attendants said to him, «See, an evil spirit from God is tormenting you. Let our lord command his servants here to search for someone who can play the harp. He will play when the evil spirit from God comes upon you, and you will feel better»" (**1 Samuel** 16:15-16). That someone would be David. "Yao ordered K'uei to compose music: when this one hit the musical stones all the beasts started to dance; when his flute was heard nine times, the bird Phoenix showed up in the sky" (**Lie-zi**). In the Hindu tradition, Heaven is Harmony and Music. Harmony or Music (*Sâma*) is the groom and the word (*Rc*) is the bride; hence, only in our world do we need words (even as verses), "the speech of birds" being music without words; the verses or the words are just a "support" for the music, which is projected from heaven to earth (Coomaraswamy, **Autorité**, pp. 79-82). The word is one of the examples that can illustrate quantity; the speech is something quantified, since without the pauses between the words we do not have coherent speech; in heaven, this quantification does not exist, therefore the music is without words, a continuous sound.

[2] Coomaraswamy considered that we should identify culture with poetry, yet, "not having in view the kind of poetry that nowadays babbles of green fields or that merely reflects social behaviour or our private reactions to passing events, but with reference to that whole class of prophetic literature that includes the Bible, the Vedas, the Edda, the great epics, and in general the world's «best books»" (Ananda K. Coomaraswamy, **The Bugbear of Literacy**, Perennial Books Ltd., 1979, p. 35).

be said to *know* what he knows *by heart*" (Coom., **Literacy**, p. 41), therefore the traditional men memorized thousands of verses, as in the case of India where the epics were told by heart without error, or in the case of the ancient Greeks. Compared to writing, oral learning allowed the live transmission of rhythm, of intonation, of harmony, all equally as important, from the spiritual efficiency point of view, as the content which was transmitted. For Coomaraswamy, the difference between oral and written literature is the same as the distinction between poetry and prose, between myth and fact; "The quality of oral literature is essentially poetical, its content essentially mythical, and its preoccupation with the spiritual adventures of heroes; the quality of originally written literature is essentially prosaic, its content literal, and its preoccupation with secular events and with personalities" (Coom., **Literacy**, pp. 41-42).

The rhythmical language – the prototype of oral poetry – is, as we have already suggested, the language of the Earthly Paradise. Similar to the traditional symbols, it has two faces, one toward the divine, the other toward the world. Only in the Earthly Paradise, that is, in the center of the integral human being, is it possible to communicate with the super-individual states and hence, to understand "the speech of birds": it is the superior face of the rhythmical language. On the other hand, the one who reached the Earthly Paradise is invested with "the gift of speech": it is the inferior face, turned toward the world.

The Rosicrucians, we saw, had this "gift of speech"; they could talk all the tongues of the earth. Yet such a skill should not be taken *ad litteram*. Rose-Cross is an initiatory degree corresponding to the *Lesser Mysteries*, symbolizing the reintegration in the center of the human being, which is also the Earthly Paradise. A Rose-Cross, therefore, speaks the rhythmical language and understands the speech of birds, being able to communicate with the angelic states. At the same time, he is invested with the gift of speech, which means, symbolically, that, reaching the Earthly Paradise, he regains the primordial Tradition, that is, rediscovers the "Lost Word," the Grail, and gathers what was scattered; he gathers, in fact, the words into the Word, the particular traditions into the one-and-only

Tradition, and, knowing the fundamental and essential unity of all the traditional and religious forms, he knows all the tongues. A Rose-Cross, René Guénon explained, due to his spiritual degree, is not bound to a specific form, or a specific place, therefore he is a "cosmopolite" in the true sense of the word (**Aperç. sur l'Init.**, pp. 237 ff.). He wears various clothing and takes different appearances, for different circumstances, and uses various languages, depending on whom he is talking to. In the same way the primordial Tradition was ramified in various traditions, all orthodox; this was necessary because there were different groups and populations. Rose-Cross being free to speak any language declared that they speak all the tongues. Because of this "freedom," Rose-Cross cannot be considered an exoteric visible organization, and that is why their meeting place was the Temple of the Holy Spirit, which was everywhere. And it is not a coincidence that the Temple of Rose-Cross is related to the Holy Spirit.

When the day of Pentecost came, they were all together in one place. Suddenly a sound like the blowing of a violent wind came from heaven and filled the whole house where they were sitting. They saw what seemed to be tongues of fire that separated and came to rest on each of them. All of them were filled with the Holy Spirit and began to speak in other tongues as the Spirit enabled them. Now there were staying in Jerusalem God-fearing Jews from every nation under heaven. When they heard this sound, a crowd came together in bewilderment, because each one heard them speaking in his own language. (**Acts** 2:1-4, 6)

The Apostles were invested by the Holy Spirit with the "gift of speech," that is, they received the quality of transmitting the Tradition in specific forms, depending on what type of individuals they would be addressing. **Acts** specified that those who understood the Apostles' tongues were "Parthians, Medes and Elamites; residents of Mesopotamia, Judea and Cappadocia, Pontus and Asia, Phrygia and Pamphylia, Egypt and the parts of Libya near Cyrene; visitors from Rome (both Jews and converts to Judaism); Cretans and Arabs" (**Acts** 2:9-11), which suggests that the Christian tradition was not destined to remain in a limited area and amid a specific people. On the other hand, it is curious that if the Christian tradition was founded having Hebrew as its sacred tongue, the **New Testament** was written in Greek from the beginning. "We may ask ourselves why the setting in writing, when it occurred, did not use the same tongue [that Christ spoke]" (Guénon, **Ésot. Chrét.**, p. 17). Compared to Arabic or Hebrew, Greek and Latin are not sacred languages.

Greek and Latin can very well play for Christianity the role of liturgical languages, yet they are not sacred. The lack of a sacred language in Christianity becomes even more striking when we note that, even in the case of the Hebrew writings, for which the primitive text existed, officially only the Greek and Latin translations were used. Regarding the New Testament, the text was known only in Greek. (Guénon, **Ésot. Chrét.**, pp. 16-17)[1]

In a review from 1938, Guénon wrote as well:

Unfortunately, in seems that in Christianity the relation between the exoteric and esoteric domains has not been established in a perfectly normal manner, as it happened in other traditions; we must admit that it is a strange «lacuna,» which was caused by multiple and complex motives (the lack of a sacred language, specific to the Christian tradition, is one example), and its explanation could drive us far away, since this forced «Christianity» to remain, in all epochs, incomplete. (Guénon, **Articles**, p. 232)

The lack of a sacred language had, no doubt, negative consequences upon the evolvement of Western society. Latin and Greek, as

---

[1] Yet even the **Old Testament** that circulated in Saint Paul's days was in Greek: we are referring to the **Septuagint**, which was read in the synagogues and churches of Greek tongue. Many of the quotations in the **New Testament** are from the **Septuagint** and not from the Hebrew text. The legend said that Ptolemy, the Egyptian pharaoh, when he built the Alexandrian Library, asked seventy wise men from Jerusalem, who spoke Hebrew and Greek, to translate, each one separately, the **Old Testament** (we note again the number 70). The seventy each gave a translation to the pharaoh, who noticed with total amazement, that all the translations were identical, making him understand that the translation was done by a divine power ("the gift of speech"). At the beginning, the **Septuagint** contained the apocryphal texts also.

liturgical languages, could not compensate completely for the lack of a sacred tongue, and maybe that is why the decline of Western society occurred faster than would have been normal[1]; today, we witness a profane language, more and more conventional and alienated.[2]

The journey of the language from sacred to profane can be imagined by comparing it to related journeys. In the traditional commentaries on **Yi Jing** it is said: "The writing cannot exhaust the speaking; the speech cannot exhaust the thinking; yet the seer's thoughts could not though manifest? Confucius affirmed: The wise man established symbols to exhaust the thoughts; he founded the hexagrams." We note the descendant hierarchy: thinking, speaking, and writing. Yet even **Yi Jing** is a good example of this journey of the language from the Word to words. The Word is One, and One is the Dragon, and the All is One, but this truth was lost in time, and therefore **Yi Jing** had to have commentaries, and the commentaries produced other commentaries, which also had to be commented upon.[3] **Yi Jing** offers a great opportunity for learning, from all the points of view. Just contemplating the form of it, in a continuous change and in accordance with the cosmic cycles, we learn more than from profane instruction. At the beginning, the Book (**Jing**) was a series of trigrams, synthetic symbols offering the vision and realization of the Truth; then, the decline of the cycle forced the symbols to become more explicit, and so the succinct forms were

---

[1] There were some attempts to prove that the Greek language was also sacred and hiding the message about Christ, a message the Greeks could not decipher. Apa Seba's manuscript is an illustration of such an attempt. The hermit said: "Here it is the mystery. God wanted, in Its providence, to use the Greek letters to force the pagans to obey unwittingly to Its religion. ... From the days of Adam and Enoch, God started to signal us the mystery of Christ and of the Holy Church" (**Les Mystères des lettres grecques**, pp. 98, 100).

[2] Frédéric Portal established a hierarchy of the language: the divine language, corresponding to God (and to the primordial Tradition, we add); the sacred language, corresponding to the priesthood (and to the particular traditions); the profane language (**Des couleurs symboliques**, Guy Trédaniel, 1979, p. 10).

[3] For this reason the Islamic tradition promoted a doctrine of Unity (*Et-Tawhid*), which contained explanations of things that *ab origo* were obvious.

born; eventually, with the increasing decadence, the commentaries were established. It is the natural journey from quality to quantity, from essence to substance: Silence – Word – words; it is the journey followed also by the Hindu tradition, for which the **Upanishads** represented an explication of the **Vêda**.

As the primordial Tradition parted into different secondary and derived branches, so the synthetic primordial symbols spread, each keeping only some aspects or meanings; and this idea must be stressed, since it is valid for any element of the manifestation, like for example human mentality or human language, which starting from the Word (which contained synthetically everything), became more and more explicit (in accordance with the fall of the human cycle), more and more elaborated; in the same way a symbol became more and more explicit and we can see today strange tautologies (the symbol being doubled by more evident explanations). Moreover, with the decay of the world, the words decayed also, multiplying, altering and desecrating their content.[1]

We might say that the moment when the multiplication and desecration of the words started is symbolically designated by the Tower of Babel episode: "Now the whole world had one language and a common speech. ... That is why it was called Babel, because there the Lord confused the language of the whole world. From there the Lord scattered them over the face of the whole earth" (**Genesis** 11:1-9). As we already suggested, the meaning of this episode can be reported on different levels: considering the entire cycle of present humanity, the confusion of the language, that is, the cutting of the primordial unique language ("Adam's language") into pieces, could symbolize the passage from the primordial Tradition to the secondary multiple traditions; considering a secondary cycle, we can envisage either the "Age of Bronze" with the revolt of the warriors (Nimrod), or the "Iron Age"; eventually, on an even more

---

[1] Hegel's opinion that the German language was much more elevate than the Chinese language is just another injustice of the modern mentality. Guénon mentioned Leibniz, who thought that his mathematical binary system was superior to **Yi Jing** (**Orient et Occident**, p. 67).

limited scale, the confusion of the language could indicate the critical times when Christianity was born and, by reflection, the modern world. We remember that Saint Paul wrote to the Corinthians: "I appeal to you, brothers, in the name of our Lord Jesus Christ, that all of you have a common speech and agree with one another so that there may be no divisions among you and that you may be perfectly united in mind and thought" (**1 Corinthians** 1:10-13), trying to end the confusion of the language; and for a while Saint Paul's endeavour succeeded: the Christian traditional society, having its apex in the Middle Ages, used the same "language," the faith in Christ. Yet, this was not for very long. Starting with the demolition of the Templars and continuing with the "one hundred years war" the Christian society lost, step by step, its unity, and after the Peace of Westphalia, there occurred another confusion of the language, since the formation of the national states meant the tearing of the one-and-only cloak and the cutting of the one language into many particular languages.

Today, the confusion has reached its extreme and we are not thinking here only of its literary meaning, but of the fact that the division among people is so acute that we do not have a common language even when we have a common tongue; today individualism makes each individual have his or her own special language. Today, many talk and few listen. Many are too preoccupied with their ego or they simply do not understand one another's language; and the words do not have profound meaning anymore.[1]

But not only did the scattering of the words reach paroxysm; the words themselves lost their true significance, being abused, altered

---

[1] The development of typography was in concert, as a necessity, with the liquidation of public "illiteracy," since who would have read otherwise the increasing quantity of printed copies. In learning to read, modern man forgot how to listen. To know how to write and read is not, from a traditional point of view, a necessary condition for a spiritual realization. Coomaraswamy wrote in a letter of 1943: "Literacy is of supreme importance only for shopkeepers and chain-belt workers, who must be able to keep accounts and be able to read the instructions that are put on the factory notice board. For the rest, it were far better not to be able to read at all than to read what the great majority of Europeans and Americans read today" (Coom., **Letters**, p. 293).

and desecrated. Metaphysics, the doctrine of pure intellect, became a non sense word: we witness expressions like "the metaphysics of *Star Trek*," "the metaphysics of nuclear energy," or "the *New Age* metaphysics," in the same way as philosophy is now a word shamelessly applied to any domain, from diet to modern art.[1]

Regarding the confusion of the language, there is another problem we should consider. Coomaraswamy mentioned oral and written literature; of course, he used the word "literature" in its general sense, even if in Latin *littera* represents mainly "written letters, inscriptions." For modern man, as well, "literature" refers firstly to written works, and especially to fiction.

In a previous book, we tried to stir interest for the domain of traditional studies using Western literature as a pretext. It was a risky endeavour, considering that nowadays there persists the opinion that humankind hides an unconscious yearning for initiatory subjects and initiatory symbolism, and has a secret need for religiosity. Such an opinion degrades the spiritual domain, bringing it down to the psychological level of individuality. And not once was the attraction towards initiatory meanings and religious implications in literary works considered a confirmation of this unwitting longing for a spiritual completion.

It is more dangerous to consider literary texts, especially the modern ones, as initiatory means. What is usually called literature belongs completely to the profane order. Modern and profane literary works have no power to transmit an initiation or to be a support for spiritual realization. Even the sacred writings do not automatically confer initiation on an individual. Reading a sacred text

---

[1] We are far away from Aristotle who called metaphysics "the primeval philosophy," or from Saint Gregory the Sinait who said: "And a divine philosopher is that one who united through deeds and direct vision with God, becoming and being named His friend, as one who loves the primeval Wisdom, more than any other friendship, wisdom or knowledge." Guénon stressed that, initially, the word "philosophy" meant "the love for wisdom," and the fall occurred when *sophia* was substituted with *philo-sophia* (**Crise**, p. 25); and Guénon added that what the modern philosophers call metaphysics has nothing to do with true and genuine metaphysics (**Crise**, p. 91).

or a thousand sacred texts doesn't allow the readers to auto-initiate themselves.

In our prior work, **The Everlasting Sacred Kernel**, we only used Western literature to introduce the essence of traditional thinking and to illustrate how the laws of sacred symbolism should be considered. We stressed the importance of looking upwards, in a *sattwic* manner, and not downwards as many are doing today. We assumed that, looking upwards, it is still possible to uncover a sacred kernel in literature, even if this became desecrated.[1] We underlined the major role of the power of discrimination to identify the traditional vestiges carried by profane literature, and in some cases we showed how these were abused and altered.

In fact, our work distinguished between two types of "literature": one initiatory and traditional, the other occult and antitraditonal. In the first category we included the biblical story of Samson, Homer's epics, the fairy tales, Dante's **Divine Comedy**, Shakespeare's plays, and two modern works, **The Three Musketeers** by Alexandre Dumas and **The Little Prince** by Saint-Exupéry; in the second category, which is extremely rich, we chose as exemplification other works by Dumas and also by Jules Verne, Mark Twain and Edgar Allan Poe. The fact that we included **The Three Musketeers** and **The Little Prince** in the first class had a purely "didactic" reason: to illustrate how we should read the dormant symbols and how we should purify our profane mentality. Yet, we never suggested that such works, belonging to profane literature, could be called "initiatory," or that they can confer an initiation, or even that their authors were some sort of initiates. Contrary to Homer, Dante and Shakespeare, who represented genuine initiatory currents (not to say more), authors like Alexandre Dumas or Antoine de Saint-Exupéry did not have any spiritual qualification and their books have nothing sacred. What happened was that literature inherited some esoteric vestiges and transmitted them further, yet they were too often altered, misunderstood, or counterfeited.

---

[1] **The Everlasting Sacred Kernel**, pp. IX-X.

In Alexandre Dumas' case, for example, **The Three Musketeers** is an exception. Dumas (and, of course, his readers) knew nothing about any initiatory symbolism and rather enjoyed "dark" subjects.[1] In **The Everlasting Sacred Kernel**, we described Dumas' interest in vampirism, ghosts and infernal characters; even in **The Three Musketeers**, there are two demonic characters: Rochefort and Milady,[2] both without real names (here it is not about a supernal anonymity, but an infernal one)[3]; nonetheless, they represent the dragon, and their roles and fate are in accord with a traditional scenario, which makes **The Three Musketeers** not a "dark" story or a parody, but a sort of fairy tale, hiding traditional data.

On the contrary, the modern Spanish novel, **El Club Dumas**, by Arturo Pérez-Reverte, is nothing else but a parody, an occultist and infernal tale, using Rochefort to stress the demonic characteristic of the story.[4] It combines fiction with non-fiction, where the non-fiction includes Alexandre Dumas' work and his sources. Since we already discussed this topic, in connection to René Guénon's sources, it is not futile to add a few words.

The interest in sources depends on the point of view. From a traditional perspective, the sources, understood in their modern sense as written references, are pointless (with the exception of the sacred texts), because a traditional teaching is not part of the public school system and the traditional lore is not modern literature. From a historic viewpoint, for the profane researcher, the sources are

---

[1] However, the modern society's attraction for the infrahuman domain was not a phenomenon limited to the 19th century, and it developed continuously in the 20th and 21st centuries.

[2] Milady appears to be a ghost from hell. Rochefort is "the cursed man, my evil genius," says d'Artagnan, "the devil," says Athos. Rochefort and Milady are "two kinds of demons," and Rochefort will salute Milady saying "My compliments to Satan!" (see **Sacred Kernel**, p. 118).

[3] Satan is the "adversary" and does not have a personal name (See Ananda K. Coomaraswamy, **Selected Papers: Metaphysics**, Princeton Univ. Press, 1977, p. 27).

[4] The movie, *The Ninth Gate* (1999), based upon the novel **The Club Dumas**, pushed the infernal and parodical characteristics to extreme.

important to establish the relative truth. The sources are also important in the case of the fake prophets and of the false spiritual masters to unveil their dishonesty and deviations. René Guénon wrote a chapter about "the source of Mme Blavatsky's works,"[1] and, in this case, the task to identify the sources makes sense, since we are dealing with a scam; consequently, the fact that Guénon was interested in Blavatsky's sources does not mean that we should hunt for Guénon's sources, since there is an essential difference between the two cases, and, once more, the "egalitarianism" concept cannot be applied here.

The Spanish novel, **El Club Dumas**, mentions **The Three Musketeers**' sources. How important is to know them? If we consider Dumas' novel a historical study, then finding the sources becomes a pertinent task; nonetheless, if we are interested in it as a fairy tale, the sources have no meaning. For example, the origin of the episode regarding the queen's twelve diamond studs is one that has its sources mentioned most often; but this episode, similar to others from many initiatory tales, symbolizes the recovery of the "light" (in this case of the twelve suns),[2] and so, knowing where Dumas found inspiration is less important than understanding the spiritual significance that survived in the novel.[3]

---

[1] **Le Théosophisme**, Éd. Traditionnelles, 1982, p. 92.

[2] D'Artagnan is taken into the queen's confidence and has to recover her twelve diamond studs from England. The purely spiritual part of the expedition comprises a double voyage: the first one, which is the trip to England, symbolizes the typical "purification rites," when the neophyte suffers a ritual death. The second voyage, following the very same itinerary from Paris to Calais, represents the rebirth and reintegration of the different levels of the total being.

[3] No doubt, the main source for Dumas' **The Three Musketeers** was **Mémoires de Mr. D'Artagnan**, written by Gatien de Courtilz de Sandras in 1700 (the edition available to us was published in 1966 at Jean de Bonnot, Paris). We find here the main characters, some episodes, including the one about Milady and her chambermaid (Bonnot edition, pp. 203, 239). The same Gatien de Courtilz wrote in 1687 **Mémoires de Mr. M.L.C.D.R.** (*Mémoires de Monsieur Le Comte de Rochefort*) (the edition available to us was published in 1710, at Henry van Bulderen), and this book is the source for the name of Dumas' Rochefort, but there were other elements that inspired Dumas and Maquet: Rochefort's journey to Brussels (**Mémoires de Mr. M.L.C.D.R.**, pp.

There is one more element. If, in some cases, finding the sources is a *sine qua non* (or seems to be), then these sources must be verified and not taken from second hand references, as it happens with many occultist and New Age works, and even with some works about traditional subjects.[1]

In **The Everlasting Sacred Kernel**, our goal was to follow the Hindu method called *Arundhati-darshananyâya*, a method based on the obvious fact that not all individuals are capable of understanding the same truth.[2] To reach the Principle – Brahma –, say the Hindu teachings, is such a difficult task for the majority of honest seekers that the master advises the student to meditate first on a physical object, let's say the physical sun (or the star *Arundhati*, which is

---

53 ff. and Alexandre Dumas, **The Three Musketeers**, Peter Fenelon Collier Publisher, 1893, p. 19); the involvement of Rochefort's father with a branded (marked with a fleur-de-lis) woman (**Mémoires de Mr. M.L.C.D.R.**, p. 5) inspired the episode about Athos and his wife; and Dumas used even a verbal expression found in Rochefort's **Mémoires**, where Rochefort admitted to be one of Richelieu's "creatures" (p. 93), and that is how Milady is described ("she was some creature of the cardinal's," **The Three Musketeers**, chapter XXXI, p. 186). The episode of the twelve diamond studs has an important place in Dumas' novel. There is more than one source for it: **Mémoires du Duc de la Rochefoucauld** and Antoine-Marie Roederer, **Intrigues politiques et galantes de la Cour de France** (Librairie de Charles Gosselin, 1832, *Les aiguillettes d'Anne d'Autriche*, pp. 195 ff.). However, the printing history of La Rochefoucauld's **Memories** is a tumultuous one, and therefore, the mentioned episode is not to be found in the early editions (the edition available to us was published in 1664, at "Pierre van Dyck," as **Mémoires de M.D.L.R.**), but much later (see, for example, **Mémoires du Duc de la Rochefoucauld**, première partie, Renouard, 1817, pp. 8-9).

[1] Arturo Pérez-Reverte, in his **El Club Dumas**, refers to all the three **Mémoires** and to Roederer's work we cited in the previous note (**The Club Dumas**, Vintage Books, 1998, pp. 14-15, 96, 196), but he adds "Mémoires of De La Porte" (p. 196) as a source for "Constance [Bonacieux]'s kidnapping." Constance Bonacieux, as D'Artagnan's mistress, appears (without a name, just as "la cabaretière") in the **Mémoires de Mr. D'Artagnan**, p. 121. Nonetheless, for "Constance's kidnapping," it is true that the **Mémoires de M. de la Porte** (the edition available to us was published in 1756, in Geneva) was the source, but in the **Mémoires** La Porte describes his own kidnapping (p. 121) and not Constance's (a character invented by Dumas, who said she was La Porte's goddaughter).

[2] In Hindu tradition, that is related to *adhikâribheda*.

usually given as example); after a while, the student will understand that the physical sun is not his real target and will move to a higher object and so on, until the spiritual Sun, the supernal Sun is reached.

This method is used in different traditions, from Yoga-mârga to Hesychasm. The neophytes simulate a state of peace and bliss, which will really become their transformed and permanent nature only after a spiritual realization. Such a *modus operandi* offers also the possibility – at least, theoretically – of integrating the series of disharmonies (the lower or external stages) into a final perfect harmony. René Guénon, writing about contrarieties and contrasts that function at the corporeal and subtle (psychical) levels, but disappear at a higher level, explains: "Who says contrast or opposition, says, by this, disharmony or unbalance, that is, something that can exist only from a very particular and limited perspective; as a whole, the equilibrium is composed of the sum of all the unbalanced parts, and each partial disorder concurs, willy-nilly, to a perfect order" (Guénon, **Hind.**, p. 15). For Guénon, this truth is so important that he uses it to explain the rank of the profane and antitraditional elements in our modern world. He states that any antitraditional, profane and even counter-initiatory actions or forces cannot surpass the individual domain (the "psycho-physical" world) and it is an illusion to think that they can oppose the spiritual order itself. Without their awareness and despite their will, these entities are subjugated to *Spiritus*, the same way everything is, even if unwitting or involuntarily, subjugated to the Divine Will. And they are used, against their will, to the realization of the "divine plan in the human domain." And Guénon added:

If we consider the matter from an overall perspective, and not only in respect to these beings [representing the counter-initiation], we may say that, similar to all the others, they are necessary in their places, as elements of the assembly, and as «providential» instruments – speaking in a theological language – of the advance of this world through its cycle of manifestation, because in this way each partial disorder, even when it appears as *the disorder*, concurs necessarily to total order. (Guénon, **Le règne**, p. 355)

The traditional vestiges, that is, the debris that survived the disappearance of different genuine traditions and traditional civilizations, could become part of these disharmonies, after the spirit withdrew and the inferior forces took control of them. A very common way is to collect all kind of vestiges belonging to various traditions and build a so-called "doctrine," which is purely and simply a fake (Guénon, **Le règne**, p. 328), without any spiritual power and often open to counter-initiatory influences. The interference of a human or individual element, that is, reorganizing, changing, abusing and altering the traditional vestiges, constitutes a significant danger. The traditional doctrines that are alive suffer the same abuse and alteration, yet their representatives can react and protect them against the "malefic" actions; on the contrary, the traditional vestiges are without protection and so, more exposed to the counter-initiatory danger. It is no surprise that Muhyiddin Ibn ʿArabî wrote:

It is better if the companions of our Way keep silent on the subject of the operative sciences of the spiritual order. More: it is forbidden to expose them in a manner that makes them comprehensible at the same time to the initiatory elite and to the common people, because the corrupters could use them in their malefic works.[1]

This kind of subversion and abuse is, today, almost impossible to stop. The least we can do is to try to restore the real meanings of the symbols that are still alive. About the importance of the symbols, René Guénon wrote:

For the people who succeeded in penetrating its profound significance, the symbol can transmit inestimably more [sacred knowledge] than any direct discursive teaching; thus, it is the only way to transmit – as possible as it can be – the inexpressible that constitutes the proper domain of initiation ... We must not forget that, if the symbolic initiation, which is merely the base and the support of the effective initiation, is inevitably the only one that can be communicated on the outside, at least this symbolic initiation can be preserved and transmitted even by people who don't understand its meaning and importance; it is enough to keep and preserve the symbols

---

[1] Ibn Arabî, **Le Livre du Mîm, du Wâw et du Nûn**, trans. in French by Charles-André Gilis, Albouraq, 2002, p. 59.

intact, and they will always be able to wake up – in those who are capable – all the concepts they contain in a synthetic mode. (Guénon, **Aperç. sur l'Init.**, p. 205)

Modern literature can serve as a preparatory exercise to understand how the fundamental symbols operate, but at the same time it shows how dangerous and pernicious are the effects of "originality," "individuality" and "inventiveness," by altering and diverting the essential meanings of symbols. A special case is that of the so-called "folklore." Folklore, like mythology, is a reservoir, which preserves the vestiges of vanished traditional societies, of sacred rituals and initiatory rites. If modern mentality didn't touch it, that is, if nobody tried to alter its content and form, "folklore" could be a valuable support in the study of traditional symbolism (**Sacred Kernel**, pp. 40 ff.); otherwise, "fabricated" folklore is no better than profane and "original" literature. We have shown, in another work, the difference between modern literature and genuine fairy tales, between pseudo-initiatory texts and the legitimate symbolism safeguarded in myths, ballads and fairy tales,[1] and hopefully one day we'll come back to the initiatory symbolism as it was transmitted orally over the ages as part of *Ars memorativa*.[2]

However, we must stress again that literature has no initiatory power and does not constitute an initiatory tool of any kind. Moreover, the popularity of the authors, or the fact that they are some famous characters in the international literary domain, means nothing. If we talk about Balzac or Patrick Süskind, for example, their works are not initiatory because the authors are profane. If the literary works carry some traditional data or initiatory symbols, it does not mean much if the author does not have the necessary esoteric qualification; on the contrary, the author's intervention can

---

[1] **Agarttha, the Invisible Center**.
[2] In Hindu tradition, for example, the **Itihâsas** belong to *Smriti*, or, in Sanskrit, the primitive sense of *smriti* is "memory"; for the modern scholars, the **Itihâsas** are only literature, similar to the fairy tales, which are considered "literature for children."

bring a counter-initiatory viewpoint, as was the case of Umberto Ecco.

In conclusion, we may view modern literature from a quadruple perspective, with respect to the author: there are authors, very few, who possess initiatory data and these are reflected in their works[1]; there are authors who, unconsciously, transmit in their works unaltered traditional vestiges; there are antitraditional authors who willingly abuse the sacred symbols and fabricate others, writing a maleficent literature; finally, there are authors who, manipulated without knowing by counter-initiatory forces, issue noxious writings.

---

[1] Of course, in the case the authors only think that they are endowed with an initiatory knowledge, fantasizing that they have the key of the secret treasure, without actually belonging to an initiatory organization or an authentic tradition, their work does not worth much.

CHAPTER XXII

THE MODERN WORLD AND THE ANTI-GRAIL

WE WITNESS TODAY AN EXPLOSION of literature belonging to the last two categories we just mentioned. It is a "sign of the times," anticipating the Wrath of the Gods. Two subjects are dealt with obsessively in this kind of literature, whether fiction or not. The first one is Jesus Christ, no more no less; the second is the Holy Grail, which, however, is related to the first. The major problem of our times is that, for the many, the capacity to look upwards, in a *sattwic* mode, is missing. Preoccupied with all sorts of daily affairs, modern people do not have time for anything else and, generally, it is much easier to look downwards. In other words, the solidification of the world is so advanced, that the human being is pulled downwards (where the heaviest element, earth, is), in contrast to the spiritual which rises by itself (symbolized by air and fire). For this reason, any attempt to rise toward Christ is impossible, and for the many it is much more convenient to bring Christ down, among humans, not as an *avatarana*, but purely and simply as a desecration.

A famous author, Nikos Kazantzakis, increased his fame by issuing a book called **The Last Temptation of Christ**. In fact, it is about Kazantzakis' temptation, and the author failed to resist, bringing to our attention old heresies from Saint Paul's days. As we have already said, the great temptation was always to bring the gods to a human level. Therefore the Greek mythology is full of gods with very human behaviour. For the same reason the much-admired art of the ancient Greeks became exclusively human; trying to copy the Nature, their art decayed into an antitraditional art. In the case of Christianity, where Christ was accepted with two natures, one divine, the other human, the temptation to make him just a man, nothing more, was even more powerful. Of course, Jesus is presented as a "holy man," yet as the Church insisted on his human nature, so others started to depict him not as a "holy man," but as a simple and common human being; and the easiest way to erase the adjective "holy" was to describe him as an individual implicated in sexual and sentimental activities, since, it is well known that the visceral area, that of the desires, and even more the psychical area, are the Adversary's domain.[1] And that is how Kazantzakis proceeded, focusing the entire book upon the relationship between Jesus and Mary Magdalene, and enveloping everything in a rough human cloak.

As we mentioned before, the idea of describing Jesus and Mary Magdalene as a couple is not new; it was already present at the beginning of Christianity, in the Gnostic doctrines. The fact that the Holy Trinity is purely "masculine," even though in an absolute sense it is neutral, like the three lights of the Hindu tradition, tempted many to suggest the existence of a couple; since Mary Magdalene was present at Jesus' crucifixion and resurrection, she was chosen for this role. Kazantzakis followed the Gnostic model and presented the famous scene found in **The Gospel of Philip**, when Jesus kissed Mary on the mouth; also he alluded to a son who was born as a result of this union.[2]

Leisegang selected, from **Pistis Sophia**, the paragraphs related to Mary Magdalene, where she is the main character, besides Jesus: "Indeed, Mary, you are the blessed one among all the women of the world, since you will be the Pleroma of all pleromas and the

---

[1] The counter-initiatory and adverse forces do not have access to the super-individual, angelic world; therefore Coomaraswamy could conclude that the devils' home is our ego (our "soul").

[2] Nikos Kazantzakis, **The Last Temptation of Christ**, Faber and Faber, 1987, pp. 457-8.

Perfection of all perfections. Indeed, Mary, you are blessed, since you will inherit the entire kingdom of light"; and Leisegang noticed the imitation in Simon Magus' Gnostic doctrine, where the prostitute Helen was an *alter ego* of Mary Magdalene (Leisegang 83-84). Gnosticism had a long life and, due to its heretical characteristic, its independence and individualism, and its "eso-exoteric" content, always found imitators; that not to say that some Gnostic sects kept interesting genuine initiatory data.

Luigi Valli, who was accused by Guénon of having a profane mentality, not an "initiatory" one (**Ésot. Chrét.**, p. 56), is a predecessor of the modern authors in this direction. He mixed together Gnosticism, Rosicrucianism, Cathars, *Fedeli d'Amore*, sometimes without much sense of distinction. An author, quoted by Valli, even wrote a book called "The Gnostic essence of Dante's thinking" (**Il linguaggio segreto di Dante e dei "Fedeli d'Amore"**, Optima, 1928, p. 422). Jean Tourniac suggested also that the Gnostic doctrine was transmitted to Masonry and the Templars, but he at least referred to the "Gnosis of the first Christians," admitting that sometimes it is difficult to distinguish between genuine and false Gnosis (**Principes**, pp. 139, 151, 155, 170-1). Guénon, in a review, wrote about an author who tried to explain the Templars' symbols "referring to the «Gnostic and Essenic» doctrines, which represent only vague labels, since we do not know much about the Essenes, and a lot of disparate things are called «Gnostic»" (**Comptes rendus**, p. 159).

The second subject is the Grail. We must stress from the beginning that, despite the historicist fantasies, the Holy Grail is not a corporeal vessel, hiding somewhere and covering some tenebrous secret. The Grail is a symbol; its sacred meaning alludes to the primordial Tradition, to the Lost Word, and to the divine Knowledge. Finding the Holy Grail crowns an initiatory quest, that is, a spiritual realization that occurs within the being. In the Christian tradition, "the quest of the Holy Grail," like in Islam, has two components: an external one, regarding the heroic deeds of the knights (corresponding to the "particular orientation" in Islam), and an inner one, when the quest aims at the Heavenly Kingdom within

The Modern World and The Anti-Graal

us, that is, the divine presence in the Heart (*Emmanuel*), *Pax Profunda* in the center of the being.

The loss of the Grail (or of one of its symbolic equivalents), explained René Guénon, represents in fact the loss of the Tradition, or even better, the occultation of it. The legend said that the Grail was handed to Adam in the Earthly Paradise and, when the fall took place, Adam lost the vessel, and from then on man was chained in the temporal sphere, far away from his original center. In other words, the loss of the "sense of eternity" is connected to what all the traditions call "the primordial state," the restoration of which represents the first stage of any genuine initiation and is the prerequisite condition to the effective realization of the super-individual states. The Earthly Paradise means exactly the Center of the World, the "Holy Land," and the "land of immortality"; it indicates, Guénon elaborated, that the Grail signifies, at the same time, two things strongly related to each other: the initiate who possesses the integral primordial Tradition, so reaching an effective degree of knowledge that essentially implies this possession, is indeed, at the same time, reintegrated into the plenitude of the "primordial state," realizing what the fairy tales name "eternal youth and life without death."

The legend said that, after Adam fell from Paradise and lost the Grail, Seth was able to come back in the center, finding the holy vessel and restoring somehow the primordial order; from Seth to Christ it is not known by whom and how the Grail was transmitted further, the Celtic influence suggesting that maybe the Druids should be considered among the keepers of the Grail and of primordial Tradition. During this "historical" adventure, the Grail no doubt was lost and found many times, at different levels. The legend also said that, eventually, the Holy Grail was carried to the "Realm of Prester John," symbolically located in *Oriens*; this last element suggests that our modern world lacks any trace of Tradition and divine presence (which have left this profane humankind called *Occidens*). Maybe that is why, today, there is a concerted attempt in the modern world to replace the true symbol of the Grail with a pure materialistic perspective, considering this vessel a very profane and corporeal "secret." In fact, what the Grail is considered to be by modern mentality is really the Anti-Grail.

Literature promoted the Anti-Grail with strange stubbornness. Recent works with great public success, best-sellers, have usually combined the two subjects, Christ and Grail, on the one hand, because in the traditional texts the Grail is the Heart of Christ, and on the other hand, because it is more efficient, more devastating, and more shocking to desecrate not only Tradition but also the Lord of the World.

A book which produced a lot of sensation in the last two decades will help us understand how this Anti-Grail campaign operates; we are not interested in the author's name and the book as such, but only in the "mechanism" regarding the tradition's desecration. We must observe from the beginning that the book is neither original, nor too well built, and it betrays the author's ignorance. The work is based, of course, as in the case of Kazantzakis, on the Gnostic couple Jesus – Mary Magdalene, a couple which becomes purely human and profane, lacking any symbolism. The author implies in his hypothesis, in order to create perfect disarray, but also for the sake of an apparent mystery and profoundness, all the usual elements employed in such cases: the Gnostics, Nag Hammadi, Jesus' kiss given to Mary Magdalene, the Cathars, Rosicrucians, Templars, the *Protocols of the Elders of Sion*, the Merovingians, and the Holy Grail. Each element is associated with a "secret." For example, the supposition is advanced that behind the Order of the Temple there was another secret Order, as if the Templars' secrets were not enough to captivate the reader.[1] The serious reader is stunned at the

---

[1] In fact, even this fantasy is not new. In 1803, Zacharias Werner wrote his **Die Söhne des Tales**, containing two dramatic plays, each written in six acts: *The Templars in Cyprus* and *The Brethren of the Cross*, in which he promoted the idea of an invisible kernel of the Templar Order, "the Sons of the Valley." A. E. Waite, in his almost unknown **Emblematic Freemasonry**, stressed that Werner was a high-grade Mason and a member of the Strict Observance, and he elaborated in his plays the traditional history (the Templar origin) of this organization. The Order of the Temple – suggests the plot of the plays – was dismantled under the invisible influence and command of the Sons of the Valley; the Order had lost its spirituality and became profane and decayed, which forced the Sons to invisibly manipulate the French king,

The Modern World and The Anti-Graal

unembarrassed manner in which the author passes from one "secret" to another, like in a television show; and the question emerges by itself: how is it possible that so many "secrets" (not just one!)[1] were carefully kept across the centuries and then suddenly a modern author is able to find and decipher them. As we said, a secret organization, but really secret, does not leave traces, and for example, if a secret Order existed behind the Templars, nobody would have known about it, much less a common author. Obviously, at the end of the book the "secrets" proved to be nothing new. Jesus was married to Mary Magdalene (the wedding at Cana being their wedding!) and they had children. The Holy Grail is in fact "the royal blood" and represents the physical children of Jesus, who were saved by Mary Magdalene and taken to Provence, in the south of France.[2] Jesus' heirs became related to the Merovingians and there was a conspiracy to dominate the whole of Europe, including the papacy. And the Crusades represented the revenge of Jesus' successors; the presence of the Templars in the Holy Land aimed at the recovery of legal documents with respect to Jesus (such as his wedding certificate and his children's birth certificates).[3] Jesus was an aristocrat, with royal blood, a legitimate pretender to the temporal throne; and, of course, his crucifixion was

---

and implicitly the Pope, to destroy the Order. Yet the Templars weren't completely abandoned; a small kernel, said Werner and Waite, was hidden in Scotland as Masons. Robert of Heredom, who was initiated by the Sons of the Valley, became the guardian of the Secret Palladium and the Master of the new Temple; after five hundred years, the Temple reappeared as Strict Observance. Interestingly enough, the Valley is described as the depository of all religions and the center of all the initiates, from Horus to Vishnu (where Jesus is identified with Osiris, and Saint Mary with Isis); and the place of Robert's initiation is a cavern. Zacharias Werner's Valley looks like Agarttha, and the Sons of the Valley (*Superiores Incogniti*) like the Masters of the subterranean center. Some of the "Guénonians," such as Jean Tourniac (**Principes et problèmes spirituels du Rite Écossais Rectifié**, Dervy, 1969, p. 97), Jean Robin (**Seth le dieu maudit**, Guy Trédaniel, 1986, pp. 172 ff.) and Jean Parvulesco (**La Place Royale**, oct. 1986, p. 52) were very interested in Zacharias Werner.

[1] This tendency to multiplication and hyperbole is typical for our modern world; even the modern individuals have noticed this abuse of presenting everything with expressions, such as "extra strong," "extra large," "super forte," etc.
[2] We observe here how the legend of the Saints Marys was plagiarized.
[3] Here absurdity and stupidity surpass all limits.

false. There is no need to add that, in the author's opinion, everything related to Christian esotericism is in fact a cover for this tremendous secret with respect to Jesus' descendants.

Very recently, the same phantasmagorias and absurdities were again considered in a work of fiction that quickly became a best-seller.[1] As other books, this one is obsessed with codes and ciphers, as Jules Verne was (see our **Agarttha, the Invisible Center**), and the "initiatory secret" (of a pure spiritual nature) being something very materialistic, and hidden by anagrams and ciphers with an occult tint. Now, the Catholic Church is attacked directly. The Templars were considered the keepers of a "secret" used to blackmail the Vatican; of course, the name of the "secret" is *Sangreal*, the Holy Grail, representing a pile of compromising documents proving the humanity of Jesus and his lack of divinity.[2] Leonardo da Vinci's masterpiece, **The Last Supper**, proves that Jesus was married to Mary Magdalene, because there the "beloved" disciple of Jesus looks like a woman. The person painted there is Mary Magdalene not John, and Mary Magdalene is the real Grail. She is the vessel containing the "royal blood," that is, Jesus' children. And, sure, again the Gnostic text regarding Jesus' kiss is quoted.[3] Then the

---

[1] The fact that such a book could become a best-seller suggests very clearly the modern mentality's flaws.

[2] It is well-known that modern man cannot imagine an oral tradition, and obeying the "syndrome of the printed word" he thinks that everything, even the most hidden secret, was put into writing to be discovered by modern individuals yearning to find all sorts of past secrets. We note also the language abuse, where for modern man secret is just an empty word, since modern life is so public, nothing is secret anymore, even the most intimate things. That is why the author, even though he talks about "secrets," does not really think that they are secrets, but some kind of gossip that you can find in any tabloid.

[3] There is a great error to believe that this kiss alludes to something sexual (even though in the modern world sex, beside violence, is promoted with an amazing obstinacy; however, "sex," in Latin *sexus*, derives from *seco*, "to cut, to divide"). In the Hindu tradition, the Great Hero, drinks *soma* directly from Apâlâ's mouth, imitating a kiss; this kind of kiss symbolizes in fact the assimilation of the immortal beverage, *soma* (Coom., **Sacrifice**, pp. 142, 144, 154-5). In the fairy tales, the hero has to kiss the maiden to start the new cycle of manifestation. The kiss transmitted by Jesus to Mary is "spiritualization." In the Middle Ages, there was the belief that the lioness brought forth the young, which appeared to be still-born. The lion cubs would give no sign of

The Modern World and The Anti-Graal

legend of the Saints Marys and Sarah is introduced. Mary Magdalene, the book says, took shelter in the south of France where she gave birth to a daughter, Sarah (the gypsies would be amazed by this invention). It is somehow amusing to follow the author's effort to be credible and the manner in which he is betrayed by his own mentality. He tells how in Jerusalem the Templars found four chests full of ancient documents describing Mary Magdalene's social status exactly.[1]

We do not think we have to continue. The examples we have given are enough to illustrate the Great Disarray of our modern world: it is the time of the Anti-Grail, when individuals think they are gods, and the gods are brought down and changed into humans; it is the time when Noah should run like crazy among us to find ten "righteous people," admonishing us with the Wrath of the Gods.

---

life, but on the third day, the lion would return and animate them with his breath (Louis Charbonneau-Lassay, **The Bestiary of Christ**, Arkana, Penguin Books, 1992, p. 10); the lion represents the "paternal spirituality," symbolizing the Sun-Father, and the "sun's kiss" gives life and spirit. **The Song of Songs** begins with, "Let him kiss me with the kisses of his mouth"; Saint Gregory of Nyssa, commenting this line, said: "The spring is the Groom's mouth, from where emerge the eternal life's words, which fill the mouth that drinks them, similar to the Psalmist who drank the Spirit." In **The Gospel of Philip** it is said: "The word would be nourished from the mouth and it would become perfect. For it is by a kiss that the perfect conceive and give birth. For this reason we also kiss one another" (**Nag Hammadi** 145). We should add St. Bernard's words: "I hold for certain that to so great and holy an *arcanum* of divine love not even the angelic creation is admitted. ... See the new Spouse receiving the new kiss, not, however, from the *mouth* but from the KISS of *His mouth*. He breathed on them, it is said. There can be not doubt that Jesus breathed upon the Apostles, that is, upon the primitive Church, and said: *Receive ye the Holy Ghost*. That was, assuredly, a kiss. What? – the physical breath? No, but the invisible Spirit. ... And so it is enough for the bride if she is kissed with the *kiss* of the Bridegroom, even if she is not kissed with His *mouth*. Nor does she think it is a slight thing or a thing to be despised that she is kissed with a *kiss*, which is nothing else than to be filled with the Holy Ghost" (**Love of God**, p. 69).

[1] Of course, the Dead Sea scrolls and the Gnostic documents found at Nag Hammadi could give the impression that it is a standard procedure, but these documents are rather an accident, generated by a serious crisis and deviation, in the critical moment of the change of cycles. And the documents did not represent in any way some kind of "memoirs."

Yet Noah is nowhere to be seen, and who really believes in the Wrath of the Gods?

CHAPTER XXIII

ORIENS AND OCCIDENS

THERE IS, HOWEVER, A SERIES OF questions not usually asked about the Great Disarray. First of all, why do we have this modern world? Modern civilization is an anomaly, an unnatural society (opposite to the meaning of "natural" as defined by the Daoist seers), so why should it exist and develop? Secondly, closely related to the first question, what generated such an anomaly? Also, why, when we say "modern society" do we think instantaneously of the Occident? What occurred in the West to produce such a profane and Anti-Grail perspective? We may ask as well, how much the West is the Occident and the East the Orient? Moreover, how much the Orient is still the Orient? Eventually, we are entitled to know the answer to the question: what the Wrath of the Gods really means?

Regularly, these questions are not part of daily human thinking. The state of facts is taken for granted. Yet if we want to have a clear perspective of the present world and the place of Tradition in it, we must complete such an inquiry. René Guénon used to say that there are not unsolvable problems, only problems wrongly put. Therefore, we are not going to follow a profane path looking for profane solutions.

As we saw in our chapter about the Near-West, René Guénon divided the world, more or less symbolically, into "Orient" and "Occident," the "Orient" containing three major traditions: the Far-Eastern, the Hindu and the Islamic tradition. This partition, even if it coincides to some extent with the present geographical situation, was viewed mainly from a traditional perspective, since Guénon specified that Islam comprises countries that are geographically as much "Occidental" as Europe is (Guénon, **Introduction**, p. 54). Moreover, René Guénon explained later: "the true Orient, the only one that deserves to be named so, is and will be the traditional Orient, even when its exponents are reduced to a minority. ... It is about this Orient that we are talking, in the same way as the Occident represents for us the Occidental mentality, that is, the modern and antitraditional mentality, no matter where it is geographically situated, since we envisage primarily the opposition of these two points of view and not just simply the two geographical terms" (Guénon, **Orient et Occident**, p. 230).

There are many reasons why we have to accept this partition. Some were already suggested in this work. But we want to point out a symbolic motive, connected to Christianity, and coming from Western heritage itself. Christian symbolism calls Jesus Christ *Oriens*, not *Occidens*. The word *Occidens* is derived from the Latin *occido*, which means "to fall, to collapse." Regardless of its immediate significance in our current language, in relation to the rising sun, more than ever *Oriens* symbolizes the residence of Tradition and *Occidens* the profane, modern and antitraditional mentality, illustrating the collapse of the traditional perspective; moreover, we might say that the world's final collapse will occur when, beside the Occident, the Orient will also be engulfed by *Occidens*. And we stress that, in accordance with Guénon's teachings, there is no profane domain, but only a profane point of view; therefore, when we refer to *Occidens*, we have in mind the modern and antitraditional mentality, and not in particular the geographical cardinal point.[1]

---

[1] We have to keep in mind that in Islamic tradition, for example, there was no discrimination between the East and the West. More than one time it is said: "Unto Allâh belong the East and the West, and whithersoever you turn, there is Allâh's Countenance. Lo! Allâh is All-Embracing, All-Knowing" (**Qur'ân**, *Al-Bakara*, 2, 115); and also: "Allâh is the Light of the heavens and the earth. The similitude of His light is as a niche wherein is a lamp. The lamp is in a glass. The glass is as it were a shining star. (This lamp is) kindled from a blessed tree, an olive neither of the East nor of the West, whose oil would almost glow forth (of itself) though no fire touched it. Light upon light. Allâh guides unto His light whom He will. And Allâh speaks to mankind

Similarly, if Jesus Christ is *Oriens*, logically Anti-Christ is *Anti-Oriens*, but it does not mean that *Anti-Oriens* is the West. Anti-Christ is beyond (or even better, below) the human world and cannot be particularize by the cardinal points; it does not have a "human" origin, in the same way as counter-initiation is non-human. The term *Anti-Oriens* should not be disregarded though; as the devil was called Non-Brother, in "opposition" to God, the Brother,[1] so Guénon used the expression "counter-initiation" to describe the adverse forces, which should not be confused with "antitradition."

René Guénon wrote:

The «counter-initiation» appears through a degeneracy... which is more profound than that of a deviated tradition or of an incomplete tradition reduced to its inferior part. There is also here something that is more than in the case of those lost traditions that were abandoned by the spiritual influence (in which case their residues can be used by the «counter-initiation» for its own purpose). Logically, this leads us to think that the degeneracy had to go back into the past; and, as obscure as its origin is, we may admit as credible that it is attached to some distortion of an ancient civilization that disappeared in a cataclysm of the present Manvantara. (Guénon, **Le règne**, pp. 351-2)

---

in allegories, for Allâh is Knower of all things" (*An-Nûr*, 24, 35); "He said: Lord of the East and the West and all that is between them, if ye did but understand" (*Al-Shu'arâ*, 26, 28); "Lord of the East and the West; there is no Allâh save Him; so choose thou Him alone for thy defender" (*Al-Muzzammil*, 73, 9). Such a perspective exists also in the Western tradition. In Masonry, in the highest degrees of the Scottish Rite, the two-headed eagle is an imperial emblem representing the reign over Orient and Occident. The 30th degree is called the "Knight Kadosh or Knight of the White and Black Eagle." A Greek legend told that Zeus sent two eagles, one from the East, the other one from the West, and they met in the center, at the white stone of Delphi, marking the "navel of the world." We can assume that the eagles are white and black, as the two ones eating a hare in Aeschylus' **Agamemnon** (104-139). Another legend said that two eagles watched on the roof of the palace in Pella the birth of Alexander the Great, a sign predicting that the new-born will become the emperor of Orient and Occident; the Arabic tradition named Alexander *El-Iskandar dhûl-qarnein*, which means "with two horns," and was interpreted as a double power, of Occident and Orient (Guénon, **Symboles**, p. 205).

[1] In fact, there is no symmetry between these two terms.

In this quotation, Guénon alluded to Atlantis, "the lost continent,"[1] and the biblical flood illustrates exactly the cataclysm that put an end to the reign of the giants: "The Nephilim were on the earth in those days – and also afterward – when the sons of God went to the daughters of men and had children by them. They were the heroes of old, men of renown" (**Genesis** 6:4).[2]

Yet Hesiod highlighted a special episode, about the "race of silver" that "could not keep from sinning and from wronging one another, nor would they serve the immortals, nor sacrifice on the holy altars of the blessed ones. Then Zeus, the son of Cronos, was angry and put them away, because they would not give honour to the blessed gods who live on Olympus" (**Works and Days**, 130-140). The "race of silver" was far before Atlantis and we should conclude that, in fact, the decadence started at the same time with the first rotation of *Dharma Chakra*, even if in the "Golden Age" the intellectuality was so pure that this decline was almost imperceptible.[3]

With regard to the doctrine of the cosmic cycles, we may say that the "Golden Age" lasted four unites of time, the "Age of Silver" three, the "Age of Bronze" two and the "Iron Age" will last one. On the other hand, the whole cycle can be considered as containing five Great Years, in which case the "Golden Age" lasted two Great Years, the "Age of Silver" one and a half Years, the "Age of Bronze" one Year and the "Iron Age" would survive half a Year.[4] Reviewing the traditional data, we may assume that the ending of the "Golden Age," at the same time as the end of the second Great Year, was marked by a double cataclysm, natural and social, the latter being the revolt of the *kshatriyas*, the warrior caste. Indeed, *Treta-yuga*, the "Age

---

[1] With regard to the entire Manvantara, Atlantis corresponds to the "red race" and the Western cardinal point, which enhances our definition of *Occidens*.

[2] As we already pointed out, some traditions considered Ham of perpetuating the teachings of the rebelious Giants and of the fallen angels, after the flood.

[3] The counter-initiation has a "non-human" origin. We may say that, at the very moment when the wheel of the manifestation started to move, the counter-initiation became active; moreover, at the same time, the *Saviour* was born.

[4] These five Years correspond to the five "suns" of the Aztecs.

of Silver" was considered under the royal (warrior) caste's control. Yet, in concordance with the law of correspondence, *Treta-yuga* itself had a "golden" beginning and it is admissible to say that this Age also (like all the other cycles) had a "divine" and a "human" period. To this "human" period, Hesiod alluded. In the Hindu tradition, Parashu Râma, the sixth *avatâra* of Vishnu, punished the revolted *kshatriyas* and ended this Age, marking the debut of *Dwapara-yuga*, the "Age of Bronze." The fourth Great Year is considered the "Atlantis Year," and half of it is situated still in the "Age of Silver," suggesting, as Plato affirmed, a "golden" or "divine" period, which could correspond to Parashu Râma's intervention, while the second half is in the "Age of Bronze," a "human" period to which *Genesis* alluded and which mentioned the giants. In any case, this last "human" period might be the source of the actual counter-initiation.

Considering the doctrine of the cosmic cycles, and the whole present human cycle (*Manvantara*), the Hindu tradition – as René Guénon affirmed – is the direct successor of the primordial Tradition, the Hyperborean (Nordic, polar) current; the Atlantean tradition is a secondary (Occidental, equinoctial) one. The former kept alive the initiatory center; the latter manifested the counter-initiation.

Compared to the "Age of Silver," and considering its place inside the Manvantara, the "Age of Bronze" was logically a "lower" Age and closer to the end of the cycle, which implies a relatively greater disarray and less chances for the future epochs to benefit by a complete restoration of the normal hierarchy. However, as we have stressed many times, the science of symbols is not systematic, but coherent, and is not methodical and simplistic, but integrative and complex, which means we have to keep the spirit of discrimination (*furqân* in the Islamic tradition, *viveka* in the Hindu tradition) fully awake. Even if Atlantis was a "lower" Age and the deviations that took place during its "human" period favored the manifestation of the counter-initiation, the same Atlantis represented in comparison to *Kali-yuga*, a better, even ideal Age, constituting a mythical past.[1] More than that: beside the seeds of counter-initiation transmitted to the new world, a genuine tradition was also communicated to posterity. Therefore, we prefer to say that "the degeneracy ... attached to some distortion of an ancient civilization that disappeared in a cataclysm of the present Manvantara" refers to *Occidens* firstly, since what eventually produced the present anomaly, that is, modern society, was a combination of more than one factor, among which the "Atlantean" influence played an important role.

We have to remember that the Occident was also the habitation of many traditional societies, as, for example, those of the Incas, Toltecs and Aztecs, and, of course, the one represented by the "Indians" of North America. The "Indians" are officially called "native people" today, but they can also be designated as "traditional people," even if the "white man" obliterated or desecrated, more or less, their spiritual heritage.[2] And there is no doubt that the

---

[1] In ancient Greece, bronze was used for purification; the ancient Egyptians had, at the entrance of their temples, rotating bronze wheels, with purificatory effects (Jane Ellen Harrison, **Prolegomena to the Study of Greek Religion**, Princeton Univ. Press, 1991, p. 591); Solomon's Temple did not contain iron but bronze. Also we should mention the Western location of the "Island of the Blessed," as a vestige of Atlantis (see Julius Evola, **Revolt Against the Modern World**, Inner Traditions International, 1995, p. 199).

[2] There are some elements that must be clarified related to this subject. First of all, from a traditional point of view, the so much eulogized era of "geographical discoveries" ventured by the Europeans was just another sign of the Western world moving away from the sacred. The word "discoveries" is an abuse and suggests a narrow-minded perspective. We should note that it was only after the end of the Christian traditional society (symbolically and historically marked by the destruction of the Templars), that these so-called "discoveries" took place. The "discovery" of America was a "discovery" only for the Europeans involved in this sort of voyages (which excluded the Near-West), and certainly not for the "traditional people" living there, this word "discovery" being, indeed, a measure of ignorance and nothing else. Yet more distressing is the fact that what promoted such enterprises was a worldly mentality, since a traditional one would never have focused on such a project built on curiosity, greed, and individualism. Even if dressed in Catholic clothes, what was exported from Europe to the other continents was modern mentality. In the history of humanity we can find examples of people invading foreign territories and obliterating other civilizations. Each time it was a critical point of the cycle, when a change was needed. In the case of the Europeans, their expansion was part of the

"traditional people" of North America were the keepers of a genuine traditional life and spirituality.[1] This is not the moment to develop this aspect but it would be interesting and instructive to compare the traditional data and rites of these "savages" to the outrageous behaviour of the Europeans who tried to "civilize" them. In any case, we see that already the modern mentality was in place in Europe and ready to be exported.[2]

We have to dissipate another misunderstanding. As for the American "traditional people" Europeans were the source of their destruction (even if at the beginning they accepted the "white man" in a mythical way), so was considered Europe by the European emigrants themselves. The future "Americans" were equipped with a

---

desecration of the world, aiming at the supremacy of *Occidens*. The consequences are well-known: the Spaniards destroyed the traditional societies of Incas and Aztecs, the French and the English ruined the "traditional people" of North America. Later the French tried to do the same thing to the Islamic tradition in North of Africa (see, among others, Titus Burkhardt, **Fez, City of Islam**, The Islamic Texts Society, 1992, and Michel Chodkiewicz, **The Spiritual Writings of Amir 'Abd al-Kader**, State Univ. of New York Press, 1995), as the English invaded India, the abode of the Hindu tradition, which Guénon considered as a direct heir of the primordial Tradition.

[1] There are today many written proofs. We would like to mention Black Elk, **The Sacred Pipe** (recorded and edited by Joseph Epes Brown), Univ. of Oklahoma Press, 1989 (it was translated in French by Frithjof Schuon – who wrote also an *Introduction* – and published as Hehaka Sapa, **Les Rites Secrets des Indiens Sioux**, Payot, 1953).

[2] Regarding the epithet "savage," which we used on purpose, there is another example of distorted mentality. Not long ago, modern man used to name all the people encountered during their "geographical discoveries" "primitives" or even "savages." Recently, mainly for political reasons and due to a dubious sentimentalism, the epithet was changed to "native." In fact, all three appellatives are wrong. These people were not "savages" but "traditional." They are not "native," in the same way the Europeans are not "native" with respect to Europe, since most probably they are heirs of lost civilizations that existed in different locations. And for sure, these populations are not "primitive." The "primitive" epithet was very convenient since it reinforced the modern (and definitely wrong) idea of indefinite progress and evolution. Guénon wrote: "We don't have to look elsewhere to find the reason why the «scientists» so relentlessly discredited any other [non-"materialistic"] conception, labeling it as «superstition» due to the «primitives'» imagination, who, for them, were nothing else than savages or people with an infantile mentality, as stated by the «evolutionist» theories" (Guénon, **Le règne**, p. 239).

"paradisiacal" dream and considered "the New World" as a regained paradise, in opposition with the old Europe, envisaged as the nest of all evil.[1] With regard to the European culture, John Cotton declared: "The more cultivated and intelligent you are, the more ready you are to work for Satan."[2] In fact, this anti-European attitude did not bring the European emigrants closer to the traditional mentality of the "native" people, on the contrary; for this reason Guénon called America "the Far-West" (which means "the Extreme-Occident" but not only geographically speaking).

It is not our task to give too many historical details, yet we still have to delve into another historical aspect. We said that the "Atlantean" influence was an important but not exclusive element that caused modern mentality in the end. Another factor was the Greco-Roman heritage. René Guénon wrote: "We are not looking to define right now the distinct characteristics of the European mentality; we just indicate that more than one influence participated to its formation: the one that played a preponderant role was incontestably the Greek influence, or, even better, the Greco-Roman influence" (**Introduction**, p. 11).[3]

Guénon meant by "Greek influence" the influence of the "classical" Greece (which was the origin of the modern mentality) and not of the "archaic" Greece (called by us "mythical"). "We agree [with the author] when he protests against the practice of considering that the entire Greek civilization belongs only to the

---

[1] About the paradisiacal utopia in relation to "the New World" see Mircea Eliade, **La nostalgie des origines**, Gallimard, 1978, pp. 169 ff.

[2] Yet the communists in Russia declared the same thing; Zinoviev said: "In every intellectual I see an enemy of the Soviet power" (see Evola, **Revolt**, p. 347). In a similar way, the Communist utopia promoted an ideal paradisiacal life, in fact a monkey-like replica of the genuine Paradise, launching slogans about "light" and "the highest acmes of welfare," changing hypotheses like the evolution theory, the linear progress and materialism into dogmas.

[3] Guénon added: "The Greek influence is almost exclusively with respect to philosophy and science. The Roman influence is more social than intellectual, since ... the Romans, with respect to the intellectual side, borrowed almost everything from the Greeks. ... We have to note also the importance, especially from a religious point of view, of the Judaic influence" (**Introduction**, p. 11).

«classical» period; moreover, we think that the previous epochs, if they could be better known, would be of much more interest than this one, since there is a difference similar to the distinction between the Middle Ages and modern times" (**Comptes rendus**, p. 9); also: "... The «classical» period marks a degeneration or a deviation with regard to the previous epochs" (**Comptes rendus**, p. 39).

The "mythical" period belongs to the second half of the "Age of Bronze" (the first half of the last Great Year), following the disappearance of the Atlantean civilization; it could be assumed that at that time the Hyperborean expansion started toward the south, and also the migration of the Atlantean currents (which escaped the cataclysm) along a West-East axis.[1] It also could be assumed that, as the Word multiplied into many words, so the Hyperborean race split into more and more branches, like a tree; and it seems that the pure sacerdotal branch arrived eventually in the present India, while the *kshatriya* and *vaishya* branches went to Europe. We stress that such a hypothesis cannot be viewed in a simplistic mode; when we affirm that *brahmana* went to the Orient, we suggest a more *principial* perspective, in the same way as the three regents of Agarttha, Brahâtmâ, Mahâtmâ and Mahânga (Guénon, **Roi**, p. 31) are *principial* functions, each one comprising spiritual authority and temporal power; hence, we should not think of the actual caste system, but only analogically with it.

On the other hand, the "Atlantean" influence was mainly carried by currents moving to the West, Near-West and Near-East; and it brought not only the vestiges of its spirituality, but also those of revolt.[2] Greek mythology kept many traces of this influence, like for example in the myth of Atlas and his daughters the Pleiades.[1]

---

[1] Concerning the evolvement of the human races, beside the decisive data transmitted by René Guénon, one could consult, with caution, Gaston Georgel, **Les Quatre Âges de l'Humanité** and Evola, **Revolt Against the Modern World** (the chapter *The Northern-Atlantic Cycle*, pp. 195 ff.).

[2] About the Atlantean influence see René Guénon, **Place de la tradition atlantéene dans le Manvantara**, in **Formes traditionnelles**, pp. 46 ff. Guénon specified that it is very difficult to determine how the junction between the Atlantean and Hyperborean currents was done; he considered that the Egyptians transmitted the Atlantean influence to the Judaic tradition, and that the Celts and Chaldeans are a

"Classical" Greece admitted receiving the influence of Egypt, Phoenicia, Chaldea, Persia and even India (Guénon, **Introduction**, p. 16).[2] Yet more than that, the myth regarding the Hyperborean Apollo and the Thracian influence with respect to Greek *Mysteries*, as well as the Trojan (Thracian) influence upon the Romans, should be added to the Oriental influences. There is no doubt that the "classical" Greco-Roman mentality was ready to assimilate intellectual data in a specific way, and, despite the *Mysteries*, the main tendency (due to the Greeks and Romans inborn nature) was toward rational thinking and experimental sciences (Guénon, **Introduction**, p. 23).

There are many other aspects, which should be elaborated in order to understand what made modern mentality what it is; yet, what we have said is enough to answer the questions we asked at the beginning of this chapter.

However, before concluding, we should heed an element which was already mentioned: the counter-initiation. As we saw, René

---

result of this junction. We may add that, as the ancient Greeks themselves confessed, the Egyptians transmitted an Atlantean influence also to the Greeks.

[1] We may note that Maia, Hermes' mother, was one of the Pleiades (that could be the reason why Hermeticism was confined to the cosmologic level).

[2] The Phoenicians' influence deserves attention. This people were called "the Canaanites" in the Gospels and we remember Jesus' reticence in dealing with them. Also, we highlighted that Ham (symbolizing the counter-initiation) was, in the **Bible**, the father of Canaan, and Noah cursed it: "Cursed be Canaan! The lowest of slaves will he be to his brothers." The name "phoenician" is considered to have been given by the Greeks, and alludes to "purple" (and maybe to the "red race"). They should be considered, beside and probably before the Greeks and the Romans, a model of the modern world. The Phoenicians were extremely skillful merchants, navigators, and masons (we should think of Solomon's Temple) and the historians regard their cities as models of democracy. The Phoenician ships reached Europe and North Africa founding cities and spreading, at the same time as their merchandise, their subtle (Atlantean) influence. The Greeks and the Romans owe the alphabet to the Phoenicians. And the fact that the modern historians consider the Phoenicians as "the great pioneers of civilization" is not a good sign from our traditional point of view. We should also mention that, as the Phoenicians and the Greeks were famous founders of many colonies, so were the Atlantean people, long before them. In fact, the Atlantean expansion towards the West and East started before the disappearance of Atlantis, through their colonies; the Phoenicians and the Greeks followed this model closely.

Guénon suggested that "the «counter-initiation» appears through a degeneracy... the degeneracy had to go back into the past; and, as obscure as its origin is, we may admit as credible that it is attached to some distortion of an ancient civilization that disappeared in a cataclysm of the present Manvantara"; and, in the same way as the Atlantean current and others spread, so the counter-initiatory elements invaded the world, trying to break the "cutting" of the sacred places, to take advantage of any fissure in the protective wall.

At any level, the greater danger did not come from a known enemy, but from the false friend, the inner adversary. In the case of spiritual realization, the worst enemies are not the outer but the inner ones; therefore, Muhammad, the Prophet, made a distinction between "the greater holy war" (*el-jihâdul-akbar*), an inner war, and "the lesser holy war," the external one. In other words, counter-initiatory centers could have invisible "locations" in the very Orient, more dangerous because nobody noticed them. René Guénon wrote:

> «Counter-initiation,» we must say, cannot be considered a purely human invention, which would be no different from «pseudo-initiation.» In fact, it is more than that, and to be so effectively, it must, in a specific mode, and with regard to its origin, derive from the unique source to which every initiation is attached, and, generally speaking, everything that manifests in our world a «non-human» element. (Guénon, **Le règne**, p. 351)

Guenon also specified in a letter that "counter-initiation always tries to establish its centers in those locations where the possibilities of an opposite order [that is, initiatory centers] exist, thus striving to combat the development of these possibilities."[1] We have to accept, beside spiritual centers with beneficial influences, the existence of satanic centers that spread evil into our world; the latter are called "the Seven Towers of Satan."[2] The Devil couldn't restrain itself

---

[1] Guénon added that "in the case of ancient spiritual centers," counter-initiation would like to establish centers close to them, "to take advantage of what these places could still have as special [vestiges], which could help the transmission of psychical influences."

[2] See **Agarttha, the Invisible Center**, p. 36.

from imitating and profaning the number seven and the symbolism of the tower. In 1927, William B. Seabrook published a curious book[1] in which he described his journey among the Arabs and Muslims, and he had a special chapter about the "Towers of Shaitan" (p. 316). Seabrook made comments on a legend, widely known in the Middle-East, about the existence of the fabulous "Seven Towers" or "Power Houses" of the Devil (p. 289), a chain of towers stretching across Asia, from Northern Manchuria, through Tibet, west through Persia, and ending in Kurdistan. In each of these towers, a priest of Satan, by "broadcasting" occult vibrations, controls the evil in the world (p. 290). Seabrook confessed that he didn't believe this legend for a moment, which seemed as mythical as the Chinese "subterranean kingdom" or the caves of Sinbad, yet arriving among the Yezidees, north of Baghdad, he saw one of the Towers (p. 316). René Guénon examined Seabrook's information in a note of **Études Traditionnelles**, confirming the existence of the "Seven Towers." He also, in some private letters, considered the towers to be in a direct relation with counter-initiation[2]; yet Guénon underlined as well that such towers, more or less important, can be found in the West too, and explained that the agents of counter-initiation use the Western pseudo-initiation. This last statement has to be understood not only as a corporeal link between these two, but also as a subtle and invisible channel, which means that we have to be careful when guessing where these "counter-initiation" centers are located.

Bhagavata Purana's text we quoted at the beginning of this study, "When reign deceit, falseness, inertia, sleep, wickedness, consternation, dismay, confusion, fright, sadness, that is called Kali-yuga, which is the dark age," considered the world as a whole and not only the Occident. What scenario can we envisage? The evident one is the invasion of Western modernism, which occurs right now.

---

[1] William B. Seabrook, **Adventures in Arabia**, Paragon House, 1991.

[2] Guénon stated, for example, that Agha Khan and his group were a "cover" for one of the "Seven Towers of the Devil." He suggested too that there could be a connection between the localization of these "towers" and the oil sources.

As a friend was saying to us, "the West is now in the East with us"; sentimental teachings, modern scientist views, blind devotion, sectarian patriotism and religious violence and extremism, in the detriment of the Intellectual Tradition are the characteristics of the modern Orient. Yet, we should not be surprised. *Kali-yuga* means a dark age also for the Orient and not only because of the West, but because of its own decadence.[1] And there is no doubt that one day this humanity has to go, not only a part of it, but all.[2]

---

[1] Regarding the destructive role of the West with respect to Eastern Tradition, it is curious that the Christian traditional society, which started its agony at the same time as the trial of the Templars, was subjected to the invasion of the Mongols from the East, that had, no doubt about it, a destructive role (similar to the function of the "Barbarian" invasions that prepared the birth of Christianity as a traditional society). This destructive role of the Mongols – Guénon admitted in a letter – could be a manifestation of Rigor (the hand of divine Justice), which raises the question that maybe the Christian society itself was degenerating as a traditional society and thus subtly causing a reaction manifested by these invasions. We always have to keep in mind this fundamental law called by Matgioi, following the Far-Eastern tradition, the law of "concordant actions and reactions" (Matgioi, **La Voie Rationnelle**, Éd. Trad. 1984); which means that we cannot accept the reaction without looking also for the action. For this reason, even if the tendency of "westernizing" the East is obvious, it could not occur if the Eastern mentality (a part, at least) had not become open and attracted to the modern influences, as a consequence of the *Kali-yuga*.

[2] Today, we can define the modern, profane world as an "extremist" civilization, which is somehow understandable, considering the fact that our cycle is reaching its extreme. Extremism is the child of ignorance, in a metaphysical sense, and a part of world's profanation. It is strongly related to all the foolish modern theories regarding the continuous evolution and progress of humankind. The modern world, because it is not traditional anymore (that is, it lacks the non-human element), lost its stability, harmony and righteousness, and it is fully consumed by the vicious and insatiable need for change, the theory of unstoppable progress being the only way the modern world could pretend that its present situation is one of order and not of chaos. These fantasist concepts of progress and evolution imply a journey towards the extreme, and the extreme is promoted today in any possible form. The goal of the so-called progress is to push individual possibilities to their limits or to create the illusion of such a thing, and, of course, what is understood today to be individual possibilities is something very incomplete and cripple. The Western world tries to depict itself as opposing the so-called religious extremism, developed especially in the Islamic countries. Unfortunately, there is no difference. All of them are duped by the Adversary; all of them strive to stretch their possibilities to the extreme, in a completely anti-traditional way. The modern world fell from the Center to the extreme and there it started to yell its anti-extremism position, negating at the same time the Center. The only normal civilization is a traditional one. A normal society is

Mircea A. Tamas

When Guénon wrote about the Anti-Christ, he stressed that this one is an impostor whose reign is "the great parody" imitating and mocking everything indeed traditional and spiritual (Guénon, **Le règne**, p. 362). René Guénon also affirmed that the "counter-initiation" is able to penetrate the traditional organizations, but only those, which both in the West and the East are decayed, or in the course of decaying.[1]

Today we witness the decadence of the whole world; but we have to understand one important thing: when we say that now the West is also in the East, considering the world as an immense *Occidens*, we do not imply that *Oriens* is no more. As Guénon explained, our world will never become purely "quantitative" or "inert," since pure quantity and inertia belong to *materia prima*, which is the support of manifestation, but not the manifestation itself. Without a trace of "quality" the world could not exist. Similarly, the world cannot exist only as a profane world; in fact, that is why Guénon was saying that there is no profane domain, only a profane perspective. The world has reality only because of its sacred kernel, which is *Oriens*. More or

---

neither extremist, nor mediocre. Today's extremists are born from the mediocre class, and, we insist, "mediocre" does not mean normal, because "normal" must be understood as related to the Latin *norma*, and we should remember that in the Chinese tradition the Principle was, as Guénon stressed, "the pivot of the *norma*." We must not confuse "mediocre" with the "middle" or "center," because a traditional civilization has the Center, the Middle, as fundament (and therefore it is "fundamental" and not "fundamentalist"), while the modern world moved away as far as possible from the central point, from the point of equilibrium and harmony, reaching the "extreme." The idea that "traditional" means "extremism" was promoted on purpose, at the suggestion of the "counter-initiatory" forces, and even René Guénon was labeled as extremist. The truth of the matter is that the only normal society is, as we said, a traditional one, and only in such a society is extremism excluded; this does not mean that such a society has to be tolerant, the same way justice does not have to be "sentimental." But a traditional society will not be traditional because some cleric or some politician declares it as such, for the simple reason that a traditional civilization is based on the "presence of God" in its center. And the "presence of God" will walk with the people as long as the people's hearts are open to God and nobody can deceive Him with words and fake oaths.

[1] Only when a traditional organization has "fissures" in its protective "wall" or "cutting," can the adversary penetrate. The same thing is valid for an entire traditional society.

less hidden, this *Oriens* is today the immutable keeper of Tradition, gathering at the same time the elements which will become the germs of the future cycle.[1] Moreover, if there still are genuine initiatory ways, they can be found only inside the Oriental traditions (within very closed organizations which counter-initiation could not penetrate), while Occident can offer, in the best of cases, just a sort of virtual initiation through some very limited initiatory organizations; we should not consider here the Hesychastic way as an Occidental spiritual possibility, but as an Oriental one (since its core is part of *Oriens* and the modern influence cannot touch it).

Let us quote again, *in extenso* this time, what Guénon wrote:

Regarding the Orient, we agree that the ravages of modernism extended considerably, at least externally; the regions which resisted longer against modernism seem now to be changing in an accelerated mode, and India itself is a striking example.[2] However, nothing has yet reached the heart of Tradition [*Oriens*], which is the only important thing in our view; it is enough that the traditional point of view, with all that it implies, is completely preserved in the Orient in an inaccessible retreat [the same *Oriens*], far from the modern world's agitation. Also, we must not forget that everything modern, even in the Orient, is nothing else but the mark of the Occidental mentality's trespassing [*Occidens*]; the veritable Orient [that is, *Oriens*], the only one that deserves this name, is and will be forever the traditional Orient, even when their exponents are reduced to a minority. It is this Orient we have in mind, in the same way as when we talk about the Occident, we have in view the Occidental mentality, that is, the modern and antitraditional mentality; it can be found everywhere, since we envisage first of all the opposition of these two points of view and not simply the two geographical terms. (**Orient et Occident**, pp. 229-230)[3]

---

[1] We have to understand that even if the whole present cycle has to die, the new cycle will be based on the old one's sacred kernel. The synthesis of spirituality will be saved by our humanity (that is, a chosen part) and this will become the kernel of the new cycle, in accordance to the continuity of the universal helix.

[2] In comparison to Islamic extremism (a sign of the modern times), let us note that in India a strong nationalism has developed (we know scholars who are convinced that everything in the world, religions, social customs, etc., have an "Indian" origin, a very modern view indeed, similar, for example, to the Western idea of a French "center of the world," which materialized in the days of Mitterrand).

[3] Guénon added these lines as an *Addendum* to the new edition of his book.

Julius Evola, in his article **René Guénon, Orient and Occident** (1954), tried, like many others, to argue that what Guénon was saying about a "traditional civilization" still existing in the Orient is no longer valid.[1] Evola affirmed:

> If we are turning to Orient, [Guénon's] considerations have to be updated; many things have changed since the first edition of his book [**La Crise du Monde Moderne**]. It becomes more evident every day that the Orient itself, considered the exponent of the traditional civilization, is on the verge of a crisis. China is not a part [of this civilization] anymore. In India, the nationalistic and modernist tendencies have become stronger. The Arabic countries and even Tibet are in disarray. Therefore, a large part of Guénon's Orient seems to become a thing of the past, and those elements of the Orient where the traditional spirit survived due to an uninterrupted continuity, and which could perform the function we discussed [that of saving the Occident], can be found only in some small closed groups.

As Guénon himself said (see the last quotation), modern mentality invaded the East too, and continues to do so. This invasion took (and takes) control over "the many" that are open to accept such influences and over the extremists that think they are rejecting them; but the traditional *oriental* core with its initiatory ways remains untouched and that is all that counts, since not quantity but quality is the nature of the sacred kernel. Evola was a Westerner by his nature; therefore he praised the royal initiation more than the sacerdotal one, action more than contemplation, and he was fond of Buddhism. And his *swadharma* did not let him correct the errors. For the same reason he tried to revise Guénon's perspective about Orient and Occident, and (in the same article which we mentioned) he invented a curious picture of the present Manvantara. Evola affirmed that it is possible to see the Occident solving its crisis and passing into a new cycle (and to a "Golden Age"), while the Orient will fall into its own "Iron Age," reaching the position in which the Occident is today. First of all, we see here again a "magical" (a word abused by Evola) perspective: a *Deus ex machina* will save the Occident... which is

---

[1] Julius Evola, **Orient et Occiden**t, Archè, 1982, pp. 40 ff.

impossible; the Occident does not have the necessary tools and means to recover by itself. Second, the laws of the cosmic cycles are not negotiable and, whether we like it or not, these laws will follow their course. Third, the present crisis is a general one comprising the entire world, but even if the Orient is engulfed by it, there still is the *oriental* sacred kernel with its more or less outwardly traditional envelopes.[1]

In 1955, Martin Lings, in his "translator's note" (the second edition of Guénon's **East and West**[2]) wrote:

Judging by outward appearances, one might say that by a sudden headlong collapse the East has reached that state of mental chaos, which was only reached in Europe after the degeneration of several centuries. Western influence shows itself in various ways: a large part of the ruling classes in the East appear to accept wholeheartedly the antitraditional outlook and to be obsessed with the idea of making themselves as Western as possible. For such people traditional belief is merely a sign of ignorance; and having rejected such belief, while still retaining the instinct for strong attachments, which they have no doubt inherited from generations of ancestors who followed faithfully the ways of their tradition, they attach themselves to modern ideas and habits with a fervour which often exceeds that of the Westerners themselves.

---

[1] Seven years later, in 1961, Evola used almost the same words in the first chapter of his book **Cavalcare la tigre** ("Riding the Tiger"), stressing again that the East becomes more and more "modern"; a traditional mentality in the East subsisted – Evola suggested – not because there is no decline there, but because the process is not so advanced as in the West (Julius Evola, **Chevaucher le tigre**, Guy Trédaniel, 1996, p. 21). And again Evola fantasized that the West will surpass by itself the crisis and will become a guide and a leader, while the East will decay completely, replacing the present West. Titus Burckhardt wrote a review about **Cavalcare la tigre**, pointing out some of Evola's errors. He stated at the end: "Considering all the prophecies, the sacred deposit of the integral Tradition will subsist to the end of the cycle; this means that it will be always somewhere an open door. For the people capable to surpass the exterior surface and driven by a sincere will, neither the decadence of the surrounding world, nor their belonging to a specific nation or milieu, constitute absolute obstacles" (Titus Burckhardt, **"Chevaucher le tigre"**, Études Traditionnelles, no. 372-373, 1962, p. 187).

[2] Sophia Perennis, Perennial Wisdom Series.

Yet Lings concluded, quoting the same text of Guénon we presented above:

As the author [Guénon] says in his post script, «it is enough that the traditional outlook, with all that it implies, should be wholly preserved in some Eastern retreats which are inaccessible to the outward agitations of our age.» Such retreats would inevitably be Eastern today, even if they happened to be situated in the West since the tradition in question would be one of the Eastern ones rather than the no longer complete Western one; but these particulars would matter little to anyone who sincerely desired the truth, since such an individual would necessarily be above sentimental attachment to the forms of any one tradition.

More recently, in 1987, Elie Lemoine, reviewing Charles-André Gilis' book, **Introduction à l'enseignement et au mystère de René Guénon**, expressed the opinion that today we cannot talk anymore about an "immutable Orient" (as Gilis does), since this "immutable Orient" has disappeared and the entire world is facing decadence.[1] And he ended the article pointing out the case of Islam: this part of the Orient decayed very fast so that "there are not too many real initiates left in the exterior world." Let us say it again: the "immutable Orient" (an equivalent of *Oriens*) cannot disappear. It is known that Satan's greatest ruse is to make the world think that it doesn't exist. Yet another ruse is also very efficiently used: the one which makes the people believe that there is no more Tradition, sacred and initiation in this world. In fact, if the world still has a degree of reality that is because the divine presence is among us. A profane domain does not have reality; there is only a profane viewpoint. And even if this world will decay completely and disappear, the sacred kernel, this "immutable Orient," will "live" forever.

---

[1] Lemoine's article was reprinted in Elie Lemoine, **Theologia sine metaphysica nihil**, Éd. Traditionnelles, 1991, see p. 210.

CHAPTER XXIV

UNITY AT THE END OF TIMES

"SUPPOSE YE THAT I AM COME to give peace on earth? I tell you, Nay; but rather division: For from henceforth there shall be five in one house divided, three against two, and two against three. The father shall be divided against the son, and the son against the father; the mother against the daughter, and the daughter against the mother; the mother in law against her daughter in law, and the daughter in law against her mother in law."[1]

Even though these words of Christ are apparently "unchristian," they were targeting in fact the end of times. If we take a moment to look around, we will see the division between Christians and Muslims, between Muslims and Jews, and between Christians and Jews, and between Christians, and between Muslims, an overall division, which makes the three religions, the only ones that can be named religions – as René Guénon has stated –, to be, at the end of times, not only a support for maintaining the spirituality in the world, but also a cause for accelerating the world's dissolution, to which we can add the false prophets who reinterpret the Scriptures: the holy words are twisted and the twisted words are taken as true.

In this context, the Ecumenical movement promoted in the West would seem to be a good remedy against division and a positive action aimed at unity, but, in fact, it is a dangerous parody, and we should remember that, as René Guénon said, at the end of times

---

[1] **Luke** 12:51-3.

everything will be a parody, an upside-down world. At the beginning of this cycle, the primordial and one-and-only Tradition stood for Ecumenical unity in its true sense, whereas now, at the end of times, we see a parody of unity, an upside-down unification of the various traditions, where truth and falsehood, orthodoxy and heresy are jumbled up; for this reason Charles-André Gilis' affirmation that, at the end, an universal exoteric Islam will dominate the world seems unlikely. Nonetheless, Gilis underlines that Ecumenism is at the opposite pole of the transcendental unity[1] and it is the parody of the *Tawhîd*. The most authorized representatives (in the spiritual sense) of the Orthodox Church consider without any hesitation that Ecumenism is a heresy, and we should mention here the spiritual community of the Holy Mount Athos which, together with other similar forces, has opposed modernism for decades, the reign of quantity[2] and the antitraditional mentality of the European Union.[3]

René Guénon explained the primordial Tradition in terms of the cosmic cycle: *Sanâtana Dharma* takes into consideration the whole duration of a *Manvantara* and represents the primordial Tradition, which is the source of all the particular traditional forms that develop from it by an adaptation to the special conditions of a specific people or of a particular epoch, yet neither one can be identified or taken for being the primordial Tradition (even if it is its image); each orthodox tradition is a reflection of the primordial Tradition or its "substitute," depending on the contingent circumstances. All these particular traditions are *principially* contained in *Sanâtana Dharma* and they all have the primordial Tradition as center. It would be a mistake to simply identify a traditional form to *Sanâtana Dharma*; the people whose horizon is limited to their own tradition often make

---

[1] **La papauté**, pp. 46, 48.
[2] A special issue was the use of optical and magnetic cards, and also of barcodes, because all of them had the number of the Beast encoded: "And that no man might buy or sell, save he that had the mark, or the name of the beast, or the number of his name" (**Revelation** 13:17). See also Guénon, **Le règne**, p. 265.
[3] Greece was for many years the only Orthodox country belonging to the European Union.

such an error, even though the representatives of each tradition could insist in good faith that their tradition is *Sanâtana Dharma*.¹ *Sanâtana Dharma* is directly connected to *Et-Tawhîd*.

"The doctrine of Unity (*Et-Tawhîd*)," René Guénon wrote, "that is, the affirmation that the Principle of all existence is essentially One, is a fundamental point common to all orthodox traditions," while "only in descending toward multiplicity differences of form appear, the modes of expression themselves then being as numerous as that to which they refer, and susceptible to indefinite variation in adapting themselves to the circumstances of time and place."² The Islamic tradition, as the last orthodox tradition descended on earth before the end of times, affirms most openly and clearly that "the doctrine of Unity is unique,"³ that is, this doctrine is everywhere and all the time the same, unchangeable like the Principle, independent of any multiplicity and of all the changes that influence the contingent applications.⁴ With the decay of the cycle and the increasing distance that separates the world from the Principle (the distance from center to circumference), this truth is forgotten, mainly because human beings live in an extreme multiplicity, and therefore the most recent traditional forms have the duty to affirm as explicitly as possible the Unity.⁵

---

¹ Guénon, **Études sur l'hindouisme**, pp. 106, 112, 113. This text is also quoted by Vâlsan (**Le Triangle de l'Androgyne**, Études Traditionnelles, no. 387, 1965, p. 38).
² René Guénon, **Aperçus sur l'ésotérisme islamique et le Taoïsme**, p. 37.
³ *Et-Tawhîdu wâhidun*. As Guénon said, in Islam, the statement of Unity is expressed in the most explicit way and so adamant that it seems to absorb all the other statements. "Moreover, this tendency increases as one advances in the development of a cycle of manifestation because this development is itself a descent into multiplicity, and because of the spiritual obscuration that inevitably accompanies it. That is why the most recent traditional forms are those that must express the affirmation of Unity in a manner most visible to the outside; and in fact this affirmation is nowhere expressed so explicitly and with such insistence as in Islam, where, one might say, it even seems to absorb into itself all other affirmations" (**Aperçus sur l'ésotérisme islamique**, p. 39).
⁴ Guénon, **Aperçus sur l'ésotérisme islamique**, p. 38.
⁵ Of course, at the beginning of the present *Manvantara*, there was no need to express the affirmation of Unity. On the other hand, today, the modern man, consumed by the reign of quantity, understands almost nothing of the doctrine of Unity; and even if he accepts the existence of three "monotheist" religions, he cannot understand that

Due to the particularities of the Islamic tradition, including the fact that it is the "seal" of previous traditions and the last tradition revealed, the Islamic terminology allows us to express the universal and *principial* truth beyond any distinction and specific form. For this reason, René Guénon, when he described the Unity, could affirm: "This luminous spherical form, indefinite and not closed, with its alternations of concentration and expansion (successive from the viewpoint of manifestation, but in reality simultaneous in the «eternal present») is, in the Islamic esotericism, the form of the *Rûh muhammadiyah*; this is the total form of «Universal Man» that God commanded the angels to adore."[1] For the same reason, the appellations "Islam" and "Muslim" have a universal essence, as any traditional man realizes their meaning, regardless of the traditional form he belongs to; "Related to this, we should recall that the proper meaning of the word *Islâm* is «submission to the divine Will»; therefore, it is said, in certain esoteric teachings, that every being is *muslim*, in the sense that there is clearly none who can elude that Will, and accordingly each necessarily occupies the place allotted to him in the Universe as a whole."[2] For the same reason, when the great seer Ibn 'Arabî declared that "Christians and, generally speaking, all «the men of the scriptures» do not change their religion when they become Muslims," he referred to the doctrine of Unity, and in this sense we have to understand Charles-André Gilis' expression, "the universal spirit of Islam."[3]

---

it is about the one and same Principle, beyond any duality, or that other traditions, like the Hindu or the Chinese one, are not "polytheist."

[1] René Guénon, **Le symbolisme de la croix**, p. 44. In accord with Guénon's sayings, Michel Vâlsan wrote that in the Supreme Center of the Primordial and Universal Tradition reigns the primordial Muhammadian Being, who corresponds to primordial Manu and to *Melki-Tsedeq* (**L'Islam et la fonction de René Guénon**, Les Editions de l'Oeuvre, 1984, p. 178). Ibn Arabî calls the Supreme Center "the Sublime Assembly" and the Islamic community is its external form, similar to the Judaic tradition where Knesseth-Israel here on earth is the expression of the celestial Knesseth-Israel.

[2] Guénon, **Le symbolisme de la croix**, p. 135.

[3] Charles-André Gilis, **L'Esprit universel de l'Islam**, Al-Bouraq, 1998, p. 205.

As we said before, the cycle could be symbolized by a circle, but also by a sphere or an indefinite spiral. The circular form is actually an image of the Principle, which manifests Itself as a universal spherical vortex or as *Rûh muhammadiyah*, and, at the same time, corresponds to the World's Egg. René Guénon said that the Ark, the inferior circumference, together with the rainbow of the alliance between God and earthly creatures, the superior circumference, compose the World's Egg, and that this circular figure, which was complete at the beginning of the cycle, before splitting into two halves, must be reconstituted at the end of the same cycle.[1] In other words, the reunification of the two halves represents the completion of the cycle through the junction of its two ends (the beginning and the end) and usually equals 10; yet, because the two halves are similar to the Arabic letter *nûn*, the value will be in fact 2 x 50 = 100, which shows that the junction takes place in the "intermediary world" or the "subtle world"; and indeed, René Guénon explained, it is impossible for this junction to take place in the inferior world (the corporeal world), where separation and division reign. Related to this, Guénon concluded that there is some sort of correlation with the historic order, where at the end of the cycle, two traditional forms meet at the junction: the Hindu tradition (with Sanskrit as the sacred language), representing the beginning as the direct heir of the primordial Tradition, and the Islamic tradition (with Arabic as the sacred language), which is the "seal of the Prophecy," being the last orthodox traditional form for the present cycle.[2]

The final conjunction, Vâlsan wrote, does not take place, of course, from an Islamic or from a Hindu point of view, as an

---

[1] René Guénon said the same thing in **Roi**, pp. 92-93. He also explained there how, when the reconstitution of the circular figure takes place, at the end of times, the horizontal circle, which separates the two spherical halves (and represents the Earthly Paradise), will be replaced by a square (representing the Heavenly Jerusalem), illustrating the transformation of the zodiacal cycle, at the same time with the ceasing of the world's rotation and its fixation in the final state, which means the restoration of the primordial state (when the successive manifestation of its possibilities ends).

[2] Guénon, **Symboles**, pp. 175-176. See also Michel Vâlsan, **Le Triangle de l'Androgyne et le monosyllabe "Om"**, Études Traditionnelles, no. 382, 1964, p. 91.

external combination or a kind of syncretism.¹ However, as Vâlsan said, we should ask ourselves what could be the role of this special conjunction between two traditional forms in the traditional world as a whole and what the situation of the other traditional forms is.² René Guénon gave the answer to this question, and Vâlsan quotes from Guénon's article **Sanâtana Dharma**: "There are reasons to consider the Hindu tradition as the closest one to *Sanâtana Dharma*, because it derives more directly than others from the primordial Tradition. (…) It is interesting to remark that the Hindu and the Islamic traditions are the only ones that affirm explicitly the validity of all the other orthodox traditions; and they do so because, being the first and the last traditions of this *Manvantara*, they have to integrate equally, even though in different ways, all the diverse forms that were produced in this period of time, to make possible «the return to origins» when the end of the cycle must join its beginning, and which, at the starting point of a new *Manvantara*, will manifest outside, again, the true *Sanâtana Dharma*."³ Vâlsan concluded that the objective of the final conjunction of Hinduism with Islam must be the integration of all the traditional forms, these two traditions playing an axial role with regard to the others.⁴ The ecumenical spirit manifested by the two forms qualifies them for this role, Vâlsan added.

The problem is that, at the end of times, the Unity of Alpha and Omega, the Unity of the beginning and the end, cannot be realized in an almost exhausted world, the same way as the "inversion of the poles" does not represent an external recovery, in the world; therefore, the Hindu and Islamic traditions will not reach a visible junction, a traditional synthesis, because at the end of times will reign a parody and an untruthful ecumenism, a parody of unity. "What

---

[1] Guénon clearly stated that it takes place in the "intermediary (subtle) world."
[2] Michel Vâlsan, **Le Triangle de l'Androgyne et le monosyllabe "Om"**, Études Traditionnelles, no. 386, 1964, p. 268.
[3] Guénon, **Études sur l'hindouisme**, p. 114. This "return to origins" is the "inversion of the poles."
[4] Vâlsan, **Le Triangle de l'Androgyne**, no. 386, p. 270. Yet it should be said that this takes place "inside."

allows this forgery to exist and to be even more perfect and more possible, as we advance in the decay of the cycle? The profound reason for this situation is the inverse analogical ratio that exists between the highest point and the lowest point."[1]; "the inversion of the poles" has as objective precisely to bring back the things to normal, and this takes place instantaneously, beyond this world.

For Michel Vâlsan, Islam is destined to remain the only form practiced on earth before the end of the cosmic cycle of the present humanity, and this because it was formed with the general human characteristics and the spiritual universality needed at the end. The function of the Hindu tradition has to be purely contemplative and of an informal order; anyway, Vâlsan underlined, in the context of the final integration, Hinduism cannot play a role in the formal order of tradition.[2] Yet will Islam remain truly *islam* until the end of the world? There is no secret that, today, Christianity is incapable of rebuilding and sustaining a traditional society; on the contrary, it concedes more and more to the modern mentality, and the most authorized representatives of the Church, even those full of faith, have no spiritual power to stop the decay and even less to remedy the situation. Yet, will Islam be capable of remaining traditional and honoring its function as the seal of prophecies, compensating for the weakness of Christianity?

Gilis considers that "Islam represents today, in the external domain, the primordial and universal tradition,"[3] but the Orthodox Church, for example, believes the same thing, and we saw how René Guénon explained why it is impossible to identify any secondary tradition with the primordial Tradition. The Masonry, on its part, could be regarded as the only one that deserves to represent, at the end of times, the Tradition. Denis Roman saw the Masonry as an Ark that saved the Western initiatory elements at the end of this cycle.[4] It allowed elements of dead civilizations to stay alive and to

---

[1] Guénon, **Le règne**, p. 195.
[2] Vâlsan, **Le Triangle de l'Androgyne**, no. 386, pp. 271-2.
[3] **La papauté**, p. 174.
[4] Denis Roman, **René Guénon et les destins de la Franc-Maçonnerie**, Les Editions de l'Oeuvre, 1982, p. 15.

be not only "vestiges" of the past, but also the "seeds" of the future. And this, Roman said, alludes to the "separation" which will take place at the end of the cycle between the things that must perish and the ones that deserve to be saved, the latter being incorporated into Masonry. The transmission of "antique" elements to the Masonry, Roman said, suggests that the Masonry has a role to play at the end of the cycle and that, consequently, it has to stay alive till the end of times: this is the very symbolism of the ritual formula stating that the Lodge of St. John is located in the "valley of Josaphat."[1] Denis Roman's statement, if read by the Christian Church, would be rejected with horror, and in the same way would be regarded by Islam,[2] because instead of accepting the truth of a unique Ark, each one is more concerned with its own ark, an ark considered the only true one.

Gilis, after admitting that, from a doctrinal point of view, Islam doesn't have a special privilege, affirms that, by its doctrine and method, Islam is qualified "to reestablish at the end of times the pure universal Religion."[3] Charles-André Gilis, it seems, refers to Mahdî who will set the world straight, and, in fact, Gilis admits eventually that "the restoration, which will come in the last period of the present cycle, previous to the Judgment marking the end,[4] will not be operated by the Christian religion or by the Islamic religion, considered as separate traditional forms, but by the initiatory Authority, which René Guénon designated as the «Supreme Center.»"[5]

Charles-André Gilis strives not only to conciliate his Islamic viewpoint with Guénon's teachings, but also to attract the Muslims to René Guénon's universal and metaphysical perspective. For this

---

[1] Roman 12-13.
[2] See Muhammad Safwat al-Saqqa Amini & Sa'di Abu Habib, **Freemasonry**, Muslim World League Publication, 1982, where Masonry is considered "satanic," against Allâh and spreading poison, heresy and non-belief.
[3] **La papauté**, p. 35.
[4] Yet Gilis mentions a tradition saying that "there is no other Mahdî but Jesus" (*Lâ Mahdî illlâ 'Isâ*) (**L'Esprit universel de l'Islam**, p. 26).
[5] **La papauté**, pp. 199-200.

very reason Gilis says that Guénon, even though he did not present himself in the name of Islam, worked discreetly as the representative of the Islamic tradition,[1] which would force us to limit the one who was always against any limitation,[2] since the *Tawhîd* is independent of the Islamic form, as well as of any other form.[3] In his endeavour to conciliate the Muslim world with René Guénon (a laudable endeavour, which we don't think will be successful), Gilis promotes the ideas that the Islamic religion is a privileged support for the universal *tawhîd*[4] and the *tawhîd* existed in the previous traditions "in a less perfect form and anyway less explicit"[5]; in fact, Guénon did not say that the *tawhîd*, in the Islamic tradition, is "more perfect," but rather expressed more directly, more openly and more categorically. Finally, Gilis, after affirming in **Introduction** that René Guénon was directly initiated by the universal Center, now says that Guénon's message is universal because the function of the Islam is itself universal,[6] which is contradictory and impossible to accept.

As we saw, Charles-André Gilis stated correctly that the restoration will not be operated by the Christian religion, neither by the Islamic religion, considered as separate traditional forms, but by the Supreme Center; and yet, he adds later that the restoration will be operated by the Mahdî, who will proclaim the universality of Islam, will transform the Islamic religion, and will end the reign of the "jurists."[7] No doubt that, from an Islamic point of view, the Mahdî has an important role at the end of times, but only if *Lâ Mahdî illlâ 'Isâ* we can talk about universality, when all these redeeming and reparative aspects will unite into One, in such a way that Elijah's mission, at the end of times, will not be limited to the Jewish people,

---

[1] Abd Ar-Razzâq Yahyâ (Charles-André Gilis), **Tawhîd et Ikhlâs**, Le Turban Noir, 2006, p. 12.
[2] Gilis knows very well that René Guénon "never presented himself as the speaker of a specific tradition or of a particular initiatory organization" (Gilis, **Introduction**, p. 45).
[3] Gilis, **Tawhîd et Ikhlâs**, p. 28.
[4] Gilis, **Tawhîd et Ikhlâs**, p. 53.
[5] Gilis, **Tawhîd et Ikhlâs**, p. 54.
[6] Gilis, **Tawhîd et Ikhlâs**, p. 57.
[7] **Tawhîd et Ikhlâs**, pp. 62-3.

but will encompass all religions,[1] when, in the case of Hinduism, even though this one does not take into consideration the Western religions, the last *avatâra*, the tenth one, will come to the whole world.[2]

Therefore, when we embrace the universal viewpoint, we cannot talk about a particular tradition, Hindu, Christian or Islamic, and the same as the Christian "guénonists" have no right to promote a universal Christian center, so it is impossible to accept a universal Islamic center, since the Center does not have appellatives.[3] It is an illusion to believe that the "Golden Age" will come now without a total rupture, because, as Guénon said, it is about the "Golden Age" of the next *Manvantara*, and it is a great illusion to believe that the new Age will be born in our present world; this is the type of illusion created by the Antichrist.[4]

Even with Mahdî's intervention, the Islamic tradition will exhaust its last possibilities, and the end of times will come, which means, as René Guénon stressed, the end of the *Manvantara* and not of a secondary cycle.[5] The idea that the Islamic tradition will become "universal" at the end is a nice illusion, but the "Golden Age" will not come without rupture and instant jump, and without the reversal of the poles. The Second Coming of Christ is something totally different than what the sentimental people hope, and the "Golden Age" will have, for example, no recollection of the Christian and Islamic traditions, these names will not exist anymore, the same way as, after the individual's death, the individual memory will not survive.

Martin Lings' opinions are more objective and reasonable. The 20th century marked the final phase for many societies – Hindu,

---

[1] Lings, **The Eleventh Hour**, Quinta Essentia, 1987, p. 90.
[2] Lings, **Ancient Beliefs and Modern Superstitions**, Suhail Academy Lahore, 1999, p. 24.
[3] Not to say about the danger of confusing the common people, who will think that they are special and saved by the simple fact that they are Christians or Muslims.
[4] Guénon, **Le règne**, p. 269.
[5] Guénon, **Le règne**, p. 268. We are now at the end of one of the four ages, and this end will be the end of the great cycle (Lings, **The Eleventh Hour**, p. 62).

Amerindian, Judaic, Buddhist and Islamic – which have partially merged with the Western world, overlapping the Western lifestyle and their own traditions.[1] In the 13th and 14th centuries, Lings affirmed, Islam was still a complete traditional society, after which a gradual decline followed,[2] and the existence of the modern world will prevent the return to a traditional civilization, which is, in fact, valid for all people, because the nations will become again traditionally civilized only when the modern "civilization" will be forced out of their lives,[3] which is most likely to occur only at the end of times. René Guénon suggested already that, "only if the West will be completely impotent to become a normal civilization again, an alien tradition could be imposed." However, Guénon added, it is not about imposing an Oriental tradition to the West, since its forms don't correspond to the Western mentality, but rather about restoring a Western tradition with the help of the East.[4]

For Lings, the very universal perspective would allow the man to understand other religions beside his own, and at least could make him understand that his own religion cannot cover the whole planet.[5] If the other religions were false, how could God allow them to reign over such large areas and for so long? For people who were not prepared to sacrifice the divine Glory to their human prejudices it became more than clear that Providence's intention was not to have one of the "world's religions" established over the whole planet; this situation does not really concern so much Hinduism and Judaism, which are limited to specific people, but Buddhism, Christianity and Islam, which, even though open to everyone, have their own population segments, and these three segments remained almost unchanged for many years and will remain so to the end of times.[6]

---

[1] Lings, **The Eleventh Hour**, p. 62.
[2] **The Eleventh Hour**, p. 58.
[3] **The Eleventh Hour**, p. 59.
[4] **Orient et Occident**, p. 221.
[5] Lings uses, after Schuon, the word "religion" instead of "tradition." The term "religion" is not proper for a universal perspective.
[6] Lings, **The Eleventh Hour**, pp. 63-64, **Ancient Beliefs**, p. 18.

The same way there are a multitude of initiatory ways, Lings says, so there are various religions for different groups of people.[1] We should mention that, due to their nature, the Arabs and Islam don't accept the religious icons, but only the calligraphic inscriptions, while for the Orthodox Christians the icons play a fundamental role. For this reason, in the "Iron Age," to have a unique tradition is impossible, the nature of the human groups being too different, and that is why Guénon did not recommend that a European join the Chinese tradition or even the Hindu one (though he made some specifications in the latter case). Even in Europe, there is a difference between the so-called Nordic people (Anglo-German) and the Latin ones, the Latin people being more similar to those of the Near East.

Martin Lings's words were addressed firstly against the intolerance noticed among the Christians. Some Christians, Lings pointed out, should know that Buddhism is also a religion, like Christianity, and in the last two thousand years it served the spiritual needs of millions in Asia, probably much better than Christianity would have done it. If they don't understand this, they think ill of Providence, and ultimately of Christianity, which entirely depends upon the Glory of God. The Christians have to understand that "All-Merciful" is not an empty word, and, therefore, God did not "choose" only one group of people or just one people; in this respect, Pope Pius XI said: "Do not think that you are going among infidels. Moslems attain to Salvation. The ways of God are infinite."[2]

The same Christians were and are still convinced that everybody will be Christian in the new "Golden Age". This idea is also strong in Islam, of course, with regard to Muslims. René Guénon, in a review, stressed: "to say that «in the new Golden Age everybody will be Christian in a Christian civilization» is to forget that this Golden Age will be the first period of another cycle, where it will be impossible to find any of these particular traditional forms which belong to the present cycle."[3]

---

[1] Lings, **Ancient Beliefs**, p. 41.
[2] Lings, **Ancient Beliefs**, p. 71.
[3] **Comptes rendus**, Éd. Trad., 1973, pp. 175-6.

And Guénon asked this fundamental question: "Among those who maintained, in spite of everything, something of the traditional spirit, how many see the truth for itself, in an entirely unselfish manner, independent of any sentimental preoccupation, of any party or school bias passion, of any concern for domination and proselytism?"[1]

It would seem that the modern Ecumenism is the antidote for religious intolerance, but – and we repeat it as strongly as possible – Ecumenism is part of the great parody typical for the end of times. René Guénon stated without equivocation: if an agreement between the representatives of various traditions is possible, this one could be achieved only from above, in such a way that each tradition will keep its entire independence, and it cannot be a sort of "fusion" by assembling elements borrowed from different doctrines.[2] The multiple traditional forms find their *raison d'être* in the variety of conditions to which they must adapt[3]; there is no inconvenience with respect to the multiplicity of traditional forms,[4] on the contrary, each one has its *raison d'être*, even for the reason that a form is more suitable to some conditions of a given milieu.[5] That is why Guénon considered that Christianity in the Western world will survive till the end of times.[6]

However, due to the lack of "religiosity" in the West, Abdul-Hadi, in an article about "the Universality in Islam,"[7] promoted the advantage of Islam, in comparison to Christianity. Abdul-Hadi rightly criticized Catholicism for rejecting any esotericism and for being just exotericism, while Islam had both; unfortunately, he used a very improper expression to define the Islamic society: "esotero-exoteric," which became later abused by various traditionalists. For

---

[1] **Autorité spirituelle et pouvoir temporel**, Véga, 1976, pp. 116-117.
[2] Guénon, **Orient et Occident**, p. 214.
[3] Guénon, **Orient et Occident**, p. 215.
[4] This is the multiplicity God gave to humankind.
[5] Guénon, **Orient et Occident**, p. 218. The difference between the external forms is a question of adaptation to various mentalities (Guénon, **Orient et Occident**, p. 144).
[6] **La crise du monde**, p. 103.
[7] **Le Voile d'Isis**, no. 169, 1934.

Abdul-Hadi, a confirmation of Islam's universality is the fact that Islam is "the best agent of spiritual communication" since there are Muslims from Atlantic to Pacific, belonging to different races. Also, Islam is the only tradition accepting the "collective reality," dealing with the problems of the world, while Christianity and Buddhism withdrew to monasticism; also, "Islam is quantitatively different from the esoteric Brahmanism, since it is vaster."

Despite what Abdul-Hadi said and despite Gilis' opinion on the best suitable traditional form for Occident's restoration, René Guénon did not choose Islam but the Hindu tradition as the traditional form that could help the West. He preferred the Hindu tradition rather than the Far-Eastern one, and considered it more advantageous than the esoteric part of the Muslim doctrine.[1] As to China, the forms of expression for its doctrines are too far away from the Occidental mentality and its methods of learning; the forms of expression belonging to the Hindu doctrines, even though extremely different from the Western way of thinking, are relatively more easily assimilated and allow for large possibilities of adaptation, especially since India is in an ideal position, right in the middle, neither too far from nor too close to the Occident.[2] In terms of the Muslim civilization, it is true that this one, with its two facets, esoteric and exoteric, and with the religious form enveloping the latter, is the most similar to what an Occidental traditional society would have meant, but it runs the risk to cause misunderstandings, which, even if without justification, are dangerous: the individuals incapable of distinguishing between the different domains might think that it is about a religious competition.[3] Therefore, Guénon did not think that the Occident should rely mainly on the Muslim esotericism,[4] and therefore the most suitable would be the study of the Hindu doctrines, which could restore the universal metaphysics in the Occident, by an exposition adapted to the Western mentality.[5]

---

[1] Guénon, **Orient et Occident**, p. 222.
[2] Guénon, **Orient et Occident**, p. 223.
[3] Guénon, **Orient et Occident**, p. 224.
[4] **Orient et Occident**, p. 225.
[5] Guénon, **Orient et Occident**, p. 228.

Unity at the End of Times

We already quoted what René Guénon said about the Hindu tradition: "There are reasons to consider the Hindu tradition as the closest one to *Sanâtana Dharma*, because it derives more directly than others from the primordial Tradition." Vâlsan considered that, even though Guénon doesn't say anything similar about the Islamic tradition, there is also, even if in different conditions, such a relation between this one and the primordial Tradition.[1] Indeed, the Islamic tradition has the capacity to express the universal: "Each new-born is in conformity with *Fit'rah*,[2] and the parents are those who make him afterwards 'Jew' or 'Christian' or 'Majûsi,'[3] a *hadhît* says.[4] Commenting this *hadhît*, Michel Vâlsan described how the being initially receives the condition of human *Fit'rah* and after birth he or she is changed following the mental and traditional form of the direct parents (and of those who represent them with regard to education); hence the qualifications like "Jew," "Christian," "Mazdean," which represent *Fit'rah*'s deformations and alterations, *Fit'rah* being considered as the primordial form. From this perspective, only the admission into Islam, understood in an absolute sense and in the totality of its virtues, can facilitate the restoration of the lost primordial condition. And this can happen only by rejecting all the restrictive conditions.[5]

Yet the admission into *Islam* does not mean the conversion to Islam.[6] Today, the Muslims are also in great need of this admission into *Islam*, and to be a Muslim in the restricted sense does not mean automatically obtaining salvation; because the admission into *Islam*

---

[1] **Le Triangle de l'Androgyne**, no. 387, p. 38. Yet, in accord with René Guénon, the same relation exists in the case of the Christian tradition, since Jesus Christ was "consecrated" by the Three Magi (Wise Men), who represented the primordial Tradition (**Roi**, p. 36), and the Christian priesthood is "after the order of Melchisedec."

[2] *Fit'rah* is the pure primordial Nature.

[3] *Majûsi* is a devotee of the fire, in Persia.

[4] Vâlsan, **Le Triangle de l'Androgyne**, no. 387, p. 41.

[5] **Le Triangle de l'Androgyne**, Études Traditionnelles, no. 388, 1965, p. 83.

[6] We should not forget that, for the Christian tradition, this would be a major sign of the end of times: "Let no man deceive you by any means: for that day shall not come, except there come an apostasy first" (**2 Thessalonians** 2:3).

does not refer to reaching the Paradise here, in our corrupted world, it does not refer to restoring the "Golden Age" on this earth, by a continuous worldly progress. The world is close to its end. The admission into *Islam* refers to a spiritual realization, to an initiatory process, to an esoteric preparation of the new cycle, and, in fact, the end of times is only for those who, looking downwards, don't see beyond this world.[1] René Guénon affirmed many times that we don't have to be pessimistic and disheartened because the terrible end is near, since, on the one hand, the whole present spiritual work is destined to prepare the new cycle, and, on the other hand, the "Iron Age" has the advantage of, somehow, recapitulating the entire *Manvantara*, not to say that, because of the extreme conditions at the end, the spiritual realization is also adapted to these conditions: "Marvelous, marvelous is *Kali-yuga*! ... The fruit of metanoia, of fasting, of the silent prayer and of other good deeds during *Krita-yuga* for ten years, for one year in *Trêtâ-yuga*, for one month in *Dwâpara-yuga*, is obtained in a day and a night in *Kali-yuga*. (...) The reward received through profound meditation in *Krita-yuga*, through sacrifice in *Trêtâ-yuga*, through adoration in *Dwâpara-yuga*, is obtained in *Kali-yuga* just by pronouncing the name Kesava."[2]

The second coming of Jesus will occur in a mode and form that nobody can imagine or predict, and therefore the very "coming" will produce the separation between the chosen and the damned ones, since the latter cannot recognize it.[3] Ibn Arabî said: "And it was not for any mortal man that God should speak to him except through inspiration or from behind a veil or He sends a messenger"[4]; yet for the men at the end of times the veil is so thick that it seems impenetrable. In fact, the veil does not become thicker, but the world becomes more and more "solid," the hearts more and more "stony," and after that, everything dissolves downwards, while a sinister and opaque crust full of misery remains over the world, a

---

[1] Guénon, **Le règne**, p. 269.
[2] **Vishnu-Purâna**.
[3] Similarly, a part of the Jews were not capable of recognizing Christ as Messiah; and, likewise, some Muslims have no capacity to recognize the Mahdî.
[4] **The Meccan Revelations**, vol. I, p. 74.

crust that rejects any celestial influence, which is considered just a superstition, a myth, the Antichrist becoming the only "reality."

CONCLUSION

THE WRATH OF GODS ?

TO ASK WHY DOES THE MODERN world still exists if it is an abnormality, is a wrongly put question. As the partial disharmonies contribute to the total order, so the modern world has its role. It exists because it has to exist, because there are such possibilities of manifestation, and because there is a last, noxious, layer of oxygen. In the same way as there are four castes, not only the *brahmanas*, or as there is more than one race and civilization, so the modern world must exist as a part of *Manvantara*.

René Guénon wrote:

The question is: for what reason is there such a period as the one we live in today? Indeed, as abnormal as the present conditions are (considered for themselves), they have to fit within the general order of things; this order, in accordance with a Far-Eastern formula, is the sum of all the disorders; this age, as painful and confused as it is, has to have, like all the others, its place in human development; and, anyway, the fact that it was predicted in the traditional doctrines, is a sufficient indication. ... The modern age must necessarily correspond to the development of some possibilities, which were originally included in the potentiality of the present cycle; and, as inferior [from the divine, *principial* point of view] as is the rank occupied by these possibilities in the hierarchy of the assembly, they have to be brought to manifest themselves like the others, in accordance with their designated order. In this respect, what, from a traditional perspective, characterizes the last phase of the cycle is, we could say, the exploitation of everything that was neglected or rejected in the previous phases. (Guénon, **Crise**, pp. 33-36)

The Wrath of Gods?

Nevertheless, we should not misunderstand Guénon's words. The fact that this modern world exists does not mean that we should accept it with fatalism. Therefore, Guénon added:

This explanation does not have to be taken as a justification. An inevitable misfortune is still a misfortune; and even if good will emerge from this evil, it will not banish the evil characteristic.[1] ... Partial disorders have to exist, because they are the necessary elements of total order; yet, despite this, an epoch of disarray and disorder is, in itself, something comparable to a monstrosity, which, even if it is a consequence of a natural law, is no less a deviation and a sort of error; or it is comparable to a cataclysm which, even though is the result of a normal process, is, taken separately, a disturbance and an abnormality. (Guénon, **Crise**, pp. 33-36)[2]

There are two aspects we should look into. On the one hand, acknowledging the flaws of our modern world, and accepting them as inevitable, will not do. On the other hand, implacably criticizing them, as many "traditionalists" are doing, without offering something in return, is futile; similarly ineffective are those who, even though criticizing the modern world, are themselves corrupted by modern mentality. Again, René Guénon is a good example. He stressed relentlessly the main errors of the modern world; yet, at the same time, he offered it a fundamental work, revealing Tradition and

---

[1] Saint Paul said the same thing: "But if our unrighteousness brings out God's righteousness more clearly, what shall we say? That God is unjust in bringing his wrath on us? (I am using a human argument). Certainly not! If that were so, how could God judge the world? Someone might argue, «If my falsehood enhances God's truthfulness and so increases his glory, why am I still condemned as a sinner?» Why not say, as we are being slanderously reported as saying and as some claim that we say, «Let us do evil that good may result?» Their condemnation is deserved" (**Romans** 3:5-8). And also: "The law was added so that the trespass might increase. But where sin increased, grace increased all the more. ... What shall we say, then? Shall we go on sinning so that grace may increase?" (**Romans** 5:20; 6:1). See also **Sacred Kernel**, p. 192.

[2] Guénon wrote as well: "*In principio*, we could say that this Occidental world is, ultimately, a part of the assembly, which became – it seems – detached at the beginning of the modern age, and at the last integration of the cycle all the parts have to be recovered in one way or another; yet this does not imply necessarily a preceding restoration of the Occidental tradition" (Guénon, **Crise**, p. 172). See also Guénon, **Aperç. sur l'Init.**, p. 292.

eternal wisdom. His whole work is addressed to the Occident, because it is not enough only to criticize and exhibit an emphatic wrath with respect to profane people.[1] And, René Guénon clearly said, "we are not attacking the Occident in itself at all, but only, and this is completely different, modern mentality, in which we see the cause of the intellectual decline of the Occident" (**Orient et Occident**, p. 115).

Therefore, Guénon's main objective was not just to open the eyes of his contemporaries, but also to straighten out the state of disorder. "[The profane state] is not a reason to remain passive and inactively witness the disarray and the darkness which seem to win at the moment, since, if it had been so, we would not have to do anything else than to keep silent; on the contrary, it is a reason to act and contribute, as much as possible, to prepare the liberation from this «dark age»" (Guénon, **Crise**, p. 15).[2]

From an individualistic or historicist point of view there is no reason to believe in the Wrath of the Gods; or that we live now in *Kali-yuga*, using the last possibilities. From a traditional perspective, on the contrary, the Wrath of the Gods is very credible. René Guénon asked in 1927: "Will the modern world descend along the fatal slope until it hits the bottom, or as in the case of Greco-Latin decadence, will a new rectification reoccur before it hits the bottom of the abyss towards which it falls?" (**Crise**, p. 32). And he answered (we insist, this happened three quarters of a century ago):

It seems evident that a halt half-way is not possible anymore, and that, following all the indications offered by the traditional doctrines, we have entered indeed the final phase of *Kali-yuga*, the darkest period of this «dark age,» this state of dissolution from which we cannot escape but through a cataclysm, since it is not about a simple adjustment that would be necessary, but about a total renovation. Disorder and confusion [the Great Disarray] reign in all the areas; they have reached a point which surpasses by far all

---

[1] For the same reason, Guénon instead of attacking and condemning the occultist journal *Le Voile d'Isis*, he transformed it in *Études Traditionnelles*.
[2] We remember how Saint Paul wrote letter after letter to square the attitude of Corinthians and others, using not only criticism but also good teachings and merciful words.

that we have seen until now, and ... threaten to invade the entire world ... it seems to be the sign of the most serious crisis encountered by humanity in the present cycle. (Guénon, **Crise**, pp. 32-33)

Such a crisis reigned also in Noah's time, with the difference that then just a part of the world was affected. Also then, like today, a part of humanity fell so low that no restoration was possible and no *avatâra* descended to operate it. Noah's mission lacked this "messianic" aspect exactly, an essential trait which stops Wrath and allows Mercy. Of course, we can ask if it would not have been contradictory for Noah to be a "saviour" in himself, when the crisis faced by the "flood generation" was without solution? As Guénon said, an initiate, a "messenger," a "missionary," regardless of the crisis, must operate with all his power toward a rectification; since, "even if it is too late to avoid the catastrophe [the end of time], his work, operated with respect to a restoration, will not be futile, but will serve to prepare a «discrimination» that will assure the conservation of the elements which will escape world's wreckage, and will become the seeds of the future world" (Guénon, **Crise**, p. 54). And from this perspective, Noah did exactly this. Even if from an esoteric and initiatory standpoint he was not a "saviour" like Moses or Christ, the Ark symbolized precisely the *Oriens*, conserving and rescuing the seeds of the new cycle.[1]

At the end of the cycle, the Ark will be reunited with the Rainbow, the end will coincide with the new beginning, and the

---

[1] Regarding the present situation of the modern world, Guénon recommended the formation of an elite, which would operate to rectify the world with a minimum of disturbance; and even if it is too late for such a thing, the elite "will have anyway another function too, even more important, the function of contributing at the conservation of what has to survive from this world, and to serve as a fundament for the future world" (Guénon, **Crise**, p. 171). And: "even if there is no more hope of reaching an effective result before the crumbling [*occido*] of the modern world, due to who knows what catastrophe, this is not a valid reason for not endeavouring a work aiming beyond this present epoch. Those who would be tempted to give up and surrender to discouragement, must think that nothing accomplished in this state of existence can be lost, that disorder, error and darkness cannot prevail but for a moment and apparently, that all the partial disharmonies and disorders necessary concur to the total harmony and order" (Guénon, **Crise**, p. 183).

"poles' reversal" will occur; the *Axis Mundi* will be straightened by *Avatâra*, whose invisible activity started with the first movement of the present cycle. *Avatâra* reunites the powers of Heaven and Earth, of Occident and Orient, and will manifest, at the same time in the domain of knowledge and of action, the double power, spiritual and temporal, power that was conserved through the centuries in the integrity of its unique principle, by the secret keepers of the primordial Tradition.

As we have already said, even if modern mentality engulfs the whole world, and the East becomes also the West, *Oriens* will guard Tradition, and will gather what was scattered. *Oriens* will guard the sacred kernel and will reunite the words back into one Word, since no "counter-initiatory" forces can penetrate such a "place." The "counter-initiation" succeeds only where the "cutting" protecting the sacred area against the "outside darkness" is feeble and fissured, but does no have access to the pure spiritual domain or to the inside of a spiritual center.

Therefore, in Christianity, the target should not be a competition between esotericism and exotericism, but rather to work for salvation. Also, in our world, the problem should not be the wrath against each other, but concentration upon mercy, not in a moral or sentimental sense, but spiritual. In the Hindu tradition, Shiva is not so much the destroyer but the transformer. In the same way, the descent to Hell is necessary to recover and reintegrate the inferior states, not just to destroy them, purely and simply. "For God did not appoint us to suffer wrath but to receive salvation through our Lord Jesus Christ" (**1 Thessalonians** 5:9).[1]

In Orphism, it was considered that Zeus' wrath gave birth to mankind, since he struck down the Titans who killed Dionysus, and from their ashes human beings were born, losing immortality. Yet,

---

[1] "All of us also lived among them at one time, gratifying the cravings of our sinful nature and following its desires and thoughts. Like the rest, we were by nature sons of wrath" (**Ephesians** 2:3); "Let no one deceive you with empty words, for because of such things God's wrath comes on those who are disobedient. ... For you were once darkness, but now you are light in the Lord. Live as children of light" (**Ephesians** 5:6, 8).

The Wrath of Gods?

the Orphic formula is: "I am a child of Earth and of Starry Heaven; *but my race is of Heaven alone* [our highlighting]" (Harrison, **Prolegomena**, p. 573).[1] The heavenly nature of man refers to the Wrath of the Gods.

In the Hindu tradition, spiritual realization and Liberation mean only apparently the ego's death and the liberation of the Self; also, only apparently, from a worldly perspective, we can say that Liberation means that *jivâtmâ* unites with *Âtmâ*, and the ego unites with the Self, which, in its turn, unites with Brahma, with the Principle. In fact, nothing, ever, was outside the Principle; in fact, the Self is not something external to the being with which this one has to unite. Actually, the Self is eternally present and only our ignorance makes us think that there is a duality or that we are the ego, the psychophysical aggregate, etc. True Liberation and Union mean to destroy the veil of ignorance through a spiritual realization, when we effectively realize that nothing is different from the Self, from *Âtmâ*, from the Principle. It is not about a formal, rational, discursive realization, nor a sentimental one through which we "feel" to be one and the same with the Self, that we are a "race of Heaven." It is about a super-individual realization, through Gnosis.

Therefore, the real problem is not that the spiritual influence withdrew from our world, and the Self hid underground, or that the gods are full of wrath against humankind. The essential problem is how thick is the veil of ignorance, how callous are the hearts. Since, "because of your stubbornness and your unrepentant heart, you are storing up wrath against yourself for the day of God's wrath, when his righteous judgment will be revealed" (**Romans** 2:5). In other words, the Wrath of the Gods exists only from the profane point of view, being a reaction to the human ignorance.

And today, Proclus' words are truer than ever: "the Wrath of the Gods does not refer any passion to them, but indicates our inaptitude to participate of them [and be indeed a race of Heaven]."[2]

---

[1] See also M. L. West, **The Orphic Poems**, Clarendon Press, 1998, pp. 164 ff.
[2] See Thomas Taylor's note in Iamblichus, **On the Mysteries**, Wizards Bookshelf, 1984, p. 263.

As Sallust added, Divinity has no joy, sadness, or wrath. "And while we live according to virtue, we partake of the gods, but when we become evil we cause them to become our enemies; not that they are angry, but because guilt prevents us from receiving the illuminations of the gods."[1] A *hadîth qudsi* concludes our study:

My Mercy precedes My Wrath (*rahmatî sabaqat ghadabî*)

---

[1] Sallust, **On the Gods and the World**, The Philosophical Research Society, 1976 (tr. by Thomas Taylor), pp. 70-71.

www.ingramcontent.com/pod-product-compliance
Lightning Source LLC
Chambersburg PA
CBHW071358300426
44114CB00016B/2095